MOON

T0300593

Copenhagen & Beyond

MICHAEL BARRETT

Contents

Copenhagen skyline

Copenhagen & Beyond

Ask anyone what Denmark is most famous for, and if they don't mention Vikings or pastries, they might say "being the happiest country in the world." And it's true—this Nordic nation consistently features at the top end of international happiness rankings. What creates this intangible sense of well-being in Denmark and its thriving capital city, Copenhagen?

Culture, nightlife, food, bicycle bridges, calming lakes, coffee shops, diversity, and work-life balance are all part of Copenhagen's way of life. Don't rush your visit. Take your time to scratch under the surface and uncover what makes the city so special. Here, happiness is more than a vague idea.

There are also many treasures just beyond Copenhagen. To the north, you'll find a giant nature reserve teeming with deer right next to a historical amusement park that brings out the child in everyone. And just across the Øresund—a strait that forms the Danish-Swedish border—is Malmö, where you can easily get a taste of Swedish life.

The southern island of Møn is only a couple of hours from Copenhagen, yet it feels like it's another world, with undulating countryside, dramatic cliffs, and a welcoming friendliness that's hard to find in any city. Helsingør and Roskilde are approachable small towns with spectacular historical edifices. The atmospheric harbor village of Dragør has a charm that cannot be denied. And, of course, there's the Louisiana Museum of Modern Art, ranking among the best in the world, located in a sleepy fishing village in north Zealand. If you're visiting Copenhagen, much of Denmark is truly within your reach.

Inderhavnsbroen bridge

10 TOP
EXPERIENCES

1 Spending the afternoon at **Tivoli Gardens**—a 19th-century amusement park—riding the Demon, strolling through a Chinese bamboo forest, and dancing to a live swing band as the sun goes down (page 51).

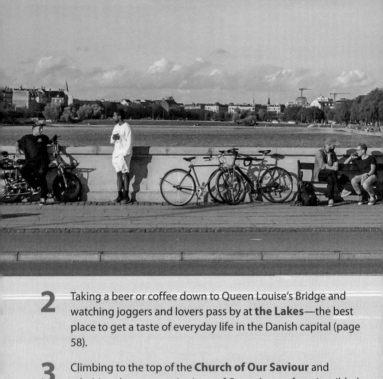

2 Taking a beer or coffee down to Queen Louise's Bridge and watching joggers and lovers pass by at **the Lakes**—the best place to get a taste of everyday life in the Danish capital (page 58).

3 Climbing to the top of the **Church of Our Saviour** and admiring the panoramic views of Copenhagen from its gilded spire (page 67).

4 **Biking** around Copenhagen and feeling the wind on your face as you cross the harbor (page 77).

5 Sampling the best of Copenhagen's **nightlife** at a hip club in **Vesterbro's Meatpacking District** (page 131) or a microbrew pub in **Nørrebro** (page 134).

6 Walking along the pebble beach and through the beech forest at the dramatic **Møns Klint,** where white chalk cliffs glisten over the turquoise sea (page 257).

7 Finding your inner bard at **Kronborg Castle,** the magnificent Renaissance palace overlooking the crossing to Sweden (page 194).

8 Visiting **Louisiana,** a sprawling modern art museum and sculpture park, and soaking in creative and ever-evolving exhibitions (page 177).

9 Taking a quick train ride across the dramatic Øresund Bridge to Malmö and going for **fika,** a Swedish coffee-and-cake break (page 307).

10 Going for a run in **Amager Nature Park,** a tranquil nature reserve where the evening sun glows orange through the reeds, birds sing, and the only sign of civilization is an aircraft on the distant horizon (page 235).

Before You Go

WHEN TO GO

High season for tourism is during the European **summer** holiday months of June, July, and August. Many Danes have several weeks off work in July, which can swell crowds and make lodging a challenge to find. Museums and other sights often extend their open hours to cope with this. Denmark's summer weather is consistently inconsistent. It might be 15°C (59°F) one day and 30°C (86°F) the next.

In **winter,** be prepared for aching cold coupled with very short days in December and January, and relentlessly freezing blasts of wind in February and March. The average temperatures for these months range −1°C to −4°C (25-30°F). Some sights, particularly ones with outdoor elements, have **shorter open hours** in the winter season or even **close** completely.

The **fall** and **spring** shoulder months—particularly September and May—can be great times to visit, with a good balance among crowd sizes, temperature, and daylight hours.

Danish Architecture Center

Daily Reminders

....

- **Monday:** Many museums, and in some instances, restaurants, are closed—double-check before you go or plan on a non-museum day. Open hours are often reduced during the winter.

- **Weekends:** Shops and markets may have earlier closing times on weekends, and some are closed completely on Sunday.

WHAT TO PACK

For Winter

Winters are harsh and long, and if you're out and about walking through town or by the harbor, the windchill is likely to make things feel even colder. Bring **warm comfortable layers,** a good pair of **gloves,** and warm headgear. If you want to fit in with the Danes, include a stylish **scarf.**

For Spring and Fall

Wet weather is common in spring and fall, so bring a **waterproof jacket** and **footwear** to protect yourself from the elements. Danes who bicycle on a daily basis consider waterproof "rain trousers" essential outerwear.

For Summer

Summer weather is unpredictable. You could find yourself needing both a rain jacket and a swimsuit. **Sunscreen,** a **hat,** and **sunglasses** are useful on the brighter days; don't forget the sun stays up until approaching midnight mid-June to mid-July.

GETTING THERE

By Air

International flights arrive at **Copenhagen Airport,** also known colloquially as **Kastrup.** It's the largest airport in the Nordic region and the third-busiest in Northern Europe, with almost 30 million passengers annually. **Scandinavian Airlines** (SAS, www.flysas.com) operates flights to a number of US and Asian cities. **Ryanair** (www.ryanair.com), **Norwegian** (www.norwegian.com), and to a lesser extent **EasyJet** (www.easyjet.com) all operate budget flights to Copenhagen.

By Car

Coming by car from either mainland Europe via **Germany** or from **Sweden** via the Øresund Bridge is straightforward, given all three countries are within the European Union's Schengen common visa area. Make sure you **carry your passport,** as Denmark retains the right to carry out random spot checks on its border with Germany. This does not mean there's a hard border, and the controls are unlikely to affect tourists.

By Train

Copenhagen Central Station (Hovedbanegården, often shortened to Hovedbanen) is linked to the **European rail network** via Stockholm to the north and Amsterdam, Hamburg, and Berlin to the south and east.

International tickets can be booked via Denmark's state rail operator **DSB** (tel. 70 13 14 18; www.dsb.dk). If you are planning an extended trip around Denmark or farther afield by rail, it is advisable to

Key Reservations

Approximate times to reserve ahead for:

- **Michelin-starred restaurants:** 2-3 months

- **Popular or highly rated restaurants:** 1-2 weeks

- **Accommodation and tours:** in high season, 2-3 weeks; low season, 1 week

- **Camping:** high season, 3-4 days

Copenhagen Central Station

What You Need to Know

- **Currency:** Kroner (DKK)

- **Conversion Rate:** 1 kr (DKK) = €0.13 (euro) = $0.15 (USD) = £0.12 (GBP); the exchange rate to the dollar and the pound are likely to vary.

- **Entry Requirements:** A valid passport that does not expire for the duration of your trip. Visitors from other European Union countries, other Nordic countries, and Britain do not need a visa. No visa is required for a stay less than 90 days if you are from the United States, the United Kingdom, Australia, New Zealand, or Canada. South African citizens who wish to travel to Denmark for 90 days or less must apply for a visa. Two new EU border systems, the **Entry/Exit System (EES)** and the **European Travel Information and Authorization System (ETIAS)** are expected to come into force in 2024 and 2025. For more information, visit the EU's website: https://travel-europe.europa.eu.

- **Emergency Numbers:** Dial 112 for all emergency services. If you want to call an on-duty medic for advice, you can use the Danish public health system's regional direct system (tel. 38 69 38 69 in Greater Copenhagen; tel. 1818 in the rest of Zealand).

- **Time Zone:** Central European Time (CET). In winter, 1 hour later than Universal Coordinated Time (UTC+1); in summer, 2 hours later (UTC+2).

- **Electrical System:** 230 V, 50 Hz; round two-pin European standard Type C outlets

- **Open Hours:** restaurants daily noon-10pm, some close 11pm or midnight; shops Mon.-Fri. 10am-6pm, some close Sat. between 2pm and 4pm, some open Sun.; museums 10am or 11am to 5pm or 6pm, many closed Mon.

look into the two main European rail passes, **Eurail** (www.eurail.com) for non-Europeans and **Interrail** (www.interrail.eu) for European residents.

By Bus

German company **Flixbus** (www.flixbus.com) operates international bus services into Denmark from both **Sweden** and **Germany.**

GETTING AROUND

By Car

Cars are **not essential** for traveling around Copenhagen. Public transportation is comprehensive, efficient, and easy to use, and the city is compact. That said, if you choose to drive, Copenhagen is quite **driver-friendly.** If you're unfamiliar with the city, you need to pay attention to the high volume of **bicycle traffic** and be aware that **bicyclists have the right of way** when you are turning right.

Outside Copenhagen, where distances increase, having a car can make travel more convenient. This is particularly the case on Møn, where public transportation is far less extensive.

By Train

Denmark's national rail company **DSB** (www.dsb.dk) operates all services between Copenhagen and the other destinations in this book, with the exception of the Øresundstog service to Malmö, run by Swedish counterpart SJ. Tickets to all destinations, including Malmö, can be purchased via the DSB's website or app.

By Bus

You can travel around Denmark with **Kombardo Expressen** (www.kombardoexpressen.dk) or **Flixbus** (www.flixbus.com). The unglamorous **Ingerslevsgade** bus terminal, which is actually no more than a parking lane on a side road near Copenhagen Central Station, will be replaced in 2024 by a new, modern bus terminal at nearby Dybbølsbro.

Budgeting

- **Cup of coffee:** 40-65 kr
- **Beer on tap:** 50-75 kr
- **Smørrebrød:** 45-80 kr
- **Breakfast:** 100-150 kr
- **Lunch:** 120-180 kr
- **Dinner:** restaurant from 250 kr, Michelin-starred restaurants 3,000-6,000 kr
- **Entrance fees for museums or art galleries:** 75-150 kr
- **Rejsekort travel card:** 80 kr (plus 70 kr credit) from machines at Metro and rail stations
- **Single Metro ticket with Rejsekort:** standard ticket 24 kr (zones 1-2)
- **Bike rental:** 100-200 kr for 24 hours
- **Hotel:** from 600 kr per person per night

BEST OF
Copenhagen & Beyond

Day 1: Nørreport and Around

Start the day with a coffee and a pastry, such as the cinnamon-infused kanelsnegl, at a **city center café.** Head to the **Round Tower (Rundetårn),** go up the cobblestone-spiraled walkway, and see the city from above. Grab lunch at a nearby restaurant or café such as **Aamanns 1921** or **Democratic Coffee.** Walk off lunch in the **King's Garden (Kongens Have).** Head into **Rosenborg Castle** to inspect the crown jewels. In the evening, go for cocktails and nibbles at a local bar.

Day 2: Greater Inner City and Slotsholmen

After eating breakfast at your hotel, make your way to the **National Museum of Denmark** for national history. It's an extensive museum, so you'll probably be ready for lunch afterward. Have a casual lunch at the **Torvehallerne** food market or, if the weather permits, a stand at the outdoor **Broens Street Food.** Head over to **Tivoli Gardens**—a legendary 19th-century amusement park—and enjoy roller coasters, gardens, and entertainment all afternoon and into the evening. There are plenty of places in the park to grab dinner before ending your day by taking in one of the theater performances or concerts.

Where To Go from Copenhagen

If You Want...	Destination	Why Go?
A quick trip outside Copenhagen	Klampenborg and Kongens Lyngby	Get a dose of nostalgia at a centuries-old amusement park or open-air museum in the suburbs
World-class art	Louisiana MoMA	Explore one of the best collections of modern art in the world in an intricately crafted coastal setting
History and culture	Roskilde	See how the Vikings lived (and died) in the former capital
	Helsingør	Immerse yourself in Shakespeare's *Hamlet* at the iconic Kronborg castle
A mix of history and nature	Dragør	Wander through the narrow alleys of the old town and the wide expanses of the Amager Nature Park
To see more of Scandinavia	Malmö	Get a taste of Swedish culture and enjoy an afternoon fika, just a short train ride away
Outdoor adventure	Møn	Spend a few days hiking, cycling, and stargazing in the wilds of Denmark, with dramatic white cliffs as a backdrop

Distance and Travel Time from Copenhagen	How Long to Stay	Page
Klampenborg: 8 mi/13 km; 25 mins by S-train Frilandsmuseet: 9.3 mi/15 km; 35 mins by S-train	½-1 day	page 158
21.7 mi/35 km 35 mins by train	1 day	page 174
21.7 mi/35 km 25 mins by train	1 day	page 209
31 mi/50 km 50 mins by train	1 day	page 189
9.3 mi/15 km about 50 mins by metro and bus; 25 mins by car	1 day	page 228
26 mi/42 km 25 mins by train	1-2 days	page 283
80 mi/128 km 90 mins by car	2 days	page 251

If You Have...

- **One day:** Pick a main attraction like **Tivoli** and focus on that, then spend the evening in the **Meatpacking District** (Kødbyen) to get a feel for the city's exceptional food and nightlife scene.

- **A weekend:** Add two or three attractions in the **Inner City** with a thorough exploration of one or two neighborhoods away from the Inner City, such as **Nørrebro**, **Vesterbro**, or **Christianshavn.**

- **Five days:** Add a climb to the top of the **Church of Our Saviour** and visit **Dragør** or **Klampenborg.** Don't miss **Louisiana,** and spend another day taking a side trip to **Malmö, Roskilde,** or **Helsingør.**

- **One week or more:** With more than a week, spend a couple nights on **Møn,** where you can explore natural Denmark on two wheels or in a pair of hiking boots.

Dragør

Day 3: Nyhavn and Christianshavn

Start the day taking in the full scope of royal Danish history at **Amalienborg.** Head to **Nyhavn** to get a bite and take pictures of the famous pastel-colored houses. Cross the Inderhavnsbro bridge to **Christianshavn.** Head to the **Church of Our Saviour,** and if you have it in you, climb the 400 steps to the top. Wander through nearby **Christiania.** Returning to Christianshavn, grab something traditionally Danish to eat at **Christianshavns Færgecafé.**

Day 4: Day Trip to Helsingør

Louisiana Museum of Modern Art

Journey north to the historical town of **Helsingør** (55 minutes by train) to immerse yourself in both real and fictional history at the imposing **Kronborg** medieval castle, a part of Shakespearian folklore. There's a nearby street food market where you can stop for lunch before going nautical at the **M/S Maritime Museum of Denmark** or strolling through the creaking alleyways of Helsingør's old town. Alternatively, devote the afternoon and evening to the **Louisiana Museum of Modern Art,** located on an atmospheric piece of coastline on the way back to Copenhagen. You won't regret it.

Day 5: Amalienborg and Langelinie

Take the Metro to **Marmorkirken** (Marble Church) station, from where you can visit royal residence **Amalienborg.** If you time it right, you'll see the changing of the guard outside the home of Denmark's king and queen. Walk to **Nyhavn** for a veggie lunch at **Apollo Bar,** then head out to Langelinie and walk along the promenade until you reach the famous *Little Mermaid* statue. With luck, you might get the perfect photo opportunity. Go back to **Nyhavn** and finish with wine and tapas near the waterfront, maybe at **Den Vandrette** or **Nebbiolo Winebar.**

Beyond the Crowds

Day 1

Stroll around the **Inner City's shopping streets,** taking in classic Danish designs and brands at places like Hay, Illum, and Magasin du Nord. Grab lunch at **Torvehallerne,** the artisanal food market, before crossing the lakes at **Dronning Louises Bro.** Pause at a bench to watch the city move around you. Walk down multicultural **Nørrebrogade,** soaking up the atmosphere. Stroll through **Assistens Cemetery** (Assistens Kirkegård) to see the final resting place of many of Denmark's most famous people. Grab dinner in **Nørrebro.** Head to the ultracool **Meatpacking District** (Kødbyen) in Vesterbro. Find a spot for food and drink such as **Magasasa Dim Sum & Cocktails** or **WarPigs.** End your night dancing at **Jolene** or **Baggen.**

Day 2

Fill a backpack with supplies and set out on two wheels for the little town of **Dragør** via bicycle route 80, which encircles the island of Amager. You'll be taken along coastal paths, around an airport perimeter, and through a nature reserve, but take time to visit **Amager Museum** and **Dragør's Old Town** while resting from all the pedal work. Combine a rest with a lunch stop at **Restaurant Beghuset.** Once you've had your fill, head back to Copenhagen for a well-earned beer and bite to eat.

Day 3

Spend the day walking on the beach at **Amager Strandpark** or in the wild surroundings of **Amager Fælled,** in line with whichever side of nature most takes your fancy. Two different branches of the Metro bring you to either destination. Near the beach, **Wulff & Konstali** is a nice stop for refreshment. If you're here in the summer, head in the evening to the **Reffen** street food market at Refshaleøen, with its atlas of different world cuisines. Stay for a craft beer at **Mikkeller Baghaven** and watch the sunset over the harbor.

Day 4

Get on the metropolitan S-train and make your way to Copenhagen's affluent northern suburbs, where you can experience herds of deer up close at **Jægersborg Dyrehave.** Stroll along **Strandvejen** and spot the many examples of signature Danish architecture, as well as a few expensive cars. For lunch, detour to the secluded **Raadvad Kro.** After head to **Bellevue Beach,** where even the lifeguard towers are classically designed, and join Danish families relaxing on the sand in nicer weather. On a rainy day, kids will love **Experimentarium.** Make your way back to Copenhagen for dinner.

deer in Jægersborg Dyrehave

If You Like...

DESIGN AND ARCHITECTURE

The **Danish Architecture Center** showcases all that is good about new architecture and urban design. For some all-time classics, find the legacy of Arne Jacobsen around **Bellevue Beach** north of the city.

FOOD AND DRINK

For fine dining, **Kadeau** and **Geranium** are among Copenhagen's leading Michelin-starred restaurants and require advance planning. Alternatively, the **Meatpacking District (Kødbyen)** has some outstanding concept restaurants. Or head to a food market, such as **Broens Gadekøkken** or **Torvehallerne** in Copenhagen and **Elsinore Street Food** in Helsingør, to sample a bit of everything.

POLITICS

Slotsholmen, the island separated from the Inner City by canals, exudes history, with **Christiansborg Palace**, an impressive palace that is the seat of Danish Parliament.

OUTDOOR RECREATION

The island of **Møn** is an idyllic get-away for outdoor recreation, with activities such as sailing, stargazing, and bicycling, as well as easy access to the popular **Camøno** hiking trail. A little closer to Copenhagen, visit the massive **Amager Nature Park** for a peaceful getaway.

ART

The classic Roman and Greek statues and French Impressionism at **Ny Carlsberg Glyptotek,** the outstanding **David Collection** of Islamic art, and the contemporary art at **Nikolaj Kunsthal** are all in Copenhagen. The crowning glory is **Louisiana Museum of Modern Art,** set in beautiful, modernist buildings and among spectacular rural coastline scenery.

ROYALTY

Amalienborg, the royal residence where a changing of the guard takes place daily, and **Rosenborg,** the home of the Crown Jewels, are essential viewing. Head north to **Kronborg Castle** in Helsingør for some Shakespearean-style palace intrigue.

Above: Danish Architecture Center

Longer Trips Around Copenhagen

If you want to explore the areas outside Copenhagen, it's possible to combine multiple destinations to the south or north without needing to return to the city to spend the night. Given their locations due east and west of Copenhagen, Roskilde and Malmö can easily be folded into either itinerary.

Northern Zealand
Number of Days: 4-5

The outlying suburbs of Copenhagen offer everything from architecture to roller-coaster rides, nature, art, and science. Starting from the north, spend a day and overnight in the town of **Helsingør,** where **Kronborg Castle** and the **M/S Maritime Museum of Denmark** are the primary attractions. Traveling south along the coast, the wonderful **Louisiana Museum of Modern Art** and its surrounding sculpture park will let you lose yourself in contemplation for a day. After spending the night nearby, a side trip to regal **Fredensborg Palace** makes for a leisurely interlude before you head to **Kongens Lyngby.**

From here, take the short journey west to **Roskilde,** once a big-hitting Viking-era city where you can now view longboats used by rampaging Danish sailors and visit the centuries-old cathedral, tracing Denmark's royal lineage via the tombs of past monarchs. Head back to Copenhagen at the end of the day, or, if you stay the night, you can linger among views of the Roskilde Fjord before returning to the city in the morning. When you're ready, the train will get you back to central Copenhagen in less than an hour.

Southern Zealand
Number of Days: 5-7

Pick up a car at Copenhagen Airport for the two-hour journey to the south—also possible by train and bus from Copenhagen—that brings you to UNESCO biosphere reserve **Møn,** an island where you can trek, cycle, stargaze, and camp to your heart's content. Following the popular **Camøno trail,** either in part or in full, is a great way to break in a pair of hiking boots and spend up to a few days wandering Møn's forests, hills, and chalky-cliff beaches. Don't miss the even smaller island of **Nyord** with its tiny hamlet and marshy plains.

white cliffs of Møns Klint

On your way back north, stop short in **Dragør,** a fishing village with a quaint old town and a surprising number of museums for its size. Afterward, drop off your car at the airport, and hop on a train to Swedish city **Malmö** via the dramatic Øresund Bridge. You'll feel like you've traveled farther than you actually have with the noticeable changes in language and aesthetics in Sweden. Plentiful options for eating, green space, and cultural fulfilment make Malmö a great place to spend a couple of days.

Copenhagen

From the pomp and history of
the Royal Quarter to anarchist Christiania,
from the shiny, clean lines of groundbreak-
ing architecture and design to the gritty in-
ner-city life and urban chic of Vesterbro and
Nørrebro, the city of Copenhagen is a thrill-
ing mix of the classic and modern, of expecta-
tions and surprises.

Visitors come to Copenhagen for a variety of reasons: to view epic architecture, live
a healthy lifestyle, eat at a Michelin-starred

Highlights

⭐ **The Round Tower:** The dizzying medieval attraction is an architectural outlier and an easy stop on your way through the historical Inner City (page 46).

⭐ **The David Collection:** This comprehensive and meticulously curated collection of Islamic Art is one of the city's underrated gems (page 47).

⭐ **Amalienborg:** The wealth of European regal tradition is on display daily during the changing of the guard at the official royal residence (page 50).

⭐ **Tivoli Gardens:** The historical amusement park mixes modern thrills and old-school leisure, retaining the charm of its 19th-century origins (page 51).

⭐ **Ny Carlsberg Glyptotek:** This elegant museum is home to Greek and Roman sculptures, Egyptian hieroglyphs, and paintings by Picasso and Monet (page 53).

⭐ **Church of Our Saviour:** Climbing the church's gilded spire is not for the faint-hearted, especially on one of Denmark's many windy days, but you'll be rewarded with stunning panoramic views of Christianshavn (page 67).

⭐ **Refshaleøen:** Grab dinner at Reffen, the expansive street food market, and enjoy the harbor view at this former industrial-area-turned-hip destination (page 70).

⭐ **Christiania:** Independent traders, autonomous cafés, artistic spaces, and improvised houses on hidden green pathways are integral to the vibe of this anarchist enclave (page 72).

⭐ **Café Culture:** Start your day with coffee and wienerbrød, enjoyed outdoors no matter the weather (page 100).

⭐ **Nørrebro and Vesterbro Nightlife:** Wash down your döner with a microbrew or two in gritty Nørrebro before heading across to Vesterbro's Meatpacking District for some seriously stylish Scandinavian nightclubs (pages 131 and 134).

restaurant, shop for designer clothes, drink coffee by the canal, or even just to see the *Little Mermaid* statue up close (and you'll need to get close to be able to see it).

These elements are part of its beauty, but Copenhagen is more than what's advertised in tourism brochures and in "happiest city in the world" articles. It's looking up into a yellowing street lamp on a misty winter night, sitting on your bicycle waiting for the light to change and thinking it never will. It's emerging from the cemetery—reclaimed by Copenhageners as a park—where Hans Christian Andersen is buried and finding yourself in the middle of Nørrebro, the most ethnically diverse neighborhood in the city. It's jogging with locals on quiet lakeside paths in the early morning, or mingling with them in the Friday-night hustle of an earthy bodega—a pub where you don't have to be a local to feel like a regular. These small moments bring the stories of Denmark's lived-in and beloved capital to life.

Orientation and Planning

Geography neatly divides the city into separate neighborhoods. Some, such as Christianshavn, are not technically districts in their own right, while others, like Frederiksberg, are distinct municipalities and don't actually have Copenhagen postcodes. I will use the popular designations rather than the technical ones.

The names of the neighborhoods Vesterbro (West Bridge), Nørrebro (North Bridge), and Østerbro (East Bridge) align with their geographical relation to the Inner City. The Inner City refers approximately to the area between Knippelsbro bridge in the east and the three lakes in the west, and from Copenhagen Central Station in the south to Østerport Station and the street Dag Hammarskjölds Allé in the north.

You might also hear the term "Medieval City" in reference to a closely-defined area within the Inner City. This is the oldest part of Copenhagen and was once within city walls that connected three gates in the west (Vesterport), north (Nørreport) and east (Østerport), all of which are now the names of rail stations. The busy square Gråbrødretorv, where a number of bars and restaurants are located today, sits approximately at the center of the Medieval City and was once the site of a monastery.

To the east and southeast of the Inner City, separated by the

---

Previous: Inderhavnsbroen bridge; Amalienborg Slotsplads; Ny Carlsberg Glyptotek.

Copenhagen

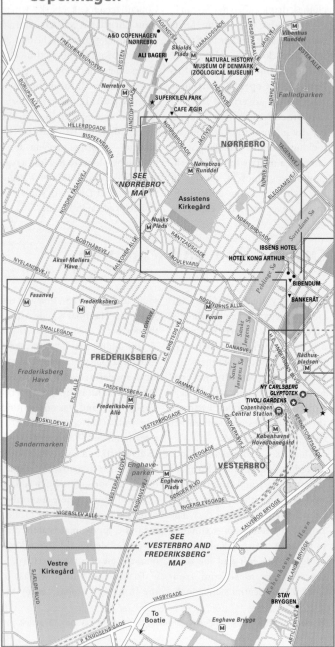

A&O COPENHAGEN NØRREBRO
ALI BAGERI
Skjolds Plads Ⓜ
Vibenhus Runddel Ⓜ
NATURAL HISTORY MUSEUM OF DENMARK (ZOOLOGICAL MUSEUM) ★
Fælledparken
Nørrebro
SUPERKILEN PARK ★
CAFÉ ÆGIR
NØRREBRO
Nørrebros Runddel Ⓜ
SEE "NØRREBRO" MAP
Assistens Kirkegård
Nuuks Plads Ⓜ
IBSENS HOTEL
HOTEL KONG ARTHUR
Aksel Møllers Have Ⓜ
BIBENDUM
BANKERÅT
Fasanvej Ⓜ
Frederiksberg Ⓜ
Forum
Rådhus-pladsen Ⓜ
FREDERIKSBERG
Frederiksberg Have
NY CARLSBERG GLYPTOTEK ✪
TIVOLI GARDENS ✪
Frederiksberg Allé
Copenhagen Central Station 🚆
Søndermarken
Københavns Hovedbanegård
VESTERBRO
Enghave-parken
Enghave Plads Ⓜ
SEE "VESTERBRO AND FREDERIKSBERG" MAP
Vestre Kirkegård
STAY BRYGGEN
To Boatie
Enghave Brygge Ⓜ

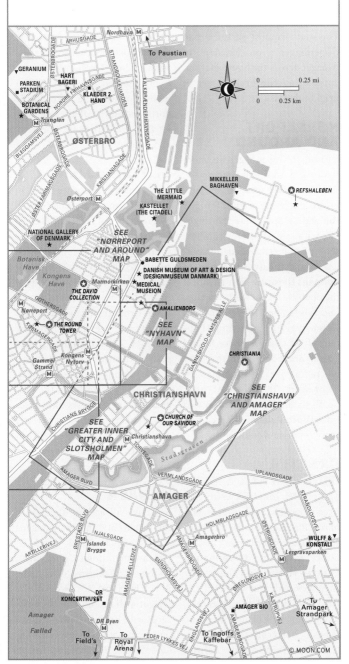

To Paustian

0   0.25 mi
0   0.25 km

GERANIUM
PARKEN STADIUM
HART BAGERI
BOTANICAL GARDENS
KLAEDER 2. HAND
Triangeln Ⓜ

ØSTERBRO

MIKKELLER BAGHAVEN
REFSHALEØEN

Østerport Ⓜ

THE LITTLE MERMAID
KASTELLET (THE CITADEL)

NATIONAL GALLERY OF DENMARK

SEE "NØRREPORT AND AROUND" MAP

Botanisk Have

BABETTE GULDSMEDEN

Kongens Have

DANISH MUSEUM OF ART & DESIGN (DESIGNMUSEUM DANMARK)

Marmorkirken Ⓜ

MEDICAL MUSEION

THE DAVID COLLECTION

AMALIENBORG

Nørreport Ⓜ

THE ROUND TOWER

SEE "NYHAVN" MAP

CHRISTIANIA

Gammel Strand

Kongens Nytorv Ⓜ

CHRISTIANSHAVN

SEE "CHRISTIANSHAVN AND AMAGER" MAP

Christians Brygge

SEE "GREATER INNER CITY AND SLOTSHOLMEN" MAP

CHURCH OF OUR SAVIOUR

Christianshavn Ⓜ

Stadsgraven

VERMLANDSGADE

UPLANDSGADE

AMAGER BLVD

AMAGER

HOLMBLADSGADE

WULFF & KONSTALI

ARTILLERIVEJ

ØRESTADS BLVD

Islands Brygge

Amagerbro Ⓜ

Lergravsparken Ⓜ

NJALSGADE

AMAGERFÆLLEDVEJ

SUNDHOLMSVEJ

ØRESLUNDSVEJ

Amager Fælled

DR KONCERTHUSET

DR Byen Ⓜ

To Field's

To Royal Arena

PEDER LYKKES VEJ

ENGLANDSVEJ

AMAGER BIO

To Ingolfs Kaffebar

To Amager Strandpark

© MOON.COM

35

Copenhagen Harbor, is the island district of Christianshavn. The southernmost part of urban Copenhagen is on the island of Amager across the South Harbor, completing the broader set of neighborhoods.

NØRREPORT AND AROUND

Visitors to Copenhagen are more than likely to spend time on the streets around Nørreport, the busy Metro and S-train hub. Strøget, the main street-esque thoroughfare with its chain stores, souvenir shops, and prestigious design outlets, connects City Hall Square to **Kongens Nytorv,** a large square at the opposite end of the Inner City, and the famous Nyhavn harbor. Købmagergade, a bustling shopping street that passes the **Round Tower** and joins with the busy Nørreport area, bisects Strøget. From here, it is a short walk north to the **King's Garden** and **Rosenborg Palace**—an area rich in museums and culture.

GREATER INNER CITY

The greater Inner City stretches from Copenhagen Central Station bordering Vesterbro in the south to the Lakes in the north. The chaotic area around **Copenhagen Central Station** and the nearby Ingerslevsgade bus terminal can feel confusing. However, careful navigation will bring you in no time to Vesterbro's pedestrian-friendly Halmtorvet. Behind

the nearby Fisketorvet shopping mall, the Cycle Snake, a winding bike bridge, takes you across the harbor (there's also a pedestrian bridge). **Tivoli,** opposite the Central Station, is a sight that can't be overlooked. The Lakes to the north and east mark the boundaries with Frederiksberg, Nørrebro, and Østerbro.

SLOTSHOLMEN

Slotsholmen is actually a small island cut onto the edge of Zealand by canals, and it is the epicenter of Danish history and politics. The southern end of Købmagergade runs into Højbro Plads, an elongated square where buskers play in front of the Illum department store. Cross the bridge at the far end of Højbro Plads and the impressive **Christiansborg,** the seat of the Danish Parliament, stands imposingly before you. Beyond Christiansborg, the harborside part of Slotsholmen faces Christianshavn on the other side of the water. From here, you can walk north along the quay toward Nyhavn.

NYHAVN

Nyhavn is directly to the east of the Inner City and the Kongens Nytorv square and north of Slotsholmen along Copenhagen Harbor. At Kongens Nytorv, the Royal Theater faces Nyhavn, the face of a thousand Danish postcards with its row of 18th-century buildings with facades in a rainbow of colors. Nyhavn once had an unfavorable reputation for housing a hive of lowlifes and tough seafaring types, until a renewal project in the 1970s began to turn it into the powerhouse of tourism it is today. The eastern end of Nyhavn connects to Christianshavn via the Inderhavnsbro bridge, which opened in 2016.

VESTERBRO AND FREDERIKSBERG

Leave Copenhagen Central Station to the west to emerge on **Istedgade,** once the heart of a tough area at the center of a drug addiction epidemic. Traces of that time are still visible today, but the street, which marks the beginning of Vesterbro, does not feel hostile. Parallel to the north runs Vesterbrogade, while just south is the **Meatpacking District,** home to a range of excellent places to eat, drink, and stay out late. Crossing Vesterbro to the north on Valdemarsgade or Enghavevej connects to middle-class Frederiksberg, a serene neighborhood that contains the regal **Frederiksberg Palace and Gardens.**

NØRREBRO AND ØSTERBRO

A long walk north through Frederiksberg on the main streets of Allegade and Falkoner Allé takes you directly to Nørrebro's **Assistens Cemetery,** a public space and the final resting place of historically notable Danes. The clay-colored wall of the northern flank of the cemetery forms one side of Nørrebrogade, the main street through the district. This leads to Nørreport via the busy Queen Louise's Bridge. **Nørrebrogade** is the beating heart of urban Nørrebro, with a cluster of eating and nightlife options around Stefansgade, Griffenfeldsgade, and Ravnsborggade. Sometimes socio-economically marginalized but a magnet for diversity, Nørrebro is a culturally important face of Copenhagen.

Head northeast on Jagtvej and you'll be between Nørrebro and middle-class Østerbro, which is marked by **Fælled Park** and **Parken Stadium,** the home of Denmark's national soccer team. Main street Østerbrogade runs almost directly north-south, leading back to the Lakes, which separate Østerbro and Nørrebro from the Inner City.

CHRISTIANSHAVN AND AMAGER

Slotsholmen connects via the Knippelsbro bridge to Christianshavn, a historical harbor area where cobbled streets, canals, and townhouses have largely retained their 17th-century layout. Heading north from Christianshavn on Prinsessegade takes you to the entrance to **Christiania,** the city's nonconformist enclave. At the far northern end of Christianshavn is **Refshaleøen,** a former dock area that has been populated with restaurants, activity centers, and a sprawling street food market. Heading south, the island Amager has urban sprawl and

Where to Stay If . . .

Christianshavn

IT'S YOUR FIRST TIME IN COPENHAGEN

Staying closely to **Nyhavn** or **Kongens Nytorv** will ensure Copenhagen's iconic sights, harbor, nightlife, and a rich choice of shopping and entertainment options are right outside your door.

YOU WANT TO SURROUND YOURSELF WITH DANISH DESIGN

Stay close to the **harbor** in the area south of the central station where the **Inner City merges with Vesterbro.** Here, you can view the Danish Architecture Center in the blocky BLOX building; the Royal Library, a.k.a. the Black Diamond, one of the most handsome buildings in the city; and the newest of the harbor's three innovative pedestrian and

is also home to Copenhagen's largest nature reserve, **Amager Nature Park.**

KASTELLET AND LANGELINIE

Kastellet and Langelinie are possibly as unfamiliar to Copenhageners as to visitors, given that these areas are somewhat removed from the residential neighborhoods and bustling commercial districts. Heading north from Nyhavn along the harbor front brings you to the grassy former military fortress known as Kastellet, and eventually to the statue of Hans Christian Andersen's *Little Mermaid,* which sits near the entrance of the Langelinie pier and promenade. Blink and you'll miss her.

cycling bridges, 2019's Lille Langebro. You'll also be a short distance from the central shopping area with its top-end interior design and furniture flagship outlets.

YOU'RE SEEKING HYGGE

Christianshavn, a 500-year-old island district of quaint bridges, canals, and historical buildings, has plenty of cafés, lakes, and parks for you to feel the cozy vibe all year round. The nearby Christiania, an anarchist alternative living enclave, has a form of hygge all of its own, which is embodied in alternative cafés and artsy surroundings.

YOUR DAY BEGINS AT 5PM

The **Istedgade** area and **Meatpacking District** of **Vesterbro** are lively at all hours. Once a rough-handed industrial area with a reputation for crime and drugs, Istedgade retains its hard edge but has been transformed by the gentrification of its immediate surroundings. The Meatpacking District's heady mix of international-class craft beers, concept restaurants, and thumping nightclubs attract crowds of attractive cool young people from Copenhagen and the world.

YOU WANT TO FEEL LIKE A COPENHAGENER

Amager, the large island to the south of Copenhagen proper, has a district that is administratively part of the city. It takes no time to reach by bicycle or Metro. Lacking in cultural attractions, it makes up for this with a wealth of nature—always a hit with Danes—and a salt-of-the-earth city atmosphere.

YOU WANT TO GO BACK TO ANOTHER ERA

Pick a spot in the **Inner City** close to **Slotsholmen,** the island district that is home to Christiansborg, the former royal palace and seat of Parliament. A wealth of museums abounds in this area, and Amalienborg Palace is only a short distance to the north.

PLANNING YOUR TIME

Copenhagen is the center of Danish politics and culture, and like other capital cities it requires an extended stay to be seen from a perspective nearing that of its permanent residents. However, given its relatively small size, **three or four days,** if well planned, can be enough to gain insight into and understanding of its layout, diversity, and history. Spend a day wandering the crowded central shopping districts of the Inner City, the royal quarters around Amalienborg, and the parliamentary quarters around Christiansborg. Then spend a second day in quaint Christianshavn and its alter-ego enclave Christiania, followed by one to two leisurely days immersing yourself in local life in the less touristy but no less international neighborhoods of Vesterbro and Nørrebro, and you'll have a good idea of what Copenhagen is about. Extra days added to this basic itinerary provide the opportunity to visit some of the city's impressive array of museums, including the National Gallery of Denmark, Ny Carlsberg Glyptotek, and the David Collection, or to wander in natural areas such as Amager Fælled and Amager Strandpark in the south.

Sightseeing Passes

Parkmuseerne

Parkmuseerne (The Park Museums, www.parkmuseerne. dk/en) is a collective term for **six attractions** in the vicinity of King's Garden: the David Collection, Hirschsprung Collection, Rosenborg Castle, the National Gallery of Denmark, the Natural History Museum of Denmark, and the Workers Museum.

A single ticket, the **Parkmuseerne ticket,** can be purchased giving access to all six attractions. It costs **295 kr,** a 50 percent saving on the overall costs of visiting each of the museums, and it's valid for an entire year, during which each of the museums can be visited once. It can be bought at any of the participating museums. At the David Collection, where entry is free, ticket holders are entitled to a 10 percent discount in the bookstore. The same discount applies in the souvenir shop in each of the other museums on the day you visit.

Copenhagen Card

The digital Copenhagen Card (https://copenhagencard.com) is a prepaid card that provides admission to **dozens of attractions** in the city as well as public transportation around it. There are two tiers: the "Discover" card (from 459 kr), which gives entry to over 80 attractions alongside unlimited use of **buses, S-trains,** and the **Metro** throughout the capital region, along with airport transfers. The slightly more expensive "Hop" card (from 475 kr) covers admission to around half as many attractions plus hop-on, hop-off sightseeing buses. Two children under age 12 are included on both types of card. Full details can be found on the Copenhagen Card website and app. Prices depend on the length of validity of the card. It can provide value for money, and it's also a convenient way to access public transportation. However, many of the attractions it covers may be closed on the day you visit, particularly Mondays, and if you want to walk or cycle around town at a leisurely pace, you may not visit enough sights to cover the costs. Overall, it's more suitable for those who prefer busy and carefully planned trips to a slower, more flexible program. The website contains a calculator where you can enter an itinerary and see potential savings.

Itinerary Ideas

COPENHAGEN ON DAY 1

This itinerary takes in the splendor of the Royal Quarter as well as some sightseeing heavy hitters.

1 Set yourself up for a full day on your feet with a hearty portion of rye bread and poached eggs at **Union Kitchen** between Nyhavn and the Royal Quarter near Amalienborg.

2 Less than 10 minutes' walk from the breakfast café, take in the full scope of royal Danish history at **Amalienborg** with a wander through the chambers of royal monarchs past, gardens, and gala halls.

3 A short walk from Amalienborg is **Nyhavn,** Denmark's most-photographed spot, with its pastel-colored houses and extensive selection of quayside restaurants and cafés, some of which are on boats.

4 Stop in for a wallet-friendly New Nordic lunch and coffee at **Apollo Bar.**

5 After lunch, take a leisurely walk along the historical **waterfront,** taking in the quayside of Inderhavnsbroen, a bicycle and pedestrian bridge. Have a look at a survivor from Nyhavn's brusquer past—the tattoo parlor in the basement of Nyhavn 17, Tattoo Ole—even if you don't want to get inked (although they do take walk-ins).

6 Cross Kongens Nytorv (King's New Square) and head directly for the **Round Tower,** a 42-m-high (138-ft) 17th-century tower smack in the middle of modern Copenhagen. The swirling snail-like stone path to the top is unlike anything else in European period architecture. Enjoy the view and don't run on the way down.

7 After descending from the Round Tower, catch your breath and people-watch on one of the benches in the leisurely regal **Kongens Have** (King's Garden).

8 Walk to **Kastellet** (the Citadel), a well-preserved example of a European medieval star fortress. Stroll around the raised rampart for views across the harbor and the surrounding historical buildings.

9 On the far side of the citadel, get your camera ready and be quick: The *Little Mermaid* sits discreetly by the water at the beginning of the Langelinie promenade.

10 **Restaurant Palægade** is a fine option to round off a day of classic Copenhagen sights: The Danish-inspired dishes served in a rustic setting are worth a little splurge.

Itinerary Ideas

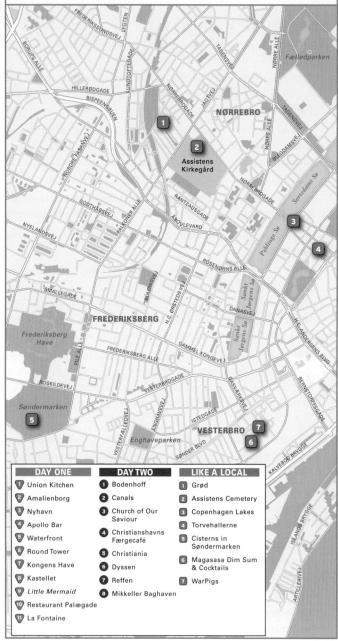

DAY ONE
1. Union Kitchen
2. Amalienborg
3. Nyhavn
4. Apollo Bar
5. Waterfront
6. Round Tower
7. Kongens Have
8. Kastellet
9. *Little Mermaid*
10. Restaurant Palægade
11. La Fontaine

DAY TWO
1. Bodenhoff
2. Canals
3. Church of Our Saviour
4. Christianshavns Færgecafé
5. Christiania
6. Dyssen
7. Reffen
8. Mikkeller Baghaven

LIKE A LOCAL
1. Grød
2. Assistens Cemetery
3. Copenhagen Lakes
4. Torvehallerne
5. Cisterns in Søndermarken
6. Magasasa Dim Sum & Cocktails
7. WarPigs

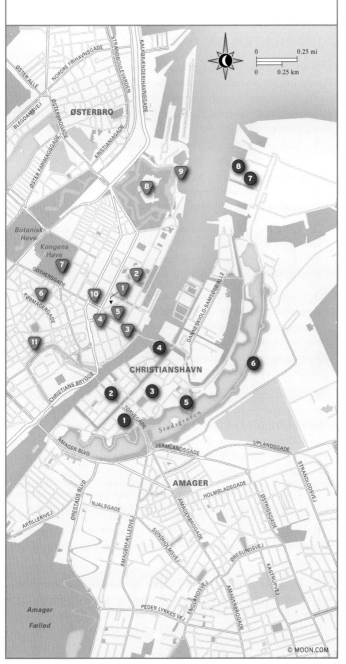

ØSTERBRO

CHRISTIANSHAVN

AMAGER

Botanisk
Have

Kongens
Have

Stadsgraven

Amager
Fælled

0   0.25 mi
0   0.25 km

© MOON.COM

11 Finish the day with a drink at legendary jazz bar **La Fontaine,** where there are regular live concerts on weekends.

COPENHAGEN ON DAY 2

Get familiar with the Copenhagen built by the industrious King Christian IV, including the charming Christianshavn and autonomous Christiania. Nearby, Refshaleøen, a purely industrial dockyard until less than a decade ago, is now the city's premier spot to grab a craft beer and some national cuisine from a food stand.

1 Start with coffee and croissant at **Bodenhoff** on the corner of Christianshavn Square, right in front of the exit from the Metro station. Seat yourself at the window and watch the morning traffic of parents with their kids on cargo bikes, suited officials on their way to ministry buildings, and international students heading to the library.

2 Cross Torvegade to the **canals,** where you can take an easy walk among the winding streets, many of which are cobbled and connected by arched stone bridges. This area is quiet and picturesque, with sailboats moored alongside the paths and plenty of nooks to explore.

3 Visit the baroque **Church of Our Saviour.** The real treat is climbing almost to the top of the 90-m-tall (295-ft) spire, where the handrail and footsteps taper to nothing, and you are left with a vertigo-inducing but spectacular panorama over the rooftops of Christianshavn. It gets busy on summer afternoons, so it's better to come in the morning during peak season.

4 For lunch, enjoy a selection of herring and salmon smørrebrød at the more than 150-year-old **Christianshavns Færgecafé,** with its black lettering and easy-to-find location on the corner of one of Christianshavn's cobbled bridges. If you're feeling brave, wash down lunch with a glass of the breathtakingly strong Danish herbal liqueur schnapps.

5 Walk a couple of blocks to nearby Prinsessegade, where you can locate the main entrance to the alternative enclave of **Christiania.**

6 Inside Christiania, cross the bridge to **Dyssen** and walk along the quiet riverside pathways flanked by the unique houses of improvised architecture.

7 Continue northeast to Refshaleøen and visit the street food market **Reffen** for dinner. The choice of stands is huge, ranging from Kurdish kebabs at Gosht to hot dogs with all the trimmings Danish-style at Nordic Hotdog (plant-based options are available).

8 Stay around and end the night with a craft beer or a few at **Mikkeller Baghaven.**

COPENHAGEN LIKE A LOCAL

Vesterbro, Frederiksberg, and Nørrebro are arguably the real Copenhagen. These primarily residential neighborhoods are crying out to be explored, either by bicycle or on foot, combined with bus, Metro, or taxi hops. Highlights include the Meatpacking District, the graves of Søren Kierkegaard and Hans Christian Andersen at Assistens Cemetery, and Frederiksberg Palace, not to mention a variety of nightlife options.

1 Start your day in Nørrebro at porridge specialist **Grød.** Its memorable selection of oats and other healthy breakfast delights should give you a good foundation for the day ahead.

2 Head to the **Assistens Cemetery** and join the locals for a morning stroll around the gravestones. See if you can spot the resting places of some of Denmark's most famous people: Kierkegaard, Andersen, physicist Niels Bohr, poet Michael Strunge, and singer Natasja.

3 From Assistens, walk along the lively Nørrebrogade in the direction of Inner City to Queen Louise's Bridge (Dronning Louises Bro) for a stroll around the **Copenhagen Lakes** and a little bit of people-watching from a bench. If you need a pick-me-up, check out one of the coffee vendors.

4 Cross Queen Louise's Bridge and venture into the Inner City for lunch at **Torvehallerne,** an indoor food market where more than 60 different food stalls are good for everything from seafood to cheese, pastries to smoked meats, and wraps to freshly ground coffee.

5 Walk about 4 km (2.5 mi) southwest of Queen Louise's Bridge (or to save time, take the Metro from Nørreport and bus 4A from Fasanvej Metro Station) to the **Cisterns in Søndermarken,** an underground labyrinth originally built to secure a water supply for the city that is now the setting for art exhibitions and other events.

6 When you're hungry, head east into Vesterbro (you can take bus 7A along Vesterbrogade) before turning right and continuing south, crossing the rough-and-ready Istedgade before eventually arriving at the Meatpacking District (Kødbyen), the embodiment of modern Copenhagen cool, for dinner at **Magasasa Dim Sum & Cocktails.**

7 Continue your evening with a few pints at nearby brewpub **WarPigs.**

Sights

Copenhagen's sightseeing opportunities span the classical to the modern, from panoramic views from church towers to scenic boat tours. The majority of the sights are found in the Inner City area, but there are several gems farther afield—the old Carlsberg district, Frederiksberg Palace, and the Cisterns, to name a few. The Metro makes it incredibly easy to switch neighborhoods with minimum fuss.

NØRREPORT AND AROUND
Church of Our Lady
(Vor Frue Kirke)

Nørregade 8; tel. 33 37 65 40; www. domkirken.dk; daily 8am-5pm; free; bus 2A Stormbroen (Nationalmuseet)

The Church of Our Lady is Copenhagen's cathedral and has been the central place of worship in the city since the 13th century. The modern church was built in the middle of the spacious Frue Plads (Square of Our Lady) in the 1810s and 1820s, designed by neoclassical architect C. F. Hansen, as evidenced by the contrast between the Greek-style columns that almost seem grafted onto the otherwise boxy edifice. Inside, sculptures depict Christ and his Apostles. A small museum (Mon.-Thurs. 11am-4pm, Sat.-Sun. noon-4pm) recounts its history. The funeral of Søren Kierkegaard, the grandfather of Danish intellectualism, took place at the church.

✪ The Round Tower
(Rundetårn)

Købmagergade 52A; tel. 33 73 03 73; www. rundetaarn.dk; Apr.-Sept. daily 10am-8pm, Oct.-Mar. Thurs.-Mon. 10am-6pm, Tues.-Wed. 10am-9pm; adults 25 kr, children 5 kr; bus 5C, 6A, 14, Nørreport, S-train Nørreport; Metro Nørreport

The 42-m-high (138-ft) tower rises above the rooftops yet appears out of nowhere in the middle of the Inner City's streets. Its swirling snail-like stone path to the top is 209 m (686 ft) in length, twisting through seven and a half circles. It was built in the 1630s at the direction of prolific builder King Christian IV as part of the Trinitatis Church at a time when a library and astronomical observatory were desired for Copenhagen University students. In modern times, the tower is used as a quirky location for temporary art exhibitions—check the website—but the primary reason for visiting is the unique climb to the top and spectacular view over Copenhagen.

Nikolaj, Copenhagen Contemporary Art Center
(Nikolaj Kunsthal)

Nikolaj Plads 10; tel. 24 22 71 27; www. nikolajkunsthal.kk.dk/en; Tues.-Fri. 11am-6pm, Sat.-Sun. 11am-5pm; adults 95 kr, under age 17 free; bus 2A Christiansborg (Vindebrogade), Metro Gammel Strand

"I'm not a church," a banner once read outside Nikolaj, Copenhagen

Contemporary Art Center, found in the former Church of St. Nicholas, dating to the 13th century. The historical surroundings are in contrast to the art center now housed in the building. Nikolaj Kunsthal is a venue for contemporary and experimental art; visitors sometimes even become part of the installations, which change regularly. Planet VR, Arto Saari, and Olafur Eliasson all had works exhibited at the museum in 2022, reflecting a mix of styles—virtual reality, photography, and visual art—as well as the combination of Danish and international art.

King's Garden
(Kongens Have)

Øster Voldgade 4; tel. 33 95 42 00; https://slks.dk/english; May-Aug. daily 7am-10pm, Sept. daily 7am-9pm, Oct. daily 7am-7pm, Nov.-Feb. daily 7am-5pm, Mar. daily 7am-7pm, Apr. daily 7am-9pm; free; bus 5C, 6A, 14 Nørreport, S-train Nørreport, Metro Nørreport

Opened to the public in the 1700s, the King's Garden is one of the most popular parks in Copenhagen. The large green space has pathways that crisscross linden boulevards and enclaves adorned with statues and benches, making it a great spot for picnicking in summer or a contemplative winter walk. Nearby Rosenborg Palace further adds to the scenery and gracious feel of the surroundings, where locals can be found taking a break on a typical afternoon. It is lined with an abundance of refreshment stops and is a short walk from Nørreport Station.

✪ The David Collection
(Davids Samling)

Kronprinsessegade 30-32; tel. 33 73 49 49; www.davidmus.dk; Tues.-Sun. 10am-5pm, Wed. 10am-9pm; free; Metro Marmorkirken

The beautiful artifacts in this private collection have been gathered from across the Islamic world—from Morocco to Indonesia—and span the 8th-19th centuries, which means that local cultural influences on Islamic art can be appreciated. The extensive museum also includes 18th-19th-century European art and a collection of early modern Danish art, including both paintings and sculptures, with a considerable collection of works by famous 19th-century Copenhagen artist Vilhelm Hammershøi. However, my favorite part of the museum is the beautiful Islamic art. With its ornate calligraphy and alternative ways of depicting perspective compared to European art from corresponding periods, as well as the surprise of Islamic works from China, Sufis, and dervishes, the entire exhibit is a pleasure. Tours lasting around 1 hour can be arranged for 650 kr for

Islamic art at the David Collection

Nørreport and Around

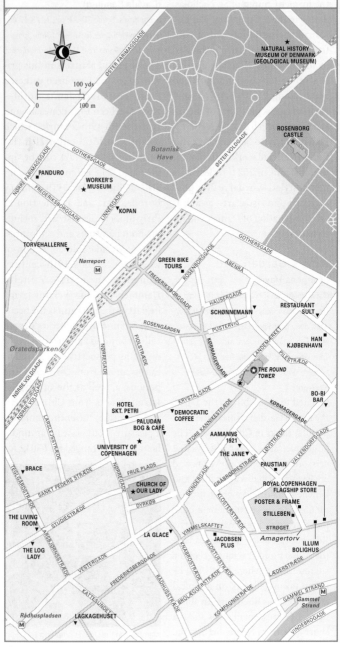

NATURAL HISTORY
MUSEUM OF DENMARK
(GEOLOGICAL MUSEUM) ★

ROSENBORG
CASTLE ★

Botanisk
Have

ØSTER FARIMAGSGADE

0   100 yds
0   100 m

GOTHERSGADE

PANDURO ▼

WORKER'S
★ MUSEUM

NØRRE FARIMAGSGADE

FREDERIKSBORGGADE

LINNESGADE

KOPAN ▼

ØSTER VOLDGADE

TORVEHALLERNE ▼

Nørreport
Ⓜ

GREEN BIKE
▼ TOURS

ROSENBORGGADE

GOTHERSGADE

ÅBENRÅ

FREDERIKSBORGGADE

HAUSERGADE

SCHØNNEMANN ▼

RESTAURANT
SULT ▼

ROSENGÅRDEN

PUSTERVIG

HAN
KJØBENHAVN ▼

Ørstedsparken

NØRRE VOLDGADE

NØRREGADE

FIOLSTRÆDE

KØBMAGERGADE

LANDEMÆRKET

PILESTRÆDE

★ THE ROUND
TOWER

BO-BI
BAR ▼

KØBMAGERGADE

KRYSTALGADE

STORE KANNIKESTRÆDE

HOTEL
SKT. PETRI ●

DEMOCRATIC
▼ COFFEE

PALUDAN
BOG & CAFÉ ▼

STORE KANNIKESTRÆDE

AAMANNS
1921 ▼

THE JANE ▼

LØVSTRÆDE

VALKENDORFSGADE

UNIVERSITY OF ★
COPENHAGEN

NØRREGADE

FRUE PLADS

SKINDERGADE

GRÅBRØDRESTRÆDE

PAUSTIAN ▼

BRACE ▼

TEGLGÅRDSTRÆDE

LARSLEJSSTRÆDE

SANKT PEDERS STRÆDE

★ CHURCH OF
OUR LADY

DYRKØB

KLOSTERSTRÆDE

ROYAL COPENHAGEN
FLAGSHIP STORE ■

POSTER & FRAME ■

STILLEBEN ■

STRØGET

THE LIVING
ROOM ▼

LARSBJØRNSSTRÆDE

STUDIESTRÆDE

LA GLACE ▼

VIMMELSKAFTET

JACOBSEN
PLUS ▼

Amagertorv

ILLUM
BOLIGHUS ■

THE LOG
LADY ▼

VESTERGADE

FREDERIKSBERGGADE

KNABROSTRÆDE

BADSTUESTRÆDE

LÆDERSTRÆDE

KATTESUNDET

RÅDHUSSTRÆDE

BROLÆGGERSTRÆDE

KOMPAGNISTRÆDE

GAMMEL STRAND

Gammel
Strand Ⓜ

Rådhuspladsen
Ⓜ

LAGKAGEHUSET ▼

VINDEBROGADE

48

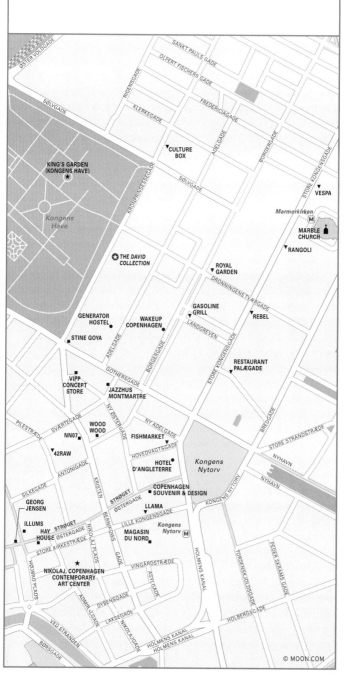

© MOON.COM

49

a maximum 12 people and are recommended; the guides are helpful and highly knowledgeable. Book at least two days in advance, but ideally before that, by calling the museum or via its website. There are also free guided tours (June-Aug. Sat. 1pm) along various themes and in English.

Workers Museum
(Arbejdermuseet)

Rømersgade 22; tel. 33 93 25 75; www.arbejdermuseet.dk; daily 10am-5pm; over age 25 115 kr, ages 18-25 90 kr, under age 18 free; bus 5C, 6A, 14 Nørreport, S-train Nørreport, Metro Nørreport

Strong labor movements are in the blood of Danish society, and the Workers Museum is a glimpse into this history. Much of the museum is dedicated to the 1950s and period goods available to the Danish working classes, such as bitter wartime-style coffee that used coffee substitutes and cakes. These can be sampled at the museum's Coffee Bar, giving you a real taste of Copenhagen during the decade. There's also a recently renovated ballroom, an exhibition where children can try out life "when grandma was young," and a history of the Danish labor movement back to the 1870s.

✪ Amalienborg

Amalienborg; tel. 33 15 32 86; www.kongernessamling.dk/amalienborg; Jan.-June and Sept.-Dec. Tues.-Fri. 10am-3pm, Sat.-Sun. 10am-4pm, July-Aug. daily 10am-5pm, hours may vary on public and school

holidays; adults 120 kr, students 78 kr, under age 18 free; Metro Marmorkirken

Royal Danish history is on full display at Amalienborg, the official home of the royal family. The chambers of royal monarchs past, gardens, and gala halls can be visited. Don't miss the changing of the guard each day at noon. The Royal Guards march through town from their barracks at Rosenborg Castle, finishing at Amalienborg for the changeover. Tours are available for groups, including inside the museum and Christian VII's Palace, as well as small guided city walks in the Royal Quarter. Private tours in English lasting about 1 hour are available; these can be requested via the website, where you can also give details of your individual needs and see a price guide.

Royal Life Guards at Amalienborg

Rosenborg Castle

Øster Voldgade 4A; tel. 33 15 32 86; www.kongernessamling.dk/rosenborg; Jan.-Apr. daily 10am-4pm; May-Oct. daily 10am-5pm; Nov.-Dec. daily 10am-4pm; hours may vary on public and school holidays;

Rosenborg Castle in autumn

adults 130 kr, students 84 kr, under age 18
free; combined ticket with Amalienborg
200 kr, valid for 2 days; bus 5C, 6A, 14
Nørreport, S-train Nørreport, Metro
Nørreport

The red brick turrets and elegant spires of Christian IV's Dutch Renaissance castle, Rosenborg, stand out splendidly in the middle of Copenhagen. Built in the early 1600s and a royal residence until 1710, the castle overlooks the King's Garden. Rosenborg Castle houses four centuries of royal treasures, regalia, and the crown jewels alongside coronation thrones, life-size silver lions, and immaculately preserved monarchs' chambers. Guided tours of Rosenborg, taking around an hour, are available in English (tel. 33 18 60 55; booking@kosa.dk; www.kongernessamling.dk/rosenborg; 995 kr plus entrance fees).

GREATER INNER CITY

TOP EXPERIENCE

✪ Tivoli Gardens

Vesterbrogade 3; tel. 33 15 10 01; www.
tivoli.dk; late Mar.-Sept., mid-Oct.-early
Nov., mid-Nov.-Dec. Mon.-Thurs. 11am-
10pm, Fri.-Sun. 11am-midnight; over age
7 from 155 kr, ages 3-7 70 kr, under age
3 free; bus 5C Tivoli v. Hovedbanegården
(Central Station); S-train:
Hovedbanegården (Central Station); Metro
Hovedbanegården (Central Station)

The iconic 19th-century amusement park Tivoli Gardens celebrated its 180th anniversary in 2023, and it remains among Denmark's most popular attractions with visitors and locals alike.

Tivoli's three roller coasters and dozens of other rides catering to all ages can be seen peeking over its walls like naughty children

Tivoli Gardens at night

from the moment you arrive. The 108-year-old original wooden roller coaster, known simply as the Rutschebane, is still going strong, while spectacular new rides such as the 28-m (92-ft) Demon also offer more modern thrills. Other amusements include arcades, an aquarium, and a concert venue. Note that the basic entrance fee does not include ride passes, but these can be incorporated into the entrance fee (from 169 kr).

The amusement park is particularly magical at Christmas. Decorated trees, the woodland smell of fir chips spread around the grounds, and the aroma of traditional Danish Christmas treats like roasted almonds, spiced mulled wine known as glögg, and small donuts called æbleskiver all help to give Tivoli an almost magical festive feeling.

An entire afternoon and evening can comfortably be spent inside the park and you won't go hungry: Tivoli counts many chain and fast food restaurants among its concessions.

National Museum of Denmark
(Nationalmuseet)

Prince's Mansion, Ny Vestergade 10; tel. 33 13 44 11; https://natmus.dk; June-Sept. daily 10am-6pm, Oct.-May Tues.-Sun. 10am-5pm; adults 120 kr, under age 18 free; bus 2A, 31 Glyptoteket (Tietgensgade)

The imposing National Museum contains a wealth of exhibits that cover 14,000 years of Denmark's history, from the Stone Age through the Vikings and up to 20th century. There are eight main exhibitions, encompassing Danish prehistory, the Middle Ages, and the Renaissance. Look for the Egtved Girl, a Bronze Age Dane whose preserved remains were discovered in a bog in Jutland in 1921. Other highlights include the Trundholm sun chariot, a 1,400-year-old gilded statue of a horse on spoked wheels pulling a disc, which originates from the Nordic Bronze Age, as well as a medieval runestone that was found in Greenland.

Ny Carlsberg Glyptotek

✪ Ny Carlsberg Glyptotek

Dantes Plads 7; tel. 33 41 81 41; www. glyptoteket.com; Tues.-Sun. 10am-5pm, Thurs. 10am-9pm; adults 125 kr, under age 27 95 kr; under age 18 free; last Wed. each month free; bus 2A, 31 Glyptoteket (Tietgensgade), 5C Otto Mønsteds Plads (Rysensteensgade)

Brewer Carl Jacobsen—yes, of Carlsberg fame—had a penchant for art and history. The philanthropist and art collector founded Ny Carlsberg Glyptotek in 1897, and it has grown over the decades into a beautiful exhibition of historical artifacts. Today, the sumptuous collection will get art lovers drooling from the moment they pass the resplendent columns and arches of the museum's entrance.

Ancient Greece, Rome, and Egypt are among the classical cultures that can be enjoyed in a stroll through the marble halls, with exhibits up to 3,500 years old. Greek and Roman sculptures abound; Egyptian exhibits include architecture from the time of the pharaohs.

These classical exhibitions sit alongside modern collections from the Danish Golden Age (1800-1850) and French paintings by, for example, Matisse, Cézanne, and Monet, as well as the largest collection of Rodin sculptures outside France. Other artists represented include Picasso and Van Gogh.

National Gallery of Denmark
(Statens Museum for Kunst)

Sølvgade 48-50; tel. 33 74 84 94; www. smk.dk; Tues.-Sun. 10am-6pm, Wed. 10am-8pm; adults 120 kr, adult with child 100 kr, under age 27 95 kr, under age 18 free; bus 6A, 23 Georg Brandes Plads, Parkmuseerne (Øster Voldgade), Metro Nørreport, S-train Nørreport

The National Gallery of Denmark has Danish and foreign art collections up to 700 years old. It includes special exhibitions as well as a permanent collection that includes the Renaissance, the Danish Golden Age, and 20th-century French art. The exhibition includes more than 260,000 Scandinavian and international paintings. Rembrandt, Cranach, and Mantegna can be listed among a weighty European

Greater Inner City and Slotsholmen

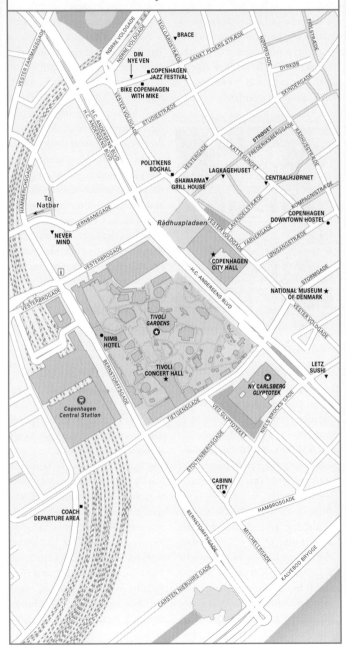

BRACE

DIN
NYE VEN

COPENHAGEN
JAZZ FESTIVAL

BIKE COPENHAGEN
WITH MIKE

NØRRE VOLDGADE

TEGLGÅRDSTRÆDE

SANKT PEDERS STRÆDE

NØRREGADE

FIOLSTRÆDE

DYRKØB

SKINDERGADE

STRØGET

FREDERIKSBERGGADE

RÅDHUSSTRÆDE

KATTESUNDET

STUDIESTRÆDE

VESTERGADE

VESTER VOLDGADE

H.C. ANDERSENS BLVD

VESTER FARIMAGSGADE

HAMMERICHSGADE

H.C. ANDERSENS BLVD

POLITIKENS
BOGHAL

SHAWARMA
GRILL HOUSE

LAGKAGEHUSET

CENTRALHJØRNET

KOMPAGNISTRÆDE

COPENHAGEN
DOWNTOWN HOSTEL

LAVENDELSTRÆDE

FARVERGADE

VESTER VOLDGADE

LØNGANGSTRÆDE

To
Natbar

JERNBANEGADE

Rådhuspladsen

NEVER
MIND

VESTERBROGADE

COPENHAGEN
CITY HALL

STORMGADE

NATIONAL MUSEUM ★
OF DENMARK

H.C. ANDERSENS BLVD

VESTER VOLDGADE

VESTERBROGADE

TIVOLI
GARDENS

NIMB
HOTEL

LETZ
SUSHI

TIVOLI
CONCERT HALL

NY CARLSBERG
GLYPTOTEK

BERNSTORFFSGADE

Copenhagen
Central Station

TIETGENSGADE

VED GLYPTOTEKET

NIELS BROCKS GADE

STOLTENBERGSGADE

CABINN
CITY

HAMBROSGADE

COACH
DEPARTURE AREA

BERNSTORFFSGADE

MITCHELLSGADE

KALVEBOD BRYGGE

CARSTEN NIEBUHRS GADE

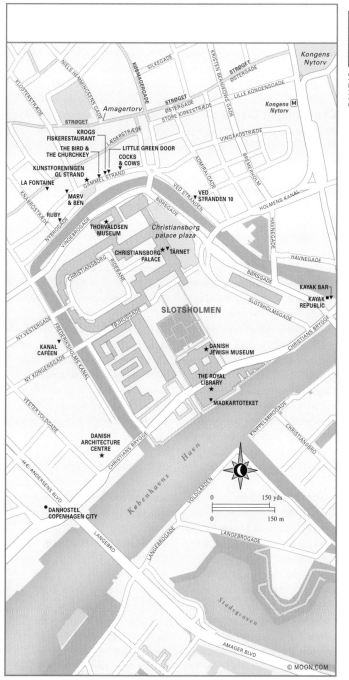

section. This is all best enjoyed at a relaxed pace over the course of an afternoon. It's included in the Parkmuseerne (Park Museums) group ticket.

Copenhagen City Hall
(Rådhuset)

Rådhuspladsen 1; tel. 33 66 25 86; www. kk.dk/artikel/rundvisninger-paa-raadhuset; guided tours in English Mon.-Fri. 1pm, Sat. 10am, tower tours Mon.-Fri. 11am and 2pm, Sat. noon; guided tours 65 kr; bus 2A, 5C, 9A Rådhuspladsen, Metro Rådhuspladsen

The big square redbrick building on City Hall Square is, of course, Copenhagen City Hall. It was built in the late 1890s in National Romantic style and is an interesting cornerstone of modern Copenhagen. It's open to the public, so you're free to walk in and look around, including in the garden (May-Sept.) and a souvenir shop. Fifty-minute guided tours can be booked via the website. Look for separate tours to the top of the 105-m-high (345-ft) tower that take visitors to a part of the building not otherwise open to the public.

Kunstforeningen GL Strand

Gammel Strand 48; tel. 33 36 02 60; www. glstrand.dk; Mon. 11am-5pm, Tues.-Wed. 11am-6pm, Thurs. 11am-8pm, Fri. 11am-6pm, Sat.-Sun. 11am-5pm; adults 90 kr, under age 27 75 kr, seniors 80 kr, under age 16 free; bus 2A Gammel Strand St., Christiansborg (Vindebrogade), Metro Gammel Strand

A leading destination for modern and contemporary art in the city,

GL Strand is located in one of the elegant canal-side houses close to Christiansborg. With no permanent exhibition, the association-run gallery seeks to promote the work of up-and-coming Danish artists. It also shows arthouse films in its in-house cinema. The gallery was reopened by filmmaker David Lynch in 2010 after extensive renovation.

Medical Museion

Bredgade 62; tel. 35 32 38 00; www. museion.ku.dk; Tues.-Fri. 10am-4pm, Sat.-Sun. noon-4pm; adults 90 kr, students 60 kr, under age 16 and seniors 50 kr; Metro Marmorkirken

One of seven museums attached to the city's university, the Medical Museion is located in the former Royal Academy of Surgeons, where thousands of Danish medical students have sharpened their dissection skills over the years. Walk through its Roman columns and imposing black double doors to reach the exhibits and artifacts on medical history, including skulls and skeletons, instruments, and medicines. The total permanent and rotating exhibition space is around 1,000 sq m (10,764 sq ft).

Danish Architecture Center

BLOX, Bryghuspladsen 10; tel. 32 57 19 30; https://dac.dk; Fri.-Wed. 10am-6pm, Thurs. 10am-9pm; adults 110 kr, students 60 kr, under age 18 free; bus 5C Otto Mønsteds Plads (Rysensteensgade), Metro Rådhuspladsen

Located in the striking BLOX

building on the quay front, the Danish Architecture Center is a showcase for architectural design in Denmark and internationally. New design trends and innovations are on show, explaining Denmark's global reputation as a design superstar. A recent exhibition considered how Copenhagen might have looked if abandoned dream projects had become reality. The center also offers various guided tours to some of the city's notable architectural achievements. Check out the roof terrace in the café for a terrific view across the harbor.

The Marble Church
(Marmorkirken)

Frederiksgade 4; tel. 33 91 27 06; www. marmorkirken.dk; church Mon.-Thurs. and Sat. 10am-5pm, Fri. noon-5pm, Sun. 12:30pm-5pm; dome daily 1pm, not during services, concerts, or bad weather; dome adults 50 kr, under age 12 free; Metro Marmorkirken

The unmistakable green dome of the Frederik's Church, more commonly known as the Marble Church, is an outlier in a city populated by spires. It was designed in the mid-18th century and was an attempt to bring character to the area around Amalienborg that would distinguish it from Christianshavn and Slotsholmen. Its construction was beset by complications before being completed in 1894—in limestone, rather than the originally intended marble. Inside, the ceiling of the dome is decorated with stunning frescoes depicting the 12 Apostles while also reflecting the 12 columns that support the curved structure.

Natural History Museum of Denmark
(Statens Naturhistoriske Museum)

Øster Voldgade 5-7; tel. 35 32 22 22; https://snm.ku.dk/english; Tues. and Thurs.-Sun. 10am-5pm, Wed. 10am-9pm; adults 105 kr, ages 3-17 50 kr, ticket includes admission to Palm House, also included in Parkmuseerne (Park Museums) group ticket; bus 23 Georg Brandes Plads, Parkmuseerne (Øster Voldgade), Metro Nørreport, S-train Nørreport

One of several museums run by the University of Copenhagen—and part of the museum district Parkmuseerne (Park Museums) located around King's Garden—the geological natural history museum has existed since the late 18th century and includes extensive collections of minerals, fossils, petrology, and meteorites. It has a strong focus on education and a permanent exhibition on the history of the solar system. Admission also gives access to the historical and serene Palm House, from where you can view the Botanical Gardens

Frederik's Church, also known as the Marble Church

and central Copenhagen through Victorian window panes.

Botanical Gardens

Gothersgade 128; tel. 22 82 94 26; https://snm.ku.dk/botanisk-have; garden Apr.-Sept. daily 8:30am-6pm, Oct.-Mar. daily 8:30am-4pm; free; bus 5C, 6A, 14 Nørreport, Metro Nørreport, S-train Nørreport

The Botanical Gardens contain Denmark's biggest collection of plants. Covering 10 ha (25 acres), a rhododendron garden, alpine plant area, observatory hill, and butterfly house surround a central lake. It also has 27 greenhouses, most notably the old Palm House from 1874 (adults 60 kr, ages 3-17 40 kr, admission included in Natural History Museum ticket). Guided tours in English can be arranged by writing to rundvisning@snm.ku.dk. In the northern corner, a new Natural History Museum is being built to house 14 million artifacts.

TOP EXPERIENCE

The Copenhagen Lakes

Dronning Louises Bro or Peblinge Dossering; free; bus 5C Ravnsborggade (Nørrebrogade), Metro Nørreport, S-train Nørreport

If the King's Garden is the green lung of central Copenhagen, the Lakes are without doubt the blue version. Flanking the northern edge of the Inner City and connecting the three bros—Vesterbro, Nørrebro, and Østerbro—the Lakes form a natural atrium that joins the various districts. In summer,

Copenhagen Lakes

the lakeside paths hum with life as Copenhageners come out to jog, picnic, or people-watch on a bench. In winter, seagulls land on the frozen surfaces. Paddle boats can be rented from **Kaffesalonen** (Peblinge Dossering 6; tel. 35 35 12 19; https://kaffesalonen.com; daily 9am-10pm; from 110 kr for 30 minutes) close to the Dronning Louises Bro-Nørrebrogade connection.

SLOTSHOLMEN
Christiansborg Palace

Prins Jørgens Gård 1; tel. 33 92 70 85; https://kongeligeslotte.dk; Royal Reception Rooms, Royal Kitchen, and Ruins July-Aug. daily 9am-6pm, Apr.-Sept. daily 10am-5pm, Oct.-Mar. Tues.-Sun. 10am-5pm, Royal Stables July daily 10am-6pm, Apr.-June and Aug.-Sept. daily 1:30pm-4pm, Oct.-Mar. Tues.-Sun. 1:30pm-4pm, Palace Chapel July daily 10am-6pm, Aug.-June daily 10am-5pm; all 4 attractions adults 175 kr, students 155 kr, under age 18 free, Royal Reception Rooms adults 105 kr, students 95 kr, under age 18 free; Royal Kitchens, Ruins, Royal Stables separately adults 65 kr, students 55 kr, under age 18 free; bus 2A, 9A Stormbroen, Nationalmuseet (Vindebrogade), Metro Gammel Strand

Fans of royal splendor should not

miss the tapestries, tiled floors, and frescoed passages of Christiansborg Palace. Although the palace is primarily known as the seat of Parliament, it is also used by the royal family for various functions of high ceremony, including state visits, funerals, and the proclaiming of monarchs. A combination ticket is the best of the admission options and includes an optional guided tour.

The **Royal Reception Rooms** are where King Frederik X receives visiting dignitaries, and during state visits the thrones (no longer used, but relics from pre-constitutional times) can be seen in a lavishly decorated chamber of marble and silk. In the **royal kitchen,** which has been restored to the furnishings and equipment of early-20th-century King Christian X, visitors can follow preparations for the King's Silver Jubilee in 1937. The **royal stables,** which have been home to the royal family's horses since the 1700s, are surviving buildings from the baroque palace of Christian VI. Christiansborg Palace was built on 800-year-old **ruins** of a castle, and some of the remains of these buildings still exist and can be visited. Here, you can learn about the brutal past of battles against pirates whose heads were put on stakes.

The Royal Library
(Det Kongelige Bibliotek)
Black Diamond, Søren Kierkegaards Plads 1; tel. 33 47 47 47; www.kb.dk; Mon.-Fri. 8am-9pm; Sat. 9am-7pm; Black Diamond free, guided tours 75 kr, under age 18 free, check ticket prices for individual events; bus 2A, 5C, 68 Otto Mønsteds Plads (Rysensteensgade), 26 Det Kongelige Bibliotek (Christians Brygge)

Denmark's national library is commonly known as the Black Diamond due to the glimmering dark architecture of the modern part of the complex, which forms one of the most characteristic features of the waterfront. Public guided tours (Mon. 3pm) and private tours are available (contact the library for details). Exhibitions, concerts, and other events are held regularly at the Diamond. A long escalator between the ground floor and the study rooms offers an impressive view into the building's atrium. It also houses a café, **Madkartoteket** (39-95 kr), where you can enjoy a bite and take in the harbor through the wide glass panes.

Thorvaldsen Museum
Bertel Thorvaldsens Plads 2; tel. 21 68 75 68; www.thorvaldsensmuseum.dk; Thurs.-Sun. 10am-5pm; adults 95 kr, under age 18 free; bus 9A, 2A Stormbroen, Nationalmuseet (Vindebrogade), Metro Gammel Strand

Another of Slotsholmen's cultural-historical treasures, the Thorvaldsen Museum houses the work of neoclassicist early 19th-century sculptor Bertel Thorvaldsen, who was born to an Icelandic family in Copenhagen and spent much of his adult life in Italy. The stately facade of the museum, which bears a passing resemblance to Berlin's Brandenburg Gate, gives a good first impression of the classical splendor within, including Thorvaldsen's personal collection of Greek and Roman sculptures as well as his own works. A free audio guide is available.

Thorvaldsen Museum, Slotsholmen

Danish Jewish Museum

Proviantpassagen 6; tel. 33 11 22 18; https://jewmus.dk/en; Sept.-May Wed.-Sun. 11am-5pm, June-Aug. Tues.-Sun. 10am-5pm; adults 100 kr, students 50 kr, under 18 free; bus, 2A Børsen (Børsgade), Metro Gammel Strand

Denmark was occupied by Germany throughout World War II, and Danes of older generations often proudly recall the efforts made by the country's citizens and small but significant resistance movement in helping Jewish Danes escape to neutral Sweden. The story is thoroughly documented at the Danish Jewish Museum, which presents Jewish life in Denmark over a 400-year period.

Danish Museum of Art & Design
(Designmuseum Danmark)

Bredgade 68; tel. 33 18 56 56; https://designmuseum.dk; Tues.-Wed. and Fri.-Sun. 10am-6pm, Thurs. 10am-8pm; adults 130 kr, ages 18-26 and students 90 kr, under age 18 free; Metro Marmorkirken

Arne Jacobsen, Bjarke Ingels, Jørn Utzon . . . Denmark is famed for its design, and Copenhagen is at the center of this, the city having been named UNESCO World Capital of Architecture in 2023. The country's heritage of design and architecture is beautifully showcased at the unsurprisingly well-arranged and renovated Designmuseum Danmark. With a library and archives alongside the exhibitions, the museum is a key center of knowledge for the discipline.

NYHAVN
Kunsthal Charlottenborg

Nyhavn 2; tel. 33 74 46 39; https://kunsthalcharlottenborg.dk; Tues.-Fri. noon-8pm; Sat.-Sun. 11am-5pm; adults 90 kr, students 50 kr, under age 16 free, Wed. after 5pm free; Metro Kongens Nytorv

Like an oasis of calm in the middle of popular Nyhavn, exhibition space Kunsthal Charlottenborg can be found almost magically. You slip away from the bustling harbor and suddenly find yourself in a calming stone courtyard at the entrance to a stately old building. In addition to its international contemporary art

Nyhavn

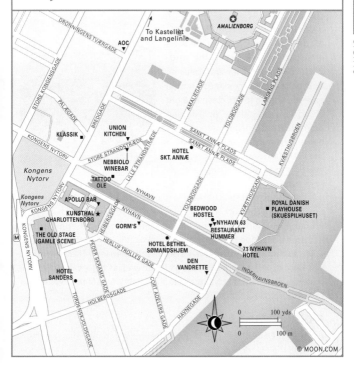

exhibitions, the building contains an arthouse cinema, a bookshop, and a bar.

VESTERBRO AND FREDERIKSBERG
Tycho Brahe Planetarium

Absalonsgade 12; tel. 33 12 12 24; www. planetariet.dk; Mon. noon-6pm, Tues.-Wed. 9:30am-8pm, Thurs. and Sat. 9:30am-8:30pm, Fri. 9:30am-9:30pm, Sun. 9:30am-7pm; movies adults 185 kr, children 115 kr; bus 7A, 26 Vesterbros Torv (Vesterbrogade), S-train Vesterport

An active and interactive space and astronomy center suitable for a family outing, the Tycho Brahe Planetarium's pride and joy is its dome theater, equipped with a 1,000-sq-m (3,290-sq-ft) screen and flight seats that show digital and IMAX films about all things space—whether it be space junk, landing on Mars, or the secrets of the universe. Some shows are in English but for those in Danish, English narration is available through headphones rented for a deposit of 50 kr at the ticket desk. Movie tickets also provide access to the center's astronomy exhibitions.

Danish Design

Danish Design is an umbrella term given to the **functionalist** style of design and architecture that emerged in Denmark in the **mid-20th century** and has since become one of the country's most famed exports. Known for its clean straight edges, timeless styles, simplicity, and high quality in both architecture and design, the movement sprang out of the **German Bauhaus school** and went on to form an identity entirely of its own.

Arne Jacobsen houses

It's not just broad stylistic themes that make design and Denmark synonymous with each other. Particular pieces such as the egg chair or the PH-lamp, or buildings like the Sydney Opera House or Copenhagen's Radisson Collection Hotel, are instantly evocative.

The **minimalist motif,** which is one of the hallmarks of Danish design, was born out of necessity. In the 1950s, as well as before World War II, materials were hard to obtain and low in quality. Out of that was born a simplistic and functional style.

FAMOUS NAMES

A range of Danish designers have achieved international recognition through their work since the middle of the 20th century. These include **Jørn Utzon,** the architect of Sydney's Opera House; furniture designer **Hans J. Wegner;** interior design master **Finn Juhl;** and modern architect **Bjarke Ingels,** founder of the Bjarke Ingels Group, which drew up building designs for New York City's VIA 57 West, the M/S Maritime Mu-

Cykelslangen

Dybbølsbro, Kalvebod Brygge; free; S-train Dybbølsbro

The Bicycle Snake is a bicycle bridge connecting Vesterbro and Amager via the Fisketorvet shopping mall. One of the most recognizable features of the harbor area, it reaches 7 m (23 ft) above the harbor at its highest point. If you've rented a bicycle during your stay, it's well worth pedaling by and seeing the city from a unique, two-wheeled vantage. Part of the Bicycle Snake is accessible only if you're on two wheels, but other bridges nearby allow pedestrians to cross the harbor at the same points and to view the bridge.

Frederiksberg Palace and Gardens

Roskildevej 28 A; https://kongeligeslotte. dk; palace guided tours in Danish last Sat.

seum of Denmark in Helsingør, and the VM Houses and Amager Resource Center in Copenhagen.

ARNE JACOBSEN

The godfather of Danish design is Arne Jacobsen, who will forever be synonymous with the iconic **ant** and **egg chair** designs. His **Series 7 chair** is remarkable, not least for its use in the famous 1963 photo of Christine Keeler by Lewis Morley. Jacobsen's cutlery, including left-handed and right-handed spoons, features in Stanley Kubrick's 1968 sci-fi classic *2001: A Space Odyssey.*

Jacobsen is no less prominent in architecture. Internationally, he designed the Royal Danish Embassy in London and Landskrona Sports-Hall in Sweden, but his legacy is most prominent in Denmark. In and around Copenhagen, the **Bellevue Theater** and **pier at Klampenborg, Skovshoved Petrol Station,** and **Radisson Collection Hotel** are particularly notable, while buildings such as **Stellings Hus,** on the corner of the Gammeltorv square in the Inner City, are more subtle examples of Jacobsen's contribution to the city landscape.

AROUND TOWN

The Danish capital's modern urban space has been directly altered and influenced by the country's design and architectural tradition. Today, square, blocky, modern buildings tessellate and make use of their space without shooting far into the sky like skyscrapers in other cities. **BLOX,** the harborside edifice that is home to the **Danish Architecture Center,** is a fitting example, but these buildings can be found all over the city, particularly in the **Ørestad** area of Amager and along the **harbor front** and parts of the **Inner City.** Just look up and around you and you're likely to see at least one structure that draws on the legacy of Jacobsen and his peers. To get a taste of Danish design under one roof, visit the **Danish Museum of Art & Design.**

of the month 11am and 1pm, contact via FAK-HO-GSE02@mil.dk to arrange a tour in English; gardens daily 6am-5pm or 10pm, depending on the season; palace guided tour 100 kr, gardens free; bus 7A Zoologisk Have (Roskildevej), 26 De Små Haver (Pile Allé)
Frederiksberg Palace, a former royal summer residence, looks grandly across the broad green Frederiksberg gardens, a perfect place for a summer picnic or a winter walk. Winding paths and babbling lakes (rowing boat tours are available) adorn the gardens, while monthly guided tours offer a chance to see inside the palace. The tours are in Danish, but private English-laguage tours can be arranged. The northern end of the gardens adjoins Copenhagen Zoo. A broad elongated palace in the baroque style, the three-story H-shaped building was completed in 1709.

Vesterbro and Frederiksberg

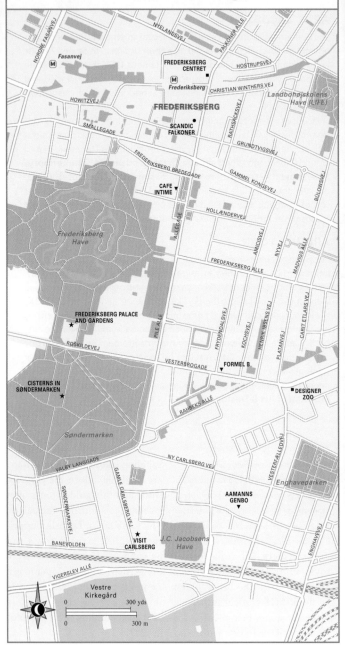

NYELANDSVEJ

NORDRE FASANVEJ

FALKONER ALLÉ

Fasanvej Ⓜ

FREDERIKSBERG CENTRET

HOSTRUPSVEJ

Ⓜ Frederiksberg

CHRISTIAN WINTHERS VEJ

FREDERIKSBERG

Landbohøjskolens Have (LIFE)

HOWITZVEJ

RATHSACKSVEJ

SMALLEGADE

SCANDIC FALKONER

GRUNDTVIGSVEJ

FREDERIKSBERG BREDEGADE

GAMMEL KONGEVEJ

BÜLOWSVEJ

CAFE INTIME ▼

HOLLÆNDERVEJ

ALLÉGADE

Frederiksberg Have

AMICISVEJ

NYVEJ

MADVIGS ALLÉ

FREDERIKSBERG ALLÉ

FRYDENDALSVEJ

KOCHSVEJ

HENRIK IBSENS VEJ

CARIT ETLARS VEJ

FREDERIKSBERG PALACE AND GARDENS ★

PILE ALLÉ

PLATANVEJ

ROSKILDEVEJ

VESTERBROGADE

FORMEL B ▼

CISTERNS IN SØNDERMARKEN ★

DESIGNER ZOO ■

RAHBEKS ALLÉ

Søndermarken

VESTERFÆLLEDVEJ

NY CARLSBERG VEJ

Enghaveparken

VALBY LANGGADE

GAMLE CARLSBERG VEJ

AAMANNS GENBO ▼

SØNDERMARKSVEJ

ENGHAVEVEJ

BANEVOLDEN

VISIT CARLSBERG ★

J.C. Jacobsens Have

VIGERSLEV ALLÉ

Vestre Kirkegård

0   300 yds

0   300 m

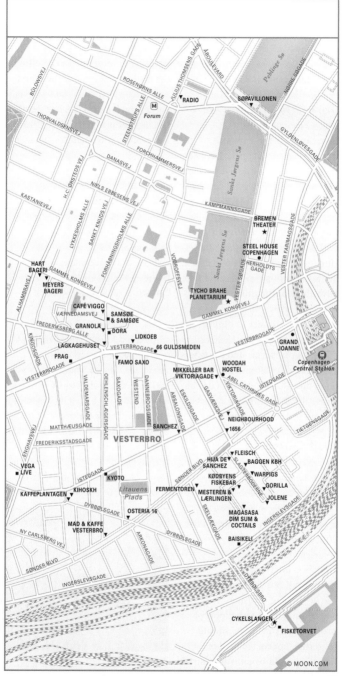

Cisterns in Søndermarken

Søndermarken; tel. 69 13 80 90; https:// frederiksbergmuseerne.dk/en/cisternerne; Tues.-Wed. and Fri.-Sun. 11am-6pm, Thurs. 11am-8pm; adults 115 kr, students and under age 27 90 kr, under age 18 free; 7A Zoologisk Have (Roskildevej)

You can find the entrance to the underground Cisterns between two glass pyramids opposite Frederiksberg Palace. They were originally built to secure a water supply for the city after a cholera outbreak in the 1850s. In modern Copenhagen, they are the setting for art exhibitions in a mix of genres and other events that take advantage of the unique architecture and very un-Scandinavian climate—humidity is almost 100 percent. Regardless of what's on, the watery underground chambers are great for exploration. It's also a good place to visit on a hot day because the underground chambers remain at a cool temperature.

Visit Carlsberg

Gamle Carlsberg Vej 11; tel. 33 27 13 98; www.visitcarlsberg.dk; May-Sept. daily 10am-6pm, Oct.-Apr. Tues.-Sun. 10am-5pm; adults 100 kr, students and under age 17 70 kr, under age 5 free, beer tasting 80 kr, guided history tour 60 kr; bus 1A Enghavevej, 8A, 26 Kammasvej

Craft beer is all the rage in Denmark these days, but that doesn't mean the heritage of Carlsberg as one of the country's biggest exports and products has been, or should be, forgotten. Located in the brewery's handsome old brick warehouses, the Visit Carlsberg experience includes horsedrawn carriage tours, tasting sessions (Carlsberg is not just lager), a museum tour detailing the history and story of the brand, and the biggest collection of beer bottles you'll ever see. A free shuttle bus leaves hourly 11am-4pm from Vesterbrogade 6 (near Copenhagen Central Station).

NØRREBRO AND ØSTERBRO
Assistens Cemetery

Kapelvej 2; tel. 33 66 91 00; www. kk.dk/brug-byen/byens-groenne-oaser/ koebenhavns-kirkegaarde/assistens-kirkegaard; Apr.-Sept. daily 7am-10pm, Oct.-Mar. daily 7am-7pm; free, digital and print guided tours available in English, call or check the website for upcoming programming; bus 5C Kapelvej (Nørrebrogade)

Assistens is not the only cemetery in the world to be a tourist attraction, but it is perhaps unique in being considered a genuinely pleasant place, and many Copenhageners take advantage of the green space in a busy part of the city for a morning jog, an afternoon stroll, or a picnic among the

Assistens Cemetery

gravestones. The calm green areas and creaking, reassuring presence of the old trees are one reason for this. Some of Denmark's most famous sons and daughters, including philosopher Søren Kierkegaard, physicist Niels Bohr, and fairy-tale author Hans Christian Andersen, are buried here.

Superkilen Park

Nørrebrogade 208; free; bus 5C
Nørrebrohallen (Nørrebrogade)

A strip of Nørrebro that is a former train track converted into an urban park area, Superkilen was designed with the collaboration of Bjarke Ingels's prestigious BIG architecture company and has an incongruous international aesthetic, with multicolored paving, a large red star at the top of a pole, and various skateboarding jumps, bicycle paths, and rock-climbing frames. The rolling concrete of the park is traversed by white lane markers, while neon signs display both a red star and a green crescent. Intended to promote a sense of community in one of Copenhagen's more marginalized areas, its internationality and diversity sets out to reflect the demographic of the area. It can be used as a park and a place of exercise.

Police Museum
(Politimuseet)

*Fælledvej 20; tel. 40 32 58 88; www.
politimuseum.dk; Tues., Thurs., and
Sat.-Sun. 11am-4pm; adults 60 kr, under
age 18 free; bus 5C Ravnsborggade
(Nørrebrogade)*

The Police Museum, housed in a former police station from 1883 in the heart of Nørrebro, tells the story of Copenhagen's law enforcement through the decades. There's a wealth of photos, artifacts, and old case files to wade through, including a macabre "murder room" with evidence from homicide cases that, to state the obvious, is not suitable for children. Some fascinating guided tours are also available with retired officers as guides. The tours can be booked online but may not be available in English—check with the museum by calling or emailing booking@politimuseum.dk.

CHRISTIANSHAVN AND AMAGER

TOP EXPERIENCE

✪ Church of Our Saviour

*Sankt Annæ Gade 29; tel. 41 66 63 57;
www.vorfrelserskirke.dk; tower 9am-8pm
daily, may close due to heavy rain, snow,
or strong wind; adults 69 kr, children 20
kr; church 11am-3:30pm daily, free; bus
2A Christianshavn St. (Torvegade), Metro
Christianshavn St.*

The gilded spire of the baroque Church of Our Saviour rises dramatically above the low rooftops of Christianshavn. Legend has it that Laurids de Thurah, the designer of the 17th-century spiral spire, threw himself from its top after realizing it had been twirled counterclockwise, but this is a myth, he actually died in his bed seven years after its completion.

The church can be visited

Nørrebro

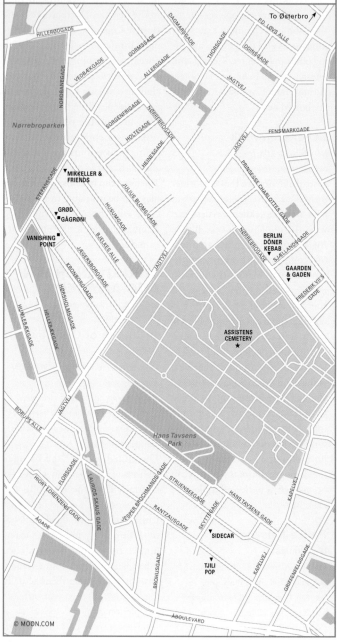

To Østerbro ↗

HILLERØDGADE
DAGMARSGADE
P.D. LØVS ALLÉ
NORDBANEGADE
GORMSGADE
THORSGADE
ODINSGADE
VEDBÆKGADE
ALLERSGADE
JAGTVEJ

Nørrebroparken

SORGENFRIGADE
NØRREBROGADE
FENSMARKGADE
HOLTEGADE
HEINESGADE
JAGTVEJ
PRINSESSE CHARLOTTES GADE

▼ MIKKELLER & FRIENDS

STEFANSGADE
JULIUS BLOMS GADE
HUSUMGADE

■ GRØD
■ GÅGRØN!
BJELKES ALLÉ
NØRREBROGADE
BERLIN DÖNER KEBAB ▼
SJÆLLANDSGADE
■ VANISHING POINT
JÆGERSBORGGADE
JAGTVEJ
GAARDEN & GADEN ▼
FREDERIK VII'S GADE

KRONBORGGADE
KRONBORGGADE
HØRSHOLMSGADE
HELLEBÆKGADE
HUMLEBÆKGADE

ASSISTENS CEMETERY ★

BORUPS ALLÉ
JAGTVEJ

Hans Tavsens Park

FLORSGADE
HIORT LORENZENS GADE
LAURIDS SKAUS GADE
JESPER BROCHMANDS GADE
STRUENSEEGADE
SKYTTEGADE
HANS TAVSENS GADE
KAPELVEJ
ÅGADE
RANTZAUSGADE

SIDECAR ▼

BROHUSGADE
TJILI POP ▼
KAPELVEJ
GREFSENFELDSGADE

ÅBOULEVARD

© MOON.COM

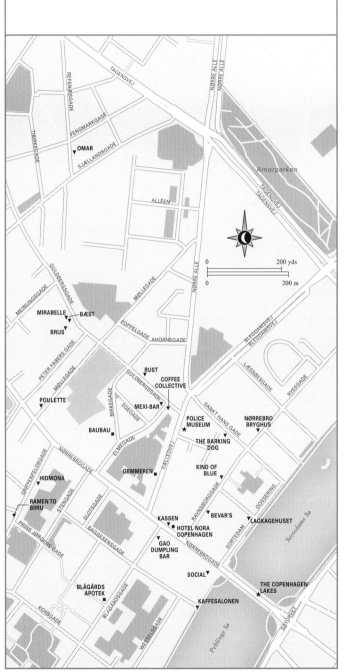

OMAR

Amorparken

TAGENSVEJ

REFSNÆSGADE

FENSMARKGADE

SJÆLLANDSGADE

ALLÉEN

NØRRE ALLÉ
NØRRE ALLÉ

TIBIRKEGADE

TAGENSVEJ
TAGENSVEJ

0   200 yds
0   200 m

GULDBERGSGADE

MØLLEGADE

NØRRE ALLÉ

BLEGDAMSVEJ
BLEGDAMSVEJ

MEINUNGSGADE

MIRABELLE   BÆST

BRUS

POPPELGADE   AHORNSGADE

LÆSSØESGADE

RYESGADE

PETER FABERS GADE

MØLLEGADE

RUST

GULDBERGSGADE

COFFEE
COLLECTIVE

POULETTE

BIRKEGADE

EGEGADE

MEXI-BAR

SANKT HANS GADE

NØRREBRO
BRYGHUS

BAUBAU

ELMEGADE

POLICE
MUSEUM

THE BARKING
DOG

GRIFFENFELDSGADE

NØRREBROGADE

GEMMEREN

FÆLLEDVEJ

KIND OF
BLUE

HIDMONA

STENGADE

SLOTSGADE

DOSSERING

RAMEN TO
BIIRU

RAVNSBORGGADE

BEVAR'S

LAGKAGEHUSET

Sortedams Sø

PRINS JØRGENS GADE

BAGGESENSGADE

KASSEN

SORTEDAM

HOTEL NORA
COPENHAGEN

GAO
DUMPLING
BAR

NØRREBROGADE

BLÅGÅRDS
APOTEK

BLÅGÅRDSGADE

SOCIAL

THE COPENHAGEN
LAKES

KORSGADE

WESSELSGADE

KAFFESALONEN

SØTORVET

Peblinge Sø

Church of Our Saviour

year-round for free, but the real treat is climbing the spire, where a view from 90 m (295 ft) above Copenhagen can be enjoyed. There are 400 steps to the top, of which the last 150 are actually on the outside of the spire, so you get a full 360-degree panorama as you go up. Be warned: The outside section is not for those who are averse to heights. Prior booking via the website is optional but advised in peak season.

✪ Refshaleøen

Refshaleøen; https://refshaleoen.dk; bus 2A (Refshalevej)

Gray concrete, the clang of steel on steel, and the clash of waves against the quayside: The holdovers of an industrial port of years gone by are now the backdrop of a popular spot on the eastern limits of Copenhagen, where the street food market **Reffen** (Refshalevej 167A;

tel. 33 93 07 60; https://reffen.dk) opened on a 10,000-sq-m (33,000-sq-ft) plot in 2018. Crowds of Copenhageners and visitors make the relatively long bicycle trip out to the converted shipping containers that are lined up in diagonal rows as far as the eye can see.

Refshaleøen is still in touch with its roots as an industrial area. Boathouses, crumbling factories, and neglected plots of land share the space with workshops and Danish craft beer icon Mikkeller, which has a large bar, **Mikkeller Baghaven,** here. **La Banchina,** with its jetty seating area, is a great spot to view the sunset over the sea while drinking a glass of wine.

You may see increasing construction activity during visits to Refshaleøen in the coming years: A gigantic government project to build an entirely new district, Lynetteholm, on land

Christianshavn and Amager

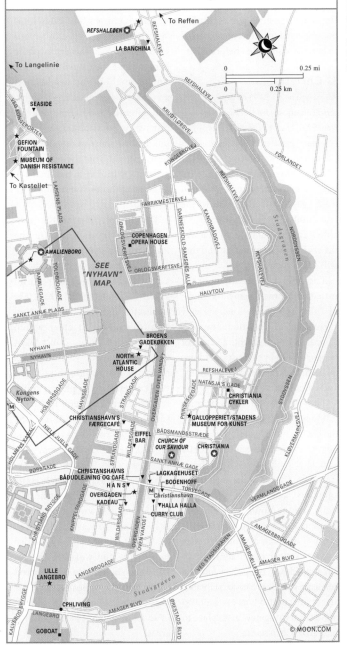

To Reffen

REFSHALEØEN

LA BANCHINA

REFSHALEVEJ

To Langelinie

KRUDTLØBSVEJ

REFSHALEVEJ

KONGEBROVEJ

FORLANDET

0   0.25 mi

0   0.25 km

SEASIDE

GEFION
FOUNTAIN

MUSEUM OF
DANISH RESISTANCE

To Kastellet

FABRIKMESTERVEJ

DANNESKIOLD-SAMSØES ALLE

KANONBÅDSVEJ

REFSHALEVEJ

NORDDYSSEN

ORLOGSVÆRFTSVEJ

Stadsgraven

LARSENS PLADS

COPENHAGEN
OPERA HOUSE

AMALIENBORG

SEE
"NYHAVN"
MAP

ORLOGSVÆRFTSVEJ

HALVTOLV

TOLDBODGADE

AMALIEGADE

SANKT ANNÆ PLADS

NYHAVN

NYHAVN

BROENS
GADEKØKKEN

REFSHALEVEJ

NATASJA'S GADE

CHRISTIANIA
CYKLER

HØJBROGADE

HAVNEGADE

STRANDGADE

NORTH
ATLANTIC
HOUSE

OVERGADEN OVEN VANDET

PRINSESSEGADE

Kongens
Nytorv

M

NIELS JUELS GADE

CHRISTIANSHAVN'S
FÆRGECAFÉ

WILDERSGADE

EIFFEL
BAR

BÅDSMANDSSTRÆDE

GALLOPPERIET/STADENS
MUSEUM FOR KUNST

CHRISTIANIA

CHURCH OF
OUR SAVIOUR

HIDLMENS KANAL

BØRSGADE

CHRISTANSHAVNS
BÅDUDLEJNING OG CAFÉ

STRANDGADE

WILDERSGADE

SANKT ANNÆ GADE

LAGKAGEHUSET

KLØVERMARKSVEJ

HANS

OVERGADEN

M

BODENHOFF

Christianshavn

VERMLANDSGADE

KADEAU

OVERGADEN
OVEN VANDET

HALLA HALLA

TORVEGADE

KNIPPELSBROGADE

CURRY CLUB

CHRISTIANS BRYGGE

AMAGERBROGADE

LANGEBROGADE

AMAGER BLVD

AMAGER BLVD

Stadsgraven

NED STADSGRAVEN

AMAGERFÆLLEDVEJ

ØRESTADS BLVD

LILLE
LANGEBRO

KALVEBOD BRYGGE

LANGEBRO

CPHLIVING

AMAGER BLVD

GOBOAT

© MOON.COM

reclaimed from the sea is underway within throwing distance from Refshaleøen, which will eventually be connected to it. It is not expected to be fully completed before 2070.

✪ Christiania

Prinsessegade; tel. 32 95 65 07; www.
christiania.org; guided tours Sat.-Sun.
3pm; 50 kr; bus 2A Bodenhoffs Plads
(Prinsessegade), Metro Christianshavn St.

"You are now leaving the EU," a sign above the entrance to Christiania used to read. The sign disappeared at some point in the late 2000s, but it epitomized the antiestablishment thought that was the essence of its founding and that still exists today.

The first "Christianites" broke into the former army barracks in 1971, and before long the new "Freetown" of Christiania was declared, its first residents a group of people united by their desire to live on principles of freedom, creativity, and community.

The occupation of the former military buildings was illegal from the outset, and throughout its history, relations between Christiania and the authorities have been fractious; the area has seen some aggressive and violent confrontations. The famous Pusher Street Market, which openly sold marijuana and related products, was a major source of the tension. By 2024, residents, the police, and the government agreed to close Pusher Street for good. Plans are afoot to build something new in its place to revitalize Christiania.

Thousands of tourists visit annually, and Christiania generally welcomes visitors: The cafés, market, and shops are open to anyone who passes by. The atmosphere here, unique for Copenhagen and unlike anything you would come across anywhere else, has a highly anti-authority and free outlook and progressive political stances underpinned by a sense of rebellion that never feels far from the surface. It's generally safe to visit, but there are a couple of things you should keep in mind.

Photography has, in the past, not been tolerated around the Pusher Street area, and anyone taking pictures could find themselves being confronted and asked to delete them. There are normally signs in Danish and English making it clear which parts Christianites don't want photographed, but when in doubt, resist the temptation to take out your camera or your phone. Police raids occurred frequently during the Pusher Street era. Anyone buying from the illicit hash trade is breaking the law and does so at their own risk. It is worth checking local news reports, such as the English-language publication *The Local Denmark* (www.thelocal.dk) or national broadcaster DR (www.dr.dk) for reports about violence in the area and warnings not to visit. You should also be prepared for the chance of passively inhaling very pungent smoky clouds in some of the cafés and outdoor areas.

Dyssen at Christiania

A **guided tour** (www.rundviser-gruppen.dk) is available for tourists, led by a "native" Christianite who presents the residents' side of the story and shows visitors around the "free state," which at 34 ha (84 acres) is larger than you might expect. Because the tour is run by Christianites, it's respectful of the space and not at all exploitative. The tour meets at the main entrance to Christiania on Prinsessegade.

Dyssen at Christiania

Prinsessegade; www.christiania.org; free; bus 2A Bodenhoffs Plads (Prinsessegade), Metro Christianshavn St. for access via Christiania or bus 5C Amagerfælledvej (Amager Blvd.), Metro Christianshavn for access via Christmas Møllers Plads

The "unknown" Christiania, Dyssen—literally "cairn," but a name with its origins in slang—is a long strip of land on the opposite side of the Stadsgraven lake, the crescent-shaped body of water that separates Christianshavn and Christiania from Amager. Not part of the former barracks, which the original squatters occupied to found Christiania in the 1970s, the 2-km (1.2-mi) stretch of land now has a variety of unusually designed houses built by Christianites. It's a remarkably quiet green area where you can stroll and listen to the birds sing. The northern end of Dyssen brings you nicely onto Refshaleøen.

Gallopperiet/Stadens Museum for Kunst

Loppebygningen, Sydområdet 4 A, 2.tv, Christiania; tel. 22 24 09 08; www.gallopperiet.dk; Tues.-Sun. 2pm-7pm; free; bus 2A Bodenhoffs Plads (Prinsessegade), Metro Christianshavn St.

Riffing on the Danish name for the National Gallery (Staden instead of Staten means the gallery belongs to

Christiania, rather than the Danish state), this gallery provides space for local artists to displays their works. Exhibitions change regularly and new ones often appear at short notice, so phone or check the website to see what's on. It's located on the second floor of a former barracks separating Christiania from Christianshavn.

Lille Langebro

Lille Langebro, Christians Brygge; free; bus 2A, 5C, 68 Otto Mønsteds Plads (Rysensteensgade), 26 Det Kongelige Bibliotek (Christians Brygge)

A little sibling to Cykelslangen, Lille (Little) Langebro bridge was opened in 2019 and conveniently connects the Christians Brygge side of the harbor, next to the Danish Architecture Center, with Christianshavn and Islands Brygge. The much older and original Langebro arches nearby, allowing heavy road traffic to head in and out of town. Pedestrians and cyclists cross the water side by side, and you get a pleasant view of the harbor, especially on more serene mornings. The bridge, which is closed to cars, rotates smartly outward when larger vessels pass along the waterway: prepare to wait among agitated cyclists when this happens.

Overgaden

Overgaden Neden Vandet 17; tel. 32 57 72 73; https://overgaden.org; Tues. and Thurs.-Fri. 1pm-6pm, Wed. 1pm-8pm, Sat.-Sun. 11am-6pm; free; bus 2A Knippelsbro (Torvegade), Metro Christianshavn St.

This welcoming nonprofit gallery has a splendid setting in one of the elegant tall houses on the Christianshavn canal. Besides having eight or so exhibitions of new contemporary and emerging art annually, its two floors also play host to small concerts, film screenings, talks, and performances.

North Atlantic House
(Nordatlantens Brygge)

Strandgade 91; tel. 32 83 37 00; www.nordatlantens.dk; Mon.-Fri. 10am-5pm, Sat.-Sun. noon-5pm; adults 40 kr, seniors 30 kr, students 20 kr, under age 12 free; bus 2A, Knippelsbro (Torvegade), Metro Christianshavn St.

Nordatlantens Brygge showcases the culture of the northern Nordic nations of Iceland, Greenland, and the Faroe Islands through its exhibitions, while also acting as a venue for performances, dance, music, films, lectures, and anything else related to the region. The official representatives in mainland Denmark of the Faroe Islands, Greenland, and Iceland are all located here, as is the restaurant Barr.

KASTELLET AND LANGELINIE
The Citadel
(Kastellet)

Gl. Hovedvagt, Kastellet 1; tel. 72 84 00 00; www.kastellet.dk; summer daily 6am-10pm, winter daily 6am-8pm; free; bus 23 Østerport St. (Oslo Plads), S-train Østerport

One of the best-preserved examples of a medieval star fortress in Europe, the Citadel—Kastellet in Danish—is still used by the

Kastellet (the Citadel)

military, which occupies some of its buildings. You might see a military ceremony if you happen to pass by on occasions such as Flag Day (September 5) or NATO Day (April 4). Much of the Citadel, which forms a pentagram surrounded on all sides by water, is open to the public, and its grassy ramparts make for a pleasant walk with great views of the surrounding area, including the barracks, the harbor, and the city. Sights include a former powder house, a church, a prison, and a windmill.

The *Little Mermaid*

Langelinie; www.mermaidsculpture.dk; free; bus 27 (Indiakaj), S-train Østerport

It needs little introduction, but Copenhagen icon the *Little Mermaid,* which was inspired by Hans Christian Andersen's fairy tale, is easy to miss. The diminutive bronze statue is tucked away on Langelinie but instantly recognizable from thousands of Copenhagen stock images, even if the real thing can feel a bit anticlimactic. If you want your photo with the mermaid, arrive early in the day or be prepared to wait your turn. To find the statue, continue to the end of Amaliegade past Amalienborg Palace, then walk past the Gefion Fountain and cross a small bridge onto the Langelinie promenade. Follow the path through a small park, and after around 180 m (200 yards), you will spot the statue below the main walkway.

Museum of Danish Resistance
(Frihedsmuseet)

Esplanaden 13; tel. 41 20 60 80; https:// en.natmus.dk; May-Aug. daily 10am-5pm, Sept.-Apr. Tues.-Sun. 10am-5pm; Metro Marmorkirken, S-train Østerport

The Museum of Danish Resistance

finally reopened in 2020 after a long period of closure caused by a fire. Telling the story of everyday life in Denmark during the Nazi Occupation of 1940-1945, scenes show dilemmas faced by Danes during the occupation, how the resistance movement began, and images from the period. Much of the narrative is presented through the perspective of five real historical people.

Gefion Fountain

Churchillparken; Metro Marmorkirken, S-train Østerport

The monumental Gefion Fountain is a relatively overlooked sculpture by Danish naturalist Anders Bundgaard, at the southern end of Kastellet near the harbor. It depicts a group of animals being driven onward by Norse goddess Gefjon, who, according to legend, ploughed the island of Zealand out of the sea between Sweden and the rest of Denmark. While many hurry past the fountain or take another route on their way to see the *Little Mermaid,* the Gefion Fountain— which is for ornamental purposes only—is no less admirable.

Recreation

Copenhageners are very outdoorsy for city dwellers and the city is primed for exploration by bicycle or by water. Take care if sailing or kayaking in Copenhagen Harbor— maritime traffic can be hectic during the summer months.

PARKS

Amager Strandpark

Amager Strand Promenaden 1; www.kk.dk/ brug-byen/vandet-i-byen/badestrande/ amager-strandpark; Metro Amager Strand St.

A 4.5-km (2.8-mi) stretch of beach with 60 ha (148 acres) of park and an artificial island, Amager Strandpark is a beautiful spot on the east coast of Amager. On a clear evening you can watch the twinkling of car headlights

Amager Strandpark, looking toward the Øresund Bridge

crossing the Øresund Bridge from Sweden, see aircraft taking off from Copenhagen Airport, and make out the coast of Malmö in the distance. The area is best during the summer, but it's also romantic in the winter if you want to brave the cold.

biking on Nørrebrogade

Amager Fælled

Artillerivej, Amager; www.kk.dk/artikel/
amager-fælled; Metro Islands Brygge

Amager Fælled is a beautiful area of grassy bush, wooded paths, and reeds that glow orange when the unimpeded low sun shines through them for hours during the long summer sunsets. The common is currently a 233-ha (575-acre) national park covering a large expanse of western Amager between Islands Brygge and the distinctive Bellacentret conference center. Much of the area has been left to grow wild, with various types of nature and terrain, including open and dense thickets, marshes, grasslands, lakes, and meadows. There are lanes and paths suitable for bicycling, and various species of wild animals and birds can be spotted.

TOP EXPERIENCE

BICYCLING
Bike Routes

With almost 350 km (217 mi) of bicycle lanes, Copenhagen is one of the least daunting cities in the world to hop on two wheels.

Cycle Superhighways (super-cykelstier, https://supercykelstier. dk) are a coherent network of "fast" bicycle connections with easy-to-follow set routes that take you in and around the city. The routes are planned to go as smoothly and with as few stops as possible with better comfort—for example, there are bicycle-height rails and foot rests to make waiting at traffic lights that much easier. The paths are well maintained, and there are pumps and other service spots located regularly along them.

Harbor Ring Route

The following 13-km (8.1-mi) route, known as the havnering or harbor ring, is actually more like a figure 8 that circles around the harbor. It starts and finishes in Nyhavn and covers some of the most famous spots in town.

Start at **Nyhavn.** Turn right onto **Havnegade** and follow alongside the harbor. After 800 m (0.5 mi), you'll reach **Christians Brygge.** Turn left on this road to keep the harbor on your left. Passing through the middle of the **BLOX building,** continue on Kalvebod Brygge for around 1.5 km (1 mi). Pass **Bølgen (the Wave),** a long, contorted wooden promenade that rolls alongside the water. Continue alongside the harbor (you will need to briefly dismount to push your bicycle up some steps near the Fisketorvet mall). Follow the cycle path as it turns toward the harbor and cross on the **Cykelslangen (the Bicycle Snake)** to reach Islands Brygge.

Turn right and follow Islands Brygge for 2.5 km (1.5 mi) until you get to **Slusen (the Sluice),** a lock which acts as a bridge, and cross back to the other side of the harbor while taking in great views of the docklands. Keep the harbor on your right. Cross the **Teglværksbroen bridge,** about 1.5 km (1 mi) along. Continue on Teglholmsgade street until you can turn right onto the busy O2 ring road, which leads through an industrial section back to the Bicycle Snake.

Cross the harbor on the **Bicycle Snake bridge** for the second time, and this time turn left on Islands Brygge. After around 1.5 km (1 mi), you'll pass under the Langebro and Little Langebro bridges. Continue on (be careful, this section is narrow and bumpy) and cross **Circle Bridge (Cirkelbroen).**

Turn right immediately after the bridge and ride alongside the canal until you can cross over Torvegade. You're now at the heart of charming cobblestoned Christianshavn. Turn right at Skt. Annæ Gade and ride for one block to see the **Church of Our Saviour.** Return to the route on Skt. Annæ Gade and make a right on Overgaden Oven Vandet. This cobbled street ends at a corner where you'll see a sign for a bicycle and pedestrian path. Follow this to get to the **Butterfly 3-Way Bridge** and take the left fork for **Inderhavnsbroen bridge** to return back to Nyhavn.

Rentals and Tours

Bike Copenhagen with Mike

Sankt Peders Stræde 47; tel. 26 39 56 88; https://bikecopenhagenwithmike.dk; summer Fri.-Wed. 10am and/or 2:30pm, fewer tours in winter; 350 kr; bus 5C Rådhuspladsen, Metro Rådhuspladsen

These enthusiastically delivered tours by the eponymous Mike take visitors around central Copenhagen on a 3-hour all-weather tour that covers a lot of ground, ticking off many of the sights and providing cyclists with local history, knowledge, and stories. You'll need to be able to

Strolling

Copenhagen Lakes

Going out for a stroll is a big deal in Copenhagen. In no other city have I found simply going for a stroll to be such a popular and everyday in-and-of-itself activity. I don't mean walking for the sake of going to the shops or the train station or to get to work, but simply because it's pleasant to do. Many spacious, green parks and waterside paths are scattered across the city. The following are some favorite places to stretch your legs and stroll:

- **Copenhagen Lakes,** the lengthy rectangular bodies of water be-tween the Inner City and outer neighborhoods, are surrounded by gravel pathways where people walk and feed the ducks or use the pavement and road bridges for a better vantage (page 58).

- In Nørrebro, **Assistens Cemetery** is also a popular spot for locals to walk, and you can combine it with the fun and perhaps a little dark di-version of hunting for the graves of historical figures—there are signs directing you to the most famous ones (page 66).

- The island of **Amager** is a great place to get outdoors, with two brac-ing options. **Amager Strandpark**—a long stretch of artificial beach with a promenade, lagoons, jetties, and views of Malmö—is blustery in the winter and exhilaratingly hip and family-friendly in the summer, and it's always refreshing (page 76). The large **Amager Fælled** nature reserve is a brambly mass of marshland and fields where bird watchers and hikers could happily spend an entire day (page 77).

bicycle in traffic. Bookings can be made by phone or the website, and helmet rental is included in the tour price.

Green Bike Tours

Rosenborggade 3K; tel. 24 85 10 07; https://greenbiketours.org; private tours only, book ahead to arrange times and rates; bus 5C Nørre Farimagsgade (Frederiksborggade), Metro Nørreport, S-train Nørreport

"We go by bike or walking and save the environment 1.1 kg (2 lbs) of carbon per person on every tour" is the pitch from Green Bike Tours, who offer sustainability-focused private bicycle tours around the city. This means you'll get to see places like bike bridges, green architecture, and city planning and wind technology, and even visit organic eateries, depending on the tour you opt for. A shorter walking version of the tour is also offered, and there is a Green Bike Tour in Malmö (as well as Berlin). The young eco-friendly guides are passionate about both the planet and their bicycles.

Christiania Cykler

Mælkevejen 83A; tel. 70 70 76 80; www. christianiacykler.dk; Mon.-Tues. and Thurs.- Fri. 9am-5:30pm, Wed. 10am-5:30pm, Sat. 11am-3pm; bus 2A, Christianshavn St. (Torvegade), Metro Christianshavn St.

The classic Christiania three-wheeled cargo cycles, commonly seen with one or more children in the front being ferried around Copenhagen by a parent, can be rented at Christiania Cykler in

Christiania Cykler cargo cycle

Christiania (550 kr per day, 250 kr per additional day, deposit 1,500 kr). If you want to splurge, they can be purchased in various models and sizes; a new bike will set you back at least 11,000 kr.

KAYAKING AND BOATING

Kayak Republic

Børskaj 12; tel. 30 49 00 13; https:// kayakrepublic.dk; May daily noon-9pm, June-July daily 10am-9pm, Aug.-Sept. daily 10am-8pm, tours May-Sept. daily 10am; kayak rental from 195 kr, tours from 395 kr pp; bus 2A Knippelsbro (Torvegade), Metro Christianshavn St.

Paddle out and see Copenhagen's harbor and canals from a true sea-level perspective with Kayak Republic, which offers guided kayak tours as well as independent kayak rental. Single and double kayaks are available, as are sea kayaks. An IPP 2 or BCU 2 certificate and ID must be presented to rent sea kayaks. You can refuel at the attached restaurant and bar, Kayak Bar, once you're done paddling for the day.

GoBoat

Islands Brygge 10; tel. 40 26 10 25; https:// goboat.dk/en; daily 9:30am-sunset; 1 hour 549 kr per boat, less for additional hours; bus 5C, Klaksviggade, Metro Islands Brygge

Go Boats are the cheapest and easiest way to get on a boat of your own on Copenhagen harbor. Go Boats are easy-to-use motorized boats that seat up to eight and have a little table where you can enjoy a picnic or even a glass of champagne with your crewmates. Boats can be operated by anyone over age 18 and no prior experience is required. Book ahead during summer.

TOURS

Stromma

Nyhavn, various hop on-hop off points around the city; tel. 32 96 30 00; www. stromma.com; boat tours from 109 kr, bus tours from 175 kr; Metro Kongens Nytorv

Stromma is one of the largest group tour operators in the city and offers a range of bus and boat tours, including a classic one-hour boat trip with a guide as well as hop-on, hop-off services. In 2018 Stromma became the first canal tour operator to bring visitors directly to the Reffen food market at Refshaleøen from the Inner City. Various combinations are available, as is a snail's pace trailer train, which takes visitors around the central sights. Audio guides are included in the ticket prices.

Boatie

Bådehavnsgade 27; tel. 60 56 66 09; https://boatie.dk; tours daily, various departure and drop-off points; from 1,500 kr

Selling itself as the most comfortable boat trip in Copenhagen, Boatie's "sofa boats" (fitted with plastic roofing for poor weather) go a long way to living up to that claim, but the most unique feature of this tour provider is its Aperol cruises (2,995 kr) in which groups of up to 12 enjoy Aperol spritz cocktails and premium snacks as they view highlights of Copenhagen Harbor. Boatie is best enjoyed on warm dry summer evenings, when you'll have plenty of company.

Nordic Noir Tours

Vesterport Station; tel. 26 10 06 33; https://nordicnoirtours.com; Sat.-Sun.; from 250 kr, depending on the number of participants; bus or S-train Vesterport

The Bridge, The Killing, Borgen, and most recently Netflix's *The Chestnut Man:* The locations of the dark drama of Nordic noir TV are the subject of Nordic Noir Tours. There are two different walks inspired by the atmospheric Scandinoir of these TV shows: One focuses on the political drama *Borgen,* and the other revolves around the darker crime fiction genre. Advanced reservations are necessary; inquiries can be made via the website or phone. Check ahead—you will receive a response the same day—whether tours are available and how many people have signed up.

SPECTATOR SPORTS

Parken Stadium

*Per Henrik Lings Allé 2; tel. 35 43 31 31;
www.parken.dk; bus 1A, 14 Trianglen, Metro
Trianglen*

Parken, the stadium of Denmark's national soccer team, is also the home of FC Copenhagen, locally called FCK, the country's best-known and most successful soccer team that competes most seasons in the UEFA Champions League or Europa League. The stadium also hosts major concerts. Tickets for big events as well as national team and Champions League matches are generally snapped up quickly, but Danish league matches are easier to attend. Tickets are sold via FC Copenhagen's website (www.fck.dk/en).

Theater and Performing Arts

Copenhagen is not lacking in fine arts, with the architectural marvel that is the quayside Opera House, the Old Stage at Det Kongelige Teater (the Royal Theater), and state broadcaster DR's concert hall, backed up by a strong supporting cast of smaller venues.

ARTS AND CULTURE

The Royal Theater
(Det Kongelige Teater)

The Royal Theater (Det Kongelige Teater) is an umbrella name used for three different cultural institutions in Copenhagen: Gamle Scene, Operaen, and Skuespilhuset.

The Old Stage
(Gamle Scene)

*Kongens Nytorv; tel. 33 69 69 69; https://
kglteater.dk; from 115 kr; Metro Kongens
Nytorv*

The stately Gamle Scene is the oldest Royal Theater building. It opened in 1874 and was designed by Vilhelm Dahlerup, the architect responsible for a number of other classical Copenhagen landmarks, including the Ny Carlsberg Glyptotek, Hotel D'Angleterre, and Dronning Louises Bro. It is an elegant mix of alcoves, archways, and sculptures. Originally built for theater, opera, and ballet, it is now primarily the home of the Royal Danish Ballet. Check the website for details and ticket availability. English-language theater tours are sometimes available. The season runs August-June.

Royal Danish Playhouse
(Skuespilhuset)

*Sankt Annæ Plads 36; tel. 33 69 69 69;
https://kglteater.dk; from 125 kr, occasional
free events; bus 26 Sankt Annæ Plads,
Skuespilhuset (Sankt Annæ Plads), Metro
Kongens Nytorv*

The 750-million-kroner harborside theater Skuespilhuset opened in 2008 with a production of the most famous play ever to be set in Denmark, *Hamlet*. The building can't be missed, with clean, low-slung square lines and glass facades almost overhanging the harbor. English subtitles are occasionally available for some productions. Occasional free events like poetry slams in the foyer and low-cost ones like morning dancing on the neighboring Ofelias Plads harbor terrace (summer, 90 kr) are alternative options to the plays.

Copenhagen Opera House (Operaen)

Ekvipagemestervej 10; tel. 33 69 69 69; https://kglteater.dk; from 165 kr; bus 2A Galionsvej (Danneskiold-Samsøes Allé)

Dramatically complementing the Playhouse from its setting on the opposite side of the harbor, the Opera House is one of the visual highlights of the entire city. Its neo-futurist style incorporates a large curved glass and metal grid front, a limestone exterior, and small canals that make you feel as though you're on an island. Inside, large spherical chandeliers designed by Icelandic Danish artist Olafur Eliasson illuminate the marble floors; the patterns and reflections change depending on the viewing angle. Concerts and operas alike can be enjoyed here.

Tivoli Concert Hall

Vesterbrogade 3; tel. 33 15 10 01; www. tivoli.dk; from 185 kr, includes Tivoli Gardens; bus 5C Tivoli v. Hovedbanegården (Central Station), S-train Hovedbanegården (Central Station), Metro Hovedbanegåden (Central Station)

The concert hall at Tivoli Gardens is a charming place to take in an evening show. It's set in the middle of the old-fashioned fairground's flowery gardens, lights, fountains, and restaurants. Orchestra, ballet, opera, and Danish folk favorites regularly appear at the venue, which is open during Tivoli's normal operating seasons.

Bremen Theater

Nyropsgade 39-4; tel. 30 32 40 90; https://brementeater.dk; from 225 kr; bus 31 Vesterport St. (ved Vesterport), 37, 68 Vesterport St. (Vester Farimagsgade), S-train Vesterport

Billing itself as an alternative to traditional theaters, Bremen is host to stand-up comedy and a fair selection of concerts. These categories include both domestic and international acts, notably US, Irish, and British comedians and European bands as well as the significant Danish contingent. The fall 2023 program included Foil Arms and Hog, Sara Schaefer, and the Amy Winehouse Band.

LIVE MUSIC

Jazzhus Montmartre

Store Regnegade 19A; tel. 70 20 20 96; www.jazzhusmontmartre.dk; from 330 kr, tables must be booked in advance; bus, Metro, or S-train Nørreport

Historical jazz club Jazz Montmartre has hosted concerts at the same Copenhagen venue since 1959 and enjoyed a heyday in the 1970s when a number of top international artists spent time in the Danish capital. It was restored and reopened in 2010 and regularly hosts concerts with up-and-coming and established acts.

Vega Live

Enghavevej 40; tel. 33 25 70 11; https://vega.dk; from 210 kr; bus 1A Tove Ditlevsens Plads (Enghavevej), Metro Enghave Plads

Vega's concert halls have a strong program of mainly indie acts with some other musical genres also represented—you maybe be lucky enough to catch one of your favorite bands visiting during your stay. The venue consists of two concert rooms: Store (Large) Vega, which has a capacity of 1,500 standing or 900 seated; and Lille (Little) Vega, for 500 standing or 160 seated. In addition to the music stages, smaller concerts take place in the attached Ideal Bar, which has been fitted with a new immersive sound setup.

DR Koncerthuset

Ørestads Blvd. 13; tel. 35 20 62 62; https://drkoncerthuset.dk; from 180 kr; Metro DR Byen

DR Koncert Hall, the super modern concert venue in DR City, the Amager neighborhood that is home to the national broadcaster DR, stands out in an already clean, futuristic-looking area around the DR Byen Metro station. Big band, swing, and the Danish National Girls Choir are regular features on a wide-ranging program. With a total space of 25,000 sq m (270,000 sq ft), the complex includes an 1,800-seat concert hall as well as three recording studios.

Royal Arena

Hannemanns Allé 18-20; tel. 32 46 04 60; www.royalarena.dk; from 300 kr; Metro Ørestad St.

Catering to the biggest names—Madonna, Diana Ross, John Mayer, and 50 Cent were among those on the 2023-2024 season program—the 16,000-seat Royal Arena is located a 20-minute Metro ride from central Copenhagen in south Amager. It also hosts sporting events like 2023's World Badminton Championships and occasionally big comedy performances—Ricky Gervais has appeared on several occasions.

Amager Bio

Øresundsvej 6; tel. 32 86 08 80; https://amagerbio.dk; Amager Bio from 260 kr, Beta 140 kr; bus 5C Amagerbrogade (Øresundsvej), Metro Amagerbro St.

The prolific Amager Bio is one of Copenhagen's most well-visited venues, with around 200 concerts yearly at its 1,000-seat converted cinema theater, as well as the smaller and more intimate Beta venue. A wide range of established stars and hopefuls from Denmark and abroad play a span of genres including rock, indie, pop, blues, metal, and jazz.

Festivals and Events

Festival peak season in Copenhagen is unsurprisingly during the summer, when, in theory, warmer weather brings people out in large numbers to enjoy the late nights and outdoor events. Distortion, a raw ode to hedonism that turns the city upside down for five days in June, is probably the most notable but perhaps also the most controversial festival, since those who are not partying often lament the morning-after condition of their local neighborhoods.

Copenhagen Jazz Festival

various locations; tel. 33 93 20 13; https:// jazz.dk; July; many concerts free

A 10-day festival sprawling across the Inner City, Vesterbro, Frederiksberg, and beyond, Copenhagen Jazz Festival is one of the best-regarded of its kind in Europe. Jazz springs up in parks, city squares, street corners, bars, and concert venues all over the city during the first half of July. It's hard to miss it. The festival has existed in its current form since 1979, but jazz and Copenhagen go back farther than this: Many prominent American jazz musicians made the city their base in the 1960s and early 1970s.

Distortion

various locations in Nørrebro, Vesterbro, Refshaleøen; www.cphdistortion.dk; May-June; full pass 550 kr per day; pass for main street parties 250 kr

Young Copenhageners come out in droves to attend the decadent street festival Distortion at the end of May or the beginning of June. Distortion is very much a street party, with mostly chaotic outdoor partying to electronic and dance music. Its buzz is infectious, although local residents are often driven to distraction by a lack of sleep and post-partying streets that resemble a scene from the movie *28 Days Later*. The event mixes free parties with concerts and festival-like programs for which you need to buy an armband ticket to be admitted. Perhaps the most famous event, the Vesterbro street party, remained free in 2023, but guests were encouraged to buy a 100-kr voluntary armband, getting a few perks in return and helping the festival organizers stay on the city's good side by helping fund the cleanup.

CPH:DOX

various locations, primarily Kunsthal Charlottenborg, Nyhavn 2; tel. 33 93 07 34; https://cphdox.dk; Mar.; individual screenings from 100 kr; bus or Metro Kongens Nytorv

CPH:DOX—Copenhagen International Documentary Film Festival—is one of the largest of its kind in the world. In 2023 it spread to include locations outside Copenhagen and achieved a record attendance exceeding 125,000. A major draw was *A Storm Foretold*, Danish filmmaker Christoffer

Guldbrandsen's hotly discussed documentary about Donald Trump's former adviser Roger Stone. The festival lasts for almost two weeks and, in addition to documentary screenings, includes audiovisual concerts, panel debates, exhibitions, and regional film events. Online streaming passes (495 kr) can also be purchased to watch the festival's films.

Copenhagen Pride

Rådhuspladsen; www.copenhagenpride.dk; Aug.; free; bus or Metro Rådhuspladsen

Copenhagen Pride is the city's annual pride festival and takes place at Regnbuepladsen (Rainbow Square, renamed in 2014) adjacent to Rådhuspladsen (City Hall Square, renamed Pride Square for the duration of the festival). The week-long program includes art exhibitions, human rights events, concerts, talks, films, and even a convention, PrideCon, before the Pride march, which since 2011 has proceeded through Frederiksberg and Vesterbro, finishing at Rådhuspladsen. Some 30,000 people and 250,000 spectators were estimated to have taken part in 2022.

VinterJazz

various locations; tel. 33 93 20 13; https:// jazz.dk; Feb.; many concerts free

The winter edition of Copenhagen Jazz Festival is actually a nationwide event and includes over 600 small and large jazz concerts and happenings in Copenhagen and Frederiksberg, as well as elsewhere in Denmark—enough to keep you moving in the depths of the winter cold.

St. John's Eve (Sankthansaften)

Midsummer is celebrated in Denmark, as it is in a number of other Northern European countries, by lighting a bonfire. The Danish interpretation of this is Sankthansaften (St. John's Eve). Held on June 23, the evening before midsummer, and in keeping with Nordic tradition, Danes typically set up a large bonfire and top it with a witch figure. After speeches and singing, the bonfire is lit and the figure goes up in flames before the festivities continue long into the bright evening.

In Copenhagen, the celebration can be seen in several places. These include Frederiksberg Gardens and Amager Strandpark, with the former, on the expansive lawn in front of the palace, one of the largest gatherings of its kind in the city.

LGBTQ+ Copenhagen

Pride colors near Regnbuepladsen (Rainbow Square)

Denmark was the first country to recognize same-sex partnerships in 1989. Same-sex marriage in churches was made legal in 2012. In 2017 the country unilaterally declassified transgenderism as a mental illness, a step the World Health Organization didn't take until 2019. Copenhagen's Pride is one of the city's largest annual events with some 250,000 estimated spectators at the 2022 parade.

Politically, there is a high degree of consensus between progressive, centrist, and conservative parties on issues such as marriage equality and the rights of same sex couples in areas like parental leave. Recent years have seen trans rights emerge as a potential wedge issue that could destabilize the existing consensus, but most parties—left and right—still share progressive views here.

Denmark and Copenhagen can claim to be at the forefront of equality now, but the 1960s saw some resistance to what was, for its time, a liberal approach to LGBTQ+ issues, with a police commissioner who encouraged officers to step in if two men were seen dancing together in public. By the time this policy was axed in 1973, the sexual revolution was truly underway in Denmark's capital.

People interested in LGBTQ+ nightlife and events while visiting Copenhagen won't be short of options, including:

- The many LGBTQ+-friendly bars in the **Inner City,** particularly around the **Kattesundet, Lars Bjørns Stræde,** and **Studiestræde** streets, just a block from City Hall Square (Rådhuspladsen)

- **Centralhjørnet,** the city's oldest gay bar (page 129)

For more recommendations or information about LGBTQ+ events, contact or drop by the **Copenhagen Pride** office (H. C. Andersens Blvd. 27; tel. 31 50 24 68; www.copenhagenpride.dk).

Shopping

Denmark is famous for its minimalist design, most prominently that of iconic architect Arne Jacobsen, whose most famous works include the ant chair and the classic wristwatch. Although these would make wonderful Danish souvenirs, they don't come cheap. Shops such as Pilgrim and Panduro offer a less expensive way to try out a bit of Danish design.

Famous clothing brands include Han Kjøbenhavn, Wood Wood, and Samsøe Samsøe, often showcasing Danes' preference for pared-down black outfits, but there are plenty of places to find vintage styles too.

SHOPPING DISTRICTS

Strøget and Købmagergade

Strøget, in the area around Nørreport, is the closest to a main shopping street Copenhagen has to offer. At its eastern end, around Amagertorv, are **flagship design and department stores,** including famous Danish names such as **Hay** and **Illum.** Nearby, **Magasin Du Nord,** just off Kongens Nytorv square, is perhaps the most recognizable store in the country.

Købmagergade, which bisects Strøget, is similarly commercial, with a number of **fashion outlets** concentrated at its eastern end near the Gammel Mønt street. All of these areas are also well stocked with **kitschy souvenir shops,** reflecting the city-center location.

Værnedamsvej and Istedgade

Tucked between Vesterbro and Frederiksberg, Værnedamsvej has **French cafés, teashops,** a **chocolatier,** and enough **boutiques** for a little window shopping. If you want to extend your shopping session in Vesterbro, head farther south across Vesterbrogade to Istedgade, where you will find **independent fashion** and **home wares** mixed in with **tattoo artists, cafés, second-hand shops,** and **liquor stores.**

Ravnsborggade

In Nørrebro, the Ravnsborggade area reflects the alternative style of the neighborhood, with a number of **thrift stores** and **vintage** or **antiques** shops.

Jægersborggade

Farther into Nørrebro, Jægersborggade also has a good smattering of independent shops, including **thrift** and **clothing stores, gifts, home wares,** and at least one **tattoo artist.**

NØRREPORT AND AROUND

The area around Nørreport is the essential destination for Copenhagen shopping, with the main brands on Strøget and Købmagergade, boutiques, department stores, and small independent specialist shops all densely packed into a small area.

Clothing and Accessories
NN07
Gammel Mønt 7; tel. 38 41 11 41; www.nn07. com; Mon.-Thurs. 10am-6pm, Fri. 10am-7pm, Sat. 10am-5pm, Sun. noon-4pm; bus or Metro Kongens Nytorv

Priding itself on equality—NN stands for "no nationality"—this independent men's fashion brand draws from its passion for international travel and food culture. The style is casual, contemporary, and simple, with a focus on high quality.

Han Kjøbenhavn
Pilestræde 30; tel. 22 30 07 16; www. hankjobenhavn.com; Mon.-Sat. 11am-6pm, 1st Sun. of the month 11am-5pm; bus 2A, 31 Gammel Strand, Metro Gammel Strand

This unique Danish brand, which recently opened a store in London's Soho, combines fashion with short film production, with the results used to present their collection of Scandinavian work wear-inspired men's fashion. It started out as an eyewear brand, and spectacle frames remain an important part of its market. The Copenhagen flagship store is itself a spectacle in the clean lines and optimal lighting of Danish design.

Wood Wood
Grønnegade 1; tel. 35 35 62 64; www. woodwood.dk; Mon.-Fri. 10am-6pm, Sat. 10am-5pm, Sun. noon-4pm; bus or Metro Kongens Nytorv

A popular choice with the Copenhagen hipster set, Wood Wood is a contemporary fashion brand now with stores in London and Berlin. The men's and women's clothing mixes high-end fashion, sportswear, and street style influences but tries to keep things grounded, as is reflected in the simple clean designs of the store's interior.

Stine Goya
Gothersgade 58; tel. 32 17 10 00; www. stinegoya.com; Mon.-Fri. 11am-6pm, Sat. 11am-4pm; bus or Metro Kongens Nytorv

Stine Goya is an ideal spot to find elegant Danish-designed women's clothes to take home. Eponymous designer Stine Goya began her fashion career in 2006 and is known for a detailed, high quality, colorful range—something of a break from Danes' penchant for black. Goya's designs have achieved international acclaim, including that of world-famous Danish supermodel Helena Christensen. The store itself is as chic as the products, with stucco coving, pastel colors, and brass railings that make for a strikingly handsome setting.

Georg Jensen
Amagertorv 4; tel. 33 11 40 80; www. georgjensen.com; Mon.-Fri. 10am-6pm, Sat. 10am-5pm, Sun. 11am-3:30pm; bus or Metro Kongens Nytorv

Founded in 1904 in Copenhagen by silversmith Georg Jensen, the Amagertorv store is the home of what is possibly Denmark's most famous jewelry brand. Its products—which include house-wares, accessories, and cutlery as well as jewelry—are character-ized by clean, sleek, graceful lines. There may be a feeling of exclusiv-ity given the high prices of most of the products—the cheapest items are just under 300 kr. Head up-stairs for vintage design and a view of Amagertorv.

Interior Design
Stilleben

Frederiksborggade 22; tel. 22 45 11 31; www.stilleben.dk; Mon.-Fri. 10pm-6pm, Sat. 10am-5pm, Sun. 11am-4pm; bus or Metro Nørreport

A fabulous collection of color-rich ceramics and glass, jewelry, glitter socks, fabric bags, kitchen gear, and artsy prints, everything for sale at Stilleben was chosen for its unique-ness—many of the products are one of a kind. Designs from around the world are included, but Danish de-sign does not take a back seat. The thoughtfully arranged shelves and framed artwork provide examples for bringing the clean Scandinavian style to your own home.

Jacobsen Plus

Vimmelskaftet 43; tel. 75 64 87 22; www. jacobsenplus.dk; Mon.-Fri. 10am-6pm, Sat. 10am-4:30pm, 1st Sun. of the month 11am-4:30pm; bus 2A, 5C Rådhuspladsen, Metro Rådhuspladsen

A good way to see the legacy of fa-mous architect Arne Jacobsen is by browsing the family-owned fur-niture store Jacobsen Plus, which is not actually named after Arne Jacobsen himself but the Jacobsen

family, whose dynasty founded the company in Jutland in the 1920s. Even though the name is coinci-dental, there are many Jacobsen de-signs available, including the classic 3107 chair in a variety of colors and finishes, and the even simpler dot stool (2,000-3,000 kr). They are not the only designs or designer on show; there's a wide range of beau-tiful lamps, bean tables, mirrors, and cabinets.

Illums Bolighus

Amagertorv 10; tel. 33 14 19 41; www. illumsbolighus.com; Mon.-Sat. 10am-7pm, Sun. 11am-4:30pm; bus or Metro Kongens Nytorv

This 3-floor store has a full range of high-quality and premium home wares, including low-hanging eye-soothing lamps, sleek kitchen uten-sils, small ornaments, and the kind of minimalist furniture that looks like it should be uncomfortable but somehow manages to soothe every joint. Illums Bolighus typifies the classic look many Danish home-owners aspire to with their inte-rior design. There are also men's and women's clothing sections and a toy department, yet Illums feels surprisingly compact given its expansive range. This histori-cal location, built in 1941 on well-heeled Amagertorv, is the site of the brand's first homewares store.

Paustian

Niels Hemmingsens Gade 24; tel. 39 16 65 65; www.paustian.com; Mon.-Fri. 11am-6pm, Sat. 11am-5pm; bus, Metro, or S-train Nørreport

Paustian offers elite design at relatively premium prices at its ostentatious store near the Strøget main shopping street. The building, a former bank, has marble columns and palazzo-style architecture, making it a fitting and expansive setting for the huge range of high-class wares, including classic chair designs, low-hanging lamps, luxurious office sofas, analog alarm clocks, and candle holders.

Vipp Concept Store

Ny Østergade 34; tel. 45 88 88 15; www. vipp.com; Mon.-Fri. 11am-6pm, Sat. 11am-4pm; bus or Metro Kongens Nytorv

Vippe is a Danish verb meaning something similar to "flip" or to quickly turn over an object. Vipp's kitchen and bathroom modules are characterized by ergonomic lids that flip open—not least the instantly recognizable kitchen trash can. The company has also branched into designing forest shelters. The resulting 150-sq-m (1,600-sq-ft) concept store is similar to a niche furniture showroom.

Royal Copenhagen Flagship Store

Amagertorv 6; tel. 33 13 71 81; www. royalcopenhagen.dk; Mon.-Fri. 10am-7pm, Sat. 10am-6pm, Sun. 11am-4pm; bus or Metro Kongens Nytorv

At Royal Copenhagen, both you and your wallet can be regal for a while. The brand is an icon, and its products are to be found in many Danish homes. The fine white crockery is instantly recognizable, but be prepared to shell out, even for a small piece, if you want to treat yourself. The flagship outlet is in a stunning 1616 three-story Renaissance building on Amagertorv and has been a Royal Copenhagen store since 1911. It exudes the delicate manners of fine china and a tradition of fine craftsmanship.

Art

Poster & Frame

Niels Hemmingsens Gade 6; tel. 31 37 51 56; https://posterandframe.com; Mon.-Fri. 10am-6pm, Sat. 10am-4pm, Sun. noon-5pm; bus or Metro Kongens Nytorv

Poster & Frame is a perfect option if you want a Copenhagen souvenir on your wall. They offer beautiful prints and depictions of many facets of the city, from its street life to landmarks to sporting achievements. There are also classic and modern art prints and postcards and posters for kids, including of popular Danish TV characters like the *Kaj and Andrea* duo. This oasis of a store is nestled between the main shopping street and the busy square. Frames are available off the shelf or handmade to order.

Panduro

Nørre Farimagsgade 74; tel. 33 15 14 01; https://panduro.com/da-dk; Mon.-Thurs. 10am-6pm, Fri. 10am-7pm, Sat. 10am-4pm, Sun. 11am-4pm; bus 5C Nørre Farimagsgade (Frederiksborggade), Metro Nørreport

You can make your own jewelry—or almost anything else you want, for that matter—if you pop in to hobby and craft store Panduro and pick up the parts you need. Originally hailing from nearby Malmö in Sweden, Panduro is hugely popular in Denmark, not least during the school holidays but also for university students putting together masquerade costumes. Products include sewing and stitching gear, decorations, paper, cards, and rubber stamps, jewelry and accessories, baking materials, and art supplies. Inside the store, the multiple well-organized sections and plethora of different objects on the shelves provide a kind of nostalgia in an intangibly Scandinavian way.

Souvenirs
Hay House

Østergade 61; tel. 31 64 61 33; www.hay.dk; Mon.-Sat. 10am-6pm, Sun. 10am-4pm; bus or Metro Kongens Nytorv

This charming shop is on several floors with a terrific view of the main Strøget shopping thoroughfare and the Stork Fountain, a popular gathering place for hippies in the 1960s. Hay is bursting with modern, sleek Danish design and is highly popular with locals. The store itself resembles an upper-class Copenhagen home with a staircase acting as its main entrance. The checkered towels and recycled plastic candy-stripe shopping bags make for affordable, but no less classy, souvenirs.

Copenhagen Souvenir & Design

Østergade 11; tel. 33 36 27 43; https:// copenhagensouvenir.com; Mon.-Thurs.

10am-6pm, Fri. 10am-7pm, Sat. 10am-4pm; bus or Metro Kongens Nytorv

Carlsberg hats, Viking magnets, *Little Mermaid* plates, clap hats (baseball caps with two hands on the peak that can be made to clap, popular among Danish soccer fans), not to mention umbrellas—you will probably find all the quintessential souvenirs and tourist fare you will need here, although there are many similar shops scattered all over the city, not least at the airport, should you miss this particular one.

Department Stores
Illum

Østergade 52; tel. 33 14 40 02; https:// illum.dk; daily 10am-8pm; bus or Metro Kongens Nytorv

Illum is a luxurious Danish department store with an impressive layout and attractive displays. It's located on the central Amagertorv square and stocks all the major Danish and international cosmetics, interior design, and clothing brands and plenty more. The store's top floor has an extensive food court and outside balcony with a fantastic view of the buskers and passersby below, as well as an eye-level view of the characteristic Copenhagen spires.

Magasin du Nord

Kongens Nytorv 13; tel. 33 11 44 33; www. magasin.dk; daily 10am-8pm; bus or Metro Kongens Nytorv

The department store Magasin du Nord started out as a draper's shop in the mid-19th century. It now has branches across Denmark, and the landmark store at the impressive French Renaissance Revival style building at Kongens Nytorv, built on the site of the earlier Hotel du Nord, boasts 7 floors of fashion, home design, furnishings, beauty supplies and toiletries, books, toys, kitchenware, and groceries, not to mention a large delicatessen. A personal shopper can be arranged by calling in advance.

GREATER INNER CITY

The end of the Inner City close to Rådhuspladsen (City Hall Square) has many chain and tourist-oriented stores, as well as a few gems, including Politikens Boghal, paradise for bookworms.

Klassik

Bredgade 3; tel. 33 33 90 60; www.klassik. dk; Mon.-Fri. 11am-6pm, Sat. 10am-4pm; Metro Nørreport

Located on salubrious Bredgade, Klassik is in equal parts history lesson and furniture store, but it's more than just a secondhand shop. The range of restored furniture is a journey into the classics of Danish design, and the staff know their stuff. The calming store resembles an extended version of an incredibly tasteful 20th-century home with its arrangements of dining and coffee tables, lighting, ornaments, and bookcases.

shop windows, Inner City

Politikens Boghal

*Rådhuspladsen 37; tel. 30 67 28 06;
https://jppol.dk/boghallen; Mon.-Fri.
9:30am-7pm, Sat. 10am-6pm, Sun. 10am-
4pm; bus or Metro Rådhuspladsen*

Politikens Boghal is home territory
for Politiken, one of Denmark's
major news media outlets and pub-
lishers. It's easy to find signed (usually Danish) books or even spot a
famous Nordic author. The store
also regularly hosts literary or cultural events and has excellent coffee in its in-house café. A large case
spanning the entire back wall has a
comprehensive selection of books
in English.

NYHAVN

Tattoo Ole

*Nyhavn 17; tel. 33 15 90 86; https://
tattooole.dk; Mon.-Fri. 10am-8pm, Sat.-
Sun. noon-8pm; bus or Metro Kongens
Nytorv*

The tattoo parlor in the basement
of Nyhavn 17 is a throwback to
days when the area was far from
the tourist attraction it is today.
The locale has had a tattoo artist
since 1884, making it the world's
oldest tattoo parlor. If you're feeling brave enough to get inked in
Nyhavn, you have a chance here:
Reservations are not strictly necessary but are recommended. The
friendly tattoo artists are generally
happy to talk to walk-ins about
their options. Inside, Tattoo Ole
drips with history, photos, and heritage. Denmark's famously inked
King Frederik IX, grandfather of
the current King Frederik X, was
tattooed here many decades ago.

VESTERBRO AND FREDERIKSBERG

Vesterbro, once known for crime,
has been redeveloped and gentrified. Its former industrial area is
now one of the trendiest bar and
restaurant districts in the entire
country, and the Værnedamsvej
shopping street, the "Little Paris"
of Copenhagen, is a cluster of cozy
cafés and shops. It still retains
enough of its edge to ensure its
history remains part of the present, however.

Clothing and Accessories

Samsøe Samsøe

*Værnedamsvej 12; tel. 29 65 91 96; www.
samsoe.com; Mon.-Fri. 10am-6pm,
Sat. 11am-5pm, Sun. 11am-4pm; bus 7A
Værnedamsvej (Frederiksberg Allé), 26
Frederiksberg Allé (Vesterbrogade), 31
Værnedamsvej (Gammel Kongevej)*

Founded by brothers Klaus
and Preben Samsøe in a small
Copenhagen shop in 1993, the
Samsøe Samsøe brand is nearly
synonymous with formal men's
clothing in Denmark, although the
company is also known for wom-
en's fashion. The style is also classically Danish, with simple lines and
colors. The Værnedamsvej branch
is small and cozy, in keeping with
local surroundings.

Dora

*Værnedamsvej 6; tel. 93 92 72 20; www.
shopdora.dk; Mon.-Fri. 10am-6pm, Sat.
10am-5pm, Sun. 10am-4pm; bus 7A
Værnedamsvej (Frederiksberg Allé), 26
Frederiksberg Allé (Vesterbrogade), 31
Værnedamsvej (Gammel Kongevej)*

A home goods store with a cluttered aesthetic and a street-corner setting, Dora touts accessories, iron-on prints for jackets, housewares, Christmas decorations, jewelry, baskets, and more.

Prag

Vesterbrogade 10; tel. 48 42 00 10; www. pragcopenhagen.com; Mon.-Fri. 10am-7pm, Sat. 10am-6pm, Sun. 11am-6pm; bus 7A Værnedamsvej (Frederiksberg Allé), 26 Kingosgade (Vesterbrogade)

Prag is a busy secondhand clothing store with well-selected accessories that range from sunglasses, hair bands, and jewelry to tights and denim jackets. Frilly dresses, 1980s power designs, and summer frocks can all be found in this trove of previously worn style, as can leather shoes, plaid shirts, and moleskin slacks. You can also buy a fabric bag with the store's logo to carry away your haul—reuse the bag for extra Copenhagener street cred. On its way to becoming a brand in its own right, Prag also has branches in the Inner City (Vestergade 10) and Nørrebro (Nørrebrogade 45).

Kyoto

Istedgade 95; tel. 33 31 66 36; www.kyoto. dk; Mon.-Fri. 10am-6pm, Sat. 10am-5pm; bus 7A Værnedamsvej (Frederiksberg Allé), 26 Frederiksberg Allé (Vesterbrogade), 31 Værnedamsvej (Gammel Kongevej)

On raw Istedgade, close to the Meatpacking District, Kyoto's fashion-conscious staff and customers could easily model for the store. Originally a male-only denim boutique in a rough neighborhood, it has now refocused on both men's and women's fashion, including shoes. There's an emphasis on known brands and simple styles for casual wear.

Interior Design
Designer Zoo

Vesterbrogade 137; tel. 51 51 54 82; https://designerzoo.dk; Mon.-Fri. 10am-5:30pm, Sat. 10am-3pm; bus 26 Platanvej (Vesterbrogade)

Championing Danish art and design in a large shop and showroom with two in-house workshops, Designer Zoo is the place to find a unique piece of Danish handicraft. A highlight in one of the two workshops is the bean table, a coffee table in the shape of, you guessed it, a bean. You can take a look at the production process and even design your own bean table, choosing between 15 models, 5 sizes, and 2 heights. Note that the tables take around 4 weeks to make.

Malls
Fisketorvet

Havneholmen 5; tel. 33 36 64 00; www. fisketorvet.dk; daily 10am-8pm; bus 7A, S-train Fisketorvet (Dybbølsbro)

Shopping mall Fisketorvet, which is quite close to Copenhagen Central Station, has a classic range of Scandinavian chain stores, including H&M, Zara, and Matas. The mall is frequented by families who use its restaurants; some chains include Ssam (Korean), Sbarro (pizza), and McDonald's. A cinema complex is also in the center.

Frederiksberg Centret

Falkoner Allé 21; tel. 38 16 03 40; https://
frbc-shopping.dk; Mon.-Fri. 10am-7pm,
Sat.-Sun. 10am-5pm; Metro Frederiksberg
St.

Frederiksberg Center, in upmarket
Frederiksberg, has a strong reputation as one of the city's leading
malls and houses mainly chain
stores, encompassing a supermarket, optometrist, jeweler, health
food, clothing, shoes, interior design, and sports. Its atmosphere is
calm and child-friendly, reflecting
the neighborhood it calls home. It
is served directly by the M1, M2
and M3 lines of the Copenhagen
Metro, adding to the location's
convenience.

NØRREBRO AND
ØSTERBRO

While more about colorful street
life and nightlife than shopping,
Nørrebro has its share of vintage
clothing shops, where you might
find the kind of bargain that would
be unlikely in the Inner City.

Clothing and Accessories
Klaeder 2. Hand

Nordre Frihavnsgade 60; https://
klaeder2hand.dk; Tues.-Fri. noon-5pm, Sat.
11am-2pm; bus 3A Hobrogade (Nordre
Frihavnsgade), 1A, 14 Trianglen, Metro
Trianglen

Klaeder 2. Hand in Østerbro is one
of Copenhagen's oldest vintage
clothing stores, having existed at
its location for over 20 years under
various guises and ownerships. It
is also one of the best regarded,

catering to the young family demographic of the area with its hip diverse clothing for women and kids.
There's a focus on exclusive brands
(and price tags), but you'll also find
pieces from H&M that will set you
back a lot less.

Gemmeren

Fælledvej 9; tel. 22 56 53 34; www.
noedhjaelp.dk/genbrug; Mon. 1pm-
6pm, Tues.-Fri. noon-6pm; bus 5C
Ravnsborggade (Nørrebrogade)

Cheap but stylish, alternative
Danish secondhand threads are
abundant at the charmingly messy
Gemmeren, where books (normally in Danish, but you might get
lucky) are also sold. Staff are always decked out in clothes from the
shop. It's also a charity shop rather
than a vintage store, although its
target market overlaps, so you can
expect to find a bit of everything.

BauBau

Birkegade 3; tel. 40 86 29 37; www.
baubaushop.com; Mon.-Fri. 11am-6pm,
Sat. 11am-4pm; bus 5C Elmegade
(Nørrebrogade)

The "revived apparel" at BauBau
has a 1980s and 1990s feel, including coats, jackets, shoes,
bags, sweatshirts, and vests; even
the walls look like distressed
denim. Brands such as Gucci and
Balenciaga and plenty of sportswear add to the high-fashion feel.
It's ostensibly a menswear store, but
there are also plenty of women customers attracted to the well-kept
vintage and handmade interior

products. Shopping here feels like an upcycling experience in itself: Closely packed racks hang from old bicycle inner tubes, and shelves are formed from driftwood.

Art
Vanishing Point
Jægersborggade 45; tel. 91 10 88 30; www. vanishing-point.dk; Mon.-Fri. 11am-5pm, Sat. 11am-4pm; bus 5C Stefansgade, Metro Nuuks Plads

A studio as well as a craft shop in Nørrebro's atmospheric Jægersborggade, Vanishing Point sells arts and crafts made by in-house or local artists or work it has acquired through collaborations with international nongovernmental organizations (NGOs). These include jewelry, hand-knitted quilts, ceramics, and art prints.

Gågrøn!
Jægersborggade 48; tel. 42 45 07 72; www. gagron.dk; Mon.-Fri. 11am-5:30pm, Sat. 10am-4pm; bus 5C Stefansgade, Metro Nuuks Plads

The 100 percent sustainable Gågrøn (Go Green) on Jægersborggade sells housewares made from recycled, upcycled, or eco-friendly materials, so you won't feel frivolous about buying souvenirs. Products include bamboo kitchen utensils, organic cotton towels, and chemical-free water bottles. The small store is also well stocked with environmental enthusiasm from the customers and staff.

CHRISTIANSHAVN AND AMAGER

Christianshavn is not known for its shopping options, although the occasional vintage clothing shop has been known to spring up in the area in the past. Over on Amager, the main street Amagerbrogade caters to most daily needs, while a little farther out is Field's, a hulking out-of-town mall.

Field's
Arne Jacobsens Allé 12; tel. 70 20 85 05; https://fields.steenstrom.dk; daily 10am-8pm; Metro Ørestad St.

Field's, the largest shopping mall in Scandinavia, is filled with 140 stores, including a complete Magasin department store and a hypermarket. The mall also boasts an entire floor dedicated to leisure, with restaurants, cafés, a fun golf course and play areas for kids, and a lounge furnished with Arne Jacobsen furniture. If you're driving, you'll probably find parking—there are 3,000 spaces.

Dining

For a city that is home to a disproportionately high number of Michelin-starred restaurants, Copenhagen's culinary experience is not just about exclusive or fine dining. Street food in Refshaleøen, food markets in the Inner City, and ethnic restaurants in Nørrebro contribute to a rich variety, while the Meatpacking District (Kødbyen) in Vesterbro is a world-class destination, as evidenced by the internationally renowned chefs that work in its restaurants.

NØRREPORT AND AROUND
Danish and New Nordic
Schønnemann

Hauser Plads 16; tel. 33 12 07 85; www. restaurantschonnemann.dk; daily 11:30am-5pm; smørrebrød 90-190 kr, 3-course set menu from 235 kr; bus, Metro, or S-train Nørreport

It doesn't get much more Danish than Schønnemann, a classic lunch restaurant where smørrebrød and schnapps are de rigeur. Crisp white tablecloths and polite service accompany the traditional fish and meat dishes, such as the grandmother's kitchen-evoking tarteletter, a small open-topped pie with a creamy gravy, meat, and asparagus filling.

✪ Aamanns 1921

Niels Hemmingsens Gade 19-21; tel. 20 80 52 04; https://aamanns.dk/aamanns-1921; lunch Mon. 11:30am-5:15pm, last order 3:30pm, Tues.-Sat. 11:30am-5pm, last order 3:15pm, Sun. 11:30am-5:15pm, last order 3:30pm, dinner Tues.-Thurs. 6:30pm-11pm, last order 8:15pm, Fri.-Sat. 6:30pm-11pm, last order 8:45pm; lunch: smørrebrød 135-285 kr, dinner: set 4-course menu from 550 kr; bus, Metro, or S-train Nørreport

Aamanns 1921, which opened in September 2017 and rose to a Michelin recommendation in 2021, serves high-quality up-to-date versions of Danish smørrebrød, made with fresh seasonal ingredients. The knowledgeable table staff are happy to present the dishes. When head chef Adam Aamann was interviewed by the *New York Times* in 2018, he was praised for his attention to such details as the choice of scented soaps in the restrooms. Courses include ravioli with rye and cheese, cold-smoked salmon on rye bread, and butter-fried and breaded plaice with the Danish remoulade dressing. There's also a sister restaurant, **Aamanns Genbo** (Kildepladsen 8; tel. 20 80 52 06; https://aamanns.dk/aamanns-genbo), on the outer limits of Vesterbro.

Restaurant Palægade

Palægade 8; tel. 70 82 82 88; https:// formelfamily.dk/palaegade; daily 11:30am-5pm, Mon.-Sat. 6pm-midnight, last order 8:30pm; à la carte mains from 150 kr; Metro Kongens Nytorv

Palægade is intimate with atmospheric lighting and lovingly

prepared and presented smørrebrød, often with an international
twist like kimchi. The restaurant's
young team stress their passion for
traditional Danish food. Dishes
include roasted turbot, white veal
with cabbage and mushrooms, and
a beef wellington for two (which
should be pre-ordered). If you have
a sweet tooth, hold out for the ka-
gevogn (cake cart) that's wheeled
around at lunchtime.

Rebel

Store Kongensgade 52; tel. 33 32 32 09;
www.restaurantrebel.dk; lunch Tues.-Fri.
noon-2:30pm, dinner Tues.-Thurs. 5:30pm-
9pm, Fri.-Sat. 5:30pm-9:30pm; menu
with 4 snacks plus wine 595 kr, starters
and other single dishes from145 kr; Metro
Marmorkirken

A foodie favorite, Rebel is a highly
rated fine-dining New Nordic
restaurant with extensive tasting menus for those who want to
"challenge their taste buds." The
Rebellious Evening menu, which
includes a glass of bubbly and
seven wines (1,595 kr per person), is the ultimate experience—
you'll need to set aside several
hours. Dishes include baked hake,
duroc pork belly, caviar, and flat-
iron steak with smoked celeriac
puree, while Rebel is particularly
known for a signature steak tartare. Reservations are necessary.
The interior is handsome with
black-framed mirrors, black furniture, and a menu written on black-
boards. The place has a bustling,
cozy vibe.

Breakfast and Diners
Restaurant Sult

Vognmagergade 8B; tel. 33 74 34 00;
www.dfi.dk; restaurant Mon.-Fri. 5pm-
10pm, Sat. 9:30am-4pm and 5pm-10pm,
Sun. 9:30am-4pm, café daily 11am-9pm;
bread and pastries from 25 kr, brunch 245
kr including drinks, evening buffet from 335
kr; Metro Kongens Nytorv

Located inside the Danish Film
Institute's buildings opposite
Kongens Have, the 300-seater
Sult—named after a seminal 1960s
Danish film by director Henning
Carlsen—is both a café and a restaurant. In the restaurant, organic
Danish-style breakfasts are on
offer, while the café has an excellent organic brunch buffet with varieties of yogurt, salmon, pastries,
eggs, rye bread, bacon, and fruit.
There are a lot of tables, and they
are close to each other, so there's
no shortage of human interaction.

Cafés and Bakeries
La Glace

Skoubogade 3; tel. 33 14 46 46; www.
laglace.dk; Mon.-Fri. 8:30am-6pm, Sat.
9am-6pm, Sun. 10am-6pm; layer cakes
from 72 kr per slice, confections from 49
kr; Metro Nørreport or Rådhuspladsen

There is often a long line outside La
Glace, supplier of the finest cakes
in Denmark. It was founded in 1870
and retains the air and elegance of
a late-19th-century confectioner.
The prices can feel steep, but this
is hardly an ordinary slice of cake
with coffee—the whipped cream is
fluffy, and the sponge cake melts
in your mouth. Seating is available

✪ Café Culture

Granola in Værnedamsvej

Danish café culture, which takes on a specific character of its own in the capital, reflects both continental European influences and the colder climate of the north. At cafés, Danes can commonly be seen outdoors, shivering under blankets, sitting at sidewalk tables at times of the year when the weather is far too chilly to be exposed to the elements. It's understandable—the winters are long, and people long to get outdoors and re-create the Italian alfresco feeling. In fact, cafés are at their best in Denmark during the winter, when you can hunker down at a table with a good **Americano** or **latte** or, in December, a mug of **glögg**—the cinnamon-flavored mulled wine synonymous with Christmas—and a **kanelsnegl** (cinnamon twirled pastry). In contrast to the grab-and-go

in keeping with the historical tea-room feel.

Democratic Coffee

Krystalgade 15; tel. 40 19 62 37; Mon.-Fri. 7:30am-7pm, Sat. 9am-5pm, Sun. 10am-5pm; Metro Nørreport

Located inside the university library opposite the synagogue on Krystalgade, Democratic Coffee is a popular bakery among students (expect to see plenty of laptops on tables). It's famed for its almond croissants and excellent light-roasted coffee. Baked goods are prepared on the premises— the croissants are so popular that they regularly sell out by noon. There's seating and window space, so you can get work done or simply people-watch.

Seafood
Fishmarket

Hovedvagtsgade 2; tel. 88 16 99 99; www. fishmarket.dk; Mon.-Sat. 11am-midnight, nature of Italian espresso culture, Danes like to linger at cafés, spending an hour or three catching up with a friend or even alone, getting some work done or reading a book.

Copenhagen itself has every type of café imaginable. The choice is yours.

- **Independent roasteries:** Enthusiasts are bound to find something they like at one of the several **Coffee Collective** (https://coffeecollective.dk) cafés spread across the city, where the beans are meticulously and sustainably sourced and the staff knowledgeable and friendly.

- **Pastry and bread specialists:** **Meyers Bageri** (https://meyers.dk) has a chain of outlets in Copenhagen and, rather than being a sit-down-and-settle kind of place, it's ideal for a to-go coffee to drink while you carry home the cinnamon pastries and pumpkin rye bread you just picked up for lunch.

- **With beer on tap or bottled microbrews:** **Din Nye Ven** (Skt. Peders Stræde 34 A; tel. 42 42 50 68; www.dinnyeven.dk) is an example of the breed of Danish cafés that have plenty in common with pubs, where you can go for a light or sturdier breakfast in the morning and come back in the evening for a beer.

- **Out-and-out bars after nightfall:** **Bevar's** (Ravnsborggade 10B; tel. 50 59 09 93; www.bevars.dk) in the Nørrebro neighborhood is good for a quiet coffee and freshly baked bread in the morning, but if you hang around long enough, you can take in a jazz concert after dark.

- **Bookish and literary:** With its heady mix of leather-bound seats and wall-to-wall bookshelves, **Paludan Bog & Café** (Fiolstræde 12, Inner City; tel. 33 15 06 75; http://paludan-cafe.dk) will have you settling in for the whole afternoon.

Sun. 11am-11pm, kitchen Mon.-Sat. 11:30am-3pm and 5pm-10pm, Sun. 11:30am-3pm and 5pm-9:30pm; starters from 145 kr; Metro Kongens Nytorv

Fishmarket is a French fish bistro with a Mediterranean-style menu, featuring fresh seafood sourced from local suppliers. The menu includes lobster, mussels, and rib-eye steak. The restaurant interior is somewhat reminiscent of an old-fashioned train carriage, with wooden and upholstered bench seats and racks to place overcoats. Choose between smaller cold dishes and more substantial warm ones. Book in advance.

Burgers
Gasoline Grill

Landgreven 10; www.gasolinegrill.com; daily 11am until sold out; burgers from 95 kr; Metro Nørreport

Gasoline Grill is a juicy fast-food burger joint offering satisfying, greasy, filling burgers to grab in a hurry. Options include a regular burger, a cheeseburger, a veggie burger, and limited outdoor seating. There are various locations across the city, including at Niels Hemmingsens Gade 20 near the main shopping streets, and at the Broens Street Food market. This one, though, is the original former gas station conversion and still has the unique grab-and-go charm.

European
Brace

Teglgårdstræde 8A; tel. 28 88 20 01; www.restaurantbrace.dk; lunch Fri.-Sat. 11:30am-3pm, dinner Wed.-Sat. 5:30pm-midnight; à la carte mains 150-410 kr, tasting menu 650-995 kr excluding wine pairings; bus 5C Teglgårdstræde (Nørre Voldgade), Metro Nørreport

Named by the *Michelin Guide* as the "32nd best Italian restaurant outside Italy," there's nevertheless a Scandinavian twist at Brace, where the chefs have chosen to infuse well-established Italian recipes with the more experimental approach of the New Nordic kitchen. Results include reginetti with rice miso butter, risotto carnaroli with elderflower, and guinea fowl with morels, but expect new innovations. It's best experienced slowly while sitting on stylish blue-gray bench seats under the tastefully calm ceiling lamps, and you can relax in the calming beer garden before being seated for your meal.

Asian
✪ Kopan

Linnesgade 24; tel. 53 57 46 88; www.kopan.dk; Tues.-Sat. 4pm-9:30pm, last order 8:30pm; mains from 99 kr; bus or Metro Nørreport

Korean food is a rare treat in Copenhagen, and Kopan does its best to supply all the kimchi you might need. One of my favorite spots in town, the friendly little restaurant on Linnesgade is complimented by the food truck parked 90 m (100 yards) or so away outside the entrance to Torvehallerne food hall. The menu is straightforward and satisfying, with bulgogi and bibimbap available with beef, chicken, and vegetables. Dumplings and pancakes are also on offer. Naturally, these can be accompanied by a shot of soju or a bottle of Seoul's own Cass beer.

Rangoli

Store Kongensgade 72; tel. 33 11 12 37; https://rangoli.dk; Sun.-Thurs. 4pm-10pm, Fri.-Sat. 4pm-11pm; mains 145-295 kr; Metro Marmorkirken

There are not as many Indian restaurants in Copenhagen as in other European cities, so Rangoli, located about halfway between Kongens Nytorv and Kastellet, is well placed. Classic curries like palak, makni, biryani, and korma, made with lamb, mutton, chicken, and tofu, are among those to choose from. There's an authentic feel about the food, while the

Rye Bread and Smørrebrød

a classic smørrebrød with fish fillet, remoulade, shrimp, salad, and caviar

While Denmark is well known for its cakes, nothing could be more quint-essentially Danish than rye bread—the dark, dense bread that forms the ballast of most Danes' everyday diet. There are various types. My personal favorite is the pumpkin seed-infused græskarrugbrød. The taste and density can take a little getting used to, but once initiated, you'll see why rye is often the first thing Danes say they miss when traveling abroad.

And, of course, rye serves as the basis for smørrebrød, the classic Danish open-faced sandwich. Don't leave Copenhagen without eating one, but beware there are some quite inflexible unwritten rules relating to the toppings. Don't just add whatever is on the table, and even more crucially, never stick another piece of bread on top to make a regular sandwich. Established combinations include rare roast beef (cold) topped with remoulade relish, grated fresh horseradish, and crispy on-ions; shrimp, eggs, and aioli with an optional topping of salmon, cucumber, lemon, or cress; and potato, chives, bacon, and onions. An easy way to avoid a smørrebrød faux pas is to visit one of the many restaurants around the city that serve delicious examples of their own.

WHERE TO EAT SMØRREBRØD IN COPENHAGEN

- **Aamanns 1921** serves high-quality updated versions of smørrebrød made with fresh seasonal ingredients. Try old-fashioned matured herring with crème fraîche and pickled elderflower (page 98).

- Savor a traditional meal of smørrebrød and schnapps at the atmospheric **Christianshavns Færgecafé** set in Christianshavn's cobbled streets. Try beet tartare with deep-fried smoked cheese (page 121).

- For a change of pace from the more traditional offerings, try some meatier smørrebrød at **Fleisch.** Try croquette on braised pork with chipotle mayo, lingonberries, salad, and walnuts (page 110).

restaurant itself has a bright, clean look with a mix of influences, but it manages to seamlessly integrate Danish-style low-hanging lamps. There's streetside seating available in the summer.

Royal Garden

Dronningens Tværgade 30; tel. 33 15 16 07; Wed.-Fri. 5pm-11pm, Sat.-Sun. noon-11pm; starters from 65 kr; Metro Marmorkirken

The always-bustling Royal Garden is a delicious and valued dim sum specialist with an authentic look right in the center of town. Self-styled as a "Chinese social dining" restaurant, you are encouraged to share dishes. Don't be reluctant to come alone: There are plenty of classic fried noodle dishes to choose from.

Latin American
Llama

Lille Kongensgade 14; tel. 89 93 66 87; https://cofoco.dk/en/llama; Sun.-Thurs. 5:30pm-midnight; Fri.-Sat. 5:30pm-2am; small dishes from 80 kr, tasting menu 450 kr; bus or Metro Nørreport

Latin American fusion restaurant Llama's menu combines the cuisines of Peru, Argentina, Bolivia, Ecuador, and Chile, as well as some Central American countries, in its range of ceviches, tacos, and beef dishes, not to mention the fiery range of spirits: pisco, mezcal, tequila, and more. Don't be put off by the colorful beaded skulls: the decor is lively, with patterned tiles adorning the walls and floor.

42Raw

Pilestræde 32; tel. 32 12 32 10; www.42raw. com; Mon.-Fri. 8am-8pm, Sat.-Sun. 9am-6pm; salads from 129 kr, breakfast bowls from 109 kr; Metro Kongens Nytorv

This intimate raw-food eatery on a narrow Inner City street is gluten-free, lactose-free, and 100 percent plant-based. The cakes are tasty and the interior welcoming, busy, and small, with a cluttered style. Truffle burger, avocado salad, sweet potato fries, and acai bowls are among the offerings.

Food Hall
Torvehallerne

Frederiksborggade 21; tel. 70 10 60 70; https://torvehallernekbh.dk; Mon.-Fri. 10am-7pm, Sat.-Sun. 11am-6pm, some stands open later, bakeries from 7am; dishes from 65 kr, cakes from 35 kr, coffee from 40 kr; Metro Nørreport

The twin glass halls of Torvehallerne are home to more than 60 different food stalls serving everything from seafood to cheese, pastries to smoked meats, wraps to freshly ground coffee. Popular outlets include porridge specialist **Grød** (tel. 50 58 55 79; https://groed.com; from 50 kr) and **Hallernes Smørrebrød** (tel. 60 70 47 80; www.hallernes.dk/ en; from 68 kr), a premium open-sandwich bar where you can wash down your salmon or potato rye bread with a schnapps. You can also stop by to window-shop the myriad fish and meat markets and grab a coffee at specialist **Coffee Collective** (tel. 60 15 15 25; https:// coffeecollective.dk).

Danish smørrebrød on display in Torvehallerne food market

GREATER INNER CITY
Danish and New Nordic
Marv & Ben

Snaregade 4; tel. 23 81 02 91; www. marvogben.dk; daily 5:30pm-1am, kitchen until 11pm; 4-course menu 450 kr, 900 kr with wine pairings; bus 2A Stormbroen/ Nationalmuseet (Vindebrogade), Metro Gammel Strand

In a small room on a quiet side street with a window to the kitchen, New Nordic Marv & Ben uses only seasonal locally produced organic ingredients. The fish is caught close to the Danish coast, and the meat is also sourced close to home. The delicate taste combinations on the menu can include scallops and green strawberries, yellow beets and trout roe, and lamb, cabbage, and black garlic. The recipient of a Bib Gourmand *Michelin Guide* distinction, Marv & Ben is nevertheless significantly more budget-friendly than Michelin-starred options.

Kanal Caféen

Frederiksholms Kanal 18; tel. 33 11 57 70; www.kanalcafeen.dk; Mon.-Fri. 11:30am-4pm, Sat. 11:30am-3pm; smørrebrød 84-165 kr; bus 2A, Stormbroen/Nationalmuseet (Vindebrogade), Metro Gammel Strand

The busy, historical Kanal Caféen's walls are adorned with an eclectic mix of pictures of local sites, maritime scenes, characters from popular television series, and commemorative plates; the low ceiling is a sturdy set of beams. In the summer, outdoor seating is available on a moored barge opposite the restaurant. The entire classic range of Danish lunch smørrebrød is here: red cabbage, roast pork, fried onion, and the bitter remoulade dressing, not to mention five types of herring. There are also lunch platters with traditional fare such as the frikadeller meatballs and fish fillets, pâté, and cheese.

Seafood
Letz Sushi

Store Kongensgade 44; tel. 53 78 67 35; https://letzsushi.dk; Sun.-Thurs. noon-9pm, Fri.-Sat. noon-10pm; starters from 52 kr, sashimi dishes from 95 kr, platters from 195 kr; Metro Kongens Nytorv or Marmorkirken

Having become synonymous with quality sushi in Copenhagen since opening its first restaurant in 2003, Letz has a string of sushi outlets across the city. The fish is freshly sourced, the menu broad, and the service quick, while the prices are competitive with the growing number of challengers. There's fast service with takeaway also available and simple, unpretentious surroundings.

Krogs Fiskerestaurant

Gammel Strand 38; tel. 33 15 89 15; www. krogs.dk/en; Mon.-Sat. 11:30am-midnight, kitchen 11:30am-3pm and 5pm-10pm; starters from 145 kr, 3-course menu 595 kr excluding wine; bus 2A Christiansborg (Vindebrogade), Metro Gammel Strand

Krogs Fiskerestaurant's prime location near Højbro Plads and its view of Christiansborg Palace are no small selling points. The restaurant is also handsome on the inside, with an elegant traditional design and some highly rated seafood platters. An extensive wine list accompanies a small but thoroughly prepared cocktail menu. The table and bar staff also deserve a mention

for their attention to detail and welcoming approach.

Burgers
Cocks & Cows

Gammel Strand 34 and other locations; tel. 69 69 60 00; https://cocksandcows. dk; Sun.-Thurs. 11:30am-9:30pm, Fri.-Sat. 11:30am-10:30pm; burgers 79-149 kr; bus 2A Christiansborg (Vindebrogade), Metro Gammel Strand

With a string of restaurant-slash-cocktail-bars across Copenhagen, bustling Cocks & Cows is a solid option for a hearty mix-and-match burger, and vegetarian options are available. Various side orders and extras can be added: I particularly like the chili mayo, and there are aioli, tarragon, and mustard alternatives. An extensive cocktail list includes the rum, cranberry juice, Cointreau, and lime Cocksmopolitan. The Gammel Strand location has the considerable extra draw of a karaoke booth.

Takeaway
Shawarma Grill House

Frederiksberggade 36; tel. 33 12 63 23; http://shawarmagrillhouse.dk; Sun.-Wed. 11am-1am, Thurs.-Sat. 11am-5am; shawarma sandwich from 75 kr; bus or Metro Rådhuspladsen

The first Lebanese restaurant to open on the central Strøget shopping thoroughfare back in 1980, Shawarma Grill House retains its reputation as one of the best kebab places outside Nørrebro. It's popular with daytime visitors as well as late-night guests, and the signature meal is still the juicy, tender lamb shawarma kebab, but a range of other Middle Eastern staples, including hummus, shish kebabs, and vegetarian options, including falafel, are solid takeaway options.

European
Vespa

St. Kongensgade 90; tel. 33 11 37 00; https://cofoco.dk/en/vespa; Mon.-Thurs. 6pm-midnight, last arrival 9pm, Fri.-Sat. 6pm-midnight, last arrival 9:15pm; 4-course set menu 295 kr; Metro Marmorkirken

Italian Vespa is an Osteria-style restaurant in one of the older parts of Copenhagen's Inner City, a stone's throw from the steepled dome of Frederik's Church. It's almost shabby-chic in style, with its mismatching chairs, good-value meals, and simple approach. Antipasti and secondi dishes include grilled zucchini, burrata, ravioli, and veal culotte, and you can quench your thirst by ordering beer or wine ad libitum.

SLOTSHOLMEN
Danish and New Nordic
Tårnet

Christiansborg Slotsplads; tel. 28 10 14 02; www.taarnet.dk/restauranten; Tues.-Sat. 11:15am-4:30pm and 5:30pm-10pm, Sun. 11:15am-4:30pm; starters from 125 kr, cakes 55 kr; bus 2A, Børsen (Børsgade), Metro Gammel Strand

There's no doubting what's unique about Tårnet, the restaurant in the tower at Christiansborg, the seat of the Danish Parliament. Operated by Meyers, which runs a chain of bakeries across Copenhagen, it has separate lunch, afternoon tea, and dinner menus. Expect high-quality Danish offerings like fried fish, salmon, potato and veal culotte cold cuts, and a generous selection of cakes. These can be enjoyed in the pompous surroundings of the tower's high-vaulted windows, busts, and other statues. Book in advance.

Cafés and Bakeries
Madkartoteket

Søren Kierkegaards Plads 1; tel. 31 38 60 71; https://madkartoteket.dk; Mon.-Fri. 8am-6pm, Sat. 9am-5pm; smørrebrød 85-90 kr, pastries from 25 kr, lunch from 75 kr; bus 2A, 5C, 68 Otto Mønsteds Plads (Rysensteensgade), 26 Det Kongelige Bibliotek (Christians Brygge)

Inside the Black Diamond, the building that houses the Danish Royal Library, you can enjoy unfettered views across the harbor from Slotsholmen as you tuck into a croissant, carrot cake, or grilled zucchini on toast at the library café. You can also just stop by for a quick cup of coffee, an option well worth considering—it's a lot better than the average canteen cup. In summer, seating (including on Fatboy beanbags) is available outside, almost inviting you to relax with a book by the water.

Burgers
Kayak Bar

Børskaj 12; tel. 30 49 00 13; https://kayakbar.dk; Sun.-Thurs. 8am-11pm, Fri.-Sat. 8am-1am; sides from 45 kr, mains 85-145 kr; bus 2A Børsen (Børsgade), Metro Christianshavn St.

Danish Cakes

kanelsnegl

Cakes are a key part of Danish culture—meeting for coffee and cake or bringing cakes to work to celebrate birthdays and other events are part of Danish everyday life. Just don't ask for a Danish pastry, as that could mean anything. The baked product known as a Danish in the United States or the United Kingdom most resembles a **wienerbrød**—literally, Vienna bread—but the most classic pastry is the **kanelsnegl,** a "cinnamon snail" consisting of a flat, twirled strip of flaky pastry flavored with cinnamon, melted sugar, and either white or chocolate frosting. But there are many more delicious options for the sweet tooth than just these. Try **hindbærsnitte,** the Danish version of Alexandertorte; chocolate-covered marshmallow treats with waffle and marzipan bases known as **flødeboller;** the marzipan and biscuit **Napoleon's hat;** and the poppy seed-topped **tebirkes.**

Bakeries where these and other Danish cakes are available include, but are certainly not limited to:

- **Albatross og Venner,** the resident artisanal bakery at **Torvehallerne** (page 104).

- **Meyers Bageri** (https://meyers.dk), the popular Copenhagen bakery with branches in Frederiksberg, Østerbro, Nørrebro and Amager.

- **Lagkagehuset** (https://lagkagehuset.dk), a large chain bakery with outlets all over Copenhagen, the rest of Denmark, and even in London, including at Torvegade 45 in Christianshavn, Frederiksberggade 23 in Inner City, Sortedam Dossering 9 and Nørrebrogade 120, both in Nørrebro, Værnedamsvej 1 in Vesterbro-Frederiksberg, and inside both the Central Station and the Magasin du Nord department store in Kongens Nytorv.

- **Bodenhoff,** on the corner of noisy, rough-and-tumble Christianshavns Torv (Square) (page 122).

Kayak Bar offers a range of café standards that include Greek salads and burgers. It is best known for its moules frites, but you can also get a continental breakfast and brunch 8am-noon. The bar and restaurant are attached to the kayak rental and tour operator Kayak Republic, which provides a lively harborside weekend vibe when the weather is suitable for sitting outdoors.

NYHAVN

Nyhavn has the highest concentration of tourists of anywhere in Copenhagen or indeed the whole of Denmark, and the extensive rows of restaurants and cafés in the historical quay-front buildings and moored boats cater well to the demand, meaning you are unlikely to struggle with finding somewhere to eat, even at busy times.

European
Gorm's

Nyhavn 14; tel. 60 40 12 00; https:// wearegorms.dk; Mon.-Wed. 5pm-10pm, Thurs. noon-10pm, Fri.-Sat. noon-11pm, Sun. 5pm-10pm; pizzas 140-175 kr; Metro Kongens Nytorv

Inexpensive fast-food pizzas are easy to come by almost anywhere in Copenhagen, but Gorm's, which has several branches in the city, steps up the game with its popular sourdough pizzas in a restaurant setting for about double the price of the common variety. Its signature location on Nyhavn offers pizzas with meatballs and truffles as well as a lot of recognizable favorites. Gluten-free options are available.

Restaurant Hummer

Nyhavn 63A; tel. 33 33 03 39; www. restauranthummer.dk; Mar.-Oct. daily 11:30am-midnight; tasting menu 450-550 kr excluding wine; Metro Kongens Nytorv

A lobster and seafood specialist (hummer in Danish means lobster), Restaurant Hummer looks over the iconic sights of Nyhavn. Whole or half lobsters, poached or grilled, can be chosen from the à la carte list, as can moules frites, halibut ceviche, and lemon sole meunière. There's plenty of atmosphere, with the location providing a constant stream of guests. The blue-tiled floors and buoys displayed on the walls give a captain's cabin feel to the decor.

Breakfast and Diners
Union Kitchen

Store Strandstræde 21; tel. 33 14 54 88; www.theunionkitchen.dk; Mon.-Wed. 7:30am-11pm, Thurs.-Fri. 7:30am-midnight, Sat. 8am-midnight, Sun. 8am-5pm; brunch plate 199 kr, breakfast dishes from 75 kr; Metro Kongens Nytorv

If you find yourself craving American-style scrambled eggs, bacon, and coffee while in Copenhagen, early opener Union Kitchen should hit the spot with its broad menu of full plates, as well as some lighter options such as salads, oats, and a filled croissant. The evening menu (from 5pm) consists of small dishes based on various international cuisines designed to complement each other. Many of these are balls, variations on the meatball concept, including pork balls, beef balls, Moroccan lamb balls, falafel balls, and several others. There's a bustling coffee shop feel, and it gets particularly busy on weekends.

Vegetarian
Apollo Bar

Nyhavn 2; tel. 27 50 32 33; https://apollobar.dk; canteen Tues. 9am-5pm, Wed.-Sat. 9am-midnight, Sun. 9am-5pm; mains 135 kr; Metro Kongens Nytorv

Apollo Bar, which is part of Nyhavn's art and cultural center Kunsthal Charlottenborg, offers a less expensive and healthy vegetarian lunch at its canteen Tuesday-Friday as well as à la carte meals with meat options from its bar, which is open until late. The canteen menu changes daily but expect couscous, beans, roasted cauliflower, broccoli, and other hearty goods. It's a good wallet-friendly—and usually less crowded—alternative to the many tourist-focused eateries around Nyhavn. Note the student discount: almost half price for the canteen vegetarian lunch. On Friday evenings there is a pre-game vibe, with DJs and plenty of students in attendance.

VESTERBRO AND FREDERIKSBERG
Danish and New Nordic
Fleisch

Slagterboderne 7; tel. 61 68 14 19; www.fleisch.dk; Sun.-Thurs. 11:30am-midnight, Fri.-Sat. 11:30am-1am, kitchen lunch daily 11:30am-3pm, dinner Sun.-Thurs. 5:30pm-9:30pm, Fri.-Sat. 5:30pm-10:30pm; lunch smørrebrød 125-155 kr, 5-course tasting menu with main course 465 kr, à la carte

starters 125-145 kr; bus 23 Gasværksvej (Istedgade), S-train Dybbølsbro, Metro Copenhagen Central Station

One of the most recognizable names in the Meatpacking District, Fleisch pays tribute to the legacy of the area with its interior design—note the antler chandeliers—and its working in-house butcher shop and hanging meat hooks. Meat is front and center: Sirloin beef tartare and short ribs are among the main courses. The bar even serves bacon-infused bourbon. There are plenty of fish courses too, not to mention a huge wine list.

Breakfast and Diners
Mad & Kaffe Vesterbro

Sønder Blvd. 68, other locations in Amager and Frederiksberg; tel. 31 35 08 80; www.madogkaffe.dk; daily 8:30am-8pm; breakfast from 115 kr; S-train Dybbølsbro

At Mad & Kaffe (Food and Coffee) you are provided with a slip of paper and a pencil, Ikea-style, on which to choose the options you would like to make up your breakfast. These include salad, dairy, bread, meat, and pastry components, and you can choose between 3 and 7 items, depending on your appetite and budget. My favorites are the avocado in chili oil, the organic sourdough rye bread, the thin crispy Danish bacon, and the grilled peaches with cheese. It's a recommended option for a flexible breakfast or brunch; you may find yourself waiting a short while to be seated on weekends.

Granola

Værnedamsvej 5; tel. 33 33 00 95;
www.granola.dk; Mon.-Wed. 9am-11pm,
Thurs.-Sat. 9am-midnight, Sun. 9am-4pm;
croissant 25 kr, breakfast platter 180 kr,
starters from 155 kr; bus 7A Værnedamsvej
(Gammel Kongevej)

French breakfast and brunch café Granola is open from early until evening, when croque monsieur and pain au chocolat give way to moules frites and a lively evening vibe in Parisian-style surroundings. Outdoor seating is available and well worth making use of in decent weather, so you can take in Værnedamsvej's stylish comings and goings. Granola gets busy in the morning.

Seafood
✪ Kødbyens Fiskebar

Flæsketorvet 100; tel. 32 15 56 56; https://
fiskebaren.dk; Sun.-Thurs. 11:30am-
midnight, Fri.-Sat. 11:30am-1am, kitchen
closed 2:30pm-5:30pm; mains 195-445
kr; bus 23 Gasværksvej (Istedgade), S-train
Dybbølsbro, Metro Copenhagen Central
Station

Kødbyens Fiskebar, a former Bib Gourmand winner, specializes in classically prepared oysters and shellfish, but you can also get fish-and-chips. The setup is informal, with meals served at the bar or at sofas as well as at tables, the white-tiled walls in keeping with the raw aesthetic of the Meatpacking District. Most of the fish and seafood is caught in Danish waterways and sourced from suppliers with an eye on sustainability. Book

ahead and expect to have plenty of company.

Cafés and Bakeries
Kaffeplantagen

Enghave Plads 1; tel. 32 11 41 14; www.
kaffeplantagen.dk; Mon.-Fri. 7:30am-10pm,
Sat.-Sun. 8:30am-10pm; coffee from 30 kr,
morning bread rolls with coffee 50 kr; bus
23 Enghave Plads St. (Istedgade), Metro
Enghave Plads St.

Perched on one side of the elongated Enghave Plads square, a lively part of Vesterbro that now boasts a Metro station, Kaffeplantagen has long been a favored stop for locals. You'll see plenty of people working on laptops on weekdays, but the computer-free weekends open up the space for a more relaxing vibe. There's a good selection of cakes on display behind the bar's glass counter, and the seating is very much outward-looking, with stools along the window and benches out front. Smaller tables inside can also be used by groups.

Hart Bageri

Gammel Kongevej 109; tel. 31 11 18 50;
https://hartbageri.com; Mon.-Fri. 7:30am-
6pm, Sat.-Sun. 8am-5pm; pastries from
32 kr, bread rolls from 16 kr; bus 31 H.C.
Ørsteds Vej (Gammel Kongevej), Metro
Frederiksberg Allé

It's easy to find Hart on a weekend morning as Copenhageners queue outside to pick up a high-quality loaf of rye bread, a cardamom croissant, or maybe a classic Danish pastry like a spandauer. The craftsmanship that goes into

Hygge: More Than Just a Cozy Place

Hygge does not always mean huddling inside by candlelight. Here it is in abundance at an outside food market.

In 2017, the *Oxford English Dictionary* added the Danish word hygge to its lexicon. How did such an unpronounceable, untranslatable word make it into an English dictionary? A BBC article in 2015 is thought to have been the start of a surge of interest in the concept, with countless articles, books, and even a board game now dedicated to the phenomenon.

Hygge is associated with pleasant activities such as drinking a cup of tea by the fireplace or sitting down to eat with friends around a candlelit table. But the word is used in a wide range of other situations too, like bumping into an old acquaintance or playing an informal game of soccer. Tasteful background music is hyggemusik. There are many ways of

the production of these baked goods is above the ordinary—Hart was founded by a former Michelin chef—but the prices are not outliers by Copenhagen standards. Having been featured on an episode of hit US television show *The Bear,* Hart is likely to become even more popular. The Frederiksberg location is the original, but there are also branches in Vesterbro (Istedgade 61), the Meatpacking District (Høkerboderne 17), Refshaleøen (Refshalevej 159A), and Østerbro (Victor Borges Plads 2).

European
Osteria 16

Sønder Blvd. 54; tel. 33 22 70 71; www. osteria16.dk; Mon.-Thurs. 6pm-midnight, Fri.-Sat. 5:30pm-1am; set menu 425 kr; S-train Dybbølsbro, Metro Enghave Plads

Simplicity is ostensibly the name of the game at down-to-earth intimate Italian Osteria 16, but the quality of the dishes might have you thinking otherwise.

creating this elusive feeling of well-being, but the search for it is almost a subconscious part of everyday Danish life. Danes will often say that the closest English synonym for hygge is "cozy," but a more accurate explanation of the concept is, in my view, simpler than that and can be summed up as "having a nice time."

HOW IS IT PRONOUNCED?

While Anglophones can be forgiven for pronouncing hygge as they read it (higgy), the pronunciation HOO-gah or HUE-guh is also a little inaccurate. Approximate pronunciation for the Danish *y* is the *u* as in put—try saying it with your jaw slightly tighter. The *e* is roughly the vowel sound in the French article *le*. The *h* and the double *g* are thankfully pronounced as you might expect: h-y-gg-e.

PLACES TO FIND HYGGE

Just as there's no definitive way of translating the word, there is also no one specific way of finding hygge. It is far more a state of mind than something embodied by a particular place. Nevertheless, here are some good places to start looking for it:

- At a low-pace café such as **Kaffeplantagen** (Enghave Plads 1; tel. 32 11 41 14; www.kaffeplantagen.dk) in Vesterbro, with its newspapers scattered across the tables and pastries enticing you behind the counter glass.

- At a rowdy pub such as Christianshavn's **Eiffel Bar** (Wildersgade 58; tel. 32 57 70 92).

- Taking a Saturday morning stroll along a quiet pathway such as the unusual **Dyssen** at Christiania (page 73).

Ingredients are mainly fresh fish and vegetables, much of which is sourced from Italy itself: Think sea bass tartare, scallops, caprese, and ravioli. There's a second Vesterbro restaurant at Haderslevgade 16 and another at Ravnsborggade 14B in the Nørrebro neighborhood.

Famo Saxo

Saxogade 3; tel. 33 23 22 50; www.famo. dk/famo-saxo; Mon.-Thurs. 5:30pm-10pm, Fri.-Sun. 5pm-10pm; 4-course menu 400 kr, antipasti 200 kr; bus 7A Værnedamsvej (Frederiksberg Allé)

Opened in 2005, Famo Saxo is something of a veteran, having been around since before the New Nordic wave took off. It's an affordable family restaurant that uses Italian ingredients. The menu changes daily but always includes a primo of pasta, risotto, or similar and a main course with meat and seasonal vegetables. Vegetarian options are also available.

Café Viggo

*Værnedamsvej 15; tel. 33 31 18 21; https://
cafeviggo15.wixsite.com/cafeviggo15;
Mon.-Wed. 10am-midnight, Thurs. 10am-
1am, Fri. 10am-3am, Sat. 11am-3am;
galettes and omelets from 95 kr, mains
from 195 kr; bus 7A Værnedamsvej
(Frederiksberg Allé), 26 Frederiksberg
Allé (Vesterbrogade), 31 Værnedamsvej
(Gammel Kongevej)*

A French bistro well in keeping with the miniature Parisian feel of Værnedamsvej, Viggo is both a café and a restaurant, with dining from around 5:30pm, when classic French dishes like foie gras and rabbit confit are on offer (depending on the season). It has a more laid-back feel during the day, when you can stop for a coffee and a filling omelet or galette for a reasonable price. A large mural of comic-book character Gaston across one wall adds some color to the traditional look.

Mediterranean
Gorilla

*Flæsketorvet 63; tel. 33 33 83 30;
https://restaurantgorilla.dk; Sun.-Wed.
5pm-midnight, Thurs. 5pm-1am, Fri.-Sat.
5pm-2am; 10-serving tasting menu 450
kr, varying-size dishes 75-235 kr; bus
23 Gasværksvej (Istedgade), S-train
Dybbølsbro, Metro Copenhagen Central
Station*

More than just a hip bar and restaurant, Gorilla has shareable snacks and fish, pasta, and meat-based, primarily Mediterranean-style dishes of various sizes, as well as a tasting menu (but there are plenty of other influences). In a large open-plan space with seating for up to 200 and an unpretentious atmosphere, the restaurant is a former meatpacking warehouse; white tiles still adorn the walls. Reservations are required at peak times. Stay on at adjoining Gorilla Bar for DJs and dancing.

Asian
Magasasa Dim Sum & Cocktails

*Flæsketorvet 54-56; tel. 33 23 80 89;
www.magasasa.dk; Sun.-Thurs. noon-
11pm, kitchen closes 10pm, Fri.-Sat.
noon-midnight, kitchen closes 10:30pm;
dim sum 55-60 kr, noodle soup 115 kr;
bus 23 Gasværksvej (Istedgade), S-train
Dybbølsbro, Metro Copenhagen Central
Station*

Tucked away in one of the quieter parts of the Meatpacking District but close enough for the area's energy to be felt, Magasasa Dim Sum & Cocktails is something of a hidden gem given its delicious combination of dumplings and drinks. The classic siu mai with pork, shrimp, and shiitake mushrooms, as well as cha siu bao buns with roasted barbecue pork are personal favorites, and the chili sour cocktail prepared with bourbon and fresh red chili has the perfect amount of kick.

Latin American
✪ Sanchez

*Istedgade 60; tel. 31 11 66 40; https://
lovesanchez.com/sanchez; Mon.-Thurs.
5:30pm-midnight, kitchen closes 10pm,
Fri.-Sat. 5pm-midnight, kitchen closes
10:30pm, Sat.-Sun. lunch 11am-3pm,
kitchen closes 2:30pm; starters from 75 kr,
dinner menu 595 kr pp; bus 7A Vesterbros*

Sanchez is arguably Copenhagen's premier Mexican restaurant, with a broad menu that delves deep into that nation's cuisine. There's a lunch menu on weekends where you can fill up on huevos rancheros or prawns a la diabla. In the evening, the main option is an impressive 5-serving menu chosen by the kitchen, where dishes can include the likes of beef tartare tostada, blue mussels in chipotle sauce, and horchata with coffee cajeta. Don't forget the cocktail menu either: The mezcal-based margarita is not to be denied. Vegetarian and vegan options are available on request. Bookings must be made through the online booking system. For something more casual, visit one of its "little sisters," the Hija de Sanchez taquerias (Slagterboderne 8 and Frederiksborggade 21 at the Torvehallerne food hall).

Organic, Vegetarian, and Vegan

Neighbourhood

Istedgade 27; tel. 32 12 22 12; www.neighbourhood.dk; Sun.-Mon. 5pm-10pm, Tues.-Thurs. 5pm-10:30pm, kitchen closes 9:30pm, Sat. 5pm-1am, kitchen closes 10:30pm; pizzas 145 kr; bus 23 Gasværksvej (Istedgade), S-train Dybbølsbro, Metro Copenhagen Central Station

Organic pizza restaurant-slash-lounge bar Neighbourhood is based in a former butcher shop in what was once the heart of Vesterbro's red-light district. Stay for a cocktail after you've finished your pizza—the thin sourdough crust eclectically topped with air-cured ham and fresh figs, sweet corn brisket, garlic shrimp, or chili salami will not overfill you. Reservations are not usually necessary.

Radio

Julius Thomsens Gade 12; tel. 25 10 27 33; https://restaurantradio.dk; Tue.-Sat. 5:30pm-midnight; 3-course menu 395 kr; Metro Forum St.

Close to the Copenhagen Lakes and Forum Metro station, the organic New Nordic Radio takes its name from the former broadcasting house in which it is located. Organic ingredients on the monthly rotating menu—like apple, parsnip, quince, or mushrooms—come from land cultivated just outside Copenhagen. Founded by veteran chef and entrepreneur Claus Meyer of bakery fame, Radio is stylish and intimate, with a reputation for service as good as the acoustics that bounce off its wood-clad walls. Certain allergies might not be accommodated, so call ahead to check. Advance reservations are required.

NØRREBRO AND ØSTERBRO

Danish and New Nordic

✪ Geranium

Per Henrik Lings Allé 4; tel. 69 96 00 20; www.geranium.dk; Wed.-Thurs. 6pm-11pm, Fri.-Sat. noon-3:30pm and 6:30pm-11.30pm, 19-course tasting menu 4,200 kr excluding wine pairings; bus 1A Aarhusgade (Østerbrogade), Metro Poul Henningsens Plads

Eating at Michelin Star Restaurants

Copenhagen has 15 Michelin-starred restaurants as of 2023, including the three-starred Geranium. That makes it the most-starred city in the Nordic region.

Noma, one of the city's most famous Michelin restaurants, announced its closure in early 2023. Head chef René Redzepi stated that the restaurant was to make way for a "food laboratory," an experimental project in which new dishes and products would be developed, possibly to be sold online.

celeriac with smoked cod roe and fermented cream with caviar at Geranium

Commentators have wondered whether the closure of Noma could herald a new era for Danish fine dining, possibly one that could see other exclusive restaurants move away from the traditional to try to innovate like Noma. That remains speculation for now, and if, like many visitors before you, the lure of Copenhagen's remarkable record for gastronomic excellence has you wanting to try a tasting menu, you have a lot of options.

- **Geranium** is likely to take over the baton as *the* Michelin restaurant in the wake of Noma's closure. Its three stars speak for its incredibly high standards, and the astonishing wine list and dramatic setting in the Parken national stadium are important parts of the experience (page 115).

- **Kadeau** (Wildersgade 10B; tel. 33 25 22 23; www.kadeau.dk) is a little piece of the far-flung Danish island Bornholm transplanted to one of Christianshavn's more peaceful side streets. The berries and fish are foraged and caught for pickling, smoking, curing, and more before

Three-Michelin-starred Geranium's reputation speaks of creative and innovative dishes that are flawlessly executed works of art. The wine list is a tome and an attraction in its own right but requires an extraordinary budget. Located high up inside Parken, the national soccer stadium, it has views of treetops, rooftops, and the Øresund. Booking ahead—up to 90 days in advance—is normally the only way to get a table; an online reservation system is available on the website. Expect unmatched hospitality and flavors that catch you unaware. The menu changes seasonally and the number of courses may vary.

their use in the Bornholm-inspired New Nordic dishes. You can almost hear the waves crashing against the rocky island cliffs.

- **AOC** (Dronningens Tværgade 2; tel. 33 11 11 45; https://restaurantaoc.dk) is another memorably located Michelin restaurant, this time in a vaulted 17th-century cellar near the royal residence. The dishes are praised in the Michelin guide for the finesse that goes into their preparation, and the definition of their flavors.

- **Formel B** (Vesterbrogade 182, Frederiksberg; tel. 33 25 10 66; https://formelb.dk) is one of the more affordable (in relative terms) of Copenhagen's Michelin restaurants. Located in a smart building in Frederiksberg with an open-plan kitchen so you can see the chefs' craftwork first hand, it is known for having an informal style. The seasonal menu consists of 10-12 dishes that the guest is invited to choose among.

TIPS

Going to an exclusive—or, at the very least, gourmet—restaurant might feel like the sort of occasion that requires smart shoes and formal attire. Generally, though, this is not an expectation at Copenhagen's Michelin-starred restaurants, where you won't be turned away even if you walk up in a pair of crocs and Levi's. That said, some guests like to treat visiting a Michelin restaurant like a special occasion—understandably so—and dress accordingly, which can be quite evident once you notice the other patrons. If you want to join in and dress up for the occasion, you should feel comfortable doing so.

Another important point to remember is to enjoy yourself, relax, and ask any questions you have. It is the job of the table staff to make sure you have a good experience, and there's a reason they are working at a Michelin-starred restaurant: They're skilled. They'll let you know if there's anything peculiar about a certain dish, or if it has to be eaten in an unusual way. They are also likely to be foodies themselves, so don't hold back—allow a rapport to build and let it enhance the experience. Nothing is expected from you as a guest, apart from footing a rather large bill, of course.

Breakfast and Diners
Grød

Jægersborggade 50; tel. 50 58 55 79; www.groed.com; Mon.-Fri. 7:30am-9pm, Sat.-Sun. 9am-9pm; oatmeal from 59 kr; bus 5C Stefansgade (Nørrebrogade)

A game changer for porridge with its selection of oats, including delicious berry, licorice, and nut-based toppings and other healthy breakfasty delights, Grød also serves a risotto, which more than holds its own later in the day. There is often ample seating space despite the busy "walk in and out on the way to work" concept. Grød has six other locations across Copenhagen, including Vesterbrogade 105b (tel.

32 15 35 35) and a stand at the Torvehallerne food hall.

Sidecar

Skyttegade 5; tel. 20 99 97 27; www.
sidecarnoerrebro.dk; Mon. 8am-4pm, Tues.-
Thurs. 8am-10:30pm, Fri. 8am-midnight,
Sat. 9am-midnight, Sun. 9am-3:30pm;
yogurt with fruit and granola 40 kr, all-day
brunch boards 169 kr, Asian street food
dishes from 75 kr; bus 2A H.C. Ørsteds Vej
(Rosenorns Allé), Metro Forum

A breakfast and brunch café that switches to Asian street food in the evening, Sidecar Nørrebro has gained recognition as one of the city's best cafés. This is a breakfast place with "all the good stuff," in Sidecar's own words. Brunches include scrambled eggs, sausages, bacon, granola, waffles, and rye bread. A vegan version of the brunch with a generous portion of avocado is also available. There is a positive welcoming energy, but like many brunch spots, it gets busy on weekends.

Cafés and Bakeries
Social

Peblinge Dossering 4; tel. 53 70 00
53; www.socialcoffee.dk; Mon.-Fri.
8am-6pm, Sat.-Sun. 9am-6pm; coffee
from 25 kr, breakfast bowls 75 kr,
salads and sandwiches 89-95 kr; bus 5C
Ravnsborggade (Nørrebrogade)

Instantly recognizable from its yellow facade and wallet-friendly coffee, Social's fresh salads and waffles complement oats, acai bowls, pastries, snacks, and more. You'll find a bohemian cozy nook with hanging plants, cushions, and bookshelves. Close to Dronning Louises Bro, where Nørrebro connects to the Inner City, this highly rated café won the *Berlingske* newspaper's award for best café in Copenhagen in 2017 and received a nomination the following year.

Ali Bageri

Heimdalsgade 39; tel. 32 57 63 42; https://
alibageri.dk; daily 8am-6pm; manakish
from 25 kr; Metro Skjolds Plads

Difficult-to-find Ali Bageri is not visible from the street: The only hint of its presence is a small metal sign on the sidewalk by the entrance to the backyard, where it is located next to a mosque. A scruffy, busy little shop, the taste of the food belies first impressions. The manakish—a flat-baked dough topped with oily za'atar, cheese, or ground meat—is its staple, as it would be at a typical Middle Eastern bakery. A second larger branch at Nørrebrogade 211 has the same basic plastic seating and quick service with less of the charm of the original, but it's easier to find.

European
✪ Bæst

Guldbergsgade 29; tel. 35 35 04 63;
https://baest.dk; brunch Sat.-Sun. 11am-
2:30pm, dinner Tues.-Sun. 5pm-10pm;
pizzas 135-165 kr; bus 5C Kapelvej
(Nørrebrogade)

Once featured on Netflix's *Ugly Delicious,* Bæst has claims to being Copenhagen's most famed—and best—pizza restaurant, and there's certainly no doubt about its popularity. The organic meats, fresh mozzarella, and wood-fired cooking all give the claim considerable substance. There are tables with chairs and stools in the ample restaurant area, which also boasts a poster of Barack Obama drinking an Americano.

Mirabelle

Guldbergsgade 29; tel. 35 35 04 63; https://mirabelle-spiseria.dk/en; Tues.-Sun. 8:30am-10pm; breakfast plate 85 kr, brunch 170 kr, mains from 145 kr; bus 5C Kapelvej (Nørrebrogade)

Once an artisanal Nørrebro bakery, Mirabelle was transformed into an Italian all-day eatery in 2023 by head chef and owner Christian Puglisi, former sous-chef at Noma. The new Mirabelle is labeled a spiseria, somewhere between the Danish all-day café and the Italian trattoria. Brioches, buns, and continental-type breakfasts are available in the morning, while later in the day you can try simple pasta dishes, focaccia, and meatballs. In the evening, there is a six-dish tasting menu for 455 kr (excluding wine), which is more than reasonable by local standards.

Burgers
Poulette

Møllegade 1; https://poulette.dk; daily 11am-8pm; chicken and tofu burgers 95 kr; bus 5C Kapelvej (Nørrebrogade)

Poulette's chicken and tofu burgers stand out among strong fast-food competition in the inner Nørrebro area. The walk-in restaurant, located next door to wine bar Pompette (with which it shares owners), is small, and seating overspills onto the street—including the pavement and curbside—on busy summer days. The burger consists of chicken breast, not processed meat, and is coated in a crisp and slightly spicy batter that has the perfect balance of crunch and moisture without being greasy. Look for the pink lettering in the window if you're finding it hard to locate. There's also a Poulette stand at the Broens Street Food market.

Ethiopian and Eritrean
Hidmona

Griffenfeldsgade 7; tel. 29 35 35 30; https://hidmona-restaurant.business.site; Mon. 2pm-10pm, Tues.-Thurs. noon-10pm, Fri.-Sat. noon-10:30pm, Sun. noon-10pm; mains from 109 kr; bus 5C Elmegade (Nørrebrogade)

A few yards from Nørrebrogade, Hidmona Ethiopian and Eritrean Restaurant offers up round metal platters of spicy food that must be eaten without cutlery, instead by picking it up with Ethiopian injera bread (the bread is made from teff flour and thus gluten-free). The decor is monotone but the food far from it, and service is extraordinarily friendly and welcoming, with English the main working language, possibly due to the multinational staff. Dishes include traditional spicy meat, garlic, butter, and vegetable platters including kitfo, misto, qey wat, and bayinat meat.

Middle Eastern
Berlin Döner Kebab

*Nørrebrogade 100; tel. 50 14 32 37; www.
berlindonerkebab.dk; Sun.-Thurs. 11am-
10pm, Fri.-Sat. 11am-4am; kebabs from 75
kr; bus 5C Sjællandsgade (Nørrebrogade)*

The stretch of Nørrebrogade opposite Assistens Cemetery, and between the two side streets Sjællandsgade and Fyensgade, is a strip of almost purely takeaway kebab restaurants. Any number of these are good enough to satisfy the discerning shawarma lover, but the pick of the bunch is Berlin Döner Kebab, evidenced by the fact it usually has the longest queue. Tender marinated meat or crisp falafels accompanied by fresh crunchy salad with a biting dressing are all neatly (until you start eating) packed into the flat bread. Once you've received your meal, you can sit on one of the benches and tables that have been installed along the street.

Omar

*Refsnæsgade 32; tel. 27 51 52 57; www.
restaurantomar.dk; Sun.-Thurs. noon-
midnight, kitchen closes 9:30pm, Fri.-Sat.
noon-1am, kitchen closes 10pm; 8-course
menu 385 kr, 4-course lunch 195 kr; bus 6A
Nørre Campus (Tagensvej)*

Low-key hygge is the vibe at Omar, a popular café recognizable from its characteristic blue- and black-tiled facade. It's loosely defined as a "no rules" kitchen but with everything from Middle Eastern to South American to Mediterranean influences, along with plenty of passion present on the menu. Try the green gazpacho, seared scallops, muhammara with pomegranate Swiss chard, and more.

Asian
GAO Dumpling Bar

*Blågårdsgade 3; tel. 34 12 46 26; www.
gaodumpling.com; daily noon-midnight;
6 dumplings from 60 kr; bus 5C
Ravnsborggade (Nørrebrogade)*

Copenhagen's oldest dumpling bar puts a flash of Chinese color into the sober surroundings of the Danish interior design. The straightforward selection, including spinach, cabbage, chicken, mushroom, and spicy pork dumplings, can be complemented with sides such as bok choy, noodles with carrot and cucumber in nut sauce, and deep-fried tofu. It's a walk-in-only restaurant with seating outside and inside. If you're in a takeaway mood, there are hole-in-the-wall branches in both Vesterbro (Istedgade 98) and Østerbro (Øster Farigmagsgade 22).

Ramen to Bíiru

*Griffenfeldsgade 28; tel. 50 53 02 22;
https://ramentobiiru.dk/norrebro; Sun.-
Thurs. 11:30am-9pm, Fri.-Sat. 11:30am-
9:30pm; ramen 135-145 kr; bus 5C
Elmegade (Nørrebrogade)*

Tokyo noodle bar meets Copenhagen craft beer at Ramen to Bíiru, where no reservations are taken. Food is ordered by inserting money into a machine, choosing your dish, pressing a button, and then taking a ticket to the counter to pick it up. Several spicy, meaty, and vegetarian options are available, but you might have to

Ramen to Bíiru

sit elbow-to-elbow with other patrons. The spicy miso is a favorite—wash it down with a Mikkeller beer. There's a stand at Copenhagen Airport should you miss out during your stay in the city.

CHRISTIANSHAVN AND AMAGER
Danish and New Nordic
Christianshavns Færgecafé

Strandgade 50; tel. 32 54 46 24; https:// faergecafeen.dk; lunch Mon.-Sat. 11:30am-3:30pm, dinner Mon.-Thurs. 5:30pm-9pm, Fri.-Sat. 6pm-10pm, Sun. 11:30am-8pm; smørrebrød from 95 kr, dinner mains 195-325 kr; bus 2A Christianshavns Torv, Metro Christianshavns St.

The archetypically Danish Christianshavns Færgecafé is unmissable in the midst of Christianshavn's cobbled streets and arched bridges, its rich orange exterior and bold letters proudly proclaiming its presence as a busy provider of victuals in an area once frequented by seafarers. Herring and smørrebrød are the order of the day, as is the homemade Skipper's Schnapps, if you're feeling brave. In the evening you'll find schnitzel, Captain's Beef Tatare with mustard,

and duck with pickled artichokes among the main course options.

La Banchina

Refshalevej 141A; tel. 31 26 65 61; www. labanchina.dk; June-Aug. daily 8am-10pm, Sept. Sun.-Wed. 8am-6pm, Thurs.-Sat. 8am-8pm, Oct.-Feb. daily 8am-4pm, Mar. Sun.-Wed. 8am-4pm, Thurs.-Sat. 8am-6pm, Apr.-May Sun.-Wed. 8am-6pm, Thurs.-Sat. 8am-8pm; bakery from 35 kr, lunch and dinner mains from 115 kr; bus 2A Refshaleøen (Refshalevej), Harbor Bus 991, 992

"Dip, eat, repeat" is the mantra at La Banchina, the year-round café at Refshaleøen. It is housed in a converted blue-washed wooden hut that was once a waiting room for ferry passengers. There is a jetty seating area that can be used to view the sunset over the sea while enjoying a fresh seafood or vegetarian dish. Inside, there are a handful of seats, and it is particularly popular among Refshaleøen visitors, which means you'll have to be quick or lucky to get a spot during peak times—especially since a no-reservation, walk-in-only system is in operation. As well as eating, you can use the facilities to take a dip in the harbor and even use the sauna (inquire ahead about availability).

Breakfast and Diners
Wulff & Konstali

Lergravsvej 57; tel. 32 54 81 81; www. wogk.dk; Mon.-Fri. 7am-7pm, Sat.-Sun. 8am-6pm; brunch 149 kr for 5 selected components; Metro Lergravsparken

Light, airy, and near the beach at Amager Strandpark, Wulff &

Konstali is an ideal spot for breakfast or lunch. Pick and mix your own breakfast and brunch from the selection of 22 different components that include croissants, eggs, grapes, melon, organic cheese, smoked salmon, and fresh bread straight from the on-site bakery. It's a busy spot, particularly on weekends or when the weather's good. There's seating along a bench table and at stools facing the window, and it also functions as a café, deli, and takeaway that serves sandwiches, smørrebrød, and salads.

Cafés and Bakeries
Bodenhoff

Torvegade 50; tel. 21 40 22 97; www.bodenhoffs.dk; Mon.-Fri. 6am-6pm, Sat.-Sun. 6am-5pm; pastries from 23 kr; bus 2A, Christianshavns Torv, Metro Christianshavns St.

Bodenhoff, a long-standing bakery chain, took over this handy location in the midst of the Christianshavn action. You can choose from a broad range of Danish-style loaves and rye breads. A good selection of cakes is also available, including staples like kanelsnurre (cinnamon bread swirls), hindbærsnitte (Alexandertorte), and brunsviger, a sugary bready cake with caramelized brown sugar on top. Grab a coffee to go with your baked goods or sandwich and sit at one of the café seats by the window, observing busy Christianshavn Square and Torvegade. Other central Copenhagen branches include Frederiksberg (Finsensvej 54) and Vesterbro (Matthæusgade 50).

HANS

Wildersgade 26; www.instagram.com/hanscoffeecph; Mon.-Fri. 7:30am-5pm, Sat.-Sun. 9am-5pm; coffee from 35 kr; bus 2A Christianshavns Torv, Metro Christianshavns St.

On a corner abutting Torvegade, the main road through Christianshavn, new café H A N S opens early, at 7:30am, with a good selection of morning pastries like the poppy seed-topped tebirkes and croissants, as well as other options like yogurt with homemade granola. The bread rolls come with a generously thick slice of pungent Danish cheese and butter, and the coffee won't let you down either. There are benches and small tables outside facing the main street, but grab a spot at one of the little round cream-colored tables inside if you're looking for something more withdrawn from the charging bicycle traffic.

Asian
Curry Club

Dronningensgade 46; tel. 28 73 43 46; www.curryclub.dk; daily 4pm-10pm; curries 110-150 kr; bus 2A Christianshavns Torv, Metro Christianshavns St.

An unassuming but colorful Indian restaurant and takeaway just off Christianshavn Square, Curry Club was opened in 2017 by two curry-mad brothers who will gladly spend 10 minutes explaining minute details of the various traditional Indian dishes. Meals can be eaten on the low-key benches inside the brightly lit restaurant or taken away. The restaurant is a

Reffen

hidden favorite of Christianshavn locals in a city where Indian food is often overlooked. I recommend the achari murghi, a strong chicken dish with chili pickles, and palak gosht, a spinach curry made using Irish lamb. Vegan and vegetarian dishes are also available.

Middle Eastern
Halla Halla

Dronningensgade 42; tel. 28 89 68 49; https://hallahalla.dk; daily 11:30am-8:30pm; pitas from 79 kr, bowls from 99 kr; bus 2A Christianshavn St. (Torvegade), Metro Christianshavn St.

Halla Halla established itself as a popular local takeaway spot in Christianshavn following its opening in 2020, becoming an instant hit with students in the university flats across the road. The Middle Eastern-inspired pita breads and bowls are ordered using a build-it-yourself menu in which you pick

and mix from a choice of main fillings (falafel, chicken, halloumi, or beef), spread (hummus, tzatziki), and dressing. Add fries or homemade chili if you prefer.

Food Market
Reffen

Refshalevej 167A; tel. 33 93 07 60; https://reffen.dk; late Mar.-late Sept. daily 11am-9:30pm, closed winter; mains from 90 kr; bus 2A (Refshaleøen), Harbor Bus 991, 992

Reffen, an open-air food market spanning 65,000 square feet on the Refshaleøen former dockland, serves world food to the masses from within the corrugated steel walls of its converted shipping containers. The 2,500 seats are laid out on a wide, dusty open space between the containers and the edge of the harbor. **Gosht** (https://reffen.dk/stadeholder/gosht) serves Kurdish kebabs, **Fuego** (https://

reffen.dk/stadeholder/fuego-street-food) offers Argentinian-style steak sandwiches, and **Ramsløg.cph** (https://reffen.dk/stadeholder/ramsloeg-cph) make fresh salads in bowls and wraps. Other businesses—including a tattoo artist—have begun to move in to Reffen, suggesting it has the potential to grow from its street food origins.

Broens Street Food

Strandgade 95; tel. 33 93 07 60; https://broensgadekoekken.dk; daily 11:30am-9:30pm, bars Sun.-Thurs. until 10pm, Fri.-Sat. until 11pm; bus 2A Bodenhoffs Plads (Prinsessegade), Metro Kongens Nytorv

Just across the bicycle-pedestrian bridge from Nyhavn, this street food market has considerably more character than many of the tourist-focused eateries along the Nyhavn harborside. It will also set you back a bit less for something comparable in quality. In the evening, lovely sunsets over the harbor can be enjoyed if you come at the right time, and the place positively hums on warm weekend nights as DJs play sets and strings of lights twinkle over the heads of hundreds of Copenhageners seated and standing around the many benches.

KASTELLET AND LANGELINIE

This area consists of a seafront promenade extending north from the royal area of the Inner City and a former medieval citadel-turned-barracks, so there are few residences or residents. If you find yourself here for sightseeing purposes—the famous *Little Mermaid* statue is just off the Langelinie shore—then walking back toward Nyhavn along parallel streets Borgergade, Store Kongensgade, or Bredgade will bring you to the closest restaurants, where there are plenty of good options.

Seaside

Nordre Toldbod 24; tel. 33 93 07 60; https://seasidecph.dk/en; kitchens Tues.-Thurs. noon-9pm, Fri.-Sat. noon-10pm, Sun. noon-4pm, bar open later; mains from 195 kr, snacks from 75 kr; Metro Marmorkirken, Harbor Bus 991, 992 Nordre Toldbod

Set in the former ferry terminal at Copenhagen Harbor with a view of Refshaleøen and the Opera House, Seaside houses seven different kitchens that offer a variety of restaurant and gastro-style meals and lighter bites. These include Asian, seafood, tartare, pasta, Nordic, and vegan raw food. There's an unusual layout, with the different kitchens clearly presented as separate entities. This doesn't seem to detract from the food, which is also good value given the lack of competitors in the vicinity and the visitors attracted by the nearby *Little Mermaid*. Seating is available outside by the harbor as well as within the restaurant.

Bars and Nightlife

Copenhagen has inexhaustible nightlife and drinking options, with a range of tastes catered to and high quality close by wherever you find yourself. However, drinking in Denmark is expensive compared to almost every other country in the world. There are savings to be had if you look in the right places, including happy hours and cheap drinks as local bodegas.

NØRREPORT AND AROUND

Copenhagen pulses with life in the evening hours around the Inner City. The possibilities for a night on the town have few limits, and one bar can quickly be swapped for another, depending on the vibe of the evening. Some of the bars along Gothersgade are rather unimaginative and best avoided, while others are worth seeking out. The area around Nørreport offers a variety of bars—everything from quiet wine tasting to boisterous pubs and lively dance floors.

The Living Room

Larsbjørnsstræde 17; tel. 33 32 66 10; Mon.-Thurs. 9am-11pm, Fri. 9am-midnight, Sat. 10am-midnight, Sun. 10am-7pm; bus or Metro Rådhuspladsen

A chilled-out and popular café during the day, coffee is swapped for relatively inexpensive cocktails as evening begins at the Living Room. With a hearth and comfy sofas on the lower floor, it can be a great way to shelter from the aching cold of the winter season. Upstairs seating has a decent view of the busy central streets, ideal for people-watching over a margarita or mocha. It's busy all day Friday-Saturday. Happy hour is daily 5pm-9pm.

The Log Lady

Studiestræde 27; tel. 26 27 93 62; Wed.-Sat. 4pm-midnight; bus or Metro Rådhuspladsen

Twin Peaks-inspired Log Lady Café is a quirky bar with a friendly vibe that does a good job of evoking the spirit of the David Lynch TV character for which it is named. There's red lighting, a good range of beers, and regular concerts. The bar has the relaxing feel of a lounge room, and you can, appropriately, sit on a tree stump while taking in the many pictures adorning the walls and other features to keep your eyes busy. Pay attention to the flooring on the way to the restrooms: The zigzagging tiles might tell you "It's happening again."

Bo-Bi Bar

Klareboderne 14; tel. 33 12 55 43; https:// bo-bi-bar.business.site; daily 2pm-2am; Metro Kongens Nytorv

Reportedly founded by a sailor during World War I, smoky Bo-Bi Bar retains the old-fashioned, rather than the consciously retro, feel of a harborside drinking establishment. Known as a place where artists and

If You're Looking For...

Mikkeller Baghaven at Refshaleøen

If you're a B-menneske, the Danish equivalent of a night owl, you probably won't be short of somewhere to go during your stay in Copenhagen. Cafés are usually closed by around midnight, and from this point onward you might be pressed for somewhere to go to sit down and have a quiet chat. This aside, you can find flashy cocktail bars, rowdy pubs, thumping night clubs, beer specialists, and very, very late openers—going all the way through to breakfast the next morning.

- **Live Music:** Amager Bio (page 84) is a prolific concert venue that hosts both new music and established artists. It gets enthusiastic crowds and has great acoustics. Book a table at throwback Jazzhus Montmartre (page 83) for jazz as it was experienced in 1970s Copenhagen, up close and personal with the artist.

writers once convened, this down-to-earth bodega is attractive to literary types for just that reason. Note that smoking is permitted inside.

The Jane

Gråbrødretorv 8; tel. 28 68 08 60; www.thejane.dk; Fri.-Sat. 8pm-5am; Metro Nørreport

There's a distinctly *Mad Men* feel to cocktail bar and nightclub The Jane, one of a number of tourist-friendly options around the Gråbrødretorv plaza, close to the Round Tower and central shopping streets. Its small rooms, dim lights, and bookcases insinuate secret doorways, and space is made for a dance floor later in the night, resulting occasionally in full-on parties.

- **Craft Cocktails:** The area around Gammel Strand Metro station—across the road from imposing Christiansborg palace—is rife with cocktail bars. These include Asian homage **Little Green Door** (page 128); **Ruby** (page 128), home of the purple mojito; and gin specialist **The Bird & the Churchkey** (page 128).

- **Breweries:** The dominant name for breweries in Copenhagen is Mikkeller. The craft beer behemoth has some great bars in various districts, including **WarPigs** (page 132) in the Meatpacking District, **Mikkeller Baghaven** (page 138) at Refshaleøen, and **Mikkeller & Friends** (page 135) in Nørrebro. For an alternative brewer, **Brus** (page 135) has a solid selection from popular Danish craft beer exporter To Øl.

- **LGBTQ+:** Head to the area next to City Hall Square (Rådhuspladsen) and you'll find **Centralhjørnet** (page 129), the original Copenhagen gay bar with decades of history behind it. Nearby **Never Mind** (page 130) pumps out pop hits until the early hours.

- **Budget friendly:** Try starting your night out with happy-hour cocktails at **The Living Room** (page 125), close to Nørreport station. From here, it's a short hop to the Nørrebro neighborhood for the student-friendly **Mexi-Bar** (page 135) and late-opener **Tjili Pop** (page 137). Cheaper than any of these options, however, would be to settle at a bodega and drink cheap bottled pilsners all night. **Eiffel Bar** (page 138) in Christianshavn is a great place to do this.

- **Dancing:** In the Meatpacking District, **Baggen Kbh** (page 133) and **Jolene** (page 134) are big local favorites and generally thronging with effortlessly stylish Danes, especially at the weekend. If you're out for the duration, **Culture Box** (page 129) is the pinnacle of Copenhagen's techno clubs.

GREATER INNER CITY
Wine
Bibendum

Nansensgade 45; tel. 33 33 07 74; https://bibendum.dk; Mon.-Sat. 4pm-midnight; bus or Metro Nørreport

One of Copenhagen's oldest wine bars, by its own estimation, diminutive Bibendum, with its candlelit tables and blackboard menus ("Wine is the answer . . . what was the question?") has a calming vibe and an enormous wine list. There's a rotating selection of organic, bio, and sparkling wines, as well as reds and whites to cater to all preferences, with Spanish- and French-inspired snacks on hand. Bibendum is located a stone's throw from the popular walking path at the Lakes and the busy Dronning Louises Bro bridge. Note that it sometimes closes in July.

Ved Stranden 10

*Ved Stranden 10; tel. 35 42 40 40; www.
vedstranden10.dk; Mon.-Fri. 3pm-10pm,
Sat. noon-10pm; Metro Kongens Nytorv*

Located in a registered historical building that dates to the 19th-century era of Hans Christian Andersen and Søren Kierkegaard, and directly facing Christiansborg Palace, there's a sense of history at Ved Stranden 10. An extensive wine list includes entries from all over the world, including a good selection of natural wines, no shortage of space, and knowledgeable staff to guide you through it. In summer you can sit outside and take in the canal-side view.

Cocktails
Ruby

*Nybrogade 10; tel. 33 93 12 03; https://rby.
dk; Mon.-Sat. 4pm-2am, Sun. 5pm-1am;
bus 2A, 9A Stormbroen, Nationalmuseet
(Vindebrogade), Metro Gammel Strand*

In a building from 1740 on Nybrogade that once housed the Georgian embassy, cocktail bar Ruby has plenty of elbow room and large comfy chairs to sink into while you enjoy a cocktail. Its stately pedigree is backed by the location opposite Christiansborg Palace, the seat of Parliament, and Thorvaldsens art museum. It carries an old-fashioned charm while still retaining a few surprises, like the unusual purple mojito that regularly appears on its changing menu. The bartenders, who are well-informed cocktail enthusiasts, are versed in the customs and traditions of their trade. The

music is not too loud, in keeping with Ruby's broad appeal.

Little Green Door

*Gammel Strand 40; tel. 31 73 73 54;
https://littlegreendoor.dk; Tues. 4pm-10pm,
Wed. 4pm-midnight, Thurs. 4pm-1am, Fri.-
Sat. 3pm-2am; Metro Gammel Strand*

Identifiable from the small emerald-green entry after which it is named, this smart cocktail bar's Asian theme extends to drinks like Tattooed in Shibuya (gin, matcha, coconut, and lime) and Dragon Eye (bourbon, raspberry, lemon, and chili bitters), along with plenty of Chinese characters and neon signs for decoration. You can also get classic cocktails like a whiskey sour or an old fashioned (although there's no Singapore sling on the menu). The guests are as well turned out as the bar, which has the look and feel of a highly polished speakeasy. The minimum age is 20.

The Bird & the Churchkey

*Gammel Strand 44; tel. 69 17 71 99; www.
thebird.dk; Sun.-Thurs. 4pm-midnight, Fri.-
Sat. 2pm-2am; Metro Gammel Strand*

The Bird & the Churchkey has more than 20 variations of gin and tonic (there are 102 different gins) and 50 beers. By the side of atmospheric Gammel Strand canal, it was recently renovated with clean lines broken up by gin cabinets, palm trees, and art prints. The atmosphere makes for a buoyant, noisy experience, and you certainly won't go thirsty. Cocktails start from 80 kr and average around 120 kr for a good quality G&T, a not unreasonable price by Copenhagen standards.

Bodegas
Bankeråt

Ahlefeldtsgade 27; tel. 33 93 69 88; www.bankeraat.dk; Mon.-Tues. 10:30am-11pm, Wed.-Sat. 10:30am-midnight, Sun. 10:30am-8pm; bus 5C Nørre Farimagsgade (Frederiksborggade)

Bankeråt almost has the appearance of an old-fashioned "brown bodega" (pub) with its deep-red walls and various stuffed animal heads adorning the walls, but the hanging fairy lights and other assorted knickknacks add a touch of the surreal. There's a good selection of local and foreign craft beers from 69 kr; Carlsberg, Tuborg, and coffee is a little cheaper. Brunch and a range of café meals are also available, including an English breakfast.

Dance and Live Music
La Fontaine

Kompagnistræde 11; tel. 33 11 60 98; www.lafontaine.dk; Mon.-Thurs. 8pm-3am, Fri.-Sat. 8pm-5am, Sun. 8pm-3am; bus 2A, 31 Stormbroen, Nationalmuseet (Vindebrogade), Metro Gammel Strand

Lady Gaga once showed up unannounced to play an improvised concert at La Fontaine, reportedly just because she liked the place. She's not the only one. Crowded and a bit rough around the edges with a slightly older crowd, this long-standing jazz bar is a Copenhagen classic. Live concerts regularly take place Friday-Saturday nights

and Sunday. There may be a cover charge of 60-150 kr for concerts.

Culture Box

Kronprinsessegade 54; tel. 33 32 50 50; https://culture-box.com; Fri.-Sat. 10pm-8am; bus 23 Kronprinsessegade (Sølvgade), Metro Marmorkirken

Culture Box is one of the few night-clubs in Copenhagen that only plays techno music, with electronic and house also included. It also stays open until the light of morning, so it can be an option after all the other bars have closed. There are two floors and three sections (Red Box, White Box, and Blue Box), all of which pump out high-tempo techno to keep you moving, often with international DJs and producers at weekly events. Check the program on the club's website or Instagram page. There's usually a cover charge of around 150 kr.

LGBTQ+
Centralhjørnet

Kattesundet 18; tel. 33 11 85 49; www.centralhjornet.dk; Sun.-Thurs. noon-2am, Fri.-Sat. noon-4am; bus or Metro Rådhuspladsen

The self-titled "world's oldest still-existing gay bar" may well live up to that claim, and it is certainly Copenhagen's first: Rumor has it that in the 1920s the army ordered conscripts not to go there, such was its reputation. In its modern form, there's a welcoming and low-key atmosphere during the day and regular events at night, such as live music, drag shows, and Sunday jazz. The gin and tonics are decent, and beers and cocktails are also on the menu. Smoking is allowed inside, adding to the sense of a throwback to a previous era.

Never Mind

Nørre Voldgade 2; tel. 21 93 76 25; https://nevermindbar.dk; daily 10pm-6am; bus 5C Teglgårdstræde (Nørre Voldgade), Metro Nørreport, S-train Vesterport

The inclusive Never Mind, which describes itself as a gay night club, announced an expansion to a larger new "VIP" premises at the distinctive Axeltorv, where there's a large dance floor and lounge, but its original premises, a 5-minute walk away at Nørre Voldgade 2, will continue. Pop hits and alcopops are popular at the long-standing club, which is welcoming of all types and looks—you certainly don't need to worry about the dress code. Smoking is allowed inside, a throwback still permitted in a small number of bars.

Nightclubs

Natbar

Nyropsgade 39-41; www.natbar.dk; Fri.-Sat. 11pm-4am; cover charge 80 kr; bus or Metro Rådhuspladsen, S-train Vesterport

Natbar (Night Bar) is located in the foyer of the Bremen Theater and opens as a nightclub on Friday-Saturday. There's a relaxed atmosphere for a club, and the high ceilings stop you from feeling closed in, which is handy, as the dance floor is usually busy. You're unlikely to hear current music but can expect to hear all manner of

genres played at some point in the evening, from funk and soul to hip-hop and rock. You must be age 23 or over to enter, but there's no dress code.

NYHAVN

Nebbiolo Winebar

Store Strandstræde 18; tel. 60 10 11 09; https://nebbiolo-winebar.com; Mon.-Thurs. 3pm-midnight, Fri.-Sat. 3pm-2am, Sun. 3pm-midnight; Metro Kongens Nyhavn

There are vintage Italian scenes on the walls, boxes of wine on the floor, and cured ham hanging from the ceiling. Wine specialists at Nebbiolo always have a large number of open bottles from throughout the Mediterranean, sold by the glass (75-125 kr). Complimentary antipasti tapas are served with the wine, and if you get a taste for a meal, a full plate can be purchased. It's a nice breather from Nyhavn's busy crowds, but it's still crowded on weekends.

Den Vandrette

Havnegade 53A; tel. 72 14 82 28; www.denvandrette.dk; Mon.-Wed. 4pm-10:30pm, Thurs. 4pm-11pm, Fri.-Sat. 4pm-midnight; Metro Kongens Nytorv

Den Vandrette is just around the corner from Nyhavn and overlooks the water, which allows you to avoid much of the area's foot traffic. With sketches of fish and bottles of wine on its facade, Den Vandrette (The Horizontal) was one of Denmark's first importers of natural wines. Wines are featured from 10 French regions along with

Den Vandrette

far more welcoming now than in the days when its name was intrinsically linked to drugs, crime, and poverty. It has become a vibrant spot with bars, bodegas (the small, rowdy, pub-like bars with tobacco-stained walls and cheap schnapps to go with the grizzled locals), and restaurants; **Viktoriagade** and **Vesterbrogade** are also good areas to seek out.

Cocktails
Lidkoeb

Vesterbrogade 72B; tel. 33 11 20 10; www.lidkoeb.dk; Mon.-Thurs. 4pm-2am, Fri.-Sat. 5pm-2am, Sun. 6pm-2am; bus 26 Frederiksberg Allé (Vesterbrogade), 7A Værnedamsvej (Frederiksberg Allé), 31 Det ny teater (Gl. Kongevej)

A long bar, boothed seating, and high taps serving quality draft beers in a clean setting with white-washed walls and matching lamps are what you'll first encounter at Lidkoeb, but there's more. Located in a three-story building that was once a pharmacy, there's a dedicated whisky bar on the top floor, open Friday-Saturday. In the middle, a function room with couch-style seating and a more laid-back feel is often open for patrons, especially on weekends.

Spain, Portugal, Italy, Germany, and the New World. Tapas-style side dishes complement the wines.

TOP EXPERIENCE

✪ VESTERBRO AND FREDERIKSBERG

The highlight of nightlife in Copenhagen is arguably **Vesterbro's Meatpacking District** (Kødbyen to the locals), which in recent years has developed into an inventive and diverse district that exudes urban chic while retaining elements of its industrial past: Many of the bars and restaurants have a white-tiled metallic aesthetic that reflects the cool sense of style of the customers. On summer weekends, the area buzzes with people sitting, standing, and dancing in and outside the many bars, clubs, and restaurants, with wide asphalt spaces ample for impromptu partying.

Elsewhere in Vesterbro, **Istedgade** is a gritty area that is

1656

Gasværksvej 33; tel. 33 91 16 56; http://cocktailkompagniet.dk; Mon.-Wed. 6pm-1am, Thurs.-Fri. 5pm-2am, Sat. 6pm-2am, Sun. 6pm-1am; bus 23 Gasværksvej (Istedgade), S-train, Metro Copenhagen Central Station

Yards from the Meatpacking

District but hidden from obvious view (keep looking if you don't see it at first), the speakeasy-style 1656, with its wooden panels and dark upholstery, has a huge cocktail menu. The sofas are comfy and the vibe intimate, with dim lighting and lively conversation. Try the 3-Star Daiquiri, named for the artisanal rum used to make it.

Beer

Mikkeller Bar Viktoriagade

Viktoriagade 8; tel. 33 31 04 15; www. mikkeller.com; Mon. 2pm-10pm, Tues.-Wed. 2pm-11pm, Thurs. 2pm-midnight, Fri. 2pm-2am, Sat. noon-2am, Sun. 2pm-2am; bus or Metro Copenhagen Central Station

The very first Mikkeller bar on Vesterbro has a classical minimalistic look, all white walls and straight lines, with simple wooden seats, black tile, and squeaky clean floors. Although no two Mikkeller bars are the same, this one is the blueprint for the Mikkeller bar you might have seen elsewhere in the world: They have been exported from Copenhagen to many, many locations over the last decade and a half. There are 20 taps dedicated to the brewery's own concoctions as well as to beers from around the world. The bartenders will help you choose and ply you with tasters to help you decide on your tipple. The offerings rotate regularly, so the service is likely to be useful each time you go back.

Fermentoren

Halmtorvet 29C; tel. 23 98 86 77; http://fermentoren.com;

Mon.-Wed. 3pm-midnight, Thurs. 2pm-1am, Fri.-Sat. 2pm-2am, Sun. 4pm-midnight; bus or Metro Copenhagen Central Station

This long-standing craft beer pub, close to the Meatpacking District, has stouts, IPAs, brown ales, and more from microbreweries from across Denmark and beyond, and the selection is rotated regularly, so you'll probably find something new every time you visit. An outdoor terrace makes for a nice spot to sit and enjoy a cold brew in the summertime. Dogs are welcome.

WarPigs

Flæsketorvet 25; tel. 43 48 48 48; https:// warpigs.dk; Mon.-Wed. noon-midnight, Thurs.-Fri. noon-2am, Sat. 11:30am-2am, Sun. 11:30am-11pm, kitchen closes 10pm; bus or Metro Copenhagen Central Station

In spacious, stark, industrial surroundings with a strong musky smell from its giant meat smokers, this Floyds and Mikkeller collaboration brewpub takes the Meatpacking District to heart. Go to the bar and order a chocolate stout and wait while it's poured from the bone-handled taps. The menu (steaks from 55 kr, sides from 35 kr) is in the style of a Texas barbecue, with ribs, pork, slaw, mac and cheese, and pecan pie.

Kihoskh

Sønder Blvd. 53; tel. 33 31 11 98; www. kihoskh.dk; Sun.-Thurs. 7am-1am, Fri.-Sat. 7am-2am; bus Copenhagen Central Station, S-train Dybbølsbro St.

It looks like a normal liquor store or a Berlin Späti from the outside, but Kihoskh is a venerable beer

WarPigs in the Meatpacking District

paradise with its cellar of new releases and rarities as well as broad range of Danish craft beers. You can bag your purchases (bring your own bag) and take them home, but there is also outdoor seating, and it is perfectly acceptable to enjoy them on the spot, reinforcing the Berlin vibe. This is more advisable during the summer. It also serves as a functioning convenience store selling baked goods, newspapers, and the like.

Mesteren & Lærlingen

Flæsketorvet 86; www.instagram.com/
mesterenoglaerlingen; Mon. 4pm-1am,
Tues.-Wed. 4pm-2am, Thurs. 4pm-3am,
Fri.-Sat. 4pm-3:30am; bus or Metro
Copenhagen Central Station, S-train
Dybbølsbro

This intimate bar is one of the smallest in the Meatpacking District and plays its music primarily from LPs. It's also open during the day but stays open late until the DJs begin flipping that vinyl. In summer, it spills onto the pavement out front where you can have a glass of cava and sometimes get a burger from the occasional barbecue.

Nightclubs

Baggen Kbh

Flæsketorvet 19-21; www.baggenkbh.
dk; Thurs.-Sat. 10pm-5am; bus or Metro
Copenhagen Central Station, S-train
Dybbølsbro

Not to be confused with Bakken the amusement park (a double *g* is pronounced the same way as a double *k* in Danish), Baggen the nightclub is a Meatpacking District veteran, with DJs, dancing, and clientele in their early 20s to early 30s. It sells relatively cheap beers in cans, and the walls, like a number of other spots in the Meatpacking District, recall the area's history with their industrial white-tiled look. There's a backyard where you can catch some air or a time-out from the dance floor. The minimum age is 18 on Thursday and 21 on Friday-Saturday.

Søpavillonen

Gyldenløvesgade 24; tel. 28 23 87 09; www.soepavillonen.dk; Thurs. 8pm-midnight, Fri.-Sat. 8pm-5am; bus 2A Vester Farimagsgade (Gyldenløvesgade), 68 Peblinge Dossering (Åboulevard), Metro Forum

Dubbed "Sø" by locals, one of Copenhagen's most famous nightclubs is also one of the easiest to spot, facing out toward the Vesterbro end of the Copenhagen Lakes. New ownership has helped turn around a once-disreputable image at this grand old nightclub, which has been here since 1965. The building itself dates to 1800. You'll find a mix of music and a generally young crowd, although the minimum age is 21. Go for something a bit smarter than everyday casual wear if your night is taking you here.

LGBTQ+
Jolene

Flæsketorvet 81-85; tel. 35 85 29 45; Wed. 4pm-midnight, Thurs.-Sat. 4pm-5am; no cover; bus or Metro Copenhagen Central Station, S-train Dybbølsbro

One of the first bars to open in the Meatpacking District in 2008, underground electronic music is still a big part of Jolene's identity. The slogan "This Is Not a F*cking Cocktail Bar" was once painted in large letters behind the bar, and although

cocktails are available (including 2-for-1 during the 4pm-7pm happy hour), the drink menu supports that claim. Drinks aside, good vibes are what you'll get at this weathered nightclub, which prides itself on an exuberant crowd, disco balls, and neon signs. The DJs occasionally give way to rock bands, and there are LGBTQ+ nights as well as other events that are listed on the Jolene Instagram account.

Café Intime

Allegade 25; tel. 38 34 19 58; www.cafeintime.dk; daily 4pm-2am; bus 8A Frederiksberg Rådhus (Allegade), Metro Frederiksberg St.

Leafy Frederiksberg is home to Café Intime, a bohemian café, jazz bar, and hangout that is busy most nights. You can't miss the name lit in bright bulbs over the door, nor the eclectic and somewhat old-school cabaret feel. Smoking is permitted inside. There is often a pianist or jazz band playing and occasional drag shows.

TOP EXPERIENCE

☉ NØRREBRO

The scene in **Nørrebro** is lively, particularly in the areas around **Ravnsborggade, Stefansgade, Elmegade, Jægersborggade,** and **Sankt Hans Torv,** where the people are as diverse as the bars, which vary from Middle Eastern-style cafés to burger bars, taquerias, and craft beer pubs. The area is lively at all times, with the side streets and squares all clustered off the congested **Nørrebrogade** main street.

In summer, Nørrebrogade is occasionally closed to traffic for small festivals and other community events, which you might be lucky enough to stumble on—on days like these, people sit on curbs eating takeaway, browse pop-up flea markets, and dance to a passing carnival band. Even on a regular evening, there's an unmistakable energy about the area.

Cocktails
Mexi-Bar

Elmegade 27; tel. 35 37 77 66; http:// mexibar.com; Thurs. 6pm-1am, Fri.-Sat. 6pm-3am; bus 5C Elmegade (Nørrebrogade)

On the corner of Sankt Hans Torv, Mexi Bar's student-friendly prices, with cocktails from as little as 80 kr, make it a popular spot for hip, young locals—and often also a crowded one due to its diminutive size. Come early. Look for the Passion Splash, a fresh sweet mix of vodka, crème de menthe, and passion fruit.

The Barking Dog

Sankt Hans Gade 19; tel. 35 36 16 00; www. thebarkingdog.dk; Tues.-Thurs. 6pm-1am, Fri.-Sat. 6pm.2am; bus 5C Ravnsborggade (Nørrebrogade)

In a basement on pleasant plaza Sankt Hans Torv, the Barking Dog is a "cocktail pub" with a broad selection of cocktails, beers, and liquors as well as a relaxed Copenhagener atmosphere. The checkered floor, cacti, and skull paraphernalia are part of its character, as are the frequently changing

and creative cocktail names, such as O.D.B., Hazy Susan, and 2023 special Hi Barbie.

Beer
Brus

Guldbergsgade 29; tel. 75 22 22 00; https://tapperietbrus.dk; Mon.-Wed. noon-9pm, Thurs. noon-10pm, Fri.-Sat. noon-midnight, Sun. noon-9pm; Bus 5C Kapelvej (Nørrebrogade)

In an old iron foundry and locomotive factory, smart brewpub Brus has a rotating on-tap selection of more than 30 microbrews by owner brewery To Øl, a Danish brand that has gained worldwide recognition. The helpful bartenders offer tasting samples before you make your choice. Grab a savory snack or something heftier, like a beef or cauliflower burger (145 kr), and settle down—there's plenty of space inside and out. There are also regularly recurring events like quizzes, concerts, and brewery tours.

Mikkeller & Friends

Stefansgade 35; tel. 35 83 10 20; www. mikkeller.com/locations/mikkeller-and-friends; Sun.-Thurs. 2pm-midnight, Fri. 2pm-2am, Sat. noon-2am; bus 5C Stefansgade (Nørrebrogade)

Mikkeller and Friends on Stefansgade offers a great chance to see the world-famous Copenhagen craft beer brand on its home turf, in a converted cellar in Nørrebro. Although the company actually started in Vesterbro, the Stefansgade bar manages to encapsulate the diverse Mikkeller styles and bars across Copenhagen, distilling them in one place. The beers on tap are rotated.

Nørrebro Bryghus

Ryesgade 3; tel. 35 30 05 30; www.noerrebrobryghus.dk; Tues.-Wed. noon-11pm, Thurs.-Sat. noon-midnight; bus 5C Ravnsborggade (Nørrebrogade)

More than just a brewery, Nørrebro Bryghus is a place where you can take a yoga class, attend a business meeting, and eat at a restaurant. The large brickwork premises close to the Lakes also house a spacious bar where bartenders are happy to share their in-depth knowledge of the 21 beers-on tap—many of which are brewed on-site. If you want some ballast in your stomach, the restaurant specializes in smørrebrød with classic Danish-style flavors using potatoes, herring, salmon, and more as toppings on a menu that can change from day to day.

Wine

Gaarden & Gaden

Nørrebrogade 88; tel. 55 55 08 80; https://gaaga.dk/en; Mon.-Thurs. noon-midnight, Fri. noon-2am, Sat. 10am-2am, Sun. 10am-11pm; bus 5C Sjællandsgade (Nørrebrogade)

You can spot Gaarden & Gaden by the large neon locksmith sign at the corner of the block. This bar holds the keys to a relaxing evening, with its range of more than 500 natural wines. Although it's much more than a restaurant, the daytime and evening menus will not leave you feeling hungry—these include

Gaarden & Gaden

croque madame and oysters (165 kr) until 2pm on weekends, and anchovies and baba ghanoush (each 95 kr) as well as larger plates in the evening. It gets busy in the evenings on Friday-Saturday, when it can be harder to find a table, but you can book ahead.

Bodegas
Café Ægir

Ægirsgade 16; tel. 35 83 10 02; Sun.-Wed. 10am-midnight, Thurs.-Sat. 10am-2am; bus 5C Stefansgade (Nørrebrogade)

A raw pub or "brown bodega" in the heart of Nørrebro, Café Ægir is a værtshus, the nearest thing Denmark has to a neighborhood pub. It won't hit your wallet too hard, and you might meet a character or two along the way. You can play billiards (more popular than pool as a bar game in Denmark) and will probably hear 4 Non Blondes at some point in the evening, although there's often live music too. Note the collection of exotic bottle openers bequeathed by foreign visitors.

Café Bars
Tjili Pop

Rantzausgade 28; tel. 35 35 90 20; Sun.-Mon. 9am-1am, Tues.-Wed. 9am-2am, Thurs. 9am-3am, Fri.-Sat. 9am-4am; bus 1A Rosenorns Allé (H.C. Ørsteds Vej)

Tjili Pop is a café-bar hybrid with good vibes in shabby-chic surroundings that gave it, along with a number of its 2000s contemporaries, the popular label "Berlinercool." But Tjili Pop has more than just a little in common with the German capital's artsy side, with its graffitied exterior, secondhand furniture, and a distressed interior doing as much to re-create the Kreuzberg style as a good selection of German beers. The Berliner-cool feel remains in place whether you come for a morning coffee, attend one of the regular small concerts, or just want to grab a pilsner.

Blågårds Apotek

Blågårds Plads 2; tel. 35 37 24 42; www. kroteket.dk; Mon.-Sat. noon-2am, Sun. noon-midnight, closes earlier in winter; bus 5A Blågårdsgade (Nørrebrogade)

All types come to gather at Blågårds Apotek, a nonprofit café that hosts live music and cultural and social events. Concerts three times a week—usually jazz or with singer-songwriters—are listed on the bar's website. There may be a 50 kr cover charge when concerts are on. The bar itself is a former pharmacy, hence the name, and what was once a medicine counter is now the bar.

Dance and Live Music
Rust

Guldbergsgade 8; tel. 35 24 52 00; www.rust.dk; Fri.-Sat. 8:30pm-5am; cover charge 80 kr; bus 5C Elmegade (Nørrebrogade)

Rust is named after Mathias Rust, who famously landed his light aircraft on Moscow's Red Square in 1987 in a daring Cold War-era protest stunt. The venue has served as a home for Copenhagen's musical underground since the 1990s and has played host to popular acts like MØ and Rufus Wainwright, but also lots of emerging artists. Check the website for upcoming events. On Friday-Saturday it becomes a raucous multilevel nightclub with a young crowd spilling drinks on the dance floor and international DJs playing electro and hip-hop.

Kind of Blue

Ravnsborggade 17; tel. 31 99 99 54; www. kindofblue.dk; Mon.-Thurs. 4pm-midnight, Fri.-Sat. 4pm-2am; bus 5C Ravnsborggade (Nørrebrogade)

There's a chilled-out jazz vibe at Kind of Blue, which is named after a Miles Davis album and has a color scheme in keeping with the name, along with comfortable seats and cushions and a decorative cello and piano. There's a decent selection of craft beers as well as cocktails. The music—the likes of Bob Dylan and Lou Reed as well as jazz—is kept to a soft volume, conducive to conversation. It's not hard to spot a first date or two taking place around the tables. Hop in for a breather from surrounding Ravnsborggade.

CHRISTIANSHAVN AND AMAGER
Beer
Mikkeller Baghaven

Refshalevej 169B; tel. 31 16 14 09; www. mikkeller.com/locations/mikkeller-baghaven; Mon. noon-9:30pm, Tues.-Wed. 2pm-9:30pm, Thurs.-Sat. 2pm-11pm, Sun. noon-11pm; bus 2A Refshaleøen (Refshalevej)

Mikkeller's large bar adjacent to the Reffen street food market on Refshaleøen oozes with the aura of a brand and a concept that knows

when it's on home turf. Outside, Trabants and other 1960s cars are regularly on display. Inside the bar, a converted shipbuilder's workshop, beers are aged in oaked vessels while a dozen or more craft brews rotate on tap. A large-scale version of the brand's logo—a mustachioed man in a bowler hat—stares down from the roof of the building. There's seating and standing space inside and out.

Ingolfs Kaffebar

Ingolfs Allé 3; tel. 32 59 95 96; www. ingolfskaffebar.dk; Tues.-Wed. 10am-10pm, Thurs.-Sat. 10am-11pm, Sun. 10am-4pm; bus 5C Smyrnavej (Amagerbrogade)

A quirky, creative interior design influenced by 1950s US diners and breakfast and brunch options, as well as a good range of beers, are the focus here. Ingolfs, hidden on a side street far into the depths of Amager (you'll know you've found it when you spot the three acrobats on the building's bright-green facade), is a hit with many students attending KUA, the University of Copenhagen's southern facility, where a number of arts and humanities disciplines are taught. In summer there's a beer garden of sorts, as the yard behind the restaurant is opened and guests flock to its picnic area.

Bodegas
Eiffel Bar

Wildersgade 58; tel. 32 57 70 92; daily noon-2am; bus 2A, Knippelsbro (Torvegade), metro Christianhavn St.

As the name suggests, Eiffel Bar has

taken the French capital's trademark and run with it. Inside, a veritable Little Paris awaits, decorated with charming vintage photos of the city, mostly the Eiffel Tower itself, the silhouette of which also appears on the bar's own-label pilsners (which will set you back a wallet-friendly 30 kr). The bar service is incredibly friendly and welcoming—very few pubs in the city can boast better. The clientele is a mixture of grizzled regulars and young students, and indie music plays loudly from the sound system. This is a great example of a Copenhagen bodega and well worth a visit.

Cafés

Christianshavns Bådudlejning og Café

Overgaden Neden Vandet 29; tel. 32 96 53 53; www.baadudlejningen.dk; summer daily noon-sunset, reduced hours in winter; bus 2A, Christianshavns Torv, Metro Christianshavn St.

A nice spot to sit in the sunshine with a cold beer or white wine, throughout the summer months Christianshavns Bådudlejning and Café draws crowds to its deck right by the Christiania canal. The seafood-based café fare can be handy if you get hungry, but the location and atmosphere are the main draws.

Accommodations

Accommodations in Copenhagen are not cheap, and even budget selections can feel steep in comparison with other Western European countries, although they are about on a par with Norway and Sweden. Chain hotels are also dominant, including international brands such as Scandic and Radisson as well as smaller Scandinavian companies such as Cabinn. Hostels are relatively few, and their quality and style vary, but there are some excellent options to be found. Booking ahead is a necessity in the peak months for these budget options.

NØRREPORT AND AROUND

Nørreport is slightly less hotel-heavy than the areas of the Inner City and Vesterbro that shoulder Copenhagen Central Station, but there are still plenty of options. Heading toward Kongens Nytorv, lodgings get more upscale, but there are also less-expensive beds in this area.

Under 500 Kr

✪ Generator Hostel

Adelgade 5-7; tel. 78 77 54 00; https:// staygenerator.com/hostels/copenhagen; shared room from 154 kr, private room from 600 kr; bus 26 Borgergade, Metro Kongens Nytorv, 177 rooms

Generator can be found on a slightly seedy-looking street a few steps from the nightlife action along Gothersgade. Don't be put off by the harsh lighting and spacey house music in the

139

stairwell—once you're inside, there's a well-trodden sense of comfort. This sprawling five-story lodging is ideal for sociable tight-budget backpackers. A giant common room and bar area are home to a long bar that serves food and often hosts live music, pub quizzes, or other social events.

500-1,000 Kr
WakeUp Copenhagen

Borgergade 9; tel. 44 80 00 00; www. wakeupcopenhagen.com; high season from 650 kr d; Metro Marmorkirken; 770 rooms

The compact budget hotel option WakeUp has small rooms that are rather pod-like, with rounded bed corners and shower cubicles, and a bright and airy lobby. Breakfast is an extra 95 kr. The place is small, clean, basic, and well organized. The Borgergade location is ideal for accessing the central Inner City on foot, but other WakeUp locations near the Central Station (Carsten Niebuhrs Gade 11) and the harbor (Bernstorffsgade 35) are also worth considering.

1,000-2,000 Kr
Hotel Skt. Petri

Krystalgade 22; tel. 33 45 91 00; www. sktpetri.com; high season from 2,150 kr d; bus or Metro Nørreport; 288 rooms

The central Hotel Skt. Petri has modern interior design in a variety of colors, a mazelike lobby floor motif, and a rooftop terrace that looks great in nice weather. Facilities include a gym with a sauna and a steam bath. Breakfast is not included but can be added

at a discount. Located on central Krystalgade, 5 minutes' walk from Nørreport station, many of the rooms on upper floors boast rooftop views over the city or Copenhagen University.

Over 2,000 Kr
Hotel d'Angleterre

Kongens Nytorv 34; tel. 33 12 00 95; www. dangleterre.com; high season 8,450 kr d; Metro Kongens Nytorv; 92 rooms

The concierges in top hats and tails tell you what to expect the moment you walk into the 5-star 250-year-old Hotel d'Angleterre, one of the most famous in Copenhagen. The elegant building looks out over Kongens Nytorv, and its central location, minutes from the Round Tower, Nyhavn, and Amalienborg, makes this an ideal base for exploring the Inner City, if you have the budget for it. The plush roomy suites have thick drapes, Bang and Olufsen TVs, and marble baths. Facilities include a spa, a swimming pool, a Michelin-starred restaurant, and, as if to make its decadence absolutely clear, a champagne bar that serves caviar and oysters.

GREATER INNER CITY
Under 500 Kr
Danhostel Copenhagen City

H. C. Andersens Blvd. 50; tel. 33 11 85 85; https://danhostelcopenhagencity.dk/en; shared room from 162 kr, private room from 1,000 kr; bus 5C Otto Mønsteds Plads (Rysensteensgade); 192 rooms

A hostel with a view to rival

anything in the city, the towering 17-floor Danhostel near the Langebro Bridge is a great option for budget travelers. It belongs to the YHA scheme and, like many Hostelling International accommodations, can lack the sense of life and spontaneity found at more independent hostels. That said, the design and cleanliness here are first class—and then there's that view—best experienced on the 17th and top floor, which consists of full apartments (from 1,499 kr). Breakfast, sandwiches, snacks, and lunch packs are all available, but be sure to book your 30-minute slot for the buffet breakfast in advance.

Copenhagen Downtown Hostel

Vandkunsten 5; tel. 70 23 21 10; www.
copenhagendowntown.com; shared room
from 275 kr, private room from 480 kr;
bus 2A, 31 Stormbroen, Nationalmuseet
(Vindebrogade), Metro Gammel Strand;
88 rooms

This is a solid backpacker hostel with various mixed dorms with 6, 8, 10, and 12 beds as well as 4-bed female dorms. Private rooms can be reserved for up to 10 people, along with double or twin private rooms. Centrally located, Copenhagen Downtown Hostel has a social atmosphere that revolves around its bar, where regular social events are arranged by staff. Bed linens are included, and guests can use the kitchen to make their own meals. If you book directly via the hostel's website, you can score a 10 percent discount at the bar.

500-1,000 Kr
Cabinn City

Mitchellsgade 14; tel. 33 46 16 00; https://
en.cabinn.com/hotel/cabinn-city; high
season from 510 kr d; bus or S-train
Copenhagen Central Station, bus 5C
Politorvet; 352 rooms

This low-cost option, part of the Cabinn chain, which has hotels in most major Scandinavian cities, is conveniently located near the rail station. Despite the high capacity, with 352 rooms and 928 beds, advance booking is necessary for the standard and economy rooms. Wi-Fi is available in every room. You can add the breakfast buffet when you book. Rooms have a clean design—many double rooms have bunk beds, in keeping with the "cabin" space-saving concept.

1,000-2,000 Kr
Ibsens Hotel

Vendersgade 23; tel. 33 13 19 13; www.
arthurhotels.dk/ibsens-hotel; high
season from 1,445 kr d; bus 5C Nørre
Farimagsgade (Frederiksborggade), Metro
Nørreport; 118 rooms

Adjoining the Hotel Kong Arthur in a charming 19th-century building, the lower-priced Ibsens Hotel shares the advantage of proximity to the Lakes and Dronning Louises Bro as well as to all the amenities of the Inner City. Compact comfortable rooms, which range from "tiny" to "x-large" in Ibsens' own terminology, have a quiet feel despite their proximity to busy city streets and are tastefully furnished with modern-style fixtures. Breakfast can be added when you book.

Hotel Kong Arthur

Nørre Søgade 11; tel. 33 11 12 12; https:// arthurhotels.dk/hotel-kong-arthur; high season from 1,600 kr d; Metro Nørreport; 155 rooms

Looking out over the Lakes, the elegant white facade of the Hotel Kong Arthur is a welcoming first impression for newcomers to Copenhagen. Amenities include spa rooms, a running club, and a gym, while fair trade and ecology are also a focus. Guest rooms are beautifully furnished in different styles of modern decor. An excellent breakfast buffet costs an additional 250 kr per person.

Over 2,000 Kr
Nimb Hotel

Bernstorffsgade 5; tel. 88 70 00 00; www. nimb.dk; high season from 3,400 kr d; bus, S-train, rail Copenhagen Central Station; 38 rooms

In the iconic 1909 Middle Eastern-style building—arches, domes, and all—overlooking Tivoli Gardens, the exclusive Nimb Hotel has spectacular history, views, and location, minutes from the central station and the heart of Inner City shopping, eating, and bars. Its high ceilings, chandeliers, and plush carpets amplify the glamour. Services include a rooftop terrace with a pool and a cocktail bar as well as a small gym. The smart, modern interior designs reflect the hotel's exterior look, with arched windows and intricately patterned quilts. Nimb consistently receives positive feedback from guests.

Hotel Bethel Sømandshjem

NYHAVN
500-1,000 Kr
Hotel Bethel Sømandshjem

Nyhavn 22; tel. 33 13 03 70; www.hotel-bethel.dk; high season from 1,095 kr d; Metro Kongens Nytorv; 30 rooms

Distinguishable by its redbrick finish and corner tower, Hotel Bethel was once a seamen's home, today down-to-earth and with a buffet breakfast included in the rates. Guest rooms, which have private baths, are basic and clean and can suffer from outside noise, particularly on the courtyard-facing side. This is balanced by an outstanding location that overlooks usually pricier Nyhavn. Corner rooms with views are available.

Nyhavn 63

Nyhavn 63; tel. 61 42 61 46; www. nyhavn63.com; capsules from 300 kr; Metro Kongens Nytorv; 11 rooms

The most attractive thing about this budget capsule hotel is its location on the Nyhavn quayside, but it also has the distinction of being the first capsule hotel in Denmark. The capsules, available in one- and two-person sizes, have code-operated locks so they can also be used for storage (although some guests have reported the locks to be faulty on occasion). In summer the capsules can feel hot; this might be a good time to consider one of the private rooms as an alternative. Some private rooms have private baths, while others, like the capsule rooms, have shared facilities. There's a lounge bar with an outdoor section where you can socialize with a beer and snacks.

71 Nyhavn Hotel

1,000-2,000 Kr
71 Nyhavn Hotel
Nyhavn 71; tel. 33 43 62 00; www.71nyhavnhotel.com; high season from 2,400 kr d; Metro Kongens Nytorv; 130 rooms

The hotel is situated in a prime spot on the corner overlooking Inderhavnsbroen and Christianshavn to the south and the masts and rooftops of iconic Nyhavn right outside the door. The rates are not the area's cheapest but breakfast is included. There are 130 rooms in two converted former warehouses that have been given a modern finish, with sturdy dark beams providing a bit of maritime atmosphere.

✪ Hotel Skt. Annæ
Sankt Annæ Plads 18; tel. 32 70 40 86; https://hotelsktannae.dk; high season from 1,595 kr d; Metro Kongens Nytorv; 145 rooms

The former Hotel Neptune, which boarded smugglers in the 19th century, is today the boutique 4-star Hotel Skt. Annæ, and there is little trace of its disreputable past. It features an airy garden-like atrium, and some rooms have air-conditioning—not ubiquitous even in expensive hotels in Copenhagen given the cold climate, but nevertheless something that can greatly enhance your stay when the summer heats up. The hotel is located on a central but quiet grassy square, very close to both Nyhavn and Amalienborg. Guest rooms are comfortable and easy on the eye in light shades of gray and blue.

Babette Guldsmeden
Bredgade 78; tel. 33 14 15 00; https://guldsmedenhotels.com/babette; small rooms from 1,145 kr d; Metro Marmorkirken; 98 rooms

In the royal quarter between the Queen's Residence, Amalienborg, and the *Little Mermaid,* diminutive

Babette Guldsmeden brings you within striking distance of famous sights, but with an emphasis on approachability, it has no regal pretentions of its own. It's still luxurious, evidenced by the rooftop spa (245 kr). The rooms are in a "Nordic-meets-Bali" style, which they pull off well with patterned throws and canopies over the beds in rooms with wooden flooring and whitewashed walls. The Guldsmeden hotel group has four other larger bohemian-style boutique hotels in Copenhagen (and one in Bali), the pick of these being 66 Guldsmeden on Vesterbrogade (Vesterbrogade 30; tel. 33 22 15 00).

Over 2,000 Kr
✪ Hotel Sanders

Tordenskjoldsgade 15; tel. 46 40 00 40;
https://hotelsanders.com; high season
from 2,900 kr d; Metro Kongens Nytorv;
54 rooms

Located on a quiet cobbled street just behind the Royal Danish Theater (Det Kongelige Teater) at Kongens Nytorv, Hotel Sanders opened in 2017 in the former Opera Hotel, where owner Alexander Kølpin, a former Royal Danish Ballet dancer, stayed on a number of occasions while performing at the Royal Theater during his career. The lobby, packed with designer sofas, rugs, and warm lighting, sets the tone for the tasteful design of the pinewood furniture in the rooms, which have nice throwback touches that include old-fashioned analog alarm clocks with bells outside their

round casings and replicas of dial telephones. À la carte breakfast is included. There are plenty of extra services and features at the hotel, including a podcast and private boat tours of Copenhagen Harbor during the summer months.

VESTERBRO AND FREDERIKSBERG

Hotels in the gentrified Vesterbro area are generally what most would consider walking distance from both Copenhagen Central Station and the long-distance bus terminal on Ingerslevsgade. With the notable exception of Tivoli, the historical attractions are farther away than from Inner City accommodations, but staying among the buzzing Vesterbro life, with its hip shops and pulsating nightlife, is a worthy trade-off.

Under 500 Kr
Steel House Copenhagen

Herholdtsgade 6; tel. 33 17 71 10; www.
steelhousecopenhagen.com; shared room
from 145 kr, private room from 650 kr;
S-train Vesterport St.; 253 rooms

Although it bills itself as a luxury hostel, the 253-room Steel House Copenhagen has a strong claim to be the least expensive place to stay in Copenhagen that isn't a couch. A stylish metallic look—the building used to house the Danish Union of Metalworkers—belies the low rates, and there are also facilities more commonly associated with starred hotels: a gym, a pool, and even a cinema, along with a communal kitchen and a café and bar with particularly comfortable armchairs. The great location is within walking distance of four neighborhoods: Vesterbro, Frederiksberg, Nørrebro, and Inner City.

Woodah Hostel

Abel Cathrines Gade 1-3; tel. 23 90 55 63; www.nakka.dk/woodahboutiquehostel; shared room from 335 kr; bus, S-train, or Metro Copenhagen Central Station; 3 rooms

This eco-conscious "small hostel with a big heart" is near the Meatpacking District and Central Station. Its 24 beds are all custom-made to fit their Japanese-style pods, and the breakfast buffet is organic and included in the price. Three rooms each contain multiple pods, and bath facilities are shared. There are daily yoga classes (book the night before; 25 kr), and you can also purchase Japanese tea and beer in the café. The decor is simple and calm with plenty of flowers, cushions, and yoga mats.

500-1,000 Kr
✪ 66 Guldsmeden

Vesterbrogade 66; tel. 33 22 15 00; https:// guldsmedenhotels.com; high season from 1,045 kr d; bus 1A Vesterbrogade (Enghavevej), 7A Frederiksberg Allé (Vesterbrogade); 74 rooms

A 15-minute walk from the Central Station brings you to the secluded-feeling bohemian 66 Guldsmeden. You'll find a colorful courtyard and patio, along with four-poster

beds in every room. You can also choose to stay in a retro trailer in the backyard. Guest rooms contain rustic wooden furniture and art made by the owner's father-in-law. The balconies and fireplace in the restaurant, which is lit in winter, indicate the keenness to elicit a feeling of hygge among guests. It's owned by the same group as the nearby larger Axel Guldsmeden (Colbjørnsensgade 14; tel. 33 31 32 66; 202 rooms) and Babette (Bredgade 78; tel. 33 14 15 00; 98 rooms).

1,000-2,000 Kr
Scandic Falkoner

Falkoner Allé 9; tel. 72 42 55 00; www. scandichotels.com; from 1,300 kr d, includes breakfast; Metro Frederiksberg; 334 rooms

There's a lot to like about the Falkoner, the Scandic chain hotel right in the center of Frederiksberg. It has a decent amount of character with its theater-themed lobby decor and shares a building with the Falkoner Salen, a concert and theater venue. It's very close to the Frederiksberg Center shopping mall and Metro station. The rooms are plush, comfortable, and a pleasure to stay in, although the first-floor rooms on the northern end of the building can carry noise up from the café and 7-Eleven store downstairs (not part of the hotel). Noise from the concert hall can likewise be heard in the lobby when there's a band playing.

Grand Joanne

Vesterbrogade 9A; tel. 78 71 40 10; https:// grandjoanne.dk; from 1,290 kr d; bus, Metro, or S-train Frederiksberg; 162 rooms

Grand Joanne reopened early in 2023 after renovations in a historical 1892 building that was previously home to the Grand Hotel. Next to the station and busy Vesterbrogade, you can choose between a city, street, or garden view. A "lifestyle hotel," it hosts events like pop-up exhibitions and yoga classes and also has a rooftop bar. Guest rooms are tastefully done in muted colors with lots of patterns, and no two are the same. Brunch and dinner are available in the hotel restaurant, where you can enjoy pancakes or eggs Benedict in the morning, and a cheeseburger or gnocchi with red potatoes and blue cheese in the evening.

NØRREBRO AND ØSTERBRO

Staying in either rough-and-ready hipster Nørrebro or middle-class Østerbro is sure to give you a different perspective on Copenhagen, simply by virtue of being away from the traditional visitor surroundings of the Inner City. As such, second-time visitors might appreciate switching their base here, but newcomers should not be put off either. Neither neighborhood is far from the central attractions, particularly if you are handy on two wheels or happy to make a few short journeys on public transportation, or if you want to walk around the pleasant Lakes, located between these two areas and the Inner City.

Under 500 Kr
A&O Copenhagen Nørrebro

Tagensvej 135-137; tel. 32 72 53 20; www. aohostels.com/en/copenhagen/kobenhavn-norrebro; shared room from 200 kr, private room from 800 kr; bus 6A Rovsingsgade (Tagensvej), Metro Skjolds Plads; 270 rooms

Budget hotel and hostel A&O Copenhagen takes you into the vibrant heart of Nørrebro. Housed in a big brick-and-glass building, all rooms are equipped with baths, and there is a spacious reception and lounge area. Linens are included only with hotel bookings. Breakfast can be added separately, and a guest kitchen is available. The communal areas, including the guest kitchen, can become crowded, but the rooms have a simple quiet feel. It's no-frills but easy on the wallet.

500-1,000 Kr
Hotel Nora Copenhagen

Nørrebrogade 18B; tel. 35 37 20 21; www. hotelnora.dk; high season from 1,300 kr d; bus 5C Ravnsborggade (Nørrebrogade); 42 rooms

This well-worn but comfortable and simple budget option is housed in an extravagant building on busy Nørrebrogade at the city end, within walking distance of Dronning Louises Bro and the Inner City and with great views from the rooftop. Breakfast is included. The light rooms come with free tea and coffee; noise can sometimes be heard from the street below.

CHRISTIANSHAVN AND AMAGER

Less hotel-heavy than the Inner City, the Christianshavn area is a great place to base yourself if you want to see Copenhagen at its most photogenic while staying within a short distance of the Inner City's big attractions and shopping.

1,000-2,000 Kr
✪ CPH Living

Langebrogade 1A; tel. 61 60 85 46; www. cphliving.com; high season from 1,690 krd; bus 5C Klaksvigsgade (Amager Blvd.), Metro Christianshavns St.; 12 rooms

Denmark's first floating hotel, converted from a former barge, is anchored between the Langebro and Little Langebro bridges, walking distance from Christianshavn—and close to shore from Islands Brygge. It's also a 15-minute walk from City Hall Square and the central shopping districts of the Inner City. All 12 of the hotel's double rooms offer dramatic harbor and city views through broad windows and French balconies, while the heated wooden floors and portholes give a simultaneously Scandinavian and maritime feel. A rooftop terrace enables guests to sit on deck and enjoy the floating vantage point. A cold-cut breakfast buffet is included.

Over 2,000 Kr
STAY Bryggen

Knud Kristensens Gade 6; tel. 72 44 44 34; https://stayapartments.dk; apartments from 1,960 kr; bus 68 Drechselsgade (Artillerivej); 172 apartments

STAY Bryggen is a complex of spacious private vacation studio apartments on Islands Brygge looking back toward Copenhagen. The 1-4-bedroom apartments are designed by the Danish interior company Hay, with a clear focus on Scandinavian minimalism. Kitchens come fully equipped, and there are also washing machines and dryers. If you don't feel like cooking, you can try the on-site breakfast service. Other facilities include a rooftop terrace and a fitness room.

Tourist Information

COPENHAGEN VISITOR SERVICE

Vesterbrogade 4; tel. 70 22 24 42; visitorservice@kk.dk; https://visitorservice. kk.dk/en; Sept.-June Mon.-Fri. 9am-4pm, Sat.-Sun. 10am-4pm, July-Aug. Mon.-Fri. 9am-6pm, Sat.-Sun. 10am-4pm

At the Copenhagen Visitor Service, you can pick up maps and brochures and buy the **Copenhagen card** that enables you to use the urban transport network. You can download guided walks on your phone, find maps for bicycle routes, and see Copenhagen from above using a VR headset. The website has a list (albeit not a comprehensive one) of events in the city. **Free Wi-Fi** is available, and there's also a selection of souvenirs like postcards, puzzles, and stamps.

In addition to the main Copenhagen Visitor Service Office, there are **eight authorized information spots** around the city where someone will be on hand to help with directions and advice. These are: Copenhagen City Hall, Tivoli Gardens, the National Gallery of Denmark, the Illum Department Store on Amagertorv, the National Museum, and the Frederiksberg Center mall, plus the library in the Nordvest neighborhood (Rentemestervej 76; tel. 82 20 54 30), north of Nørrebro, and the old telephone kiosk in the middle of the plaza at Nytorv 1F.

Getting There

BY AIR

International flights arrive at **Copenhagen Airport (CPH),** also known colloquially as Kastrup after the suburb of Amager that neighbors the airport (Kastrup, the suburb, has its own separate Metro stop—make sure you don't get off there when traveling to the airport).

Getting to the City Center
Metro and Train

The easiest way to reach the city center from the airport is usually the **Metro.** Transfer to the **M3 or M4 lines** at Kongens Nytorv station get to Copenhagen Central Station or to an **S-train** at Nørreport station, which is slightly faster if a little less simple. The full journey from the airport to the railway station shouldn't take more than 30 minutes whichever option you choose. Trains run around the clock, departing every few minutes during the day and every 15-20 minutes at night.

You can also take a **direct train** from Copenhagen Airport to Copenhagen Central Station. These leave approximately every 10 minutes and take around 20 minutes. Most trains traveling west (as opposed to east toward Sweden) from the airport stop at Copenhagen Central, but check departure boards to be sure. Trains cover the journey to Copenhagen Central Station faster than the Metro but leave less frequently.

Tickets for the train or Metro cost the same 30 kr and can be purchased from machines in the terminal, or you can check in using a Rejsekort if you have one, spending 23.50 kr of prepaid credit.

Bus
A number of bus lines travel between the airport and the city. Although these take longer than the Metro or S-train, they can be useful if your destination is close to one of the lines (check the location of bus stops at https://dinoffentligetransport.dk). The most frequent and convenient is **bus 5C,** which plies a route from one end of the city to the other with the airport at one end of the line. Tickets can be purchased from the driver using cash up to a 200 kr note, or you can check in with a prepaid Rejsekort. Prices are the same as on the train and Metro. Expect just under 45 minutes for the bus journey if you're going to the rail station.

Taxi
Taxis are normally easy to pick up from the stand outside **Terminal 3.** You should be able to pay by credit card. The fare will likely be 400 kr or more, depending on traffic and your destination in the city. Unless it's rush hour, you should be at your accommodations within 20-30 minutes.

Car
The airport's **Car Rental Center** is a short distance from the terminal entrances and is open daily 7am-11pm, although the individual rental companies may open and close their desks at different times. Free buses connect the airport to the Car Rental Center.

BY CAR
Coming by car from either mainland Europe via Germany or from Sweden via the Øresund Bridge (440 kr for cars for a single journey) is relatively straightforward, although there are occasionally border controls in the form of ID spot checks on both borders. Overall, being stopped on the border for a spot check is unlikely but does occur, so make sure you have your passport in hand. The E20 highway leads from the Øresund Bridge toward the city and connects with the O2 ring road, the main artery from major roads to the north, south, and west.

BY TRAIN
Copenhagen Central Station
(Hovedbanegården, often abbreviated to Hovedbanen; Bernstorffsgade 16-22), at the western end of the Inner City on the boundary with Vesterbro, is

linked to the European network via Stockholm to the north and Amsterdam, Hamburg, and Berlin to the south. Trains arrive regularly from Sweden—Malmö is a commuter town for many working in Copenhagen—while there are also regular services from Germany via southern Denmark or Jutland.

International tickets can be booked via Denmark's state rail operator **DSB** (tel. 70 13 14 18; www.dsb.dk).

For travel within Copenhagen and between Danish cities, the essential resource is **Rejseplanen.dk,** which can be accessed via the website or app (an English-language version is available). Part-owned by local travel authorities, Rejseplanen suggests the fastest and easiest routes between destinations, combining bus, Metro, S-train, Harbor Bus, and regional train connections, and tells you how much it will cost.

BY BUS

German company **Flixbus** (www.flixbus.com) is the dominant international coach operator and offers services to Denmark from both Sweden and Germany.

Buses leave and depart from a single **terminal,** which as of June 2024 is an all-new facility on **Carsten Nieburhs Gade.** The new bus terminal is accessible from the Dybbølsbro S-train station and city bus lines 7A and 11, as well as **Copenhagen Central Station.**

BY BOAT

DFDS (www.dfdsseaways.dk) operates overnight boats to Copenhagen from Oslo, for which inexpensive tickets can usually be procured in advance. Cabin prices range 600-3,100 kr for a single voyage, from 2-person economy cabins to 5-person cabins with sea views. A car costs an additional 700 kr per person. There's a restaurant and tax-free shop on board. Overnight voyages depart daily and take 16 hours, 30 minutes. Ferries arrive at the DFDS terminal at Dampfærgevej 30 in Østerbro, close to the Langelinie pier.

Getting Around

BY PUBLIC TRANSIT

Copenhagen's public transportation system is comprehensive, consisting of **bus** and **Metro** systems as well as an above-ground metropolitan rail known as the **S-tog (S-train).** The **Rejseplanen app,** available in English, is a must-have for instant planning of journeys that combine all of the networks. In addition to Rejseplanen, transport operator **Din Offentlig Transport (DOT)** (https://dinoffentligetransport.dk) is a good resource for updated public transportation information and timetables. You can also purchase tickets through the app.

Petty and violent crimes, including against tourists, do occur in Copenhagen, as in any large city, but there are no specific reasons to avoid public transportation in any part of the city or at any time due to safety considerations.

Tickets and Passes
Rejsekort

If you plan to use public transport in Copenhagen for more than a couple of days, the Rejsekort (www. rejsekort.dk) may be a good option. The Rejsekort is valid for use on city buses, Metro, S-train, and Harbor Bus, as well as regional trains. The card itself costs a nonrefundable 80 kr plus 100 kr credit for travel. The ticket machines (look for their neon-blue cladding) can be used to add credit to the card. The physical Rejsekort is gradually being replaced by an app, which might ease some of the inconvenience and cost of obtaining a card. Both card and app are valid for the Metro in the transitional phase. More details are available on the Rejsekort website (www.rejsekort.dk).

Alternatively, single tickets can be bought at Metro and S-train stations and from bus drivers. This is more expensive than the Rejsekort. As a visitor to the city, however, it may be easier to buy single tickets as you go, given that the Rejsekort costs 80 kr plus 100 kr in credit that the card won't let you fully use up on travel (you must have a balance of at least 70 kr to check in for a journey). You'll also need to return the card to get the remaining balance back, and this isn't a straight-forward process; you have to call the customer service center (tel. 70 11 33 33) and request a form.

When using the Rejsekort, you must "check in" by holding the card over the sensor inside the bus or on the train platform at the beginning of your journey. The check-in points, with their front-facing domed sensors, are easy to spot. You "check out" from the separate checkout sensor (there's a red sign on the sensor with the words "Check ud") when you are at or about to reach your destination. If you connect to a different bus or train, you should not check out, but you must check in again on the second bus or train after transferring. You then check out for the entire journey when you reach your destination.

City Pass

Alternatively, you can travel on a **City Pass,** which gives you unlimited travel on buses, trains, and the Metro all day and all night. These can be valid for 24 hours to five days and 80-600 kr, depending on the area you want to cover. They are available on the DOT website (https://dinoffentligetransport.dk/citypass) and app or from station machines. Two children under the age of 12 can travel for free on each adult City Pass.

Metro

The **Copenhagen Metro** opened

entrance and sign at Forum Metro station

in 2002 and was significantly upgraded in 2019 when two new lines and 17 new stations were opened, vastly improving the Metro's coverage of the city.

The **M3 City Ring** connects the Inner City, Østerbro, Nørrebro, and Frederiksberg districts and includes stops at Copenhagen Central Station and Rådhuspladsen (City Hall Square). It also connects to the older M1 and M2 lines at Kongens Nytorv and Frederiksberg stations; the M2 line terminates at the airport. The new 2019 line, **M4,** is a small branch from the **M3** after Østerport station, heading to two stations at Nordhavn and Orientkaj. The two original lines, M1 and M2, connect Amager and Christianshavn in the south of the city directly to the Inner City and Frederiksberg. Line **M2** terminates at the airport and also stops at Amagerbro and the

Amager Strand beach and lagoon area; **M1** has stations at Islands Brygge and Vestamager, where you can access the Amager Fælled national park and Amager Nature Center. M1 and M2 also both stop at Nørreport Station, the main hub for local rail in Copenhagen, where you can transfer to rail and S-train services.

Expansion of the Metro continues: In 2023 the city government greenlit an extension of the M4 with two new stations. There has even been talk of an M5 extension that could put a Metro station in the Swedish city Malmö, but realizing this idea is still quite a ways down the track.

Open 24 hours, Metro trains run every 2-4 minutes at peak times, 3-6 minutes during the day, and every 15-20 minutes on weeknights, and every 7-8 minutes during the night on weekends.

Train

The **S-train (S-tog)** is an extensive urban and suburban rail network comprising **7 lines** and **85 stations** serving the Greater Copenhagen area, with the exception of Amager and Christianshavn. It connects Copenhagen Central Station with Nørreport, from where there are S-train connections to stations in all the other neighborhoods mentioned in this chapter, as well as Jægersborg, Klampenborg, and Hellerup, north of Copenhagen. S-trains pass through the Central Station and depart regularly throughout the day **5am-12:30am**—there is a train every 10 minutes until the evening, and every 20 minutes until around midnight. All-night services with 30-minute departures run on some lines on weekends.

If you're using the S-train, the website and app of national rail operator DSB (www.dsb.dk) can be used to search journeys and purchase tickets, but you can also do this with the local DOT app. Fares are the same on both platforms.

Bus

Buses can be used to get to many areas of the city and are generally reliable. Primary routes have an A in their route number, with the exception of the 5C, an iconic and often maligned route that crosses the city. This route was in fact called 5A until 2017, when it got a makeover, new carbon-neutral vehicles, and a new identity. The A routes (and the 5C) run daily 24 hours, while other routes stop between 1am and 5am. For the majority of journeys among the parts of Copenhagen covered by this chapter, the Metro is likely to get you close to where you're going without the need to take a bus. On the other hand, buses often get you closer to the door, and there are still a couple of small areas not served by Metro, like the eastern end of Nørrebrogade.

Boat

Havnebussen (The Harbor Bus) is a great way to see Copenhagen from the harbor without taking an expensive tour, but the boats also act as an efficient means of transportation. For the price of a normal bus ticket you can connect the harbor pool at Teglholmen in the south with Refshaleøen and Orientkaj in the north by traveling between stops at Islands Brygge, the Royal Library (Det Kongelige Bibliotek), Knippelsbro (at Slotsholmen and Christianshavn), Nyhavn, and the Opera. There are normally two departures hourly **7am-7:30pm**—the timetable is available at https://dinoffentligetransport.dk and is also on the Rejseplanen app (route numbers 991 and 992). The Harbor Buses are distinctive squat yellow vessels with green dashes on the side to denote their electric-powered operation.

ON FOOT

Copenhagen is largely pedestrian-friendly and rewarding to walk around, although some of the cobblestones can leave your ankles feeling sore if you're not used to them. The Inner City and Christianshavn have cobblestone paving. There are few pedestrian streets apart from Strøget.

Almost all roads in Copenhagen and the rest of Denmark have designated bicycle lanes. This means there are two curbs: one between the sidewalk and the bicycle lane, and one between the bicycle lane and the road. Don't mistake the bicycle lane for the sidewalk and dawdle or walk in it. Similarly, look carefully when stepping off buses into a bicycle lane, which you have to cross to get to the sidewalk: Cyclists are not obliged to slow down for you (although they will if they see you, of course).

When crossing roads at pedestrian crossings, you'll notice that the locals tend to wait patiently for the green crossing signal to flash before crossing, even when there's no traffic. Jaywalking is against traffic laws, and breaking them can land you a fine. When crossing, keep an eye out for right-turning vehicles. Motorists are allowed to turn right on green-lighted pedestrian crossings if they are clear. Danish drivers can have an impatient bent and will sometimes hurry to make their turn just before or after you cross the street, which can be unsettling.

BY BIKE

Copenhagen's flat terrain and broad bicycle paths make it ideal for exploration on two wheels.

From the Inner City, all outer districts are within a 15-30-minute bike ride, depending on your fitness level: Copenhagen's flatness makes things as painless as possible if you're not accustomed to cycling. Be careful of the heavy traffic when bicycling in the city center. The busy multilane roads within central Copenhagen are usually fine to travel by bike—you'll see plenty of others doing so—but there are areas in the Inner City, particularly around Kongens Nytorv, Gothersgade, and Nørreport Station, where you might feel a little exposed, particularly during rush hours (Mon.-Thurs. 8am-9am and 4pm-5pm, Fri. 8am-9am and 3pm-4pm).

Bike Rental

Many **hostels** and **hotels** operate their own **bike rental** services, but there are countless other options. These include relatively inexpensive secondhand bikes from nonprofit **Baisikeli** (Ingerslevsgade 80; tel. 26 70 02 29; www.baisikeli. dk; full day from 125 kr, discounts for longer periods). You can rent a genuine Christiania cargo bike with **Christiania Rent a Bike** (Fabriksområdet 91; tel. 70 70 76 80; https://christianiacykler.dk; 1st day from 550 kr, subsequent days 250 kr).

Donkey Republic (www. donkey.bike/cities/bike-rental-copenhagen) is a Europe-wide app that allows you to find, unlock, and rent a bicycle. It is highly visible in Copenhagen.

Rules

Bicycles are allowed on trains, S-trains, Metros, the Harbor Bus, and city buses, apart from the Metro in peak periods (Mon.-Fri. 7am-9am and 3:30pm-5:30pm). This also applies to A buses, the 5C, and lines numbered 1-100.

On the S-train, Harbor Bus, and local trains, bikes travel free, but you'll have to pay for a separate bicycle ticket on the Metro, buses, and longer distance trains. Bike tickets (14 kr, 80 kr outside Greater Copenhagen) can be bought on the Rejsekort prepaid card, on the DOT app, or at ticket machines.

Bicycle helmets are not required by law, and surprisingly few Danes wear them, although bike rental shops will provide them. I strongly recommend taking the option for your own safety. Accidents can and do happen, regardless of the city's excellent bicycle lanes.

The bike paths, normally broad enough for two bicycles, are available on the vast majority of roads through the city. They are usually marked by a curb, clearly distinguishing them from the road and sidewalk on each side. Where there is no curb, for instance when a bicycle path crosses an intersection, there will be clear markings painted on the road.

On the relatively few streets where there are no bicycle lanes, make sure you keep to the right side and rejoin the bicycle path once it reappears on a later street.

Bike Parking

Bikes can be parked on most sidewalks, and you will see long rows of them lined up with their front wheels jammed into the metal bike stands provided by the city. You don't have to use a stand if you can't find one, but some shops and businesses place "No Bicycle Parking" signs on walls and in windows. These usually use the phrase cykler fjernes uden ansvar, literally "bicycles will be removed with no liability." Bicycles are normally secured using a locking device that fits to the back wheel, consisting of a metal bar that clicks into place between the spokes, preventing the wheel from turning, and requiring a key to unlock it. An alternative method is the old-fashioned chain lock. Some people use both: Bicycle theft is, unfortunately, all too common. If you're leaving a bicycle parked overnight, strength in numbers is a good idea: Try to leave it in a stand with other bikes rather than conspicuously on its own.

BY CAR

Although bicycling is as much an ingrained part of the Danish mindset as a convenient form of transportation, Copenhagen is quite suitable for exploring by car if you are traveling between neighborhoods. Within individual neighborhoods, distances are generally too short to warrant the use of a car. Rush hours—Monday-Thursday 8am-9am and 4pm-5pm, Friday 8am-9am and 3pm-4pm—can cause delays but are usually severe than in major US cities.

All parts of the city are easy to reach by car, and parking is usually possible, even if it can take patience to find a spot in popular areas. All cars in Denmark display a parking disc, which looks like an analog clock (some cars have automatic digital ones), on the inside of the windshield. This must be set at the time you leave your car if you are parking in an area that does not have a parking charge but does have a time limit. If there is a time limit for parking, it will be displayed on a signpost on the street or parking lot, hence the need to display the time you arrive. Failure to set your parking disc or parking illegally can result in your vehicle being issued with a ticket or clamped.

Many private parking lots have their own payment and ticketing systems that don't use the parking discs. For these, the best way to pay is by downloading a parking payment app and registering your car's license plate number to it, along with your payment card. You can also set up number plate registration, so the timer starts when you enter the parking lot and payment is made automatically when you leave. These apps include EasyPark, ParkOne, and Apcoa Flow, all of which work in most paid parking lots. If you don't want to use an app or don't have smartphone coverage, ticket machines are usually available and accept card payment.

BY TAXI

Taxis are a reliable and easy way to get around. They come at a premium: The base price is 39 kr, and the meter (taxis use meters as standard) moves quickly: 10 kr per km or 6.75 kr per minute Monday-Friday 6am-6pm, and more at peak times.

It is possible to hail a taxi on the street. Look for a green "FRI" (vacant) sign in the window or a lit taxa or taxi sign on the car. Taxi stations are located around the city, including at the Central Station and outside the airport terminal. Almost all taxis accept credit cards, but check with the driver to be certain. Be sure to use only officially marked taxis.

Taxi companies operating in Copenhagen include **DanTaxi** (tel. 48 48 48 48), **4x27** (tel. 27 27 27 27), and **Taxa 4x35** (tel. 35 35 35 35), which has an app that can be used to book journeys. The **taxi. eu app,** which connects taxi services in several European countries, can also be used to book cabs in Copenhagen.

RIDESHARE

Uber does not operate in Denmark. It withdrew from the country in 2017 following regulation that was introduced favoring traditional taxi businesses.

The only form of Rideshare is **GoMore** (https://gomore. dk), which is only used for longer journeys between cities, not for short trips. If you're leaving Copenhagen, it can be a good alternative and sometimes a cheaper option to the train, and it gives you an opportunity to meet Danes and others who live in Denmark. Search the journey you want on the GoMore app and you'll be shown rides that match it. The driver is usually a private vehicle owner who is driving the route that day and wants to take passengers to save costs (driving across Denmark can be expensive due to the bridge tolls). You can see the driver's rating on the app.

Klampenborg and Kongens Lyngby

Nature and nostalgia are plentiful, and there's an engaging mix of working-class entertainment, earthy history, bracing outdoors, and upmarket real estate in the areas north of Copenhagen.

Bakken is the most famous attraction in the area and one of the world's oldest amusement parks. Its history traces back to a mythical event in the 16th century when a spring was found in the forest. The area later became a draw for Copenhagen gentry and, later, hosted carnival rides and roller coasters. The amusement park

Highlights

⭐ **Dyrehavsbakken:** More commonly known as Bakken, this retro amusement park makes serious attempts to outdo Tivoli Gardens (page 160).

⭐ **Jægersborg Dyrehave:** This embracing expanse of protected Danish open space sprinkled with ancient trees, historical buildings, and wild animals is waiting to be explored (page 164).

⭐ **Frilandsmuseet:** Ride a horse-drawn cart into Denmark's rural past at this out-of-town outdoorsy museum (page 170).

lies within the Jægersborg animal park, a 10-sq-km (3.8-sq-mi) wild area with a baroque hunting lodge in the middle and hundreds of deer roaming the grounds. Head to the coast and you'll find a sandy beach and surrounding affluent streets with the timeless imprint of architectural icon Arne Jacobsen, while farther inland, one of the largest open-air museums anywhere will transport you back through industrialization to Denmark's roots as a rural agricultural society. Straddling the city and the countryside, Copenhagen's northern suburbs allow you room to breathe. Perhaps that's why so many Copenhageners as well as visitors find themselves drawn to this part of the city.

ORIENTATION

Klampenborg and Kongens Lyngby, the two primary areas covered in this chapter, are both part of the greater Copenhagen metropolitan area and are located around 10 km (6.2 mi) north of the city. Klampenborg is to the east on the coast, and Kongens Lyngby is inland to the west. From Copenhagen, the journey to both is 20-40 minutes by car or rail, depending on the time of day and your destination. Travel between the two takes 35-50 minutes by public transportation (sometimes it's faster to travel back to Copenhagen to change buses or trains) or 20 minutes by car.

Previous: Dyrehavsbakken amusement park near Klampenborg. **Above:** Dyrehaven, including Hermitage lodge; Frilandsmuseet.

Itinerary Idea

A DAY TRIP TO KLAMPENBORG

1 After breakfast in Copenhagen, take an S-train to Klampenborg. As you exit the station, go left and enter **Jægersborg Dyrehave,** a large forested park where you can take a calming walk in the woods.

2 Raise your heart rate by entering **Dyrehavsbakken** for some old-school fairground fun, including a ride on a nonagenarian roller coaster with a wooden frame that arguably cranks the thrill factor as high as any modern alternative.

3 You can also stop for lunch here at one of the **Restaurants at Bakken.** There's an array of options, from more traditional restaurants to casual cafés that cater to various tastes and levels of appetite.

4 Leave Bakken in the late afternoon and spend the rest of your day walking along the **Strandvejen coast,** spotting the exclusive mansions and assorted Arne Jacobsen-designed sites.

5 For dinner, head to the secluded **Raadvad Kro,** an affordable New Nordic restaurant in an idyllic spot that feels a lot farther from the city than it actually is.

Klampenborg and Around

The Klampenborg suburb, as with many neighborhoods of Greater Copenhagen along the Øresund coast, is a well-to-do area, its status embodied by the big houses, real estate agents, and law offices along Strandvejen, a road that's synonymous with affluence in the city. It's not an area that is charmless or exclusive, however; it draws people from across Copenhagen, particularly in the summer, with sandy Bellevue Beach, the historical working-class amusement park Bakken, and the expansive Jægersborg Dyrehave—all attractive destinations for holiday day trips. A cluster of 1930s buildings and structures designed by Arne Jacobsen, the grandfather of modernist Danish design, can be spotted in the area.

SIGHTS
✪ Dyrehavsbakken

Dyrehavevej 62, Klampenborg, 2930; tel. 39 63 35 44; www.bakken.dk; end of Mar.-Apr. Sat.-Sun., May-late Aug. daily, late Aug.-2nd weekend in Sept. Fri.-Sun., limited days in Oct., end of Nov.-last weekend

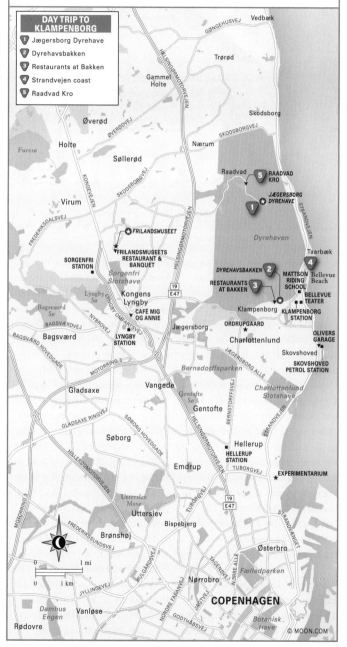

Klampenborg and Kongens Lyngby

DAY TRIP TO KLAMPENBORG
1 Jægersborg Dyrehave
2 Dyrehavsbakken
3 Restaurants at Bakken
4 Strandvejen coast
5 Raadvad Kro

Vedbæk
GØNGEHUSVEJ
Trørød
HELSINGØRMOTORVEJEN
Gammel Holte
Skodsborg
Øverød
ØVERØDVEJ
SKODSBORGVEJ
Holte
Furesø
Søllerød
Nærum
Raadvad
5 RAADVAD KRO
SKODSBORGVEJ
KONGEVEJEN
Virum
JÆGERSBORG DYREHAVE
1
FRIDERIKSDALSVEJ
FRILANDSMUSEET
Dyrehaven
FRILANDSMUSEETS RESTAURANT & BANQUET
Taarbæk
SORGENFRI STATION
Sorgenfri Slotshave
DYREHAVSBAKKEN 2
4
HELSINGØRMOTORVEJEN
MATTSON RIDING SCHOOL
Bellevue Beach
19
E47
RESTAURANTS AT BAKKEN 3
BELLEVUE TEATER
Lyngby Sø
Kongens Lyngby
CAFÉ MIG OG ANNIE
Klampenborg
KLAMPENBORG STATION
Bagsværd Sø
LYNGBY OMFARTSVEJ
NYBROVEJ
BAGSVÆRDVEJ
ORDRUPGAARD
OLIVERS GARAGE
Bagsværd
LYNGBY STATION
Jægersborg
Charlottenlund
Skovshoved
BAGSVÆRD HOVEDGADE
MOTORRING 3
JÆGERSBORG ALLE
SKOVSHOVED PETROL STATION
Bernsdorffsparken
Gladsaxe
Vangede
Charlottenlund Slotshave
GLADSAXE RINGVEJ
SØBORG HOVEDGADE
Gentofte Sø
BERNSTORFFSVEJ
HELSINGØRMOTORVEJEN
STRANDVEJEN
Søborg
Gentofte
Hellerup
HILLERØDMOTORVEJEN
HELLERUP STATION
TUBORGVEJ
EXPERIMENTARIUM
Utterslev Mose
TUBORGVEJ
19
E47
Bispebjerg
STRANDVÆNGET
MOTORRING 3
FREDERIKSSUNDSVEJ
Utterslev
Brønshøj
Østerbro
JYLLINGEVEJ
HULGÅRDSVEJ
FREDERIKSSUNDSVEJ
Fælledparken
TAGENSVEJ
ÅBOULEVARDEN
NØRRE ALLE
Nørrebro
Damhus Engen
Vanløse
NØRDRE FASANVEJ
JAGTVEJ
GODTHÅBSVEJ
COPENHAGEN
Botanisk Have

0   1 mi
0   1 km

© MOON.COM

KLAMPENBORG AND KONGENS LYNGBY
KLAMPENBORG AND AROUND

161

candy shop in Dyrehavsbakken amusement park

before Christmas Fri.-Sun., noon-10pm or 11pm, check the website for times; entry free, rides from 25 kr, passes and multiple-ride discounts including full-pass wristband from 279 kr, 1-day kids pass 179 kr

Dyrehavsbakken, or Bakken, to use the vernacular that has become its popular name, is an institution in Copenhagen. It's a large traditional theme park in a centuries-old forest outside the city. It might be the oldest amusement park of its kind in the world, founded in 1583 after the mythical discovery of a natural spring. The area was once owned by the nobility and closed to the public. Now it is anything but: The old-fashioned rides and amusements belong to the people, who still attend in huge numbers at the peak of the season, when there are dense crowds and long queues. Visiting Bakken can feel like a time warp, a throwback to the days when your parents took you to the fairground

and you bought as many ride tokens as you could with your pocket money. Bakken's payment system can feel as confusing now as fairground tokens did to me when I was a youngster, but individual rides are not expensive.

Nostalgia is threaded throughout many other aspects of Bakken. The **Korsbæk på Bakken** area is a loving tribute to *Matador,* an iconic 1970s television series set in the fictional town of Korsbæk in the early 20th century. The series is close to the hearts of Danes of all generations. Visitors can walk around period streets and enter shops and establishments true to the era and to the series. And while Bakken has countless rides, the highlight is **Rutschebanen,** literally "The Roller Coaster," a wooden coaster that opened in 1932. The timber of its frame looks like the structure of a half-built church in an old

the Rutschebanen

Western movie. Reaching a maximum height of 22 m (72 ft) and top speeds of around 75 km/h (47 mph), it holds its own on the adrenaline front.

Other popular rides include the **Tornado,** a steel spinning coaster from 2009, as well as the **Ladybird** and the **Wild Mice,** both favorite roller coasters for kids. There are spinning coffee cups, bumper cars, and of course a horse carousel. Indoors there are slot machines, cabarets, and circus-style performances.

Bakken enjoys widespread affection and popularity among Copenhageners and people from across Zealand and Denmark, and it can become overcrowded on warm summer days, particularly weekends. Peak times are normally noon-2pm, and queues are generally shorter later in the day. Wristbands can be purchased in advance on the Bakken website and are cheaper if you book 6 or more days ahead of your visit. Redeem your online ticket at the park's sales and information counter, either on your phone or as a printout.

It should be noted that Bakken is primarily a summer excursion: The rides are packed away and the stands roll down their shutters by mid-September. Everything opens again for the Danish autumn holiday in October, when schools are closed and many people have time off work. In December, a festive atmosphere falls over the park like layers of snow as Bakken opens in full Christmas costume on weekends from the second-to-last week in November until the weekend before Christmas. Check the website for exact hours, and dress very warmly if you're venturing out in the winter months.

Ordrupgaard

Vilvordevej 110, Charlottenlund; tel. 39 64 11 83; https://ordrupgaard.dk; Tues. and Thurs.-Sun. 11am-5pm, Wed. 11am-7pm; adults 130 kr, ages 18-26 and students 95 kr, under age 18 free

Ordrupgaard is a museum that specializes in 19th- and 20th-century French Impressionist and Danish Golden Age art, a period of prodigious creativity in the country, inspired by German Romanticism. The museum houses one of Scandinavia's finest Impressionist collections, with works by Monet, Cézanne, Gauguin, and Matisse, among others. Among the prominent Danish artists exhibited is Vilhelm Hammershøi, a painter known for poetic subdued interiors that at times perhaps match the calming atmosphere at Ordrupgaard itself. Set in a beautiful early-20th-century mansion, the museum opened in 1953, and the original building is still used to exhibit the permanent collection of Danish and French works. Monet's *Waterloo Bridge, Women Bathing* by Cezanne, Manet's *Basket of Pears,* and *Sunset* by Henri Rousseau are just a handful of the standouts.

In 2005, the museum was expanded by prize-winning architect Zaha Hadid, who added a stark glass-and-concrete element to the original structure. Large temporary exhibitions are held in the new space, adding to the draw of the museum. As a result, this section is often busier than the mansion, which means there is a quieter atmosphere in the permanent exhibitions. Both Hadid's addition and a more recent one by Norwegian architecture firm Snøhetta create an architectural profile that is part of the museum's attraction.

As with the permanent collection, temporary exhibitions often feature Impressionism and works from the 19th and 20th centuries. Frida Kahlo, Edvard Munch, and Henri Matisse have been featured in the past. In 2023, Anna and Michael Ancher, prominent artists from the Skagen school, along with installation artist Veronica Hodges were the subject of special exhibitions. The Hodges exhibition saw a huge treelike installation in the

newly renovated greenhouse, which dates from 1918.

Ordrupgaard also caters to children. The garden installations in particular are known to capture kids' attention—the steaming, raining, tall vertical bronze ring *Vær i vejret* (Be In the Weather) by Danish-Icelandic Praemium Imperiale laureate Olafur Eliasson is just one example. During school holidays, creative workshops for children take place alongside activities like treasure hunts and tours around a miniature version of the museum called Villapük. Kids can be signed up for these activities in advance, and dates and details are available on the museum website.

Ordrupgaard is a 40-minute walk from Klampenborg Station, served by both local rail and the S-train, or a 25-minute walk from Ordrup S-train station. Bus 388 from Klampenborg Station goes to the stop at Vilvordevej, close to the museum, and takes around 15 minutes. You can use the same ticket or Rejsekort journey you used to take the train from Copenhagen, so there is no extra cost. The total travel time from Copenhagen Central Station is approximately 50 minutes.

RECREATION
✪ Jægersborg Dyrehave
Dyrehaven, Klampenborg; https://eng. naturstyrelsen.dk/experience-nature; daily 24 hours; free

Famous for the herds of deer in the park, Jægersborg Dyrehave (Animal Park or Deer Park) is a

10-sq-km (3.8-sq-mi) slice of wild Danish countryside not far from Copenhagen. It boasts ancient oak trees, glacial streams, and views of the sea, and it's beautiful year-round, not least during the outbursts of color in spring and fall. As painters and poets were drawn to this natural park in the past, so are photographers today.

Enter through the red gates near Klampenborg Station and Bakken and head toward Kirsten Piil's spring, the natural water source around which the park was formed. Legend has it that a mysterious woman named Piil discovered the spring in 1583. The baroque 18th-century Hermitage hunting lodge, 300-year-old oaks, ponds, plains, monuments, and wildlife all await.

Deer are emblematic of the park, with around 2,000 living throughout its approximately 1,000 ha (2,470 acres). Different species include fallow deer, red deer, and sika deer. The animals have adapted to the presence of people, so it is possible to see them up close, which provides some great photo opportunities. Visitors can't feed the deer or get too close, however, as they must remain wild animals. Deer can be seen in most parts of the park, but it's useful to note that the female red deer and their fawns stay in the southern part, while the stags keep to the north. They normally only mix during the mating season—the rut—in September-October.

In addition to the wealth of deer,

Jægersborg Dyrehaven

birds, and other animals, it's likely you'll see other people, particularly on weekends and during summer, as well as during the rut, which is a popular attraction. The close proximity of the park to the Technical University of Denmark and residential suburbs mean it's a popular spot for people out running or taking some fresh air.

There are five walking or bicycling tours within the park, passing attractions that include the Hermitage Palace. The five routes are described in the Danish Nature Agency's hiking tour leaflet no. 134, which can be picked up from stands at the entrances to the Dyrehave or downloaded from the Danish Nature Agency's website (https://naturstyrelsen.dk/media/pqlbjjvb/parforce_jaegersborg22_web_uk.pdf).

Bellevue Beach
Strandvejen 340, Klampenborg, 2930; daily 24 hours; free

Bellevue is the sandy beach and sloping grassy park area at Klampenborg that covers a 700-m-long (2,300-ft) stretch of the north Copenhagen coast close to the southern end of Jægersborg Dyrehave. Look for the blue-striped lifeguard towers and geometric kiosks: They were designed by Arne Jacobsen, the preeminent Danish designer and architect. Jacobsen lived most of his life in the municipality of Gentofte, where Klampenborg is located, and left a permanent legacy with his buildings. Bellevue remains a popular spot for Danes hoping to catch some sun and take a dip on warm days in summer, when it can still get crowded, even though its popularity has waned a little since the advent of the Amager Beach Park and bathing facilities at the Copenhagen Harbor during the 2000s. Refreshments are sold at the kiosks, and public restrooms can be found at the beach, which has lifeguard service during the summer season.

lifeguard tower at Bellevue Beach

Strandvejen Coastal Walk
The area around the beach or close to the coastal road in Klampenborg is rich in the influence and legacy of Arne Jacobsen, who lived nearby most of his life and had a studio and office in the area. Many of the Jacobsen-designed houses were built in the 1930s, early in the architect's career, while some also date from the 1950s. While the clean minimalistic style associated with Jacobsen is recognizable

Bellevue Theater

in most of the buildings, they also reflect how the designer experimented with different methods of construction and types of material.

Some of the highlights of Jacobsen's work can easily be viewed while walking around Klampenborg. You can see the lifeguard towers, the kiosk complex, and the kayak club at Bellevue Beach; the Søholm apartment complex, which includes Jacobsen's former home; the Mattson Riding School; the Bellevue Theater; and a couple of miles farther south, the striking Skovshoved Petrol Station. Excluding the gas station, a walk taking in these sights can be comfortably completed in much less than an hour; add another 30-40 minutes to include the walk to the gas station at the end. The tour is entirely on sidewalks, although you have to cross several roads.

Leave Klampenborg Station onto Peter Lieps Vej and turn right, crossing the railway bridge in the direction of the coast. After the bridge, turn right onto Bellevuevej. Immediately on your left you'll see **Mattsson Riding School** (1933-1934)—a hangar-like building in Jacobsen's signature white with a curved roof—on the left side, facing the rail tracks. Turn back to Peter Lieps Vej and walk down to the main road, Strandvejen, and turn right. About 100 m (330 ft) along you'll reach **Bellevue Teater** (1936) (www.bellevueteatret.dk), one of Jacobsen's most famous buildings, unmistakable with its distinctive blue period lettering and the green ivy that now covers its broad rounded corners. Cross Strandvejen and head to the beach, where you'll quickly be able to spot the quirky-looking **lifeguard towers** with splayed legs and horizontal marine-blue stripes, along with the geometric **kiosks** and **Klampenborg Kayak and Canoe Club** (https://klampenborg-kajak.dk), just south of the theater.

No more than 200 m (650 ft) south of the theater on Strandvejen, roughly opposite where the beach ends, the **Søholm housing complex** (1951) marks a departure from Jacobsen's white functionalism to a more modernist Danish style, the neatly tessellated brick buildings fitting together in jigsaw patterns. **Strandvejen 413** is where Jacobsen lived. Located at the end of the row facing the water, it is unlike the other houses in that it has a small extension that was used as a drawing studio by the architect, who lived here from 1951 until his death in 1971.

From here, it's a bit more exercise if you want to finish the walk at the **Skovshoved Petrol Station** (1936). Stay on Strandvejen and head south for 2.5 km (1.5 mi). You'll have grassy lawns on one side and the sea on the other, and in clear weather you'll be able to see Copenhagen in the distance. The still-operating gas station is unlike any other: its art deco clock, white tiles, and flying saucer-esque circular roof are quite incongruous with the surroundings. Originally commissioned by Texaco as a new standard model for its gas stations, the design was never implemented. The station at Skovshoved is now a registered historical building. At a side door of the station you'll find the small takeaway bar, **Olivers Garage,** offering ice cream and burgers, among other refreshments. There are benches and plenty of other outdoor seating options—including the nearby jetty and promenade at the harbor.

Returning to Copenhagen, you can avoid walking back to Klampenborg by taking bus 23 or bus 179 from Strandvejen and transferring to an S-train at Hellerup or Charlottenlund station, connecting you to Nørreport and Copenhagen Central Station. The ticket can be purchased from the bus driver (40 kr) or you can use the Rejsekort (30 kr).

FOOD

Restaurants at Bakken

Dyrehavevej 62, Klampenborg, 2930; same hours as Bakken; prices vary by restaurant

Bakken has 26 restaurants. Many are buffets, and all live up to similar standards while providing for

a range of preferences. Perhaps the best known is **Bakkens Perle** (tel. 39 64 31 64; www.bakkensperle.dk; lunch buffet 169 kr, dinner buffet 189 kr), a traditional-style restaurant that offers a range of steaks and meat-based dishes along with a salad bar on its evening buffet. Classic Danish offerings that include herring, fish fillets, and meatballs are available at lunch.

A filling kebab can be had at **Shawarma Hytten** (tel. 22 76 09 01), which also serves falafel and hummus and has a terrace as well as indoor seating. **Jernbane Restauranten** will feel familiar to anybody who has seen iconic TV series *Matador*—a replica of the old-fashioned restaurant in the show where the characters met for a beer and a chat throughout the years. **Elverdybet** (tel. 20 65 30 28; www.elverdybet.dk; sandwiches from 62 kr, desserts from 40 kr, coffee from 30 kr) is a café and ice cream bar partly concealed under a grass-decked roof and located next to the Ladybird kids' roller coaster. It sells meaty sandwiches and a vegetarian option, smørrebrød, and salads as well as burgers, ice cream, banoffee pie, waffles, and other cakes to satisfy the sweet tooth. There are picnic basket options (order ahead; from 225 kr per person) if there's good weather and you want to enjoy the ample outdoors space. You can also just stop in for a filtered coffee, latte, or hot chocolate with marshmallows.

Raadvad Kro

Svenskevej 52, Kongens Lyngby, 2800; tel.
45 80 61 62; www.raadvadkro.dk; Tues.
noon-3pm, Wed.-Sat. noon-3pm and 6pm-
9pm, Sun. 10am-3pm; brunch 375 kr pp,
lunch 2-course set menu 365 kr, à la carte
mains from 155 kr

Raadvad Kro feels far from the busy traffic and crowds of Copenhagen. It's set in a tranquil pocket surrounded by narrow lanes, trees, and a small lake. The menu is an uncomplicated take on New Nordic food—shellfish, poached eggs, fried beef tartare with pickles and beets, and fish with clam sauce are some examples from the menu. It's worth booking ahead in peak season.

Olivers Garage

Kystvejen 24, Charlottenlund, 2920; tel.
44 11 39 11; www.oliversgarage.dk; summer
daily 9am-10pm, winter daily 9am-9pm;
burgers from 87 kr

Situated in the famous Arne Jakobsen-designed Skovshoved gas station, Olivers Garage describes itself as a pit stop for burgers and ice cream. Sandwiches include tuna, avocado, or hummus, and you can eat in your car or sit on one of the nearby benches or convenient walls by the harbor jetty 90 m (100 yards) or so away. It's not uncommon to see a selection of classic sports cars parked in the adjoining parking lot as owners meet up on impromptu or organized convoys. A regular gas station store this is not.

GETTING THERE
By Public Transit

From Copenhagen, the most common ways to reach Klampenborg is line C of the S-train, which terminates at Klampenborg, or a regional train toward Nivå. From Copenhagen Central Station to **Klampenborg Station,** the journey takes 20-25 minutes and costs 40 kr for a standard adult ticket, or 30 kr using the Rejsekort. These trains leave approximately every 10 minutes during the day.

The entrances to **Bakken** and **Jægersborg Dyrehave** are within walking distance from Klampenborg station. Turn left out of the station and you'll see the red gate of the animal park. Head through it to enter the forest and continue straight ahead to reach the entrance to Bakken in 200 m (650 ft). A northern gate to Dyrehaven is within walking distance from Skodsborg Station, which is also served by the Nivå regional train (40 kr, Rejsekort 30 kr).

To get to **Ordrupgaard** from Klampenborg Station, take bus 388 toward Lyngby (get off at Vilvordevej, Ordrupgaard/ Klampenborgvej), from where the museum is a 10-minute walk. The bus journey itself takes a few minutes, but there are only a couple of departures every hour. The ticket is the standard 24 kr, Rejsekort 18 kr. You can also walk the 3 km (1.9 mi) from Klampenborg to Ordrupgaard in approximately 40 minutes. From Peter Lieps Vej, outside Klampenborg Station, turn left onto Bellevuevej, veer right after a short distance on Dyrehavevej, continuing on Christiansholmsvej before taking a right turn on to Klampenborgvej; Ordrupgaard is signposted from here. Follow this road for about 2 km (1.2 mi) until you reach the junction with Vilvordevej. Turn onto this road, and the museum is on the left.

By Car

If you are traveling by car from Copenhagen, leave the Inner City, crossing the Lakes on Tagensvej, passing Copenhagen's main hospital, Rigshospitalet, on your right. Turn right on Nørre Allé; this is a busy intersection, so get in the right lane early. Follow Nørre Allé as it becomes the multilane Bernstorffsvej/Route 19, keeping right as the road forks to stay on Bernstorffsvej (the left fork is Route 19). Continue straight for around 3 km (1.9 mi) until you reach Vilvordevej, where you pass Ordrupgaard Museum on your right. Turn right at the intersection just past the museum and follow Klampenborgvej to Klampenborg and Bakken's parking area. The 13-km (8.1-mi) journey should take around 30 minutes, depending on traffic and where you start from in Copenhagen.

Kongens Lyngby

Kongens Lyngby is the commercial center of the suburban Lyngby-Taarbæk Municipality, which neighbors Arne Jacobsen's Gentofte and includes the large Jægersborg Dyrehave within its boundaries. Its central shopping street, Lyngby Hovedgade, is suburban and pleasant, but the standout reason for venturing this far from central Copenhagen is the excellent Frilandsmuseet, an expansive open-air museum set in the green countryside, with a huge collection of buildings from Denmark's rural past and an atmosphere to match.

SIGHTS
✪ Frilandsmuseet

Kongevejen 100, Lyngby, 2800; tel. 41 20 64 55; https://en.natmus.dk/museums-and-palaces/the-open-air-museum; Tues.-Sun. *10am-4pm, limited day at Christmas and Easter; adults 120 kr, 110 kr off-peak, under age 18 free*

An open-air museum, Frilandsmuseet has both outdoor and indoor exhibits that allow you to escape to Denmark's agricultural past. You can ride a horse-drawn cart and peruse as many as 50,000 historical artifacts, including tools used by weavers, millers, and other craftspeople of centuries gone by, along with items used by peasants in their homes and by the poor of the workhouse. But the museum's most significant exhibit is the buildings themselves: farms, houses, mills, and shops from various periods and areas of Denmark that were collected and relocated here over the course of 100 years.

Take a Detour: Experimentarium

a staircase in the shape of a DNA helix at Experimentarium

Tuborg Havnevej 7, Hellerup, 2900; tel. 39 27 33 33; www.experimentarium.dk; daily 9:30am-5pm; adults 215 kr, ages 2-11 135 kr, under age 2 free

If you're traveling with kids, **Experimentarium** in Hellerup is a nice stop on your way to Bakken. The family-focused science museum has 18 exhibitions on three floors, all of which are interactive. There are also daily workshops, demonstrations, and activities, so kids and adults alike can learn about physical forces, chemical reactions, and bodily functions. There are exhibitions about traffic safety, mathematical puzzles, space travel, and even COVID-19 and how viruses work, but that really only scratches the surface of the wealth of scientific discovery and educational value on offer.

Take line B or C of the S-train from Copenhagen to Hellerup Station, a trip that takes 17-18 minutes and costs 24 kr, Rejsekort 18 kr, for a morning of experimenting before hopping back on line C and hitting up the rides at Bakken.

There are more than 100 buildings, arranged so as to present Danish life in different parts of the country, and even in other countries and regions with close to connections to Denmark, such as the Faroe Islands and Skåne in Sweden. Opened in 1897 and covering as much as 40 ha (99 acres), it is thought to be one of the world's oldest and largest open museums. It's possible to spend the best part of a day wandering around its farm buildings, mills (the oldest is a post mill from 1662), and houses and their surrounding grounds. Look for the station town, with its old gas pump, workshop, garage, and stores showcasing the changes wrought by industrialization on

Frilandsmuseet

small-town life in the late-19th century. The old station building from Øresundsvej on Amager, torn down to make way for the Copenhagen Metro, will eventually be added to this section.

A range of tours with various themes (the lives of farmers, countryside homes, children's play and lives, town life in the interwar period) are offered by the museum for a range of prices, starting at 900 kr for an hour, plus a 250 kr "language fee" for private tours. Call at least two weeks before your visit to inquire about options and arrange a tour. Tours can be canceled with at least three days' notice.

Frilandsmuseet's gift shop has a range of books, souvenirs, and knickknacks as well as toys and candy, including old-fashioned Christmas decorations during the festive season.

FOOD

Frilandsmuseet's Restaurant and Banquet

Kongevejen 100, Kgs. Lyngby, 2800; tel. 45 85 34 80; www.frilands-restaurant.dk; Apr.-Oct. Tues.-Sun. 10am-4pm, Oct.-Mar. Sat.-Sun. 10am-4pm, hours vary with local holidays; smørrebrød from 82 kr, lunch buffet 415 kr pp

Frilandsmuseet's restaurant and café is located in a spacious building within the museum grounds and mostly sticks to Danish tradition in keeping with the surroundings, serving herring and capers, beet tartare, quiche, and slow-roasted pork among the dishes in its buffet, while eggs, shrimp, chicken salad, fish fillet, and beet and avocado are on the sandwich and smørrebrød café menu. It looks a bit formal, with white tablecloths and candles, but it is praised for friendly service.

Café Mig og Annie

Lyngby Hovedgade 70b, Lyngby, 2800; tel. 45 87 18 34; https://migogannie.dk; Mon.- Fri. 9:30am-9pm, Sat. 9:30am-8pm, Sun. 9:30am-6pm; yogurt and fruit bowls 65-70 kr, pancakes 75 kr, smørrebrød 99-119 kr

A family-run café that has been a part of the scenery on Lyngby's semi-pedestrianized main shopping drag for over 20 years, Café Mig og Annie can be found on a leafy corner next to a flower shop, with which it competes for sidewalk space. The food mixes Danish and American café classics: pancakes, fruit and yogurt, bread rolls and cheese, avocado and fried egg on rye bread, and burgers. The café is cozy and casual.

GETTING THERE
By Public Transit

The easiest option for traveling to Frilandsmuseet from Copenhagen is to take line E of the S-train toward Holte to **Sorgenfri Station** and walk the final 800 m (0.5 mi) to the museum. From Copenhagen Central Station, this trip takes around 35 minutes. A standard ticket costs 46 kr or 37 kr using a Rejsekort. To go via the center of the suburb of Lyngby, where there is a semi-pedestrian main street with shops and cafés, leave the train at **Lyngby station** (one stop before Sorgenfri on line E; the faster line A also stops here). This is a 3-km (1.9-mi) 30-minute walk from Frilandsmuseet.

An S-train and bus combination is also possible for the same fare, bringing you closer to the museum than walking from Sorgenfri Station. Taking S-train line E toward Hillerød, get out at Lyngby, and take bus 184 (Holte) or bus 194 (Nærum). The bus stops outside Frilandsmuseet.

By Car

The drive from central Copenhagen to Frilandsmuseet takes 20 minutes in good traffic. Start out on the same route as for Klampenborg: Leave the Inner City, crossing the Lakes on Tagensvej, and turn right on to Nørre Allé; this is a busy intersection, so get in the right lane early. Follow this road north as it becomes the multilane Bernstorffsvej/Route 19. Here you diverge from the Klampenborg route. Keep left, taking Route 19 (Tuborgvej). Following this road for 9 km (5.6 mi) as it becomes Route 201, passing an IKEA warehouse, then taking you through Lyngby. Turn right on to Skovbrynet and left shortly afterward on Kongevejen to reach the museum. The total distance is 15 km (9.3 mi).

Louisiana Museum of Modern Art

Louisiana Museum of Modern Art
is situated in a spacious park in Humlebæk—a
small coastal Zealand town between
Copenhagen and Helsingør—with a view
across the Øresund toward Sweden. This location has been crafted over decades to reflect
the museum's position as a world-class art
complex, grounded in the natural beauty of
Denmark. Inside, you'll find permanent and
temporary exhibitions of major international
modern and contemporary art, encompassing
artists such as Pablo Picasso, Yayoi Kusama,

Highlights

⭐ **North Wing:** The emblematic Glass Passage of the North Wing leads to one of Louisiana's signature collections (page 179).

⭐ **South Wing:** This wing plays host to exciting special exhibits at Louisiana. A must-see is Yayoi Kusama's installation *Gleaming Lights of the Souls* (page 180).

⭐ **Louisiana Sculpture Park:** A key exhibition at the museum, the park's 60 sculptures blend seamlessly with their coastal natural surroundings (page 181).

Yves Klein, Asger Jorn, Louise Bourgeois, and Andy Warhol. On the museum grounds you can lounge on the sloping lawn, enjoy a first-class smørrebrød on the terrace of the café, gaze across the sea, and stroll through the Louisiana Sculpture Park and landscaped gardens. Louisiana is known by many art and culture lovers as one of Denmark's most beautiful spots, and for good reason.

Humlebæk, the tiny town in which Louisiana is located, is itself a quiet place, even though it has two harbors: Humlebæk Harbor, which neighbors Louisiana, and Sletten Harbor, around 2.5 km (1.5 mi) to the south. Of these small marina areas, Sletten is the more interesting, with atmospheric lanes and thatched houses, along with the highly rated Sletten restaurant in its immediate vicinity. The royal summer residence at Fredensborg, 10 km (6.2 mi) west of Humlebæk, weighs in with a serious amount of grandeur, bringing splendor and occasion to this serene corner of Zealand.

The tourist information website **Visit Nordsjaelland** (www.visit-nordsjaelland.dk) provides tips on attractions and events in the area, including in Fredensborg and Humlebæk.

Previous: the Sculpture Park at the Louisiana Museum of Modern Art.
Above: the Giacometti Gallery in the North Wing; the Old Villa.

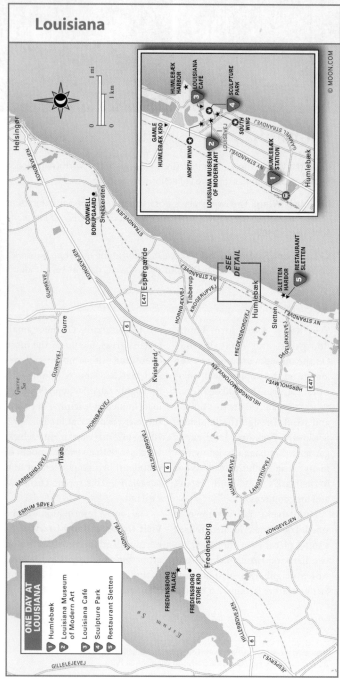

Louisiana

© MOON.COM

ONE DAY AT LOUISIANA
1. Humlebæk
2. Louisiana Museum of Modern Art
3. Louisiana Café
4. Sculpture Park
5. Restaurant Sletten

Detail:
- HUMLEBÆK HARBOR
- GAMLE HUMLEBÆK KRO
- LOUISIANA CAFÉ — 3
- SCULPTURE PARK — 4
- NORTH WING
- LOUISIANA MUSEUM OF MODERN ART — 2
- SOUTH WING
- HUMLEBÆK STATION — 1
- Humlebæk
- GAMMEL STRANDVEJ
- NY STRANDVEJ
- LOUISIANAVEJ

SEE DETAIL

- Helsingør
- Snekkersten
- COMWELL BORUPGAARD
- Espergærde
- Tibberup
- Kvistgård
- Tikøb
- Gurre
- Gurre Sø
- Fredensborg
- FREDENSBORG PALACE
- FREDENSBORG STORE KRO
- Esrum Sø
- Humlebæk
- Sletten
- SLETTEN HARBOR
- RESTAURANT SLETTEN — 5

Roads/labels: KONGEVEJEN, GURREVEJ, HARRESHØJSVEJ, ESRUM SØVEJ, GILLELEJEVEJ, HORNBÆKVEJ, HELSINGØRSVEJ, STRANDVEJEN, NY STRANDVEJ, KROGERUPVEJ, FREDENSBORGVEJ, HELSINGØRMOTORVEJEN, HUMLEBÆKVEJ, LANGSTRUPVEJ, DAGELØKKEVEJ, HØRSHOLMVEJ, KONGEVEJEN, ENDRUPVEJ, HILLERØDVEJEN, JESPERVEJ, E47, 6

Scale: 1 mi / 1 km

Itinerary Idea

ONE DAY AT LOUISIANA

Louisiana is more than just a museum visit.

1 Take an early train or bus from Copenhagen to **Humlebæk.**

2 Spend the morning exploring the **Louisiana Museum of Modern Art,** Denmark's showpiece contemporary art museum. See the famous Giacometti Gallery and Glass Passage, immerse yourself in the special exhibits, and get into a dreamy headspace at Yayoi Kusama's *Gleaming Lights of the Souls* in the South Wing.

3 Enjoy a Nordic-style lunch and coffee as you gaze at a panoramic view of the Øresund at **Louisiana Café.**

4 Spend the afternoon wandering around Louisiana's **Sculpture Park** and enjoying the beautiful rural coastal setting. Download the museum's mobile guide for more information on each of the sculptures that you spot.

5 Leave the museum and head to the pleasant Sletten Harbor for a seafood dinner at **Restaurant Sletten.**

Sights

TOP EXPERIENCE

LOUISIANA MUSEUM OF MODERN ART

Gl. Strandvej 13, Humlebæk; tel. 49 19 07 19; https://louisiana.dk/en; Tues.-Fri. 11am-10pm, Sat.-Sun. 11am-6pm; adults 145 kr, students 125 kr, included in Copenhagen Card "Discover," Louisiana members free (membership 490 kr per year, discounts for seniors and under age 30)

Louisiana is one of the primary modern art museums not just in Denmark, but anywhere. Set on the grounds of an old mansion along the serene northeastern coast of Zealand and overlooking the waters of the Øresund, the clean, square, modernist rooms of the museum house top-class international contemporary art year-round. Permanent installations like *Gleaming Lights of the Souls* by Yayoi Kusama will leave visitors—art buffs or not—in a dream world.

Louisiana's buildings consist of the original villa and four wings that were added in stages. The modernist style dates from the 1950s, when founder Knud W. Jensen commissioned architects to extend the museum by blending

Louisiana Fast Facts

- **Number of wings:** 4, all connected in a ring around the Sculpture Park

- **Recommended duration of visit:** 3-6 hours

- **Least crowded times:** You'll have more space late on weekday evenings—the museum stays open until 10pm. But that would mean missing out on the beautiful views of the sound (unless it's midsummer), so try weekday mornings instead.

- **Most famous wing:** The North Wing's Glass Passage is perhaps the most recognizable part of Louisiana. It includes paintings by Danish artist Asger Jorn and sculptures by Swiss modernist Alberto Giacometti.

- **My favorite exhibit:** Yayoi Kusama's *Gleaming Lights of the Souls,* a beautiful mirrored chamber of endless polka-dot spotlights.

- **Underrated gem:** If it's on display when you visit, don't miss Shilpa Gupta's *Singing Cloud,* which I can best describe as a giant swarm of microphones. Part cloud, part insect plague, it emits a quiet buzzing as you approach. Nearby, a replica of an analog-style airport departure board flips numbers and letters in a random sequence, adding to the disorientating sensory effect.

- **Social media:** Visit @louisianamuseum and @louisianabornehus on Instagram to be inspired and to keep up with current goings-on at the museum and children's wing.

new gallery buildings with the surrounding natural environment. The result is an unobtrusive but nevertheless remarkable Nordic look. The height of the buildings is constant: some are actually built underground and into the hillside. The lawns and leaves of the Sculpture Park, which is encircled by the museum and also looks out over the sea, is the final element of a sprawling mosaic.

You can spend anywhere from two hours to a full day at Louisiana. The circular layout of the museum's four wings makes it possible—and logical—to simply follow one exhibition to the next, and this is the easiest way of making sure you visit each exhibition.

It's equally easy to step outside and walk through the Sculpture Park at any point during your tour, and doing this halfway through can be a good way to refresh your senses. The Louisiana Café is situated between the East and North Wings, more or less halfway around the museum, and also makes for a nice stopping point.

The museum's huge collection is regularly rearranged into new presentations with the intended effect of constantly providing new perspectives. You can visit a year or even a season later and barely recognize the floor plans of the galleries (so it should be noted that works may be found in different locations than what is described in this chapter, which refers to the layout of the museum at the time of writing). The temporary exhibitions are often huge draws in their own right. All this means that no two visits to Louisiana are the same.

Lectures, debates, and other events are regularly hosted in an auditorium that connects to the Louisiana Café, and an amphitheater sometimes hosts small concerts and events, such as during the annual Louisiana Literature festival. You'll also find a large gift shop, the main attraction of which is the range of prints depicting promotional posters from past Louisiana exhibitions. Whether you're a fan of Arne Jacobsen, Gabriele Münter, or Andy Warhol, you'll find something of interest, and there's an interactive screen you can use to browse and select the prints and picture frames.

Tickets and Practical Information

Tickets (over age 18 145 kr, students 125 kr) can be purchased at the museum. Tickets can also can be bought via the Louisiana website and shown either as printouts or on smartphones.

There's a small **parking lot** outside the museum, and parking is free. Alternative parking is allowed at the nearby shopping area, Humlebæk Center, behind the rail station and a 10-minute walk from the museum.

Visiting Louisiana

A few hours is enough to get a real feel of what Louisiana is about, even if you can't see everything in one visit, and the layout of the museum means you can follow your nose and see each wing in turn. If you are looking to see a particular artist or exhibition in detail, it makes sense to plan which wings you want to concentrate on.

✪ North Wing

The North Wing of the museum, with its glass corridor and views of the Sculpture Park, has a gallery dedicated to the sculptures of **Alberto Giacometti,** one of the most important sculptors of the 20th century. The Giacometti room, with its balcony, brown tiles, and giant window looking down the hill, is emblematic of Louisiana. Don't miss the gallery dedicated to **Asger Jorn,** arguably Louisiana's signature Danish artist, with its airy, wooden roof work.

You'll also find the **Glass Passage** here, another of the museum's most recognizable spots. A long glass-walled corridor lets in light from both sides and affords views of the Sculpture Park and natural surroundings enveloping the museum. The space encourages a moment of reflection.

the reflecting pond in the North Wing

✪ South Wing

The South Wing, built in 1982, is an exhibition room with a higher ceiling than the older buildings, built into the surrounding terrain to keep the horizontal profile of Louisiana constant. It has perhaps the museum's best view in the panoramic **Pause Room.**

The South Wing is home to many of the **special exhibitions** hosted by Louisiana every year. Some of these are quite spectacular: In 2018, a special exhibition to mark the 50th anniversary of the Apollo 11 moon landings included a collage by American artist Robert Rauschenberg, who was invited to the 1969 launch by NASA. *The Irreplaceable Human* offers an expansive look at AI, how humans are set apart from it, and how it threatens human creativity.

One of the permanent exhibits in the South Wing is the spectacular **Yayoi Kusama** installation *Gleaming Lights of the Souls.* You'll definitely spot the queue of people waiting to go inside and lose themselves in the limitlessness of its multicolored hanging polka dots. It's in a room of only 4 sq m (43 sq ft) but feels infinitely bigger.

East Wing

On its completion in 1991, the addition of the East Wing meant that Louisiana's buildings were now connected in something approaching a circle. A curving underground passage with brick paving, this is one of the most architecturally interesting parts of the museum.

The East Wing also hosts **special exhibitions:** Be sure check out the museum's website before visiting for an idea of the aesthetic treats on offer. It was here that Andy Warhol's *Mao Tse Tung* series, in which the Chinese leader is shown in a style reminiscent of Warhol's celebrity portraits, was on display during a 2018 exhibition entitled *Men and Masculinity.* It's a piece that belongs to the Louisiana collection and is worth looking out for during your visit. The *Pussy Riot* exhibition drew international headlines and huge crowds in 2023. It was replaced in 2024 by the first exhibition of Chaïm Soutine, a distinctive expressionist from the School of Paris and featured around 70 paintings by the artist.

West Wing

The West Wing, one of the older parts of the museum, has large spaces and has been used for a diverse range of exhibitions. It leads from the Old Villa toward the North Wing adjacent to the Calder Terrace, where there's a great view of the sound. The arrangement of the ongoing exhibition can make its changing floors and rooms feel deceptively expansive. In recent times, **Shilpa Gupta**'s gigantic *Singing Cloud,* a buzzing insect swarm-microphone hybrid, was displayed here.

The Children's Wing

Tues.-Sun. 11am-6pm, workshops 11am-5:30pm

Children are well catered to at Louisiana. The Children's Wing, a tangent to the main circle adjacent to the North and West Wings, has a range of creative and fun activities in facilities spread over three floors. The highlight of the Children's Wing is the **open workshops,** which get kids creating based on the current exhibitions in the museum, including activities like building space rockets, clay sculpting, or creating storytelling images. Activities are organized and led by Louisiana's arts professionals.

✪ Louisiana Sculpture Park

Louisiana's Sculpture Park, while part of the main museum, is an attraction in its own right. It is from the Sculpture Park that the unbeatable location of Louisiana and panoramic views can be best appreciated, as can the design of the buildings and their integration into the wooded slopes of the museum grounds. You won't want to miss this part of the museum, open year round.

You can spend many hours wandering through it without spotting all of the **45 sculptures,** many of which blend organically into the surroundings; some were created specifically for the site. There's an array of styles among the sculptures, including the jagged metronomic *Little Janey Waney* by sculptor **Alexander Calder** on the terrace; the colorless but disorienting *Square Bisected by Curve* by **Dan Graham;** *Phase of Nothingness* by **Nobuo Sekine,** in which the viewer's reflection looks as though it's about to be crushed by a falling rock; and **Henry Moore's** *Reclining Figure*

No. 5 (Seagram), perhaps the most memorable of the figures gracing the famous view across the Louisiana lawn.

Look out also for the works visible from inside the North Wing through the glass corridors. These include the excellent ***Pars Pro Toto*** by **Alicja Kwade,** a collection of stone spheres that resemble a planetary system.

A personal favorite is ***House to Watch the Sunset*** by Swiss artist **Not Vital.** Its reflective steel surface beams back natural greens, browns, and whites during the changing seasons, and the jagged edges of its steps and central column are at once evocative of an M. C. Escher illusion and the trees themselves.

A **mobile guide** to the park that provides helpful insight into the works can be downloaded for free. It can be found on the Louisiana website (https://guide.louisiana.dk/en).

HUMLEBÆK HARBOR

Humlebæk; tel. 21 29 71 91; https://humlebaekhavn.dk

Often ignored given that Louisiana itself overlooks the sound, Humlebæk Harbor—a stone's throw from the art museum—is a small, quiet corner that exemplifies Denmark's fishing and sailing heritage with a slight hint of a present-day active sailing industry. There's not much in the way of facilities, but the area makes for a pleasant walk, and the harbor has

Louisiana MOMA sculpture courtyard

a pleasing natural look with boulders and wood far more prominent than concrete. The harbor celebrated its second century in 2010: It was rebuilt in the years after the bombardment of Copenhagen and destruction of the Danish fleet by the British in 1807. More recently, it has undergone renovation and repair in recent years and still sees hundreds of guest boats mooring each year.

SLETTEN HARBOR

Sletten Havn 1; tel. 20 40 27 72; https://slettenhavn.dk

In the southern part of Humlebæk, the harbor at Sletten is part of what was once a fishing village, and it remains an idyllic place with around 130 old fishing families' houses, now restored and privately owned. It's possible to take a short walk along the marina, possibly after a meal at nearby Sletten Restaurant, from where there are views across the sound and of the old houses in the village.

FREDENSBORG PALACE

Slottet 1B, Fredensborg; tel. 20 20 10 12; https://kongeligeslotte.dk/en; public areas year-round, private gardens open in July; free

Around 10 km (6.2 mi) west of Humlebæk, Fredensborg Palace, the autumn and spring residence of the royal family, was beloved of the late Prince Henrik, husband of Denmark's Queen Margrethe and father of the current King Frederik X—perhaps because of its French-inspired baroque style. The palace, which is well used by the modern royals, is often the scene of important state events. Its grounds contain gardens, sculptures, and fountains of cultural note, and while some areas of the gardens are open to the public year-round, access is best during the summer months, when guided tours are available for 125 kr (adults) and 50 kr (children age 7-17). Guided tours in English take place quarter-hourly from 1:45pm-2:45pm (July 1-August 6).

The palace interior and some areas of the gardens—the Private Garden—are normally reserved for royal use, and as such it's not generally possible to visit. During the summer season, however, it is possible to see parts of the palace. The Private Garden, as well as the Herb Garden, are open throughout the month of July daily 9am-5pm. You can also visit inside of the palace with guided tours in English daily at 1:45pm and 2:45pm. Tickets for guided tours can be reserved on the National Museum's web shop (https://shop.natmus.dk) in the spring, prior to the open dates.

Features of the palace interior include the Dome Hall, a setting for banquets and royal functions with a vaulted domed roof and a characteristic black-and-white star-patterned marble floor. The red-framed windows at the top of the dome provide atmospheric lighting within the hall, which has hosted Danish wedding receptions

Fredensborg Palace

for centuries, including that of the Crown Prince Frederik and Crown Princess Mary in 2004. It is also famous for its windowpanes, on which tradition dictates that visiting kings and presidents scratch their signatures.

The Baroque Gardens, created in the image of Versailles by 18th-century Francophile King Frederik V, consist of broad avenues radiating out from the palace. Boxwood hedges and linden trees line the avenues, and sculptor Johannes Wiedewelt was commissioned by the king to create eight sandstone pieces for the central Broad Avenue (Brede Allé), depicting war trophies and scenes from ancient mythology. There is also an ornamental garden in front of the palace. The gardens and sculptures were restored in 2013 to resemble how the grounds appeared in Frederik V's heyday.

The Private Garden contains a small bridge, statues of its own, rose beds, rhododendrons, yellow yarrows, and a half-timbered 1960s playhouse for the royal children. Also in the gardens, the Valley of the Norsemen is a large collection of 70 sculptures of Norwegian and Faroese farmers and fishermen, commissioned by Frederik V. It is unusual in that it was rare for images of commoners to adorn royal gardens at the time, making them a unique record of how people of the period dressed and the tools they used. The sculptures were made between 1764 and 1784.

Festivals and Events

LOUISIANA LITERATURE

Gammel Strandvej 13, Humlebæk; tel. 49 19 07 19; https://louisiana.dk/en; late Aug.; included in Louisiana museum admission

Literature festivals are a popular summer event in Denmark, and Louisiana is in on the trend. Its international literature festival takes place indoors and outdoors in late August, combining the atmospheric surroundings with authors' voices and prose.

During the busy 4-day festival, around 40 authors from Denmark and abroad take part in readings, panel discussions, and literary events that cover a diverse range of genres and traditions. The festival takes place during normal museum hours. Previous festivals have included appearances from some huge names, including Haruki Murakami in 2023. Earlier versions have welcomed Sally Rooney, Margaret Atwood, Zadie Smith, Patti Smith, Chris Kraus, Tomas Espedal, Karl Ove Knausgård, Alaa Al Aswany, David Mitchell, and Michel Houellebecq. Past talks and interviews from the festival can be viewed via the museum's Louisiana Channel (https://channel.louisiana.dk).

Dining

Louisiana Café

Gl. Strandvej 13, Humlebæk; tel. 49 19 07 19; https://en.louisiana.dk/louisiana-cafe; Tues.-Fri. 11am-9:30pm, Sat.-Sun. 11am-5:30pm; lunch 189 kr, dinner from 125 kr

While it's permitted to bring a packed lunch to Louisiana and eat outdoors (follow the signs for the Lake Garden Pavilion for the best spot), I recommend using the Louisiana Café. Prices are slightly higher than a regular Copenhagen café, but you get what you pay for: floor-to-ceiling windows allowing the sunlight and views of the Sculpture Park surroundings to flood in, contrasted by the characteristic Louisiana brown tiles; table service that's fast and efficient even at busy times like weekends; and, not least, the memorable food. The menu contains various mainly Danish options and typical cakes like krænsekage—the crispy marzipan and almond cake often associated with celebrations—as well as kid-size dishes. My preferred choice is the "smørrebrød of the week" (119 kr), one of the cheapest items on the main lunch menu; it will fill you up for a few hours of browsing the galleries. The salmon, lemon, and crème fraîche variant is possibly among the top three smørrebrød I've had in Denmark.

Louisiana Café

Restaurant Sletten

*Gl. Strandvej 137, Humlebæk; tel. 49 19 13
21; https://formelfamily.dk/sletten; lunch
Tues.-Sat. noon-4pm, dinner Tues.-Thurs.
6pm-11pm, Fri.-Sat. 6pm-midnight; lunch à
la carte from 155 kr, dinner 4-course menu
700 kr excluding wine*

At Sletten Harbor, south of
Louisiana and Humlebæk Station,
Restaurant Sletten shares its owners with Michelin-starred restaurant Formel B in Copenhagen, and
the emphasis on high-quality local
ingredients is just as evident here
as at the more famous establishment in the capital. Surrounded
by fishing huts and with its own
view of the Øresund, the menu
is influenced by both the sea and
the cuisine of Formel B: Expect the
likes of scallops, steamed dover
sole, and pickled gooseberries to
be among the delights on the tasting menu. Advance reservations
are advised.

Gamle Humlebæk Kro

*Humlebæk Strandevej 1A, Humlebæk; tel.
49 19 02 65; www.gamlehumlebaekkro.
dk; lunch daily noon-4:30pm, dinner daily
5:30pm-9pm; entrées from 145 kr*

Gamle Humlebæk Kro is an old-
fashioned inn that serves simple,
tasty staple Danish dishes, including
smørrebrød, roast pork, and fiskefri-
kadeller (fish meatballs) on its lunch
menu. The evening menu is in more
unusual territory: The three-course
menu, for example, includes elk with
game sauce. Vegetarian options are
limited. There's no shortage of history under the thatched roof of the
inn, which has been in place since
1740. Its old-fashioned carpets,
grandfather clock, and mounted
antlers and animal heads are testament to the traditional feel, as are the
checked tablecloths and candlesticks.
There's also a large terrace area for
outside seating during the summer.
Reservations are recommended.

Accommodations

There are scant places to spend the night in Humlebæk itself, but a couple of good options farther afield offer visitors a good opportunity to combine a visit to the museum with other attractions nearby or a trip to Helsingør.

Comwell Borupgaard

Nørrevej 80, Snekkersten; tel. 48 38 03 33; https://comwell.com; 149 rooms; high season from 892 kr d

Comwell Borupgaard, located in Snekkersten between Humlebæk and Helsingør, is a hotel with conference facilities in a country manor-type property with modern buildings appended. It has a spa and is a 10-minute walk from the beach. Buffet breakfast is included. All rooms have a modern clean style with large en suite baths and flat-screen TVs. Free parking and electric car charging is available in the hotel's car park.

Fredensborg Store Kro

Slotsgade 6, Fredensborg; tel. 71 71 21 21; www.storekro.com; 100 rooms; high season from 1,295 kr d

With Fredensborg Palace a few hundred yards down the boulevard, it is easy to pick up on the regal countryside vibe at Fredensborg Store Kro, which was originally built in 1723. A bistro restaurant (tel. 71 96 96 44) is open for lunch daily noon-3pm and for evening meals Monday-Saturday 6pm-10pm. Breakfast is not included in the room rates. Some of the renovated and chic individually decorated rooms are furnished with antiques; some of the suites have garden or palace views and balconies.

Getting There and Around

GETTING THERE FROM COPENHAGEN
By Train

Regional trains run by **DSB** (www.dsb.dk) leave up to four times hourly from Copenhagen Central Station to **Humlebæk** and cost 74 kr for an adult single ticket. The journey takes 35-40 minutes. Check www.dsb.dk or www.rejseplanen.dk for departure times. The Rejsekort travel card can be used to pay for the journey, provided you have enough credit, and reduces the fare to 47 kr.

Louisiana is around 1.2 km (0.7 mi) from the train station, a 15-20-minute walk along a main road. The museum is clearly signposted from the station; alternatively, follow the many other visitors at peak times. You can also take the northbound **388 regional bus,** across the road from the train station. Get off at the second stop and you'll find yourself at the turn-off for the museum entrance. The fare is the same if you use the bus in addition to the train—just purchase a ticket to Louisiana rather than Humlebæk Station. If using the Rejsekort, do not check out after leaving the train; check in again on the bus and then check out when leaving the bus. **Taxis** can also be hailed or called at the station. A reliable taxi company is **Dantaxi** (tel. 48 48 48 48); the journey from the station to the museum takes a few minutes and should cost at most 100 kr.

By Car
Head north from Copenhagen on **Route 152 (Strandvejen)** along the Øresund coast or via the **E47** highway. Louisiana is around 35 km (22 mi) north of Copenhagen, and the journey should take around 35 minutes from the center of the capital.

GETTING THERE FROM HELSINGØR
The train from Helsingør to Humlebæk takes 10 minutes and costs 30 kr, or 24 kr using the Rejsekort, leaving around four times per hour. If you're driving, head south on the **E45** or **Route 152 (Strandvejen).** You should cover the 10 km (6.2 mi) to Humlebæk within 20 minutes.

GETTING AROUND
The easiest way to travel between Humlebæk and **Fredensborg** is with direct bus **370R,** which leaves from Humlebæk Station and takes 25 minutes and costs 30 kr. Two buses leave every hour. The Rejsekort (19 kr) can also be used for this journey. If traveling from Copenhagen to Fredensborg, you should take the train to Humlebæk and then transfer to bus 370R. A second option is to take an S-train on Line A from Copenhagen to Hillerød, and then the local rail service 930R for three stops from Hillerød to Fredensborg. This is the slightly faster option at 50 minutes; both routes cost 74 kr (Rejsekort 48 kr).

Helsingør

It's impossible to miss the sense of theatrical occasion as one approaches Helsingør along the northeast Zealand coast as the colossal Kronborg Castle, immortalized by Shakespeare's *Hamlet*, comes into view. It stands on a spit as if held at arm's length from the medieval town that still dominates it, expecting to receive its Sound Dues, the toll for passing ships on which the city's wealth was founded.

The town's signature attraction is this UNESCO World Heritage Site, with its

Highlights

⭐ **Kronborg Castle:** This iconic castle juts out from the coast over the Øresund. Its evocative courtyard, soaring cannon tower, dramatic royal chambers, and poignant underground chamber of Holger Danske are all experiences not to be missed (page 194).

⭐ **M/S Maritime Museum of Denmark:** Denmark's seafaring tradition, shown in an innovatively converted dry dock, deserves a detailed look (page 199).

⭐ **Hamletscenen:** See a Shakespeare play in the setting imagined by the Bard himself (page 203).

baroque and Renaissance interiors and iconic features, but Helsingør has plenty more to offer, including a broad harbor area with an impressive maritime museum in a deep dry dock, a new street food market, and a well-preserved old town. Meanwhile, seagulls squawk and sailboats crisscross the water, with the Swedish city of Helsingborg visible beyond on most days—nowhere else is the Øresund narrower than here.

ORIENTATION

The harbor area, including the maritime museum, Elsinore Street Food, and Kronborg, are north of the train station and the main bus terminal, which are a short walk of less than 1 km (0.6 mi) along the harbor or through the town. Moving inland from the coast, three streets—Stengade, Sct Olai Gade, and Sudergade, as well as the perpendicular Sct Annagade, Sophie Brahes Gade, and Stjernegade—run parallel to the coast and demarcate the old town, laid out as it was in the 15th century. This is the best area for exploring the oldest surviving buildings and streets. The very oldest building in the city, the 13th-century St. Olaf Cathedral, sits at the southeastern corner.

Previous: Kronborg from the sea. **Above:** Kronborg in winter; Maritime Museum of Denmark, Helsingør.

PLANNING YOUR TIME

Kronborg itself is worth half a day to a full day, so a day trip or an overnight stay are a good fit for a Helsingør visit. Your next priority after the castle should be the M/S Maritime Museum of Denmark, and don't forget to spend an hour or two wandering the old city center. It survived redevelopment in the 1960s and 1970s and retains the layout that has been in place since medieval times.

Itinerary Idea

ONE DAY AT HELSINGØR

Head north to the mythical home of Hamlet for the day.

1 After breakfasting in Copenhagen, catch a train to Helsingør. From the rail station, head north and spend an hour or so wandering through the **Old Town.**

2 Head toward the harbor—and down under sea level—to the **M/S Maritime Museum of Denmark** for an afternoon of seafaring exploration.

3 Grab a sandwich at **Kadetten,** located in a lieutenants school just outside Kronborg Castle.

4 With your stomach full, step inside the majestic **Kronborg Castle** and spend the rest of the afternoon immersing yourself in Renaissance intrigue. Don't miss scaling the cannon tower for sweeping views of the city.

5 For dinner, there's no better place than the **Elsinore Street Food/ Værftets Madmarked.** Choose Argentinian barbecue, French crepes, ramen, or Syrian mezze—or have a little bit of everything.

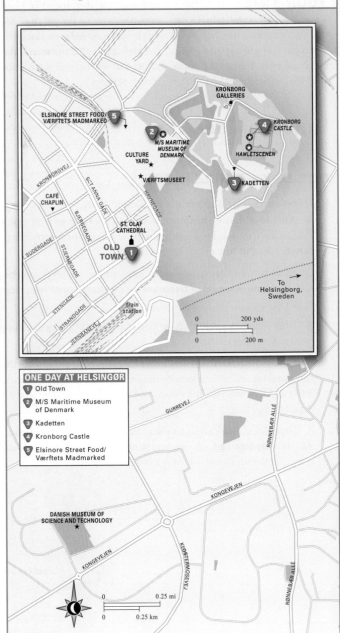

Helsingør

KRONBORG
GALLERIES

ELSINORE STREET FOOD/
VÆRFTETS MADMARKED 5

2
M/S MARITIME
MUSEUM OF
DENMARK

CULTURE
YARD

VÆRFTSMUSEET

4 KRONBORG
CASTLE

HAMLETSCENEN

3 KADETTEN

KRONBORGVEJ

CAFÉ
CHAPLIN

SCT ANNA GADE

HAVNEGADE

ST. OLAF
CATHEDRAL

OLD
TOWN 1

BJERREGADE

SUDERGADE

STJERNEGADE

STENGADE

STRANDGADE

train
station

JERNBANEVEJ

To →
Helsingborg,
Sweden

0   200 yds

0   200 m

ONE DAY AT HELSINGØR

1 Old Town

2 M/S Maritime Museum
of Denmark

3 Kadetten

4 Kronborg Castle

5 Elsinore Street Food/
Værftets Madmarked

GURREVEJ

RØNNEBÆR ALLÉ

KONGEVEJEN

DANISH MUSEUM OF
SCIENCE AND TECHNOLOGY

KONGEVEJEN

KLOSTERMOSEVEJ

RØNNEBÆR ALLÉ

0   0.25 mi

0   0.25 km

© MOON.COM

Sights

• •

TOP EXPERIENCE

✪ KRONBORG CASTLE

*Kronborg; tel. 49 21 30 78; www.kronborg.
dk; Jan.-Apr. Tues.-Sun. 11am-4pm, May.-
Oct. daily 10am-5pm, Nov.-Dec. Tues.-Sun.
11am-4pm; adults 125 kr, students 115 kr,
under age 18 free, admission included in
Copenhagen Card*

There's no mistaking the majesty and significance of Kronborg as you walk through the gateway into a fully enclosed courtyard. The imposing masonry immediately evokes the court machinations of centuries past.

History

The presence of a fortress at Kronborg dates to the 15th century, when Danish king Eric of Pomerania decided that ships entering the Baltic Sea through the narrow Øresund Strait should pay a toll—known as the Sound Dues—for the privilege. At the time, the other side of the water also belonged to Denmark; it was lost during a series of disastrous wars with Sweden in the 1600s. That meant Denmark was able to control all navigation through the area, which the medieval kingdom quickly monetized.

It was in the stone chambers of Kronborg that a king's residence was established, and in the late 1500s King Frederik II built the castle into a towering Renaissance stronghold as it entered a golden era of renown throughout Europe. Its cannons threatened passing ships, and the presence of the authoritative fortress persuaded captains to pay their Sound Dues. The king's coffers were thereby filled, allowing Frederik II to endow the castle with spires, towers, sandstone masonry, and copper roofing. Seafarers, merchants, diplomats, and royals sent reports back to their homeland about the majesty and pomp of the court at Helsingør.

A devastating fire in 1629 destroyed art, tapestries, and roofing and signaled the beginning of the end of royal presence at the castle. The loss of Skåne—the region on the other side of the channel—to Sweden in 1658 after a series of costly wars under kings Christian IV, also known for building many of Copenhagen's historical areas, and his successor, Frederik III, greatly weakened Denmark's influence over the strait. The castle was even occupied and plundered by Swedish king Karl X Gustav in 1658-1660.

In later years, Kronborg was used as a military fortress, with new defenses and ramparts built around it. In the 1700s it became a prison, with soldiers from the military barracks just outside the walls guarding the convicts.

In 1857 the Sound Dues were finally abolished, and in 1938 Kronborg was opened to the public, eventually becoming literally one of the biggest attractions on the island of Zealand, with 250,000 visitors annually.

Visiting the Castle

The castle is an imposing and memorable sight, both inside and out, and details such as the cannons outside its far walls—still pointing threateningly at Sweden a short distance away—and the iron water pump in the courtyard, bring its history to life. There's plenty to do and see here, and I recommend taking at least half a day to visit so you can adequately take in and explore the castle and its grounds.

Kronborg has many different areas. Although you'll often move naturally from one area to the next as you walk through the castle, no particular order is better than another. What all visitors will see first, though, is the walk from the harbor, crossing it via two bridges and then turning left to walk around the castle with its wall to the right and earthen defenses to the left. A third bridge takes you across the moat and into the outer battlements of the castle itself, where you'll get a first view of the Renaissance and baroque influences on its construction, with reliefs, statues, and pillars at the entrance to the main courtyard, a spectacular walled-in square of sandstone, towers, and narrow rectangular windows. From this courtyard, signposts direct you to all the attractions within the castle itself.

courtyard at Kronborg Castle

The opulent **Royal Apartments** are where King Frederik II, who spent a fortune building and furnishing the castle in the late 1500s, lived with the queen Sophie, whom he married in 1572, when she was 14 years old. The rooms are not original, as they were destroyed in a later fire, and much of the furniture was acquired after Frederik's time, but the chambers have been set out in a reconstruction of the King's design. Look for a monogrammed shield containing the letters F and S—perhaps the royal medieval version of a heart engraved on a tree. There are ceiling-high **tapestries** that once completely covered the walls of the ballrooms; sleeping chambers with carved wooden four-poster beds, one each for the king and queen; and an officelike room, the chancellery, where the king's correspondence was kept in cabinets. Some of the more spectacular features elsewhere in the apartments include ceiling paintings that depict members of the royal family and a 62-m (200-ft) ballroom with an impressively checkered tile floor.

The **chapel,** built in 1582, survived the fire, occupation, and bombardments of the castle's heyday and is therefore an accurate representation of how it was originally decorated. The ceiling is arched and whitewashed, and the floor is a chessboard of tiles. The detailing on the pews and altar are ornate, with floral patterns and figures on the ends of the rows.

The **Cannon Tower**, with a view across the water and of the city of Helsingør, is well worth the effort required to climb its 142 stone steps. It is in the southwestern corner of the castle: The entrance is on the far right side as you enter.

From the heights of the tower, you can go straight to the murky depths of the **Casemates,** the damp underground passages where you will find the statue of **Holger Danske** (Ogier the Dane), a legendary knight of Charlemagne who, it is said, will rise to Denmark's protection in its direst hour of need. The statue underneath Kronborg, a cast of a 1907 original by H. P. Pedersen-Dan, sits cross-armed with head bowed, as if to underline the magnitude of the castle's symbolism.

Near the entrance, the year-round photo exhibition **Hamlet on Location** pays tribute to actors to have played Hamlet here at Kronborg—including Laurence Olivier, Derek Jacobi, and Jude Law.

Tours and Practical Details

Crowds at the castle increase on weekends and during the summer, as well as during the middle of the day. Timing your visit to include the last hour before closing is a good way to enjoy a relatively deserted Kronborg. This is a great time to get a clear view at the top of the Cannon Tower and maximize the spookiness of the Casemates.

There are two main **daily tours** included in the price of Kronborg

Holger Danske

admission: **Kronborg in Brief,** which focuses on the castle and its history, and **Hamlet's Castle,** which revolves around *Hamlet*. These can't be booked in advance but are frequent and easy to find: Look for information on the blackboard in the courtyard or find a tour guide; they will be holding a "Guide" sign.

These two tours are sometimes offered as short versions that cut the tour length from 45 minutes down to around 15. These provide a concise overview of themes and exhibitions before leaving you for more immersion on your own. Occasionally, **themed tours** like Secrets of Kronborg and Kronborg Queens are also available. These are less frequent, and you are more likely to find them offered during off-peak periods.

For an additional cost, four different **guided tours in English** are available at Kronborg. The tours are around 60 minutes in duration and cost 975 kr. For an additional 2,000 kr, you may be able to arrange a visit outside regular hours, giving you the chance to feel like you have the expanses of the stone wall and ancient chamber all to yourself. Reservation requests for these tours should be made well in advance (tel. 49 21 30 78; email kronborg@natmus.dk). In your request, include details such as your name, contact details, date and time of your visit, and the number of participants, and specify you want the tour to be in English.

While **private guided tours** are generally similar in theme to the daily open version, they go farther than the regular tours. For example, the **Hamlet's Castle Tour** involves diversions into hidden nooks and crannies, and the guide lets you into locked rooms;

Experiencing *Hamlet*

inside Kronborg Castle

Shakespeare's longest play is inextricably connected to Kronborg, the castle at which it is set, even though the Bard himself never visited Denmark and set the play based on his formidable imagination. Many spots at the castle are referenced in the play, and these can be found if you look around (and use your own imagination a little):

- On the castle **ramparts,** Prince Hamlet gets a shock when he meets the ghost of his dead father. You can evoke this scene without having to go into the castle itself, as Kronborg's ramparts are outside the castle wall.

- In Act III, Hamlet and Gertrude's showdown takes place in the **Queen's Chamber,** located within the **King's Apartment** in the real castle, while Polonius listens in from behind a **tapestry.**

- In the **chapel,** in front of the altar, Claudius surrenders and admits to murdering the king.

- The dramatic climax in Act V Scene II was set by Shakespeare at "a hall in the castle": For this, see Kronborg's **grand ballroom,** located within the castle's royal quarters.

You can also partake in a daily castle tour that follows the footsteps of Hamlet, Claudius, Ophelia, Laertes, and company: **Hamlet's Castle.** The tour is included in the ticket price and takes place in English several times a day, with shorter and longer versions available. The exact times of tours vary seasonally—check the chalkboard in the courtyard when you arrive at the castle, or find a host with a "Guide" sign.

the **Kronborg Queens** tour takes in private chambers and intrigue-driven myths about the powerful women of Kronborg through the centuries. If you take the **Secrets of Kronborg** tour, you can expect to go into cellars, up towers, and on ancient staircases. The fourth private tour, **All About Kronborg**, is a comprehensive trip through the history of the fortress, built around the story of King Frederik II and Queen Sophie, whose chambers are part of the tour.

It should be noted that these tours are offered year-round, and form the program at the time of writing, but they are subject to change. Check the museum's website for upcoming events, as plenty is on offer during seasonal peak times, including afternoon tea, Christmas concerts, and spooky storytelling in the dark after closing time.

There is no restaurant or café within the castle but several just outside the entrance and near the ticket office. There's also a lunch room inside the castle where packed lunches can be eaten. If you're lucky, the weather might be nice enough to use the picnic area outside. Bring a bottle of water if you visit during the summer. Tickets can be purchased on arrival: Look for the last of the orange brick buildings in the barracks area outside the castle, then turn the corner and head toward the bridge at the entry gate. You can also purchase tickets in advance via the Kronborg website, which accepts major credit cards. If you have the Copenhagen Card from your stay in the capital, it can be used for entry here at no additional cost.

○ M/S MARITIME MUSEUM OF DENMARK

Ny Kronborgvej 1; tel. 49 21 06 85; https:// mfs.dk; Sept.-June Tues.-Sun. 11am-5pm, July-Aug. daily 11am-6pm; adults 135 kr, students 100 kr, under age 18 free

From a distance it's almost invisible, but get up close and you can see right down into the depths of the M/S Maritime Museum of Denmark in its 19th-century converted dry dock. The museum is simultaneously an architectural marvel and a fine telling of Denmark on the waves through the centuries. It was designed by the famed Bjarke Ingels architectural firm and opened in 2013. From the outside, it takes a moment or two to realize the museum is actually a museum, given its appearance as a giant rectangle cut into the concrete of the docks, with glass down its sides and an angular staircase sinking into its depths. Inside, the focus is less traditional than it might be at other maritime museums, with fewer models of ships (although these are by no means absent) and more emphasis on telling the stories of Danish and international mariners. Presentation is also untraditional, with lighting, coloring, and display cases made to feel like parts of a ship or the sea itself.

Quirkier exhibitions include a buoy back-illuminated in a way that makes it look like a disco light and a range of figureheads fixed to the wall like an array of ornaments. Models range from a giant Maersk container ship to a huge display of ships in bottles and other scale miniatures that opened in 2023.

There are several engaging permanent exhibitions with topics that include the sailor's life experience, complete with a mock-up of port temptations, tattoos, hostels, and seafarer's churches; globalization; technology and navigation; and the evolution of ship design. Look for BIG Dock, the story behind the choice of the old Helsingør dry dock as the museum's location and insight into Ingels' architectural thought process, complete with before and after images and scale models.

The museum is relatively compact and can therefore be combined with a day visit to Kronborg. Some of the exhibits are interactive. Guided tours can be arranged at least three weeks in advance: Contact booking@mfs.dk for prices, information, and reservations.

Not far from the entrance (the staircase down) to the Maritime Museum, you can find the sculpture *HAN*—a male version of Copenhagen's *Little Mermaid* statue, echoing the original's size, style, and demeanor. Walk across the harbor area near the museum entrance to the end of the jetty.

DANISH MUSEUM OF SCIENCE AND TECHNOLOGY

Fabriksvej 25; tel. 49 22 26 11; https://tekniskmuseum.dk; Tues.-Sun. 10am-5pm; adults 110 kr, under age 18 free

It looks incredibly unspectacular from the outside, but don't let the gray cardboard factory-warehouse look mislead you: Inside it's like an aircraft hangar full of transportation, technology, and other fascinating objects from the 20th century. With a self-confessed "childlike fascination" with machinery, function, and mechanics, Helsingør's Danish Museum of Science and Technology takes pride in everything from engines to aircraft to 25-year-old cell phones, which are as antiquated to today's teenagers as a Model T Ford. A spectacular model railway, crafted lovingly by local enthusiasts and filling an entire exhibition room, showcases the history of train travel in Denmark until the 1960s, depicting the Roskilde-Copenhagen line along with windmills, a hot-air balloon, and early-20th-century factories, with lighting in the room alternating between night and day. This is only one example of the visual enjoyment on offer, and there's plenty of interactive fun too.

The Gaming exhibition offers the chance to try classic early 1980s arcade games like *Space Invaders* and *Pac-Man*. You can also learn about AI, space travel, black and green energy, early aviation, and, appropriately for Denmark, the history of the bicycle. There are vintage bicycles alongside fire engines, cars, and all sorts of aircraft, from old prop planes to wrecked fuselage to an old Danish Air Lines craft, which you can enter and sit in the cabin. The museum is hands-on—there are signs saying which buttons and levers you can try out at the exhibits. There's no heating in the hangar, so it can get cold in winter.

HELSINGØR'S OLD TOWN

Sudergade-Strandgade, Sophie Brahesgade-Stjernegade

Helsingør boasts a well-preserved historical center spanning a small area three by four blocks no more than 1-2 km (0.6-1.2 mi) from the harbor. The streets of Stengade, Skt. Olaigade, and Sudergade, which run roughly east to west, are crossed by Sophie Brahesgade, Skt. Annagade, Bjergegade, and Stjernegade in a somewhat north-south direction. The street plan is thought to be the work of King Eric of Pomerania, who also built the original structure of Kronborg in the 14th century. Only one older building, the 13th-century **St. Olaf Cathedral,** breaks this surprisingly regular pattern.

The names of the streets carry their own stories about the town's history: **Stengade (Stone Street)** was the well-to-do quarter where the first stone houses were built, and **Sudergade** was the shoemaker's street; the word suder is

St. Olaf Cathedral

not from Danish but is the Low German word for shoe.

One block south of Stengade, **Strandgade (Beach Street)** is nearer the coast and was built at some point after the original old town. Streets connecting these two parallel roads include **Gl. Færgestræde (Old Ferry Passage)** and **Brostræde (Bridge Passage).** Narrow Gl. Færgestræde is perhaps the most atmospheric in old-town Helsingør, its cobbled stones still laid out the way they were in the Middle Ages, uneven enough to force you to tread carefully. The buildings, painted dark yellow-orange in their wooden frames, feel high and enclose each side of the narrow passageway. It's almost enough to make you think someone is about to empty a chamber pot from one of the windows directly above. The open gutter (not in use) that runs down the middle of the street does little to shatter this illusion. This street is so narrow that it's easy to miss: Look for it on the left as you walk along Stengade from the harbor end of town. You'll see the entrance and an old sign painted into the wall reading "Gl. Færgestræde" shortly before you reach the city hall.

Elsewhere around the old town, **old merchant's houses** retain handsome wooden carvings on their colorful facades, and backyards and alleys feel untouched by modernity. **Stengade** is a testament to Helsingør's former position as a strategic location for shipping trade routes, with a number of surviving Renaissance-period houses that bear the influence of the international craftspeople likely to have been involved in construction of Kronborg. Now the town's main shopping street, Stengade also has its share of modern and functional architecture, but there are also older buildings, like the baroque Stengade 64, dating to 1739, a few meters from Færgestræde. If you have time, explore the surrounding streets for further glimpses of old Helsingør.

ST. OLAF CATHEDRAL
(Skt. Olai Kirke)

Sct. Anna Gade 12; tel. 40 18 68 14; www. helsingoerdomkirke.dk; May-Aug. daily 10am-4pm, Sept.-Apr. daily 10am-2pm; free

The oldest building in the city, St. Olaf Cathedral dates originally from the 13th century; the present building was completed in 1559. Remains of the original church's decorations can be seen on the interior north wall. A classic redbrick church with a tall copper spire, it sits at the southeastern corner of the old city between Stengade and Skt. Olufgade, making it an ideal component of a wander around old Helsingør. Its design has both Gothic and baroque elements. Inside, there's a 16th-century fresco in one of the nave vaults, which are otherwise whitewashed. The interior is quite beautifully decorated, with ornate chandeliers depicting St. Olaf—the Norwegian king and saint for whom the church is named—and alabaster altarpieces.

VÆRFTSMUSEET
(The Shipyard Museum)

Allégade 4; tel. 49 28 18 00; https://helsingormuseer.dk/vaerftsmuseet; Mon.-Fri. 10am-5pm, Sat.-Sun. 11am-4pm; free

The clash of metal on metal and the glare of welding torches are part of the heritage of the former Helsingør Shipyard, located on the corner of the harbor, and the Shipyard Museum tells the story of the more than 400 cargo ships, ferries, and frigates that were constructed at the site from the late 19th century until it closed in 1983.

There are two exhibitions related to shipbuilding, including one where visitors can learn about the craft of constructing seaworthy vessels and even attempt some of the metalwork methods, such as stamping their name onto a metal sheet. You can also inspect a re-creation of the boardroom and may be able to speak to a former worker, who will be able to give insight into the shipyard's huge importance to the town as its biggest employer for many years. Display information in English is limited. Private tours may be possible (60-90 minutes; 950 kr) by sending an inquiry to frehe@helsingor.dk.

Entertainment and Events

THE ARTS
✪ **Hamletscenen**

Kronborg 13 and 16; tel. 70 20 20 96; https://hamletscenen.dk; individual plays 260-360 kr including fees

"Denmark's Shakespeare theater" Hamletscenen couldn't have a more apt setting with Kronborg Castle rising behind it. It's open year-round, with a specially built outdoor stage for summer and indoor Thalia Hall for when it's colder. You can take in classic Shakespeare plays besides *Hamlet*, along with modern retellings and Shakespeare-adjacent productions. The program for 2023 included *The Tempest, Othello,* and *King Lear* as well as a reimagining of *The Merchant of Venice* and a play about an aging actor who is offered the role of Hamlet. Be sure to check whether the play is in English or Danish before you book. Subtitles may be offered in some cases.

Every year in August, Hamletscenen host the Elsinore Shakespeare Festival, bringing *Hamlet* and other Shakespeare plays staged by acclaimed theater companies and production artists to a specially built open-air theater near Kronborg Castle. A unification of art, cultural heritage, and nature, these plays are given unique character by the Danish outdoor elements and the cawing of seagulls. With a stunning backdrop of the moat and castle walls, things can't get much more atmospheric.

production of *Hamlet* at Elsinore Shakespeare Festival

Plays are performed in the evening, so bring warm waterproof clothes: Even though it's summer, it can be chilly and wet. The theater has its own bar (from 6pm daily). During intermission, you'll be able to buy drinks and snacks. You can also preorder a picnic, which can be collected from the nearby Culture Yard two hours before the performance and enjoyed outdoors with views of the castle, the sea, and the stage (bring your own blanket). Picnics must be preordered 24 hours in advance. If you don't opt for the picnic, eat before you arrive.

The festival program and ticket prices are generally announced in spring, with tickets on sale by May.

The Culture Yard
(Kulturværftet)

Allégade 2; tel. 49 28 36 20; https://kuto. dk; Mon. 10am-6pm, Tues.-Wed. 10am-7pm, Thurs. 10am-8pm, Fri. 10am-6pm, Sat. 10am-4pm, Sun. 11am-4pm, hours may vary during holidays, events, and concerts; ticket prices vary

The Culture Yard is a cultural house located on the shipyard, a mishmash of glass and brick almost equidistant from the Kronborg and St. Olaf spires. Bright colorful reading rooms on the upper floors have great views of the castle and the bay. The café, **Spisehuset**

The Culture Yard

(Mon.-Fri. 10am-7pm, Sat.-Sun. 10am-5pm) has warm and cold dishes like a pancake and sausage brunch or smørrebrød as well as a variety of snacks and cakes. In summer, there's an ice cream cart outside on the harbor. A library and resource center by day, the 13,000-sq-m (140,000-sq-ft) facility hosts hundreds of events annually, including theater, concerts, comedy, crafts workshops, a literature festival, seasonal events like New Year's celebrations, and special film showings. There are two concert halls, and some events take place on the harbor front. Check the website to see what's happening and to buy tickets.

Kronborg Galleries

Kronborg; www.kronborggallerierne.dk; individual galleries listed in the brochure on the website

The Kronborg Galleries are a series of creative spaces located in the former barracks buildings around the castle perimeter. They are often open to the public (look for raised banners outside the entrances) and include shops and arts and crafts workshops featuring a range of specialties, including glass, jewelry, ceramics, photography, and painting.

Dining and Accommodations

✪ Elsinore Street Food/ Værftets Madmarked

Ny Kronborgvej 2; tel. 49 20 02 01; www. vaerftetsmadmarked.dk; daily 11am-8pm; entrées from 70 kr

Opened in 2017 with the aim of bringing locals and visitors together in a public space attractive to all, Elsinore Street Food is a scaled-down version of the larger street food markets of Copenhagen but with the same sense of choice and accessibility. About a dozen stalls have set up in the high-roofed surroundings of the former Elsinore Shipyard—bits of boat and netting hang from the ceiling to add to the maritime feel. It's a great place to go for an easy and budget-friendly meal and a drink, and options include Argentinian steak sandwiches, tandoori, ramen, Moroccan tagine, Syrian mezze, and gastro burgers—or you could stick with the shipyard theme and grab a portion of fish-and-chips.

Kadetten

Kronborg 10A; tel. 42 90 10 11; https:// kadetten.dk; Tues.-Fri. 10am-3pm; open-face sandwich from 85 kr, brunch 150 kr

A second lieutenants training school just outside the castle and within the outer entrance in the Kronværksbyen barracks area, Kadetten is an organic café and socially responsible business that harvests many of its ingredients from the gardens of military buildings. A particular source of pride at the café, which aims to provide jobs to people with special social needs, is its homemade rye bread made in the style of the rations given to cadets studying at the school in times past. Other classic menu items include herring, potato, salmon, and pesto madder (open-face rye bread sandwiches).

Café Chaplin

Kampergade 3; tel. 30 53 54 56; www. cafechaplin.dk; Mon.-Fri. 10am-3pm; brunch buffet 185 kr

It's only open on weekdays, but if you're in town at the right time, Café Chaplin serves a solid inexpensive brunch-lunch buffet and will help you fuel up for a full day of sightseeing. The buffet is stocked with favorites of the Danish café brunch genre: bacon, scrambled eggs, cocktail sausages, pâté, herring, salmon, and various cheeses with fresh rye and sourdough bread baked on-site. It has a handy location on the corner of the Axeltorv square at the edge of the old town, along with widely praised service.

✪ Danhostel Helsingør

Ndr. Strandvej 24; tel. 49 28 49 49; www. danhostelhelsingor.dk; shared room from 225 kr, private room from 395 kr

Located by the sea with a beach at the end of the grounds, this extensive hostel is a preferred location of large school groups as well as independent and older travelers—so there may be noise at times. It's in spacious and welcoming surroundings with a large main building and several outbuildings. It's a short bicycle ride (bicycles can be rented from the hostel) from Kronborg. Breakfast is available, and there is free coffee for guests.

Marienlyst Strandhotel

Ndr. Strandvej 2; tel. 49 21 40 00; www. marienlyst.dk; high season from 1,493 kr d

This sprawling seaside hotel a stone's throw from Kronborg was built in 1861 and in its early years was a favorite summer destination among the nobility of Copenhagen, Denmark, and farther afield. According to its own legend, Denmark's King Christian IX summered in room 15 while the Tsar of Russia ate lunch in the restaurant during its 19th-century heyday. There's still plenty of evidence of its exclusive past, but its whitewashed walls and wooden balconies are perhaps the features that give it its overriding charm. There is a range of room options, including some with great sea views. There's a spa, three restaurants, a casino, and a small gallery on-site.

Tourist Information

Local tourism organizations **Visit Nordsjælland** and **Helsingør Turistbureau** have a self-service tourist information center inside **The Culture Yard** (Allégade 2; tel. 49 28 28 28; www.visit-helsingoer. dk; Mon.-Fri. 10am-9pm, Sat.-Sun. 10am-5pm), where information and brochures can be picked up for Kronborg, the Maritime Museum, and other events and attractions. Maps and free Wi-Fi are also available.

Getting There and Around

GETTING THERE
By Public Transit
Direct trains leave from Copenhagen Central Station to **Helsingør Station** (Stationspladsen 2, Helsingør; 88 kr, Rejsekrot 57 kr) three times per hour during the day. Discount tickets can sometimes be found on DSB's website for as little as 37 kr. The journey takes 46 minutes, and Helsingør Station is an easy 10-15-minute walk from both the historical part of Helsingør and from Kronborg. Check https:// dsb.dk or https://rejseplanen.dk for departure times. The Rejsekort travel card can be used to pay for the journey, provided you have enough credit. Replacement buses sometimes take over rail services on weekends, which result in longer and more crowded journeys. If replacement buses are operating, you will be diverted to them directly from train departure points.

By Car
Leave central Copenhagen on the main street Tagensvej, which runs between the Østerbro and Nørrebro districts. Keep right and turn onto Nørre Allé just after you pass the hospital, Rigshospitalet. At the Vibenshus Runddel junction (there is also a Metro station here), go straight and slightly left onto Lyngbyvej, which then becomes Route 19 heading north out of Copenhagen. From here, continue north until you are outside the city, at which point it will be possible to follow signs to Helsingør. Route 19 merges with the E47 highway. As you reach Helsingør, follow Kongevejen into town and stay right to continue onto Jernbanevej. This will take you to the old town and harbor area, where you will be able to park close to Kronborg and the surrounding attractions, or the old town if this is your first destination. The Museum of Science and Technology has its own car park.

The journey is approximately 50 km (30 mi) and should take around 40 minutes.

GETTING AROUND

Kronborg, the Maritime Museum, Helsingør Old Town, and Helsingør Station are all within a 10-15-minute walk of each other. To get to the **Danish Museum of Science and Technology,** take local rail service from Helsingør Station to nearby Snekkersten Station, where bus 803 goes directly to the museum, which has its own bus stop (18 minutes; 24 kr). You can also walk there by heading away from the castle, past the station, and toward the outskirts of town on Kongevej for around 3.5 km (2 mi) until you meet a large traffic circle with the O3 circular road. Take the first road on the right, then the second left onto Fabriksvej. The museum is around 500 m (0.3 mi) ahead on the left side. It will take around 1 hour to walk.

Roskilde

Only 20 minutes from Copenhagen, Viking capital Roskilde can lay claim to being the most historically significant city in Denmark. This is embodied by the town's two major attractions: the Viking Ship Museum, where an impressive set of preserved longboats overlooks the Roskilde Fjord, and the towering Roskilde Cathedral, where royal tombs spanning centuries are testament to the longevity of Denmark's royal family.

The town sits at the southern point of the

Highlights

⭐ **Viking Ship Museum:** Five Viking longboats recovered from the waters of the Roskilde fjord and painstakingly restored are the centerpieces of the story of Viking Scandinavia told at this museum (page 214).

⭐ **Roskilde Cathedral:** This brick Gothic church, the final resting place for centuries of Denmark's monarchs, exudes authority over the city's skyline (page 215).

⭐ **Roskilde Festival:** Attend this annual music festival, the largest of its kind in Northern Europe, for the big headliners, all-hours parties, and an all-around head-spinning experience (page 219).

Roskilde Fjord, a 41-km-long (25-mi) waterway that is an offshoot of the larger Isefjord, with the neighboring fjords turning a large part of the map of Zealand blue. These waters are intrinsically connected to the Viking past and the discovery of the ancient longboats, which are meticulously preserved and displayed at the ship museum. The fjord has a peaceful air: Motorized boats are not allowed in the bay due to its status as a nature reserve. The flat reedy banks and calm shores allow you to look far into the distance on a clear day.

Back in town, Roskilde has nothing of the pretense you might expect for a city boasting an enormous cathedral, dozens of buried monarchs, and the title of former capital. It's small enough to visit all the major sights in one day with time to spare, and it is uncomplicated and rewarding. The central shopping streets are a little tired and generic looking, but you'll probably be too busy looking at the cathedral to notice.

If you're here around the beginning of July, expect the downtown area to resemble a Scandinavian *Mad Max,* as the Roskilde Festival, Northern Europe's largest music festival, takes over a huge green area neighboring the town. If you don't have a ticket, it might not be the best time to come. If you decide

---

Previous: the towers of the Roskilde Cathedral. **Above:** Roskilde Cathedral; the Viking Ship Museum.

to brave it, be prepared for a messy city center.

ORIENTATION

Roskilde Station is south of the city center. The town is compact, and bearing north from the station will inevitably take you to, or very close to, Roskilde Cathedral and the City Park (Byparken) on your way to the fjord. From the station, cross Hestetorvet square and walk along the narrow Store Gråbrødrestræde and Lille Gråbrødrestræde, or take the more direct Hersegade north from the station to arrive at Algade, a pedestrian main street that runs east-west across the city center. At the western end is Stændertorvet, a large market square with the very noticeable spires of Roskilde Cathedral rising at the northern edge. Directly north of the cathedral, the sloping Byparken, which has tree-sheltered paths and open grassy areas, leads down to the fjord. Roskilde Harbor and the Viking Ship Museum are located on the southern shore of the fjord, at the edge of the town. It's less than 2 km (1.2 mi) and about a 20-minute walk from the station to the museum.

PLANNING YOUR TIME

It makes sense to spend a full day in Roskilde, split between a half-day at the Viking Ship Museum and the harbor area and half in the city, with around two hours devoted to the cathedral. This allows time to spare to see other peripheral sights. A half-day visit including both the Ship Museum and the cathedral is doable but would entail a tight schedule. Traveling times from Copenhagen are very short, making a visit easy to plan. Overnight stays are not essential if you have lodging back in the capital.

Itinerary Idea

. . . .

ESSENTIAL ROSKILDE

Did the Vikings really have undercut hairstyles and tattoos? Was Harald Bluetooth, King of Denmark and Norway, really buried at Roskilde Cathedral? Find out on a day trip to Denmark's Viking capital.

1 After arriving on an early train from Copenhagen, stop into **Kaffekilden** for a coffee and bread roll.

2 Head first to the **Roskilde Cathedral,** a UNESCO World Heritage Site that is almost impossible to miss as you wander through the city, given its sheer size relative to everything else around it.

3 After an hour or two of touring the crypts, nooks, and crannies

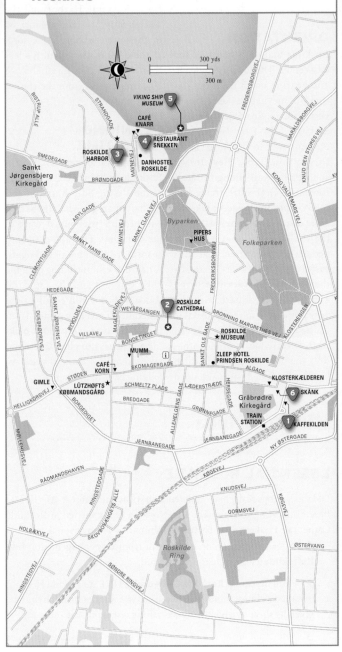

Roskilde

0   300 yds

0   300 m

VIKING SHIP MUSEUM **5**

CAFÉ KNARR

RESTAURANT SNEKKEN **4**

ROSKILDE HARBOR **3**

DANHOSTEL ROSKILDE

Sankt Jørgensbjerg Kirkegård

STRANDGADE

BISTRUP ALLÉ

SMEDEGADE

HAVNEVEJ

BRØNDGADE

SANKT CLARA VEJ

FREDERIKSBORGVEJ

HARALDSBORGVEJ

KNUD DEN STORES VEJ

KONG VALDEMARS VEJ

Byparken

Folkeparken

PIPERS HUS

ASYLGADE

SANKT HANS GADE

CLEMONTGADE

HEDEGADE

SANKT JØRGENS VEJ

DUEBRØDREVEJ

VILLAVEJ

BYVOLDEN

MAGLEKILDEVEJ

WEYSEGANGEN

FREDERIKSBORGVEJ

DRONNING MARGRETHES VEJ

KLOSTERENGEN

ROSKILDE CATHEDRAL **2**

BONDETINGET

MUMM

CAFÉ KORN

SKOMAGERGADE

SANKT OLS GADE

ROSKILDE MUSEUM

ZLEEP HOTEL PRINDSEN ROSKILDE

ALGADE

KLOSTERKÆLDEREN

SKÄNK **6**

GIMLE

STØDEN

LÜTZHØFTS KØBMANDSGÅRD

SCHMELTZ PLADS

BREDGADE

LÆDERSTRÆDE

ALLEHELGENS GADE

GRØNNEGADE

HERSEGADE

Gråbrødre Kirkegård

TRAIN STATION

KAFFEKILDEN **1**

HELLIGKORSVEJ

BORGEDIGET

JERNBANEGADE

JERNBANEGADE

NY ØSTERGADE

MØLLEHUSVEJ

RÅDMANDSHAVEN

RINGSTEDGADE

SKOVBOULANGENS ALLE

KØGEVEJ

KNUDSVEJ

GORMSVEJ

KØGEVEJ

HOLBÆKVEJ

SØNDRE RINGVEJ

Roskilde Ring

RINGSTEDVEJ

ØSTERVANG

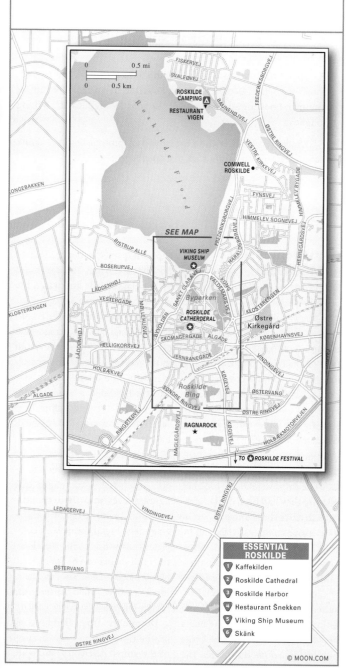

0   0.5 mi

0   0.5 km

FISKERVEJ

SVALEVEJ

ROSKILDE CAMPING

RESTAURANT VIGEN

BAUNEHØJVEJ

FREDERIKSBORGVEJ

VESTRE KIRKEVEJ

ØSTRE RINGVEJ

COMWELL ROSKILDE

FYNSVEJ

HIMMELEV BYGADE

HERREGÅRDSVEJ

HIMMELEV SOGNEVEJ

FREDERIKSBORGVEJ

Roskilde Fjord

LONGEBAKKEN

BISTRUP ALLÉ

BOSERUPVEJ

LADDENHØJ

VESTERGADE

KLOSTERENGEN

TØHUSVEJ

LADDENHØJ

HELLIGKORSVEJ

HOLBÆKVEJ

ALGADE

SEE MAP

VIKING SHIP MUSEUM

SANKT OLAVSVEJ

MØLLEHUSVEJ

BYVOLDEN

Byparken

ROSKILDE CATHERDERAL

SKOMAGERGADE   ALGADE

JERNBANEGADE

Roskilde Ring

SØNDRE RINGVEJ

RINGSTEDVEJ

MAGLEGÅRDSVEJ

RAGNAROCK

KONG VALDEMARSVEJ

HARALDSBORGVEJ

KLOSTERENGEN

Østre Kirkegård

KØBENHAVNSVEJ

VINDINGEVEJ

KØGEVEJ

ØSTERVANG

KØGEVEJ

ØSTRE RINGVEJ

HOLBÆKMOTORVEJEN

↓ TO ⭐ROSKILDE FESTIVAL

LEDAGERVEJ

VINDINGEVEJ

ØSTRE RINGVEJ

ØSTERVANG

ØSTRE RINGVEJ

ESSENTIAL ROSKILDE

1 Kaffekilden
2 Roskilde Cathedral
3 Roskilde Harbor
4 Restaurant Snekken
5 Viking Ship Museum
6 Skänk

© MOON.COM

of the cathedral, head to **Roskilde Harbor** for a brisk stroll and great views of the Roskilde Fjord.

4 For lunch, pop into **Restaurant Snekken** by the harbor. Sit outside if the weather is nice.

5 Spend the afternoon at the **Viking Ship Museum,** the second-most-important site on a trip to Roskilde. If you're here during summer, book ahead for a tour of the fjord in a replica of a Viking longboat.

6 Unwind with a beer and a cheese and charcuterie board at **Skänk** before hopping on a train back to Copenhagen.

Sights

✪ VIKING SHIP MUSEUM

Vindeboder 12; tel. 46 30 02 00; www. vikingeskibsmuseet.dk; May-Oct. daily 10am-5pm, last week of Oct.-Apr. daily 10am-4pm; adults 125-160 kr, depending on the season, under age 18 free

In 1962 the remains of five Viking longboats were discovered in a channel at the bottom of Roskilde Fjord. The discovery was hugely significant for the study of the seafaring ways of the Vikings, a warrior-farmer people who lived during approximately 800-1000 CE. The ships were found together because they had been deliberately sunk to block the channel as part of a defensive strategy carried out by Roskilde's Viking-era inhabitants.

The discovery led to a painstaking recovery and preservation process that took decades and resulted in the opening of the Viking Ship Museum in 1969. The boats are displayed together in a large exhibition room built over the shoreline, on the beach next to Roskilde's Harbor. You can stand by the glass facade and watch the waters lap the shore beneath your feet as you pause next to the reconstructed longboats, allowing you to get close enough to see the detail in the Viking shipwrights' craftsmanship. The boats vary in size and type, related to their different purposes—two warships, two cargo ships, and one fishing boat. Ranging in length 3.8-17.3 m (12.5-57 ft), the boats look skeletal—their surviving pieces have been recovered, restored, and rebuilt like jigsaw pieces into their original positions in the hulls of the five longboats. Metal framework completes the outline of the vessels, so their full shapes can be appreciated where pieces of the wooden structures have been lost to the centuries spent underwater.

Despite its atmospheric setting on the fjord close to the location of the ships' discovery, there are only a few years left to enjoy the museum in its current form. The existing building is threatened by climate change, particularly storm surges that cause the fjord's water levels to rise. Meanwhile, the large amount of light allowed in by the windows is slowly breaking down the ancient wooden beams. A new improved museum is planned to open in 2030.

The museum has more to offer than just the boats. The basement has a large space for rotating displays, while there are also permanent exhibitions setting out the history, trade, seafaring practices, and culture of the Vikings. Visitors can try on Viking period clothing, and there is a small activity area for kids.

It's also possible to take **sailing trips** on the fjord during the summer months, May-September. Tickets for the one-hour trips (130 kr) in traditional Nordic sail boats—descendants of the museum's Viking longboats—can be bought at the museum's ticket office, where a timetable for the trips can also be seen. Safety equipment and a briefing are included. The sailing trips are part of a number of outdoor activities offered at the museum in summer, which also include daily guided tours and a "living" Viking shipyard where period shipbuilding techniques are on display.

Free guided tours of the museum are offered daily in summer and occasionally at other times of the year, such as during the school year and

Christmas holidays. Conducted by history and archaeology students, the 50-minute tours, which can't be booked in advance, detail the life and use of the ships and what their discovery tells us about Viking maritime culture. Call ahead or check at the museum's information desk for the tour schedule on the day of your visit.

✪ ROSKILDE CATHEDRAL

Domkirkestræde 10; tel. 46 35 16 24; www. roskildedomkirke.dk; Mon.-Sat. 10am-4pm, selected days until 6pm, Sun. 1pm-4pm, hours change with church functions; adults 70 kr, students and seniors 50 kr, under age 18 free, free with Copenhagen Card

Roskilde Cathedral

Surrounded by quiet cobbled streets and historical houses, Roskilde Cathedral's three spires tower over the city's modest skyline and are difficult for observers on the Cathedral Square to fit into a photo frame. But it's only

sarcophagus of Queen Margrethe I in Roskilde Cathedral

inside—walking through the various crypts, vaults, and staircases, and coming face-to-face with the sarcophagi of Denmark's monarchic past—that the importance of the cathedral really becomes apparent.

A church was first built at this location by Harald Bluetooth, a former King of Denmark and Norway who died around 985 CE. According to medieval chronicler Adam of Bremen, Harald was "buried in the town of Roskilde, in the church he himself built to the honor of the Holy Trinity." No traces of Harald's wooden church have ever been found. The structure that stands today was begun in the 1170s, shortly after the advent of brickmaking in Denmark. Although the body of the building was completed around a century later, chapels and extensions have been added throughout the years,

leaving an array of styles within, including neoclassical, Romanesque, and Byzantine.

The cathedral has been the main burial site for Danish monarchs since the 15th century. This makes walking through the crypts and chapels a history lesson in itself, given the tidbits of information about the monarchs that are on display throughout in both Danish and English, and the evolving styles of the coffins. Look for the statues at Christian IX's sarcophagus, known as "The Little Mermaid's Sisters"—they were sculpted by the same artist, Edvard Eriksen.

There is plenty more to see and admire: The nave and the chapel have their own stories to tell, and there is a museum high up within the upper-floor galleries. Here the cathedral's history over its 1,000-year lifespan is told through items that include a copy of Queen

Margrethe I's golden dress and photographs of the devastating 1968 fire that destroyed one of the spires. Most of the information here is in Danish. There is also a scale model of the cathedral from 1730, reproducing the church as it was at the time.

Be sure to look up before leaving: Above the right side of the entrance you'll see the mechanical clock, dating to around 1500, responsible for the hourly chiming of the cathedral bells.

The cathedral has regular open hours, but check the website or call to make sure it's open before setting out. It is still used for services and religious ceremonies and can sometimes be closed to visitors.

One-hour private guided tours (800 kr) of the cathedral, titled "1000 Years in One Hour," must be booked at least a month in advance by emailing the cathedral (post@roskildedomkirke.dk). Include your name, a phone number, preferred time and date for the tour, and the number of participants. You should also request the tour in English; Spanish and German may also be available, as is Danish.

ROSKILDE MUSEUM

Sankt Ols Stræde 3; tel. 46 31 65 00; www. roskildemuseum.dk; June-Sept. daily 10am-4pm; Oct.-May Tues.-Sun. 10am-4pm; adults 60 kr, under age 18 free, included in Copenhagen Card

Roskilde's city museum is in the center of town in two adjoining registered historical buildings, a former sugar refinery and a former merchant's house. The history of the town in the museum takes in its golden age as a center of religion and learning, the subsequent decline after the bishopric was moved to Copenhagen, and the 20th-century history of Roskilde and today's status as a market town near the capital. Archaeological objects and newer exhibits tell the story, organized across three floors, with a natural history section on the ground floor, a Middle Ages section in the middle, and a look at the modern town of Roskilde on the top floor. There is also a section for children as well as rotating exhibitions, which in 2023 spanned subjects like recycling and Viking burial grounds. Information is provided in Danish and English.

LÜTZHØFTS KØBMANDSGÅRD

Ringstedgade 6-8; tel. 46 35 00 61; https:// lützhøftskøbmandsgård.dk; mid-June-Aug. Thurs.-Fri. 11am-5pm, Sat. 10am-2pm, Sept.-mid-June Wed.-Fri. noon-4pm, Sat. 10am-2pm; free

A cross between a museum and a shop, this old-fashioned købmand (grocery store) has all sorts of delights on display: yo-yos and licorice, shoe brushes and watering cans. The goods are packed into jars and baskets and stacked on shelves. Visitors are welcome to look behind the counter and go through to the office in back, where stocks of goods are piled up in storage. Be sure to take a look in the yard behind the store, an extension to the museum where, on the upper floor of the old grain ware-house, you can see a collection of crafts from the hands of carpenters, furniture makers, wood sculptors, and clog makers; a textile shop fills the ground floor.

ROSKILDE HARBOR

Strandgade 2; www.roskildehavn.dk; free

Next to the Viking Ship Museum, the small pleasant harbor area is a popular place for locals to take a walk and stop for ice cream. There are plenty of benches to enjoy the view of **Roskilde Fjord,** a 41-km-long (25-mi) protected body of water that's home to a variety of birds and plant life. The Restaurant Snekken and Café Knarr are nearby if you're feeling hungry. A nice way to head back to the city center is via Kirkegade, a picturesque street with thatched cottages.

RAGNAROCK

Rabalderstræde 16; tel. 46 31 68 54; https://museumragnarock.dk; Tues. 10am-5pm, Wed. 10am-10pm, Thurs.-Sun. 10am-5pm; adults 110 kr, under age 18 free

A golden inverted L-shaped build-ing with a lipstick-red foyer that looks like it should be the home of some megalomaniac glam rocker, Ragnarock is an ode to all things musical, adding a splash of variety to the primarily nautical, religious, and historical themes of most visits to Roskilde (unless you're here for the Roskilde Festival, in which case music will of course be the focus).

The interactive exhibitions take visitors on a trip through

Lützhøfts Købmandsgård grocery store and museum

the history of modern youth culture, with themes of fan culture, the emergence of different genres, and the relationship between music and dance. You can sample historical music through dozens of headphones attached to a wall and try your skills as a light or sound mixer. You can even take a ride on a giant record player. Elsewhere, the Fanboys and Fangirls exhibition looks at the influence of superstar acts on young fans, tracing the phenomenon back to the Beatles. There are many references to Danish music history, but the spirit of the museum will resonate with music lovers from anywhere. A good portion of the information is available in English.

Recreation

PARKS
Byparken
Byparken; free

Byparken stretches downhill between the cathedral and the harbor. It makes for a pleasant outing regardless of the season: There are great views of the fjord among the ponds, treelined paths, and moments of contemplation amid the trickling sound of the streams that run through it. A thatched cottage, **Pipers Hus** (tel. 46 36 56 96; https://pipershus.dk; Mon.-Fri. 11am-10pm, Sat. 10am-10pm, Sun. 10am-5pm), serves food throughout the day, and nearby is a large grassy slope occasionally used for free summer concerts as well as Skt. Hans celebrations.

Festivals and Events

✪ ROSKILDE FESTIVAL
Darupvej 19; tel. 46 36 66 13; www.roskilde-festival.dk; last week in June-first week in July; full festival pass 2,400 kr excluding fees; day pass 1,200 kr excluding fees

For thousands of young Danes, the Roskilde Festival, commonly referred to simply as "Roskilde," is as much a rite of passage as school graduation parties and moving out of your parents' home for the first time. Its significance goes beyond that, with the live music festival attended by people of every generation and Danish artists' careers often taking off after an appearance at the summer event.

The nonprofit live music event has around 30,000 volunteers who work each year in exchange for festival passes. Many of these volunteers come from abroad—2,200 in 2023. Their work helps to turn the festival area, located in farmers' fields south of Roskilde, into

Roskilde Festival

a temporary city with a population of 130,000—complete with its own rail station, unofficial post office, and expanses of tents visible from the highway. The huge camping area is organized into different suburbs with different subcultures that range from quiet and clean to full-on partying, as well as one dedicated to participants with accessibility and other needs. The main musical program is arranged over four days Wednesday-Saturday, but the camping area is open for an entire week, and early arrivals rush for prime tent locations—a ritual known as "breaking down the fence."

Unpredictable summer **weather** can wildly change the overall experience from one year to the next, or from one day to the next. One year, relentless rain turned the area into a soggy mess. The next, a week of glorious sunshine left the festival zone looking more like Arizona than Zealand. Regardless of rainfall and temperature, the "orange feeling"—a sense of freedom and openness felt by those camping at the festival, named after the main stage, the Orange Stage—is one of Roskilde's strongest connotations.

Roskilde takes **sustainability** seriously. The cleanup operation after the festival closes takes months, with organizers insisting every last scrap of paper and cigarette butt be lifted from the grass. There are dozens of sustainability initiatives, with new ones sprouting each year focused on principles such as green procurement, responsible waste management, recycling, and circular economy. Specified goals include a 30 percent waste reduction by 2024 compared to 2019—equivalent to 600 tons of waste—and a 55 percent increase in recycling.

Safety: Reports of isolated harassment incidents and sexual assaults at the Roskilde Festival are not unknown. Generally, however, the festival is a safe place to be if you take normal nightlife precautions. There is a phone number (tel. 46 36 66 13) to call when assistance is needed with practical matters like finding a toilet or similar problems. Staff in orange vests are instructed to assist anyone who approaches them requesting help, or to contact their supervisor if further action is needed.

Music

It is actually possible to forget that the primary reason to go to Roskilde is to see live music, and rumors abound of people who never manage to leave the party scenes around the campsites. To do so would be a mistake, however, because as many as 200 acts play on eight stages across the event. Within the last five years, headliners have included Nick Cave and the Bad Seeds, Eminem, Dua Lipa, and Blur. Paul McCartney played the main Orange Stage in 2015, as did Prince in 2010. Bob Dylan appeared on several occasions during the 1990s and 2000s. There is also plenty of concert time devoted to Danish and Scandinavian acts, so you can discover new music too.

Camping

There are several camping options for festival guests, so depending on the amount of background noise you can put up with and the level of sleep and comfort you prefer (although these will never reach the levels of a real bed, particularly by the end of the week), you can purchase add-ons to your festival ticket, which includes the basic camping pass. These camping products are announced early in the year via the website.

Information and Services

Tickets usually sell out sometime before the festival, and one-day options are available, so be sure to monitor the Roskilde Festival website well in advance. One-day tickets normally go on sale in the early part of the year once the lineup, or the main part of it, has been announced. There is also a monthly payment option available through the Roskilde website.

Parking is available at the site, but given its close proximity to Copenhagen, it is often easier to arrive via train to Roskilde, where a shuttle bus or special rail service will take you on to the festival area. Roskilde city takes on a markedly different look during the week, as bleary-eyed campers shuttle to and from town to stock up on supplies, bringing the unmistakable festival spirit with them.

Dining

DANISH AND NEW NORDIC

Mumm

Karen Olsdatters Stræde 9; tel. 46 37 22 01; www.mummroskilde.com; Tues.-Sat. 5:30pm-midnight; 170 kr per dish, 4-6 dishes recommended, set menus including wine 1,010-1,625 kr

Mumm, tucked away on a quiet side street, serves French and New Nordic-inspired gourmet food that belies its modest setting. Depending on the rotation, the intricately presented small dishes may include milk-poached halibut, salted and grilled oyster mushrooms, veal brisket, and quail with sage. Dishes are made with fresh organic ingredients and seasoned with homegrown herbs in the style favored by leading Danish Michelin-starred restaurants. Call ahead to reserve.

Restaurant Vigen

Baunehøjvej 5; tel. 46 75 50 08; www.vigen.dk; May-Aug. Tues. 5pm-10pm, Wed.-Sun. noon-10pm, Sept.-Dec. and Mar.-Apr. Wed.-Sat. noon-10pm, Sun. noon-5pm, Jan.-Feb. Tues.-Sat. noon-10pm, Sun. noon-5pm; 6-dish menu from 750 kr excluding wine, lunch set menu from 350 kr, smørrebrød from 95 kr

Located about 2.4 km (1.5 mi) north of the city center next to the Roskilde campground, with a nice view of the fjord, Vigen was originally built in the 1930s as a restaurant and dance hall. Its lunch and evening menus are based on locally sourced ingredients and salmon, halibut, beef tartare, and porridge-based dishes. Call ahead to book.

Pipers Hus

Frederiksborgvej 21; tel. 46 36 56 96; https://pipershus.dk; Mon.-Fri. 11am-10pm, Sat. 10am-10pm, Sun. 10am-5pm; brunch 175 kr, salads 140 kr, smørrebrød from 78 kr, lunch platters 198 kr; evening mains 180-268 kr

Housed in a picturesque, thatched cottage in the Byparken park, with views of the fjord and the cathedral in close proximity, Pipers Hus offers traditional Danish fare for both visitors and locals. The lunch platter includes herring, fish fillet, roast beef with relish, pickled red onions, brie, and rye bread, combining many popular smørrebrød elements. In the evening 5pm-9pm, the menu switches to à la carte dishes. These include wiener schnitzel, veal brisket with red wine sauce, and steak with potatoes and fried mushrooms. There's seating inside the house and on the terrace, and views of the fjord can be had from both.

INTERNATIONAL

Restaurant Snekken

Vindeboder 16; tel. 46 35 98 16; https://snekken.dk; Mon.-Fri. noon-10pm, Sat.-Sun. 10am-10pm; weekend brunch buffet 225 kr, mains 169-345 kr

Conveniently located between the Viking Ship Museum and the harbor, this roomy restaurant serves burgers, steaks, and pasta along with seafood mains like moules frites and fish-and-chips. Vegan and vegetarian options are limited. A large weekend brunch with free juice refills is on offer, as are kids dishes. With something for almost everyone, it makes a good stop for a quiet coffee with a view and can also serve as a cocktail bar if you come on Friday-Saturday evening. There is ample seating inside, and the outdoor section has a great view of the fjord.

CAFÉS AND LIGHT BITES

Kaffekilden

Hestetorvet 7; tel. 32 14 60 30; www. kaffekilden.net; Mon.-Fri. 8am-8pm, Sat. 9am-7pm, Sun. 10am-7pm; coffee from 28 kr, cake from 27 kr

A rustic, cozy-chaired, brick-and-woodwork coffee bar by the station, Kaffekilden is an ideal place to get a caffeine fix if you are arriving after the short rail journey from Copenhagen. Brownies, cookies, croissants, bread and butter rolls, and skyr natural yogurt are all available to complement your brew.

Café Knarr

Vindeboder 12; tel. 46 30 02 53; www. vikingeskibsmuseet.dk/cafe-knarr; Mon.-Wed. 10am-5pm, Thurs.-Fri. 10am-10pm, Sat.-Sun. 10am-5pm; dishes from 79 kr

Located on the Museum Island as part of the Viking Ship Museum, Café Knarr offers the rare opportunity to try food prepared as "New Nordic Viking Food,"

meaning only ingredients available to the Vikings are used, and the dishes fit the modern Nordic style. This means you won't be tucking into potatoes, tomatoes, or cucumbers but will be able to fill up on flat bread, fish, berries, bacon, and barley. The view takes in the harbor and the replica wooden boats moored outside the museum.

Café Korn

Skomagergade 42-44; tel. 35 12 40 00; https://cafekorn.dk; Mon.-Thurs. 10am-9pm, Fri.-Sat. 10am-10pm, Sun. 10am-4pm; mains 169-239 kr, brunch from 159 kr, light morning snacks 49-89 kr, lunch burgers, salads, and sandwiches 159-179 kr

Café Korn has spacious seating around a semi-open kitchen area with more seating in The Stable in back. There's no shortage of space, and during the warmer season the seating spills on to the street in front of the entrance; these seats are heated in winter. The menu includes a range of burgers, sandwiches, salads, and lighter open-face sandwiches with meatballs, potatoes, or simply cheese and marmalade (burger orders come with a free refill on fries, if you ask nicely). You can also try the bøf-sandwich (steak sandwich), a traditional dish that was Denmark's answer to the hamburger. It consists of a beef patty on bread with mustard, pickled cucumber, beets, and onions drenched in a thick brown gravy. Service is friendly and informal.

Bars and Nightlife

LIVE MUSIC

Gimle

Helligkorsvej 2; tel. 46 37 19 82; www.gimle. dk; café Tues.-Sat. 4pm-11pm; see program for ticket prices, some concerts free

In a low brick building that once housed the city's waterworks, Gimle is a regional concert venue, meaning it receives state support to help develop musical talent. This is reflected in the program, which includes a lot of well-known Danish acts and some that are more up-and-coming. Forthcoming concerts and events can be checked on the website. Entry is often free for recurring events like jazz concerts and jam sessions. There are 12 full-time staffers and hundreds of volunteers who ensure the venue hosts hundreds of concerts and culture nights annually. Check out The Raven, an on-site bar run by five European volunteers, where orders must be placed in English.

BARS

Klosterkælderen

Store Gråbrødrestræde 23; tel. 31 17 11 14; www.klosterkaelderen.beer; Mon.-Thurs. 2pm-11pm, Fri. noon-2am, Sat. 11am-2am

As an intimate bar near the station, Klosterkælderen has a great range of 15 craft beers on tap and up to 350 bottled varieties. The on-tap beers are rotated regularly, and there are plenty of samples of akvavit schnapps, a stingingly sharp Danish spirit, to try. The stone walls reflect the name: Klosterkælderen translates literally to "the monastery cellar."

Skänk

Hestetorvet 10; tel. 44 18 56 20; https:// skaenk.dk; Mon.-Thurs. 4pm-11pm, Fri.-Sat. 2pm-2am

Skänk is a modern-style wine and beer bar in a room adorned by wooden furniture, barrels, and beams. With eight Danish-brewed craft beers on tap and wine tasting (from 150 kr), it's a pleasant place to while away an afternoon or evening. There's also cheese and charcuterie available should you want some nibbles with your drinks.

Accommodations

UNDER 500 KR
Danhostel Roskilde

Vindeboder 7; tel. 46 35 21 84; www.danhostelroskilde.dk; private room from 625 kr high season, linen rental 85 kr; 40 rooms

Roskilde's family-oriented Danhostel is in the thick of the fjord action, perched between the harbor area and the Viking Ship Museum. Rooms range from singles to six-person family rooms. There are pictures of longboats on the walls and views of longboats from the windows. With a guest kitchen, laundry room, TV lounge, Wi-Fi, and parking available, the spacious and clean facilities are ample budget accommodations. A breakfast buffet is available.

1,000-2,000 KR
Comwell Roskilde

Vestre Kirkevej 12; tel. 46 32 31 31; www.comwellroskilde.dk; high season from 1,429 kr d; 159 rooms

In the northern part of the city, with views over Roskilde Fjord in the "standard small view" room category, Comwell Roskilde is a modern conference-style hotel that was renovated in 2016. A walk in the hotel grounds is pleasant, with pavilions, terraces, and small nooks and courtyards. Facilities include a restaurant, a gym, a bar, and a game room with table football, darts, air hockey, and a video game console; the breakfast buffet is included.

Zleep Hotel Prindsen Roskilde

Algade 13; tel. 70 23 56 35; www.zleep.com/da/hotel/roskilde; high season from 1,440 kr d; 75 rooms

Although it's part of a chain, Roskilde's Zleep Hotel has the appearance of a long-standing part of town and manages to retain an individual feel, owing to its location on the main street in an impressive historical building formerly occupied by another hotel, the Prindsen (as evidenced by the building's facade). It's handsome on the inside too, with a rococo-style interior. Breakfast (129 kr per person) is not included in the room rates.

CAMPING
Roskilde Camping

Baunehøjvej 7; tel. 46 75 79 96; https://roskildecamping.dk; Apr.-Sept.; high season camping from 105 kr, rooms from 450 kr, cabins from 650 kr

Camping is located about 3 km (1.8 mi) north of Roskilde city center and with great views over the fjord, so you might spot a passing Viking ship. Roskilde Camping can accommodate tents, trailers, and campers, while cabins are also available. Facilities include a play area for kids and a pier for bathing. The campground recently introduced a "glamping" option (high season from 900 kr d), giving you a luxury tent with pillows and duvets, armchairs, your own terrace, and a coffee machine, among the long list of perks.

Tourist Information

Visit Fjordlandet

Roskilde does not have a permanent staffed tourist information bureau, but the local tourism website Visit Fjordlandet (www.visitfjordlandet.dk/en) is a useful resource for attractions and accommodations in and around Roskilde, and also provides a guide to local walks along with cycling and hiking routes in the Fjord Country surrounding the town.

Getting There and Around

GETTING THERE
By Train

It is quick and straightforward to reach Roskilde from Copenhagen Central Station. Regional and some Intercity services stop at Roskilde, so there can be as many as eight departures hourly during daytime hours. The journey takes 20-25 minutes and costs 66 kr, 43 kr with Rejsekort. **Roskilde train station** is located at Jernbanegade 1.

By Car

The easiest route by road is via the O2 ring road south of Copenhagen, exiting at Route 21, where signs will direct you to Roskilde.

GETTING AROUND
By Bus

Local bus 203 from Roskilde Station takes you closest to the Viking Ship Museum: Get off at the Vikingeskibsmuseet (Sankt Clara Vej) stop (8 minutes; 24 kr, 14 kr Rejsekort). Buy a ticket on board or use your Rejsekort. To the cathedral, bus 201A (Stændertorvet) takes you closest, but the bus journey (24 kr, 14 kr Rejsekort) only takes 3 minutes; it might be easier to walk. Between the museum and the cathedral, take bus 204 or bus 209 to and from Stændertorvet to the stop closest to the Viking Ship Museum, Sankt Clara Vej (Frederiksborgvej) (3 minutes; 24 kr, 14 kr Rejsekort).

On Foot and By Bicycle

Roskilde is a very walkable town, particularly if you are headed to the cathedral and the Viking Ship Museum. The cathedral is a 10-minute walk from the station, mainly along the Algade pedestrian street; the walk from the museum to the fjord, where you'll find the harbor and the museum, takes around 15 minutes through the city park (Byparken).

The town is also comfortably accessible for bicycles, if a little more hilly than Copenhagen. You can bring a bicycle with you on the train from Copenhagen by purchasing the bicycle ticket upgrade at station machines (20 kr, 13 kr Rejsekort). The **Donkey Republic** company has bicycles in Roskilde; these can be unlocked for short meter-based rentals using the Donkey Republic app. **Roskilde Cykelcenter** (Blågårdsstræde 3-5; tel. 46 35 08 28; Mon.-Thurs. 9am-5:30pm, Fri. 9am-6pm, Sat. 9am-2pm) rents pedal bikes (from 100 kr per day) and electric bicycles (from 200 kr per day).

Dragør

Dragør is at the southeastern tip of Amager and is an intimate harbor town that can be reached via a bicycle trip or short bus ride from Copenhagen. A walk through the superbly preserved historical town center, with its winding cobbled streets and single-story 19th-century buildings painted in pastel oranges and yellows, shows why much of Dragør is protected as a heritage area. There's a summer feel to the harbor, where ice cream stands, local history museums, and the crash of the waves against the dock make you want

Highlights

⭐ **Dragør's Old Town:** Go back in time with a stroll around the cobbled alleys of this immaculately preserved old town (page 232).

⭐ **Amager Museum:** Learn about the local trade and history of Store Magleby at this quaint museum (page 235).

⭐ **Amager Nature Park:** A wealth of outdoor life awaits at the enormous nature reserve area on the western half of Amager (page 235).

to linger until the sun sets. A 3,500-ha (8,500 acre) nature reserve outside town is a huge draw, literally and figuratively, that further enhances Dragør's charms, making it a great destination for a day trip from Copenhagen.

ORIENTATION

Dragør is about 12 km (7.5 mi) south of central Copenhagen on the far coast of the island of Amager, which itself is closely connected to Copenhagen by several bridges (much of Amager is part of Copenhagen's municipality). The main road leading into town from the rest of Amager, Kirkevej, terminates at the northwestern corner of the old quarter of this small compact town, a few

hundred meters from the harbor. The old town is demarcated by the streets Kongevejen (a continuation of Kirkevej), Strandlinien, Rønne Allé, and Vestgrønningen. The old town itself, much of which is not accessible to vehicles (there's ample parking just outside it), is a winding maze of narrow alleyways and the old-fashioned houses of fishing families, where ivy hangs and the sun glimmers on late summer evenings. There's not much need for orientation in this small area—wander, get lost, and take it all in. You'll easily find your way out again, even if you don't necessarily want to.

The harbor, old pilot's tower, and Dragør Museum are all directly to the east of the old town,

---

Previous: Dragør street corner. **Above:** Amager Nature Park; Dragør's old town.

and a flat grassy area stretches out toward the old fort and a sandy, grassy stretch of beach to the south of the town.

Around 2.5 km (1.5 mi) back west along Kirkevej, the village of Store Magleby is probably seen by most visitors before Dragør as they travel through it to reach the coastal town. Tiny Store Magleby has a handful of streets, the most important being Hovedgaden (literally Main Street), which leads north from near the church to the Amager Museum at the edge of town, close to the perimeter of Copenhagen Airport.

Directly west of Dragør, Amager Nature Park is a huge wild area, taking up almost a quarter of the island of Amager and stretching to the city area in the north. It can be reached via Metro from Copenhagen and by bus, bicycle, and on foot from Dragør.

PLANNING YOUR TRIP

Its close proximity to Copenhagen and small size means that Dragør can be visited almost on a whim: You can travel to the town, see the old town and harbor, and return the same day. If you want to explore the wilds of Amager Nature Park, you will need to plan because of its size, but the park can be even easier to get to than Dragør—the Copenhagen Metro takes you almost to the gate.

Itinerary Idea

ONE DAY IN DRAGØR

Centuries-old fishing village Dragør is only a stone's throw from Copenhagen, but get your visit right and you'll feel like you've been to the opposite end of the country—in the nicest possible way.

1 Start your day in Dragør's old town with a morning coffee and pastry at **Hallöy Café.**

2 After breakfast, walk about 2 km (1.2 m) west to the even smaller village of Store Magleby. Visit the **Amager Museum** to learn all about the village's quirky history and Dutch influence.

3 Head back to Dragør for lunch at **Café Dragør Sejlklub,** where you can enjoy a view of the marina and the Øresund, including the Øresund Bridge, while savoring freshly delivered seafood.

4 Rejuvenated by lunch, head to the Kongelunden forest in **Amager Nature Park** to spend the afternoon biking or walking through the beech and elm woods. Look for birds (and planes) flying above you.

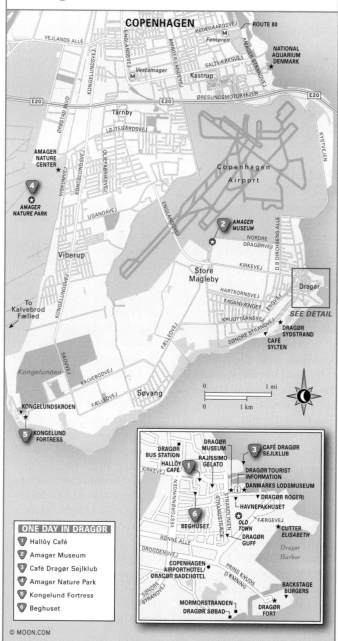

Dragør

ONE DAY IN DRAGØR

1. Hallöy Café
2. Amager Museum
3. Café Dragør Sejlklub
4. Amager Nature Park
5. Kongelund Fortress
6. Beghuset

© MOON.COM

231

5 In the late afternoon, visit the **Kongelund Fortress,** the site of a lookout built during World War I. You can explore parts of the now defunct facility, but the best thing to do here is to just sit and enjoy the coastal views.

6 After all the walking you've done, you're probably famished. Visit **Beghuset,** a homey wallet-friendly Danish restaurant in a beautiful example of one of the old town's listed houses.

Sights

DRAGØR
✪ Old Town

between Toldergade and Rønne Allé,
Dragør

When you wander around the tightly wound alleys of Dragør's old quarter, life seems to stand still. The old town is one of the best-preserved settlements in Denmark. Founded in the late 1600s and expanded in three periods around 1770, 1830, and 1890, creating a patchwork effect, a large number of the buildings and the original layout of the town remain much as they once were, even surviving serious fires in the mid-19th century.

The cluster of 18th- and 19th-century houses nestled in the cobbled alleyways between Kongevejen and Rønne Allé, with their characteristic clay-tiled roofs and mustard-colored walls, are the highest concentration of listed buildings in any small town in Denmark, with 76 in total along with 5 more at the harbor. A good mix of homes and businesses make up the old town. In summer, calm descends over the streets in the evening. Clothes hang on lines and windows are opened to let in the evening light. Small squares open around narrow corners, and ivy grows on the walls.

Guided tours (tel. 50 99 40 38; hellebjorholm@stofanet.dk) in English are available in the summer season by booking ahead or through the Dragør Visitor Center (tel. 28 96 58 82; visitorcenter@ museumamager.dk). The time and place of the tour can be arranged with the guide, and the tour takes in the architecture and history of the old town along with the stories behind its quirks. There are various themes: a classic tour of the city, the escape to Sweden of Danish Jews during World War II, and the women of Dragør. A group tour for 20-25 people lasting 1 hour 30 minutes costs 1,500 kr during high season or 1,350 kr off-season. Shorter tours of 45 minutes for up to 10 people are also available for 800 kr (off-season) to 1,000 kr (high season). Call ahead to inquire and make reservations—tours must be arranged in advance.

Dragør's old town

Dragør Museum

Strandlinien 4; tel. 28 96 58 82; www.
museumamager.dk; May-Sept. Tues.-Sun.
11am-4pm; adults 65 kr, under age 18 free

By the old harbor in one of the town's oldest houses, dating to 1753, is Dragør Museum. Exhibits in the renovated space tell of the town's seafaring and fishing past, including a collection of paintings by local artists and a feature on Johan Blichmann, the 17th-century builder responsible for many of the houses in the old town. Although it's small, there is plenty to see, and there's very much a maritime feel, with model ships and pictures of historical seafaring scenes. The Skipper's Living Rooms, created using inventory from some of Dragør's oldest houses, give a glimpse into traditional life in the town. Flugten 1943 (The Flight of 1943) looks at the escape of Jews from occupied Denmark to Sweden during World War II through the eyes of the harbor town, which was the launch point for many escape boats. Modern Dragør is not forgotten—the Amager 2019 feature showcases local identity today. There's a touchscreen that can be used to catch herring or navigate a schooner across the seven seas.

Danish Pilots Museum
(Danmarks Lodsmuseum)

Dragør Gl. Havn 11; tel. 28 96 58 82; www.
museumamager.dk; May-Sept. Wed. and
Sat.-Sun. 2pm-4pm; free

Dragør, with its important vantage point looking across the Øresund, has had a pilots station since 1684, when local mariners began helping vessels navigate the strait. The Danish Pilots Museum, a small attraction housed in the two stories of the former station (the current facility is elsewhere on the harbor), is easily located—it is right next to the 16-m-high (52-ft) pilots tower (not open to the public). The museum showcases everyday life in the pilots station in a 20th-century context, not a 17th-century one, with an old-fashioned office and communication equipment, charts, log books, uniforms hanging from a hook on the wall, and lodgings with a small bed and a kitchenette as it was in 1984, the year the station marked its 300th anniversary.

Cutter *Elisabeth*

Dragør Gl. Havn; tel. 28 96 58 82; www. museumamager.dk; late June-mid-Aug. Sat.-Sun. 2pm-4pm; free

The cutter *Elisabeth,* moored in Dragør harbor close to the Pilots Museum, is famous for being part of a scraped-together fleet of private boats used by Danes to assist Jews fleeing Nazi persecution in October 1943. The boats were used to helped hundreds escape to neutral Sweden, with the *Elisabeth*'s skipper, Einar Larsen, helping up to 70 people before fleeing himself. The *Elisabeth,* one of the few remaining vessels from the transport operation, was donated to the Amager Museum in 2007 and is now given a prominent place in the harbor.

A 9-m (30-ft) fishing boat, the now restored gleaming-white *Elisabeth* can be visited during short windows on weekends in the summer, where local volunteers on board can tell you about the cutter and its dramatic past.

STORE MAGLEBY

The village of Store Magleby, a short distance from Dragør, is also known as "the Dutch village." There is little trace today of the Netherlands beyond the appropriately flat landscape and Dutch names on some of the church's gravestones, but the settlement was in fact a Dutch colony of sorts from the time King Christian II invited families from the Netherlands to live in the village in 1521, wanting to improve the quality and variety of vegetables on offer at the palace in Copenhagen. The Dutch farmers were allowed to take over existing farms and land and were given special privileges such as exemption from taxes and military conscription. It is not known to what extent this upset the natives or whether there were recriminations against the new Dutch farmers. Three centuries later, the use of Dutch in the village, by this time mixed with the local Danish and German spoken by priests, finally faded out.

Despite major fires during the 17th-century wars with Sweden, as well as in the 19th century, Store Magleby has retained its original village and road layout. In later years in much of Denmark, many farmers' houses were moved away from villages and closer to the land being worked. No buildings from the original Dutch period remain, but policies to protect the village in recent decades prevented it from expanding through modern developments on its outskirts, so it is possible to gain a sense of how it might once have looked. On Shrove Tuesday, Dutch traditions are upheld as riders gallop through the town on horseback, smashing barrels left out as targets.

✪ Amager Museum

Hovedgaden 4, Store Magleby; tel. 28 96 58 82; www.museumamager.dk; July-Aug. 13 Tues.-Sun. noon-4pm, May-June and Aug. 16-Sept. Wed.-Sun. noon-4pm; adults 80 kr, under age 18 free

Two old farmyard buildings in Store Magleby are home to the Amager Museum, a collection of cultural relics that illustrate the unique character and culture of the rural area around Dragør, separated from the rest of Denmark by Copenhagen but with a different identity from the capital—not least due to the influx of Dutch farmers in the 16th century. There's a room dedicated to neighboring Dragør, with various items brought back by the town's seafarers: blue tiles from Holland and wooden engravings from England. Elsewhere, there are portraits by local artists and even a small exhibition on tulips, illustrating the Dutch connection.

Several examples of Amager's traditional clothing are on display, which is another example of the Dutch culture in the village, since local dress is far less commonplace in Denmark than in the Netherlands or other Scandinavian countries. The clothing is characterized particularly by the wide flat silk hat for the men, known as the floshat. The use of these hats persisted until the 1800s, and their size even increased—whether this was out of habit or a pride in the Dutch ancestry is unclear. Women wore patterned skirts and blouses and hats that signified whether the wearer was married, a maiden, or in mourning.

The museum also includes an extensive garden where root vegetables, cabbages, dahlias, and in the spring, tulips grow.

While the museum is worth visiting any time its doors are open, July is when it really comes to life. Staff in period costume carry out the daily tasks of a preindustrial farm, and visiting children are invited to try on old-fashioned outfits. Daily activities vary and can include digging up vegetables, repairing clothes, or weaving, and children are encouraged to learn about what's going on. If your visit is outside the summer season, you might still be able to visit: The museum opens for special activities during the October school holiday, as well for seasonal events on weekends in the run-up to Christmas, beginning in November.

TOP EXPERIENCE

✪ AMAGER NATURE PARK

Granatvej 3-15; tel. 31 47 52 75; https:// naturparkamager.dk; Mon.-Fri. 9am-2pm, Sat.-Sun. 10am-4pm; bus 33 Foldbyvej (Otto Bachés Allé), Metro Vestamager

Amager Nature Park is a gigantic nature reserve covering most of the western half of Amager. It is made up of four distinct sections: **Amager Fælled, Kongelunden,**

Dragør Sydstrand, and the largest, **Kalvebod Fælled,** comprising 2,000 ha (4,940 acres) of the total 3,500 ha (8,650 acres). The entire reserve boasts 25 km (15 mi) of coastline, 300 bird species, 450 types of plants, 20 sites for camping including shelters, and hundreds of cycling and hiking paths. With its vast expanses of rolling open land, marshes, hills, ponds, canals, ditches, bird reserves, forests, paths, and shelters, there's enough to keep explorers and nature lovers enthralled for days. Remarkably, these wild green landscapes are just a few Metro stops from the bustle of central Copenhagen or a bus, hike, or bicycle trip from Dragør (the park spans both municipalities). Lush in summer, it is also beautiful at other times of year, whether under a layer of snow or so rainy and windswept you'll be unable to resist channeling your inner Brontë.

There are a number of ways to access the park, the primary one being **Vestamager Metro** station, a few minutes' walk from Amager Nature Center. The nature center is an excellent resource, with a café and a tourist information center, and you can borrow a bicycle to get around the park. It is also possible to enter the park at many other points around its perimeter through distinctive red wooden gates, should you want to visit a specific spot far from the nature center. From the inland (eastern) side of Kalvebod Fælled, **bus 33** tracks along the Kongelundsvej road between Dragør, northern Amager, and Copenhagen. From this road you can hop off the bus at a number of different stops and walk around 500 m (0.3 mi) west to reach the perimeter of the reserve.

Kongelunden and **Dragør Sydstrand** are closer to the town of Dragør and easier for shorter visits of at least half a day; I recommend a full day for Kalvebod Fælled, more if you want to camp. They can be reached by bicycle or bus, or on foot if you have a little more time.

Amager Nature Center

Granatvej 3-15; tel. 31 47 52 75; friluftshuset@amsh.dk; www. naturcenteramager.dk; Mon.-Fri. 9am-2pm, Sat.-Sun. 10am-4pm; bus 33 Foldbyvej (Otto Bachés Allé), Metro Vestamager

I recommend Amager Nature Center as the starting point and base for exploring and wandering Amager Nature Park. It is close to public transportation connections, and there are parking options outside the gate to the reserve (but note the 6-hour time limit). The center comprises two main buildings, Friluftshuset and Traktørstedet.

At the tourist information desk at **Friluftshuset** you can talk with friendly khaki-clad guides who can advise you on the various walking and cycling routes inside the reserve, shelters for camping (these can also be booked in advance by calling or emailing the center), wildlife to look out for, and which locations are particularly worth searching out at the time of your visit. Bicycles can be rented from the center for the outstandingly inexpensive price of 50 kr per day, while cargo bikes (100 kr per hour) and children's bikes (50 kr per day) are also available. Equipment and guidelines for campfires and barbecuing can also be purchased here.

Friluftshuset also facilitates various activities throughout the year, including the use of picnic areas and sites where barbecuing is permitted. Private guided bicycle tours (from 2,500 kr for up to 4 people, includes bike and helmet rental) can be reserved by calling or emailing the center. The tours last 3 hours and take in natural and constructed landmarks on the nature reserve and also venture into the modern architectural world of the adjacent Ørestad neighborhood.

Traktørstedet (tel. 22 55 32 65; https://traktoerstedetvestamager.dk; Tues.-Sun. 10am-6pm; coffee from 30 kr, breakfast platter 145 kr, cakes from 30 kr, soup or salad from 95 kr, children's meal 60 kr) is a welcoming café with wooden pillars, red-and-white checked tablecloths, and a great view of Kalvebod Fælled to give it a picnic-like feel. The organic menu is fairly extensive, including everything from a continental breakfast to burgers to a kids meal of rye bread with sausage or vegetarian toppings and fruit. Returnable flasks of coffee and tea can be purchased to take with you onto the commons, as can beer, water, and soda and even a dough for the popular activity of baking snobrød (twist bread) over a campfire.

To get to the Nature Center from Dragør, take bus 33 (3 buses per hour; 24 kr) to Foldbyvej (Otto Baches Allé). From Copenhagen, take the simple 14-minute Metro trip to nearby Vestamager station (frequent departures; 24 kr). It's around 8 km (5 mi) from Dragør by bicycle. You can cycle out of town through Store Magleby on Kirkevej, which becomes Englandsvej/ Route 221. Follow this for around 6 km (3.7 mi) until you reach Løjtegårdsvej. Turn left here and continue for less than 2 km (1.2 mi). You'll see the signs to the center.

Kalvebod Fælled

Until the end of the 1930s, the 2,000-ha (4,942-acre) area known today as Kalvebod Fælled was underwater. The shallow area was dried out by a dam that was built along what is now the coastline between 1939 and 1943. Rumor has it that the Danish government used the project to keep as many men as possible working to prevent them being sent to the war by occupying Nazi Germany, although this has never been proved. A total of 2,480 ha (6,128 acres) was reclaimed from the sea, including part of what is now Amager Fælled to the north, and two pumping stations and a network of channels and ditches were built to dry out the area. These ditches can be seen today in what is now a huge nature reserve enticingly close to central Copenhagen. It includes an international bird sanctuary, Denmark's largest self-sown birch forest, pathways, small

Kalvebod Fælled, Amager Nature Park

hills, marshes, forests, purple butterflies, edible frogs, blue irises, and herds of sheep and cows.

The **Bird Sanctuary,** in the southwestern part of the common, is off limits to visitors, but it can still be seen from the vantage point of a series of birdwatching towers on the coastal path that goes around the western edge of the sanctuary (along the dam structure that created it), as well as from a covered viewpoint for birdwatchers (a great place to spot kingfishers). This spot is just to the west of **Pinseskoven,** the largest self-sown birch forest in Denmark. The forest was created by seeds that were blown across the Øresund from Sweden in the years after the area was reclaimed. It's an ideal area for camping. The **Birkeholm** area can seem a bit noisy compared to the rest of the reserve—it is not far from a highway—but

it is a less visited, open-forested area with places to camp and fish. **Svenskehøj** and **Villahøj** were originally built by the military as lookouts during Kalvebod Fælled's time as an army exercise area (it was not completely opened to the public until the 1980s). Now, the two raised areas can be used to observe the park's drainage ditches and are also a good place to spot wading birds such as ruffs. If you've brought a picnic, this is a great spot to enjoy it. To reach this area and the nearby Pinseskoven, follow Granatvej in a straight line southwest from the Nature Center for just under 2 km (1.2 mi). If you're looking for a viewpoint a little closer to the Nature Center, try **Store Høj,** around 750 m (0.5 mi) west of the information center. This is an easily accessible area with shelters, a lake, and an area for making small bonfires. The top of the hill, with its outlook over the flat and open rolling land, is positively melodramatic on a windy day. Between here and the main entrance to the park is **Himmelhøj,** a 60-m-long (200-ft) sculpture in the shape of the hull of a boat, or perhaps an ark. With rocks and places to climb inside, it's a great natural playground for kids.

There are paths and tracks crisscrossing the entirety of Kalvebod Fælled, except the Bird Sanctuary, and paths are clearly marked and suitable for both boots and bicycles. Four color-coded routes, ranging 2.5-14 km (1.5-9 mi) in length, are marked by signposts and can also be followed with a map available for free from Friluftshuset. The 27-km (16.8-mi) **Amarmino,** marked by signs shaped like water droplets, is a trail that crosses the entire island of Amager, taking in the varied landscapes of the nature reserve as well as the urban part in the north and Dragør to the south. There are several marked camping areas as well as four sleeping shelters. These are basic wooden cabins with no amenities in which you can sleep with slightly better cover from the elements than in a tent. As with camping, the use of shelters is free and open year-round, but they must be reserved ahead—contact the center before setting off.

Kongelunden

Kongelunden is primarily forest at the southern end of Amager and east of Kalvebod Fælled. The woods include deciduous and coniferous

areas. It is teeming with flowers, birds, and wild-growing fruits like blackthorn and apples. In the spring you can pick wild chives, and cherry plums can also be foraged. As you wander through the woods, look up to spot a nightingale or a wood warbler; there's also a good chance you'll see an aircraft coming in to land at Copenhagen Airport. Bicycle and walking-friendly paths, bonfire sites, picnic benches, and hundreds of oak and elm trees make this area ripe for outdoorsy fun.

There are two marked routes through the forest, one 3.5 km (2.2 mi) and the other 5.5 km (3.3 mi), along with the wheelchair-accessible **Collin's Path,** which ends in a great view out from the elm trees toward the marshland, the beach, and the sea. Many of the oak trees here are 150 years old, and **Kroneegen** (the Crown Oak) is 180 years old. It can be found at **Collin's Stone,** a memorial to Jonas Collin, the councilor who founded the forest in the early 1800s by persuading villagers in Store Magleby to plant trees on some of their land. Also to be found in this area is **Knirkebøgen** (the Creaking Beech), so named because of its propensity to moan during high winds. To the north of the Collin's Path area, a "tree landscape," **Landskabstræet,** is an area in which 52 different trees have been planted around a path layout that forms the shape of a tree when viewed from above.

In the middle of the forest,

Collin's Path is crossed by the Kongelundsvej Road, which bisects Kongelunden. There is a car parking area here: look out for **Løvenskjolds Mindestøtte**, a rectangular monument to a royal hunt master who brought pheasants to the area. The hunt no longer exists, but pheasants still live in the forest. Parking is opposite the monument.

If you are traveling to Kongelunden using public transportation, take bus 33 from either the bus station in Dragør (2 buses per hour; 25 minutes; 24 kr) or from City Hall Square in Copenhagen (2 buses per hour; 40 minutes; 30 kr) and get off at Kongelunden (Skovvej). You'll find yourself in the middle of the forest, a few meters from Collin's Path. On some occasions, however, the bus does not pass this stop, in which case you can get off at the alternate Skovvej (Kalvebodvej) stop, a short walk to the south of the forest. You can bicycle to Kongelunden from Dragør in 30-40 minutes and walk in around an hour and a half: Take Engvej out of town to the southwest, turn left on to Krudttårnsvej after 2 km (1.2 mi), and follow this road for around 2.5 km (1.5 mi) before turning left on to Fælledvej. Take a right on to Kalvebodvej and then a final right turn on to Skovvej, which takes you into the forest. Alternatively, a path runs from Dragør along the coast through Dragør Sydstrand, and then travels through the forest before continuing to Kalvebod Fælled.

Kongelund Fortress
(Kongelundsfortet)

Kalvebodvej 265; tel. 32 89 01 00; www. dragoer.dk/kultur-og-fritid/steder-i-naturen/kongelundsfortet; daily 8am-8pm; free

A military bunker built during World War I, the Kongelund Fortress is a hefty clump of concrete just south of Kongelunden. With a great view of Køge Bay, the fort is an interesting insight into a period when Denmark, like much of Europe, felt the need to protect itself from its close neighbors. There's an old radar station, built in 1959, with rickety metal steps and a lookout post among the Cold War-looking distressed structure. It is free to walk around and has been renovated with play and barbecue areas, so you can bring along a picnic. There is no access to any of the buildings. There are often activities and events such as paddling, organized camping, and litter cleanup held by various organizers at the fort. These are often very cheap to take part in. The best place to keep abreast of what's going on is on the fort's Facebook page, www.facebook.com/kongelundsfortet.

To get to Kongelundsfortet, take bus 33 to Sydvestpynten (Kalvebodvej), from where it's a short walk. On foot or bicycle, follow the route as for Kongelunden, but instead of turning on to Skovvej, continue on Kalvebodvej until you reach the fort. Alternatively, follow the coastal path from Dragør to Kongelunden via Dragør Sydstrand—this path passes through the forest close to the fort.

Dragør Sydstrand

The closest part of Amager Nature Park to Dragør, this marshy area runs along the south of Amager for around 6 km (3.5 mi) and has a coastal path starting just outside Dragør that connects it to Kongelunden. It's replete with salty lagunas, grasses, ducks, and wading birds resting on the flats. If you're lucky you might spot a seal in the bay or even on the beach. The terrain is sometimes sandy, sometimes grassy, and changes with the effects of coastal erosion. Its flatness makes it a popular spot for morning joggers, although the bracing winds can make even light exercise take a little more energy than usual. It's easy to reach from Dragør: Just walk south of the harbor and fort to Batterivej and follow it toward the coast.

The sandy seabed and clean water are suitable for bathing, and the end of Batterivej is also where you will find **Dragør Søbad** (Batterivej 15; tel. 32 89 04 50; www.hollaenderhallen.dk; May-Aug.; adults 25 kr, children 15 kr), a sea swimming facility accessed by a pier, and **Mormorstranden** (Grandmother's Beach). The beach, which is sandy with shallow waters and has a volleyball net, is child-friendly, and there's a jetty at its southern end if you want to jump into deeper water. Don't expect the water to warm you up.

National Aquarium Denmark
(Den Blå Planet)

Jacob Fortlingsvej 1; tel. 44 22 22 44; https://denblaaplanet.dk/en; Mon. 10am-9pm, Tues.-Sun. 10am-5pm; adults 210 kr, 185 kr online, ages 3-11 110 kr, 100 kr online, under age 3 free; Metro Kastrup Station, bus 5C (Den Blå Planet)

Secreted away past the far end of Amager Beach Park is the largest aquarium in Northern Europe. Officially called National Aquarium Denmark but better known as The Blue Planet after its Danish name, this huge whirlpool-shaped attraction is easily reached on the way to or from Dragør or Store Magleby if you're visiting from Copenhagen. A vast number of aquariums support both cold- and warm-water habitats, letting visitors get up close to hammerhead sharks, watch piranhas being fed, view a squid dissection, and see the seahorses. The clown anemonefish made famous by Disney's *Nemo* films can be spotted here among the reefs and tropical touch pools, as can octopuses, eels, sea urchins, and countless other wonderful species. There are also some fascinating exhibitions, which include displays like prehistoric marine life and ocean sustainability. The Blue Planet is a great option if you're looking for a rainy day activity to keep the kids entertained.

It's easy to reach from Copenhagen on either the Metro or bus 5C (24 kr), and takes around 45 minutes from central Copenhagen by bicycle. From Dragør, take bus 35 to Copenhagen Airport and then switch to bus 5C, or bike around the airport perimeter if you don't mind navigating a couple of traffic junctions (which have bicycle crossings) as you pass the airport approach roads.

Entertainment and Events

FESTIVALS

Dragør Harbor Festival
(Dragør Havnefest)
Strandlinien; tel. 32 53 00 75; www.
dragoerhavnefest.dk; Aug.; free

This weekend-long local festival takes place during the summer, usually in mid-August, at Dragør Harbor. Its small size gives a real sense of community. There's a raft of concerts by Danish pop and folk artists, local hopefuls, children's entertainers, and cover bands. Kids can try pony rides, hop on the bouncy castle, or get their faces painted, and there are ice cream and food stands.

Sankthans
Dragør Harbor; July 23

Sankthans, the Danish version of Midsummer, does not go unnoticed in Dragør. A bonfire is lit around 10pm on June 23 at the harbor, and there is usually entertainment in addition to the traditional speech and song. Festivities normally include a pop-up street food market and a live DJ and bar. Recent years, notably 2018 and 2023, saw the event under threat of cancellation due to fire risk related to exceptionally dry weather, so check ahead in such conditions if you're thinking of attending. The highlight of spending Sankthans here is the view from the harbor side or coast after the fire has been lit: Bonfires can be seen stretching along the coast as well as in Sweden on the opposite side of the strait.

Dragør Art Festival
Strandlinien, Dragør; July; free

Dragør's annual art festival weekend first took place in 2009 and is now held at the old harbor around the pilots tower, Lodstårnet, and along the coast-facing street Strandlinien. More than 40 artists exhibited in the most recent Dragør art festival, with painting, sketching, stone and glass sculpture, photography, and handcrafts on show and for sale. The art is exhibited outdoors under open-sided tents to protect it from the elements, and there's a relaxed weekend fair atmosphere.

Recreation

BICYCLING

There are no bike rental shops in the town of Dragør, but you can rent one at the Amager Nature Center for cycling in the nature reserve, and many hotels in the area offer bike rentals to guests. Alternatively, the **Donkey Republic** company has a few bicycles in Dragør, including a stand at the harbor on Strandlinien. These can be unlocked using the Donkey Republic app and are suitable for short meter-based rentals. Another option is to rent one in Copenhagen and cycle to Dragør—a trip that takes 45 minutes to 2 hours, depending on your pace.

Munkevejen Route 80
www.munkevejen.dk

Route 80 is a regional cycling trail that takes you through almost the entirety of Amager, including some of its natural areas. Cycling the section that goes through Dragør and the wild areas of Amager Nature Park, including Kongelunden, is a great way to see the area.

The 38-km (24-mi) route starts on the promenade by the Amager Strandpark beach close to the Femøren Metro station. Heading south, it passes Den Blå Planet aquarium and then connects to the coastal road, Amager Strandvej. From here, the cycle path guides you under and around major traffic junctions past the entrance to Copenhagen Airport onto Kystvejen, which follows the outer perimeter of the airport between its fences and the Øresund. This makes for quite a hair-raising and dramatic ride as you cycle a long straight section with the sea on one side and aircraft roaring in to land just overhead. If you can time it right, it's spectacular at dusk.

After rounding the airport, turn left onto Ndr. Strandvej and follow this road all the way into Dragør, skirting around the old town on Kongevejen and Vestgrønningen before continuing out of town on Sdr. Strandvej, which runs alongside **Dragør Sydstrand** (of course, you could decide to stop for a rest in Dragør). It then enters **Kongelunden,** crosses **Kalvebod Fælled** via **Pinseskoven** to the west coast of Amager, and eventually passes close to **Amager Nature Center.** It then makes its way past Field's shopping mall and into Amager Fælled, finally entering the built-up northern end of Amager, and finishing in the Islands Brygge subdistrict, across the harbor from central Copenhagen. You'll be cycling mostly on asphalt. The Dragør and Nature Park sections will offer a combination of mild hills and flat sections, windy coastal stretches, and more sheltered areas, including forests.

The trail is not signposted, but the route can be found and GPS coordinates downloaded from the Munkevejen website. You should

Summer in Dragør

Dragør's charm is present year-round, but there's no doubt the area really comes to life in the summer, when the ice cream shops stay open well into the daylit evening and visitors come to take in the festive harbor atmosphere. The sounds of masts clinking and the Øresund lapping against the marina are but a few distractions. Some of the best things to do here in the summer include:

Dragør in summer

- Exploring the wilds of **Kalvebod Fælled**

- Enjoying an **ice cream** while sitting by the **harbor**

- Visiting the **Amager Museum** in **July** when the staff are gussied up in period costume (kids can also try on the old-fashioned outfits)

- Seeing all the bonfires stretching up and down the coast during **Sankthans** on June 23

- Celebrating **Havnefest** in August with the locals by the old port

reserve a day for cycling the entire route at a less than strenuous pace.

HIKING

Amarminoen

https://naturparkamager.dk/oplevelser/amarminoen

The "Amarmino" is the latest in a number of Danish hiking trails to be named with a word play on "camino." It's a 27-km (16.8-mi) marked walking route which crisscrosses much of the island of Amager's natural areas, starting at the DR-Byen Metro station at the Copenhagen end and finishing in Dragør; the trail can be followed in either direction. On the way, it passes through Amager Fælled common and the larger Kalvebod Fælled with its forests and bird reservation, along with Kongelunden forest, also passing Kongelund Fort.

To follow it, look for the water droplet-shaped markings on the trail signposts. The trail begins at the Ørestads Boulevard/Grønjordsvej traffic circle a short walk from DR-Byen Metro station, leading on to Amager Fælled. In Dragør, you can find the trailhead at Prins Knuds Dæmning, the approach road to Dragør Fort. A printable PDF map can be found on the website. The trail can be used for anything from an hour-long breath of fresh air to a two-day camping hike with as many birdwatching breaks as you care to take.

Dining

DRAGØR
Danish
Dragør Rogeri

Gl. Havn 6; tel. 32 53 06 03; https://dragor-rogeri.dk; Thurs.-Sun. 10am-5pm; salads from 44 kr, fish fillet and fries 65 kr

This is a busy fishmonger-slash-café by the harbor that sells fresh fish with salads, potatoes, or fries and the sour-tasting Danish relish remoulade. Plenty of types of white fish, including hake, cod, plaice, and the signature smoked salmon are popular among locals—you may have to wait to make your order at the counter. The smoked fish can be packed so you can eat it as a takeaway on the harbor.

Seafood
Restaurant Beghuset

Strandgade 14; tel. 32 53 01 36; www.beghuset.dk; Mon.-Sat. 11am-10pm, Sun. 11am-6pm; smørrebrød and warm dishes from 73 kr

Beghuset is located within one of the yellow-washed tiled-roofed old buildings that give Dragør its charm. It recently changed ownership and now serves unpretentious classic Danish dishes like open-face sandwiches (smørrebrød) and tarteletter, a flaky pastry pie with a creamy chicken and asparagus filling. You can also get home-made toast or a slice of apple tart for as little as 35 kr. You may

Restaurant Beghuset

also be able to try the dish of the day (129 kr), likely to be a Danish classic like brændende kærlighed (mashed potato topped with bacon and onions) or forloren hare, a kind of meatloaf wrapped in bacon and accompanied by steamed vegetables. The prices, like the building, appear to come from another era, namely the end of the 2010s, before inflation sent prices at Denmark's restaurants up several notches. It's worth calling ahead to reserve.

Burgers
Backstage Burgers

Prins Knuds Dæmning 2; tel. 60 51 27 91; www.backstageburgers.com; Tues.-Fri. 4pm-8pm, Sat.-Sun. noon-8pm; burgers 95 kr, meal deal 140 kr

A windswept shack on Dragør Fort is the location of this burger bar, which started life as a food van outside the Royal Arena concert venue in Copenhagen, hence the name. There's some seating inside if it gets too blustery. The location comes into its own on a warm summer evening when you can take in the nearby fort and harbor, but it's probably Dragør's best burger option regardless of the prevailing conditions. The menu includes beef, chicken, and veggie burgers, and you can upgrade the meal deal to include an IPA or a weiss beer if you're feeling fresh.

Cafés and Ice Cream
Café Dragør Sejlklub

Strandlinien 1B; tel. 22 52 15 19; http://cafedragoersejlklub.dk; Dec.-Sept. Mon.-Sat. noon-10pm, Sun. noon-8:30pm, Oct.-Nov. Mon. and Fri.-Sat. noon-10pm, Sun. noon-8:30pm; starters 129-145 kr, mains 199-295 kr

By the pier just off the old harbor, Café Dragør Sejlklub has perhaps the best of all the sea views of any of Dragør's restaurants, and there's plenty of competition. Freshly delivered ingredients are used to make dishes from tapas to homemade fish-and-chips. The restaurant also serves as a café with a lunch menu (mains 169-329 kr) with a French-style platter, chicken salad, Danish herring on rye bread, and a burger among the options.

Rajissimo Gelato

Kongevejen 13B; tel. 50 52 76 29; www.rajissimo.com; daily 11am-7pm; ice cream, waffles, churros from 50 kr

Rajissimo also has four branches in Copenhagen, but its outlet in Dragør often sees the longest queues in summer as the popular ice cream takeaway serves its long list of flavors to sweet-toothed visitors. Ice cream is mixed daily; waffle sticks and churros are also available and become the main sellers during the colder months.

Dragør Guff

Strandlinien 51; hours vary; ice cream from 50 kr

Dragør's oldest ice cream shop is known for its crisp homemade waffles and ice cream from famous maker Hansen's. It can be found in an extension on a large white-and-blue house on the corner of town, facing the sea across a grassy plain. Try the strawberries and cream in early summer, or put homemade jam on top of your cone.

Hallöy Café

Kongevejen 11; tel. 31 19 20 47; Mon.-Tues. 10am-5pm, Wed.-Thurs. 8am-5pm, Fri. 9am-5pm, Sat.-Sun. 9am-6pm; sandwiches 68-78 kr; salads 99 kr

At the end of Kongevejen, a main street of sorts, you can grab a sandwich, salad, or ice cream at Hallöy. There's seating on the small square outside, a nice spot to take in the seaside atmosphere and check out Dragør Bio, the quaint 1928 cinema that closed in 2023 but still retains its charming facade. If it's cold, try the butternut soup (especially around Halloween) or warm æbleglögg (spiced apple juice) in December.

Café Sylten

Søndre Strandvej 50; tel. 30 50 60 19; https://sylten.dk; Apr.-Oct. Wed.-Fri. noon-5pm, Sat.-Sun. 10am-5pm; starters 75-125 kr; mains 165-170 kr

By the beach, away from the busiest section of town, Sylten offers filling café standards that include nachos, burgers, sandwiches, salads, and a vegetable stir-fry. The menu changes monthly.

AMAGER NATURE PARK
International
Kongelundskroen

Kalvebodvej 270; tel. 32 53 31 57; www. kongelundskroen.dk; Mar.-Dec. Thurs.-Sun. noon-5pm; lunch 95-230 kr

In a charming setting at the end of the coastal road near the Kongelunden forest and overlooking the sea, Kongelundskroen serves its French-Danish fusion dishes in the traditional-looking setting of a kro (inn). You can try smoked salmon on a spinach pie, fish soup à la bouillabaisse, or braised pork with potato roulade. An outside terrace can be used in the summer, and there's a friendly atmosphere inside the homey restaurant, which has a traditional look with patterned wallpaper and low ceilings. It's open primarily for lunch Thursday-Sunday. Evening bookings can be made any day for groups of at least eight adults.

Accommodations

Copenhagen Airport Hotel/ Dragør Badehotel

Drogdensvej 43; tel. 32 53 05 00; www. badehotellet.dk; high season from 895 kr d; 32 rooms

This three-star hotel has balcony rooms looking toward the Øresund Bridge, marina, and fort. The rooms in the hotel's annex have noticeably less charm than those in the original building. Although it's ostensibly an airport hotel due to its close proximity to Copenhagen Airport, it has a homey feel and is just outside the old town in Dragør, and it's a good option if you want to stay in the town.

Dragør Fort

Prins Knuds Dæmning 2; tel. 32 53 13 15; https://dragorfort.dk; shelter from 995 kr

Built in the early 20th century on an artificial island to the south of the harbor and connected by a short causeway, Dragør Fort rises like an anomalous green blob across a broad flat area to the south of the harbor and old city. The 32,000-sq-m (344,000-sq-ft) fort was built to protect the coast from hostile advances and was later used as a shooting range by the occupying Germans during World War II. The fort was purchased by a private owner in 2002 and public access is therefore

harbor in front of Dragør Fort

limited. One way to see it is by staying at the outside shelter—an open cabin with basic sleeping accommodations. The shelter accommodates three adults or two adults and two children. Unlike most shelters, such as those in Amager Nature Park, it offers a range of amenities including electricity and running water. Bookings are made via the fort website. Points of interest on the fort grounds include several concrete relics from its previous military use, among them a fire watch post and a cannon base. There is a nice vantage point from which to view Dragør.

Tourist Information

Dragør Tourist Information

Gamle Havn 14; tel. 28 96 58 82; www. visit-dragoer.dk/dragoer/dragoer-turistkontor; May-Sept. Tues.-Sun. 11am-4pm

Dragør's tourist information office can be found in a small house by the harbor and provides information on local sights and attractions. Maps of the area are available, as are coffee and soft drinks.

Getting There and Around

GETTING THERE
By Public Transit

From Copenhagen, the most direct route is to take bus 250S from Copenhagen Central Station directly to **Dragør's bus station** (every 20 minutes at peak times; 1 hour; 30 kr, Rejsekort 20 kr). This bus travels via Amagerbrogade, Amager's central traffic artery and shopping drag, and can be picked up at the Amagerbro Metro station. If you want to connect from the Metro, this is a handy route. An alternative option is to take the Metro or a train all the way to the airport and switch to bus 35, thereby cutting out some of the central Copenhagen traffic. The fare is the same.

For Amager Nature Park, the Copenhagen Metro takes you almost to the doorstep: **Vestamager station** is about 500 m (0.3 mi) from the entrance to the park and the Amager Nature Center. Bus 33 travels close to other parts of this large nature reserve as well as the Nature Center and is therefore a useful alternative transport option. It terminates in Dragør, so you can also take it from Dragør to get to the park. Taking bus 33 from Copenhagen all the way to Dragør takes 1 hour and costs 30 kr; to the Nature Center it's around 45 minutes and 24 kr from Copenhagen and 45 minutes and 24 kr from Dragør.

By Bicycle

Munkevejen Bicycle Route 80 (www.munkevejen.dk) is a scenic trail that you can pick up from Islands Brygge near Copenhagen Harbor or from the Amager Strand beach.

Alternatively, head out of Copenhagen via Christianshavn, cross to Amager, and head directly south on the main shopping street Amagerbrogade. Follow this road for around 5.5 km (3.4 mi), where it turns right on to Tømmerupvej, close to the airport. After 1.2 km (0.75 mi), take a left on to Englandsvej/Route 221. From here, it's another 4.5 km (2.8 mi) to Dragør; you can follow the road all the way, passing through Store Magleby as you go. Plan at least an hour for the ride, which is on a flat trajectory.

By Car

By car from Copenhagen, the fastest route is via Langebro to Amager, then following Ørestads Boulevard for 3 km (1.8 mi) before taking a left turn on Vejlands Allé close to the distinctive Bella Center hotel and conference center. Then, after 1 km (0.6 mi), right on to Englandsvej, which you can follow all the way to Dragør. This 15-km (9.3-mi) journey takes 25 minutes.

GETTING AROUND
By Bus

Bus 33 traverses the southern end of Dragør, linking the town's bus station and harbor with Store Magleby and the natural areas to the southwest, including Kongelunden and Kalvebod Fælled. Single journeys cost 24 kr, 20 kr using Rejsekort. Journeys to and from the nature park by bus take 15-45 minutes depending on which part of the reserve you're headed to. Departures are every 30 minutes in peak periods. Use the travel planner at https://rejseplanen.dk to plot your route and find departure times.

On Foot and By Bicycle

Dragør itself should be explored on foot—the cobbled alleyways are not suitable for anything else. Bicycle lanes and paths connect Dragør with its surroundings, including Amager Nature Park. The lanes are in good condition and size and are easy to find.

Møn

What was once a tough, windy, and remote corner of Denmark is now a jewel in the crown of its natural attractions. After crossing the bridge from Zealand, an air of calm seems to descend as you travel across the flatlands and rolling fields, through the well-preserved former regional capital of Stege, and all the way to Møns Klint, the dramatic white cliffs that rise up from the coast. While these are an unexpected geological formation, keeping in mind the flat sandy coastlines of the rest

Highlights

⭐ **Møns Klint:** The white cliffs of Møn ruggedly define the eastern coast and are visible from forest paths above and rocky beaches below (page 257).

⭐ **GeoCenter Møns Klint:** The multimillion-kroner museum at the gateway to the white cliffs is the place to discover the island's geology and the "birth of Denmark," and there is even a dinosaur exhibition (page 258).

⭐ **Thorsvang Collector's Museum:** Built from scratch over decades by a local restaurateur turned nostalgia buff, this incredible collection of knickknacks will have you feeling wistful for the past (page 269).

⭐ **Camøno:** This 175-km (109-mi) calm and often strikingly beautiful "friendliest trail in the kingdom" across the island takes in forest, field, coast, and starry sky (page 270).

⭐ **Møn Is Farm Shop and Dairy:** Sample the fresh rich flavors of Møn's locally produced ice cream right at the source (page 277).

⭐ **Stargazing:** Møn has some of Denmark's clearest skies due its small size and proximity to the calm Baltic Sea, and there are plenty of ways to participate in amateur astronomy (page 280).

of the country, the cliffs are far from the only variation on Møn. Stargazing, abundant birdlife, hiking, and local history supported by a well-organized but not overcrowded tourism infrastructure are all part of what makes Møn a highlight of any Denmark trip.

ORIENTATION

Møn is a small island connected to Zealand by bridge on its northwest coast. The road from the bridge heads directly into Stege, the largest town and formerly a municipal capital before administration was moved to the larger island. Northeast from Stege, you'll find

---

Previous: Møns Klint. **Above:** Geocenter Møns Klint; trail marker to Møns Klint.

Møn

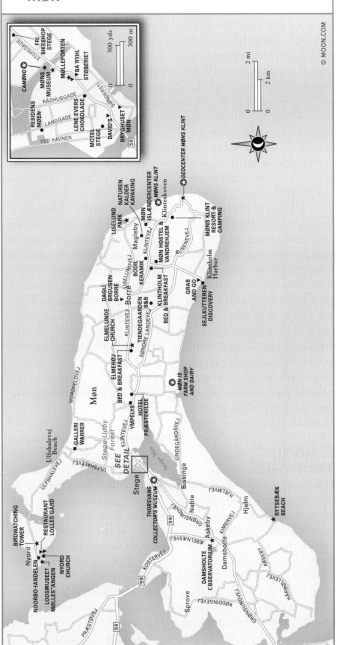

Detail Inset (Stege)

STOREGADE
FRI BIKESHOP STEGE
BIKESHOP STEGE
MØLLEPORTEN
CAMØNO
BA RYKH
STØBERIET
MØNS MUSEUM
RÅDHUSGADE
SØNDRIST
RESIDENS MØEN
LENE EVERS CHOKOLADE
LANGGADE
MOTEL STEGE
DAVID'S
BRYGHUSET MØN
VED HAVNEN
59

300 yds
300 m

© MOON.COM

2 mi
2 km

Main Map

GEOCENTER MØNS KLINT
NATUREN KALDER KAYAKING
LISELUND PARK
MØN ISLÆNDERCENTER
MØNS KLINT
Klinteskoven
Magleby
MØN HOSTEL & VANDREHJEM
MØNS KLINT RESORT & CAMPING
KLINTEVEJ
LISELUNDVEJ
BODIL KERAMIK
Klintholm Harbor
DAGLI BRGUSEN BORRE
Borre
KLINTEVEJ
KLINTHOLM BED & BREAKFAST
GRAB AND GO
Klintholm
ELMELUNDE CHURCH
TIENDEGAARDEN BED & BREAKFAST
SEJLKUTTEREN DISCOVERY
KLINTEVEJ
SØNDRE LANDEVEJ
ELMEHØJ BED & BREAKFAST
NORDFELDVEJ
Møn
HOTEL PRÆSTEKILDE
YMPELVEJ
MØN IS FARM SHOP AND DAIRY
GALLERI WARRER
LINDEGARDSVEJ
Stege Udby
Ulvshalevej Beach
Stege Nor
Bissinge
SEE DETAIL
KLINTEVEJ
ULFSHALEVEJ
Nable
Stege
THORSVANG COLLECTORS' MUSEUM
59
BIRDWATCHING TOWER
RESTAURANT LOLLES GARD
Askeby
GRØNSUNDVEJ
ABELNÆSVEJ
Hjelm
RYTSEBÆK BEACH
HJELMVEJ
Nyord
KOSTERVEJ
KIMERVEJ
NOORBO-ANDELEN
LODSMUSEET MØLLESTANGEN
NYORD CHURCH
DAMSHOLTE OBSERVATORIUM
Damsholte
Sprove
RØDDINGVEJ
GRØNSUNDVEJ
ÅSSEBY
HARBØLLEVEJ
PRÆSTØVEJ
59

the flat reedy island of Nyord, with its sandy coastal pathways, tiny town, and octagonal church, via a narrow concrete bridge. Heading directly east from Stege, you'll pass through the blink-and-you'll-miss-them villages of Elmelunde, Borre, and Magleby before arriving at the coast, where the showpiece geological attraction, the white cliffs at Møns Klint, are located at the top of a gravelly approach road. The southwest of the island is where you'll find the town of Askeby and the smaller island of Bogø. This is the quieter part of Møn, though it has several attractions of its own, including a beachy southern coast.

Route 59 is the main road that connects the island to Zealand. Route 287 links the island from east to west, and from Route 287 on the west, you can cross a bridge to Bogø. Driving the full length of the island from east to west takes around 45 minutes. Møn is small enough to navigate by following your instincts most of the time, and there's nothing wrong with asking a passerby for directions.

PLANNING YOUR TIME

Møn boasts a rich variety of nature to explore both day and night, and it's ideal for stargazing. There are also charming and enjoyable museums on offer. As such, this nature-abundant, serene island is well suited for a weekend visit. Day trips by car from Copenhagen, taking in the white cliffs of Møns Klint along with a couple of other attractions, are also viable and worthwhile,

given the relatively small size of Møn and its manageable 1.5-hour drive time from the capital.

Many Danes are keen Tour de France fans, and you can enjoy a similar though less physically extreme challenge on Møn. The mostly flat landscape can be covered by bicycle in 2-3 days, and there are plenty of routes to follow. Unlike in the cities, however, there are plenty of roads that do not have bicycle lanes, so cycle with care. Since the island is part of the N9 Berlin-Copenhagen bicycle route, there is good access to the island on two wheels, with routes and destinations mapped out. If you have a week to spare and prefer walking to wheels, the Camøno trail is an increasingly popular and rewarding way to become intimately acquainted with all the island has to offer.

If you're not visiting primarily to walk or bicycle, having a car makes Møn a lot easier to see, since the island's bus network is not comprehensive.

In early 2024, a landslide caused by severe winter weather damaged some of the viewpoints at Møns Klint. While small landslides are common, damage to the lookout points is rare; this was the biggest landslide since 2007. It's advisable to check ahead for weather warnings with Denmark's national meteorological agency DMI (www.dmi.dk) and for any recent changes to the area around Møns Klint.

An excellent website for tourist information for the island is www.southzealand-mon.com.

Itinerary Ideas

MØN ON DAY 1

Start your trip to Møn with a visit to the dazzlingly white signature Møns Klint.

1 Stege, Møn's largest town with a population of 3,800, can be used as a base and is a good place to begin your visit. Head to **David's** to pick up a white bread roll with jam or cheese and a coffee, or stop for brunch if you're feeling hungry.

2 Head to **Møns Klint,** across the island from Stege, and stop at the GeoCenter Møns Klint for some insight into the geology of the cliffs and Denmark's natural history. Children will be enthralled by the dinosaur exhibition.

3 Pop into the café at the **GeoCenter Møns Klint** for a quick lunch of smørrebrød.

4 After lunch, take one of the staircases down to **Møns Klint beach** and spend an hour or two wandering the coastline and admiring the rugged beauty of the cliffs from below.

5 After ascending the stairs, try some of the local Møn **ice cream** or just grab a coffee at the ice cream stand opposite the entrance to the GeoCenter.

6 Head to **Liselund Park,** only 1 km (0.6 mi) or so to the north of Møns Klint, for a picturesque early evening walk around the monuments and small buildings.

7 End your day with a hearty meal and a pint or two of locally brewed beer in Stege at **Bryghuset Møn.**

MØN ON DAY 2

Take a look into the island's past and present and experience the meadows and history of Nyord.

1 After breakfast at your lodging, spend some time walking around **Stege.** Don't miss the Mølleporten, one of the few medieval town gates anywhere that still marks the limits (or thereabouts) of the town.

2 Visit the **Thorsvang Collector's Museum** for a poke around the various treasures and trinkets collected over the decades by the museum's owner, a dyed-in-the-wool Mønbo (Møn islander).

3 Chow down on a hearty traditional Danish **lunch at the museum**

Itinerary Ideas

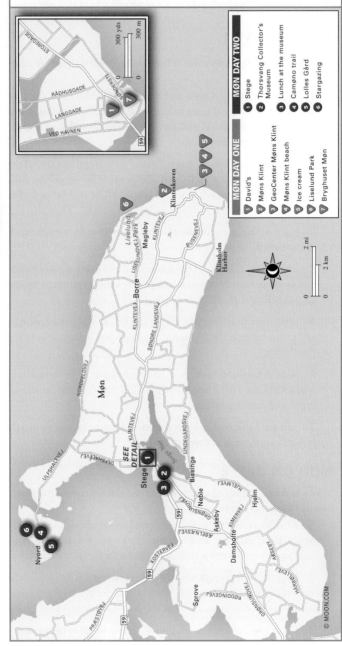

RÅDHUSGADE
LANGGADE
VED HAVNEN
STORGADE
SØNDERSØ

300 yds
300 m

MØN DAY ONE
1. David's
2. Møns Klint
3. GeoCenter Møns Klint
4. Møns Klint beach
5. Ice cream
6. Liselund Park
7. Bryghuset Møn

MØN DAY TWO
1. Stege
2. Thorsvang Collector's Museum
3. Lunch at the museum
4. Camønø trail
5. Lolles Gård
6. Stargazing

Klinteskoven
Liselund Park
Magleby
Busenevej
Klintevej
Klinteholm Harbor
Borre
Klintevej
Liselundvej
Søndre Landevej

Møn
Nordfeltvej

Stege Nor
Ulvshalevej
SEE DETAIL
Klintevej
Lindegårdsvej

Stege
Bissinge
Nebie
Askeby
Grønsundvej
Hjelm
Hjelmvej
Kimervej
Abelnæsvej
Damsholte
Sprove
Grønsundvej
Kostervej
Røddingevej
Prastovej
Harbøllevej
Ørslev

Nyord

2 mi
2 km

© MOON.COM

before leaving Stege behind for Nyord, a separate island about 8 km (5 mi) northwest of Stege. There is no public transportation connecting Stege and Nyord, so you'll need to travel by car, bicycle, or on foot.

4 Once you've crossed the bridge to Nyord, you'll feel like you've entered to a different ecosystem. Spend the rest of the afternoon exploring the island, hiking part of the **Camøno trail** through Nyord's meadows.

5 After your hike, you'll be more than ready for a hefty portion of schnitzel at the restaurant **Lolles Gård** in Nyord, which you can enjoy in their garden if the weather is good.

6 If the good weather holds and the night is clear, head to the bird-watching tower for a serene night of **stargazing.**

Møns Klint and Eastern Møn

The white cliffs of Møns Klint are the island's showpiece attraction, located on its far eastern coast. Nearby and along the way, the tiny towns of Elmelunde, Borre, and Magleby offer a few sights and other points of interest as well as places to stay the night.

SIGHTS

✪ Møns Klint
(Cliffs of Mon)
Stengårdsvej 8, Borre; www.moensklint.dk; daily 24 hours; free, car park 35 kr

In Denmark, which has no mountains, Møn feels almost alpine in places. Climbing from sea level to 143 m (470 ft) in the space of 1 km (0.6 mi), the white cliffs of Møns Klint are melodramatic by Danish standards and seem to rise out of nowhere from the trees of western Møn. The cliffs stretch along 6 km (4 mi) of the island's east coast and reach 128 m (420 ft) above sea level at their highest point. The chalk edifice topped by peaceful forests is one of the country's natural wonders and the pinnacle of the Møn UNESCO Biosphere Reserve.

Adventure movie-evoking beech trees grow right up to the edges of the cliffs in Klinteskoven, the forest above Møns Klint. The leaves of these unusual trees are a lighter green as a result of the high chalk content of the soil. After walking through the forest, take one of Møns Klint's two long wooden staircases down to the peaceful pebbly beach and enjoy the awe-inspiring sight of the steep white slopes above.

Late spring, summer, and early fall are great times to visit Møns

Klint, which looks spectacular in all three seasons. Denmark's climate is generally unpredictable, including on Møn, so come prepared for colder and wetter weather than you expect. That way, you'll only be positively surprised. In winter, tourist services are much sparser, and the outdoors can be relentlessly cold, but the bare forests and cliffs retain great natural beauty.

Visitors traveling by car to see Møns Klint can park at the GeoCenter Møns Klint parking lot (45 kr). Your car's license plate will be registered automatically at the parking lot entrance. You then enter the registration number to pay for parking at the machine near the entrance.

✪ GeoCenter Møns Klint

Stengårdsvej 8, Borre; tel. 55 86 36 00; www.moensklint.dk; Apr.-Oct. daily 10am or 11am-5pm or 6pm, late Oct. daily noon-4pm, check website for exact hours; adults 155 kr, ages 3-11 100 kr, parking 45 kr

A trip to Møns Klint can be substantially expanded by visiting GeoCenter Møns Klint, a child-friendly museum with dinosaur bones, a 3-D cinema, virtual-reality glasses, and lessons about glaciers, supervolcanoes, and meteors. The museum also offers geological insight into the local landscape.

The building that houses GeoCenter Møns Klint, opened in 2007, is a modern boomerang-shaped construction with a café on the terrace that faces the trees of the surrounding Klinteskov forest and

Møns Klint white cliffs

Møn, Denmark's First UNESCO Biosphere Reserve

In 2017, Møn was named as a UNESCO Biosphere Reserve—an area consisting of land, marine, and coastal ecosystems. It is currently the only place in Denmark to have such status, which reflects the presence of most of Denmark's various ecosystem types within Møn's 450-sq-km (174-sq-mi) biosphere area: woodlands, grasslands, pastures, wetlands, coastal areas, ponds, and steep hills.

The status gives the island extra clout as a world-class natural area and is also recognition of the contribution made by the Mønboer (Møn islanders) to the natural areas on the island: in order to qualify for the UNESCO designation, an area must be considered a place where solutions are found to enable local people and nature to exist in balance. In Møn's case, Stege and the island's villages and farms, with their total population of 10,000, are able to live and work while making sure the ecosystems continue to thrive.

Møn has a series of landscape types, each with its own characteristic animal and plant life and contained within the biosphere zone. These include the cliffs at Møns Klint with ridges and hills created by glaciers at the end of the last ice age, and the landscape around Nyord, which was created by marine erosion and sediment transportation.

There are different types of sea around the island too, from brackish in the west to salty in the east—hence, the blue-green hue of the shallows at the bottom of Møns Klint, which form a striking contrast with the white of the cliffs.

Up to 18 species of orchids, rare plants, fungi not found anywhere else in Denmark, and semi-endangered birds such as the peregrine falcon and the red kite are cited by UNESCO's Ecological Sciences for Sustainable Development in its listing of this natural and ecological treasure trove as a listed biosphere.

Møns Klint. Inside, there's color, sound, interactivity, and plenty of visual stimulation to maximize the attraction and educational value for kids.

The high-tech installations include fossils and life-size reproductions of fearsome-looking dinosaurs to spark kids' imaginations, along with the films, taking you not only to the dinosaur kingdom but also underwater among sea monsters and into the midst of extreme weather systems. There's also a virtual-reality installation where you can take off and attempt to catch prey from the air.

The exhibition Where Denmark Was Born, in a room dug into the cliff itself, is built as a journey through time, presenting the Cretaceous and Tertiary Periods and the glaciers of the later Quaternary Period, tying together everything about how Møn's geology was created. As a whole, there is a strong emphasis on interactivity, with both young and old visitors able to get their hands on fossils, make souvenirs, study natural materials, and follow in the footsteps of paleontologists.

Other highlights include a climbing wall, an "indoor glacier," and a huge number of belemnite fossils—the museum is attempting to gather the world's largest collection with specimens from the beach at the bottom of the nearby cliffs, and visitors are encouraged to add their own finds to be included in the collection.

Guided tours through the surrounding forest are also available. These can include fossil hunts, zip lines (peak season daily noon-4pm; free with admission), and guides to local plants and wildlife. Options vary according to the season, so check ahead or ask at the museum's reception.

Guided tours by mountain bike (peak season daily 2pm-4pm; free with admission) are also available. Guides will present geology, flora, and fauna as you bike through the terrain. Tours are first-come, first-served, but you can reserve a spot by calling ahead, which is recommended. You must be over age 12 to join, and helmets are included.

Liselund Park

Langebjergvej 4, Borre; tel. 55 81 21 78; https://en.natmus.dk/museums-and-palaces/liselund; daily 24 hours; free; Liselund House guided tours July-Aug.

Wed.-Sun. 11am and 1pm; adults 60 kr, under age 18 free

In the far northeast of Møn, north of neighboring Møns Klint, Liselund Park is like something out of a fairy tale. A thatched-roofed cottage, Chinese tea pavilion, Norwegian cabin, lakes, streams, and monuments give this charming park an unquestionably romantic feel—there are few better places to bring a picnic. The park is a labor of love created by Antoine de la Calmette, a late-18th-century landowner, as a country home for his wife, Lisa.

The park is arguably one of Europe's best-preserved romantic gardens, with winding paths, hills, small lakes, trees from far-off lands, and slopes with monuments and pretty buildings. These include a pagoda-evoking Chinese summerhouse, a thatched cottage called the Swiss House, and the Norwegian House, so named for its location in a hilly area supposedly reminiscent of Norway's fjords.

The old manor house, Liselund Gammel Slot, is a small country home in the French neoclassical style, built in 1792; the park itself was purchased from the crown about 10 years earlier. The rooms include nine bedrooms and an impressive entry and have tasteful colors and delicate decorations—oval mirrors, chandeliers, and marble-topped tables. The white building with its thatched roof, light-blue columns, and decorated spire look out over a small waterfall and pond.

If you arrive early in the day in

Liselund Gammel Slot

summer, you can take a guided tour of the well-preserved interior, still much the same as it was laid out by its 18th-century court decorator. If you come later in the day, you'll have the park almost to yourself, which can make for an atmospheric sunset walk in the grounds and surrounding forest.

Although the house is only open to visitors in the summer, the garden is open year-round and admission is free. The park is small enough to walk around in 1-2 hours, and there are gravel paths among the ponds, trees, and buildings.

Elmelunde Church

Leonora Christines Vej 1, Elmelunde; tel. 40 18 40 72; www.keldbyelmelundekirke.dk; year-round daily 8am-3:45pm; free

The church at Elmelunde is a classic Nordic-style church on the outside, with high whitewashed walls and tiled pitched roofs. The interior is remarkable for its ceiling frescoes: Painted on the Gothic vaultings over the nave and choir by an artist known as the Elmelunde Master, probably in the late 15th century, they were hidden for centuries following the Reformation before being restored in the 1960s. Today, visitors can admire the vinelike floral patterns and chevrons; religious and biblical figures in medieval dress; and animals, including

Elmelunde Church

deer, horses, and a human-headed serpent, depicted in the intricate frescoes.

RECREATION
Beaches

The beach at Møns Klint is a serene sight. Shallow turquoise water—its color transformed by the chalky sea bed—laps against the pebbles of the beach with thousands of fossils scattered among them, preserved for eons before being released by the advancing geology of the cliffs. The beach stretches across 6 km (4 mi) of Møn's east coast, but most visitors walk only the short 1.5-km (0.9-mi) section between the wooden staircases leading up to Klinteskoven Forest and the GeoCenter. It's not a beach for sunbathing, even on warm days, due to its contours and inaccessibility—Møn has other beaches more suited to lounging.

There are three wooden staircases close to the GeoCenter that lead from the top of the cliffs down to the beach. The closest of the three, **Maglevand Steps,** is opposite the entrance to the GeoCenter and is clearly signposted, as are the paths into the forest and to lookout points. You can follow any of the staircases up and down, which take 15-30 minutes to descend or ascend, depending on your fitness, the weather, and the care required in wet conditions. The **Røde Udfald Steps,** around 1 km (0.6 mi) north of the Maglevand

Møns Klint beach

Steps, zigzag down the hill and are less steep until you reach the final section. A third set, **Gråryg Fald Steps,** is south of the GeoCenter. Do not attempt to climb these if you are likely to have any physical difficulties. At the top of the cliffs, winding forested paths take you between the two staircases; there's no set route. At the bottom, simply follow the arc of the coast and admire the glistening white cliffs, serene atmosphere, and sea air.

Walks

Walking Route: Klinteskoven Forest and the Møns Klint Coast

Start: *GeoCenter*

Distance: *2.7 km (1.5 mi)*

Hiking time: *1-2 hours*

Walk north from the GeoCenter to Dronningestolen (the Queen's Chair), the highest point on the cliff face, 128 m (420 ft) above sea level. The path is well marked from the starting point and easy to follow through the forest, with dramatic vantages over the cliffs. Continue north, passing another viewing point, Vitmunds Nakke (Vitmund's Neck). Turn right onto the Røde Udfald Steps, which wind back and forth through the forest and take you down to the beach through leafy wooded slopes until you reach the final descent to the shore. Turn right and walk south along the beach, taking in the clear water and the view of Møns Klint from below. After around 1 km (0.6 mi) you'll find yourself at the popular Maglevand Steps, which are steep and almost straight and take you back to the GeoCenter.

Hiking

Hiking Route: Liselund Park, Klinteskoven, and the Less Explored Beach

Start: *GeoCenter or Liselund Park car park*

Distance: *14.5 km (9 mi)*

Hiking time: *12 hours*

This route requires a good level of fitness and familiarity with hiking. It leads through the Klinteskoven Forest, the grounds of Liselund Park, and the less-trodden section of the Møns Klint beach that abuts it, along with a wild nature area which adjoins the two parks. You can start anywhere along the route, but I recommend beginning at Liselund. Make sure you have plenty of water, start early in the day, and have a sturdy pair of shoes, regardless of the time of year. The route passes through **Liselund Park,** passing its old Manor House, Swiss Cottage, and other buildings of interest in the rolling gardens, before ducking into the forest. Here the trail crosses babbling brooks and winds through the trees before descending the steep **Djævlekløften** (Devil's Gap) stairs down to the beach. If the tide is high, there's not a lot of room along the pebbly shore, so tread carefully. In some cases, it's necessary to climb over roots or rocks to progress along the beach. As you head south, you'll see the cliff line jut out, separating this section from the more neatly curved cliffs below Klinteskoven.

Around 1.5 km (0.9 mi) south of the Djævlekløften steps, you'll be able to ascend back into a narrow section of the forest via a second set of stairs, **Jydeleje Fald.** Turning left, follow the path through the forest, stopping to take in the vistas from the **Store Taler Feld** and **Hylldals Slugt** viewpoints before the path takes you past **Svantestenen,** a rock that, legend has it, was thrown by a Swedish troll woman at the twin church spires in Magleby. One of the spires broke off and flew into the sea, while the other landed in the forest.

The trail winds its way through the forest before coming out at the GeoCenter at around the halfway point, an ideal time to stop for refreshments at the center's café. It then winds deeper into the forest and farther into the cliffs before exiting at wild plains called **Jydelejet,** where there's a wealth of nature to take in, and the raised **Aborrebjerg** viewpoint. There's also a camping area, Lille Ørnebjerg, which you pass in the final miles before the trail completes its loop to arrive back at Liselund.

It should be kept in mind that all the trails mentioned above are part of the living nature of the area. Because of its geology, the cliffs crumble, and rubble occasionally slides into the sea. It's forbidden to throw stones and other objects over the edge, and straying from the marked trails is associated with high and potentially life-threatening risk, the Danish

Nature Agency states. Climbing on the cliffs is also strictly forbidden. Because the forest is protected, picking flowers and other plants is not allowed.

Boat Tours
Sejlkutteren *Discovery*

Klintholm Havneby, Borre, 4791; tel. 41 42 90 36; www.sejlkutteren-discovery.dk; Apr.-Sept. daily 2-6 departures, check website or call for timetable; adults 200 kr, ages 3-11 100 kr

You can view the white cliffs from the sea by taking a boat trip aboard the cutter *Discovery,* owned by local fisherman Bjarne Larsen, who bought the vessel in 2012. Larsen has sailed the Baltic Sea since the 1980s and is a partner of the Visit Møn tourist board. Call ahead to book your chosen trip—space on board is limited and reservations are necessary. The 2-hour tours have departures daily during the summer season, weather permitting.

Horseback Riding
Møn Islændercenter

Moenavej 7, Borre, 4791; tel. 55 81 28 10; www.moen-ishest.dk; year-round daily, tours usually 11am and 3pm; 550 kr pp

Icelandic horses clip-clop their way through the forest near the cliffs on tours provided by this family-run business. Both new and experienced riders are welcome, and the pace and route are tailored to suit the participants, with two guides joining if there is more than one skill level among the riders—so you might get to try a gallop if you're comfortable enough. Tours last around 90 minutes.

SHOPPING
Bodil Keramik
Sømarkevej 2, Magleby, 4791; tel. 55 81 20 61; http://bodilkeramik.dk; daily 10am-5pm
This small pottery workshop produces uniquely designed, traditionally made teapots, dishes, bowls, vases, and cups. Its walls and tables are stacked with locally made pottery, each hand-thrown on a kick wheel. All products are on sale in the well-stocked shop adjoining the workshop.

DINING
GeoCenter Mons Klint Café
Stengårdsvej 8, Borre; tel. 51 54 14 84; https://cafemoensklint.dk; Apr.-Oct. daily 10am or 11am-5pm or 6pm, late Oct. daily noon-4pm, check website for exact hours; sandwiches, smørrebrød, and salads 65-180 kr
Unless you've brought a picnic with you to enjoy on the benches outside the museum, in the forest, or even on the beach (all good options), the café at GeoCenter Møns Klint is the only place for lunch. It has a good selection of smørrebrød, fruit, pastries, and sandwiches, along with warmer dishes like frikadeller, Danish meatballs that come with a salad of your choice.

ACCOMMODATIONS
Under 500 Kr
Møn Hostel and Vandrehjem
Klintholm Havnevej 17A, Borre, 4791; tel. 55 81 24 34; Mar.-Sept.; dorm from 300 kr, private room from 400 kr

Located close to Møns Klint in rural surroundings and 3 km (1.8 mi) from Klintholm, this large hostel with 29 rooms and 96 beds opened in 2013 after moving from elsewhere on the island, but the building still gives off a retro holiday vibe. Bicycle rentals are available. There is a guest kitchen; breakfast and packed lunches (from 75 kr) can also be purchased. Bed linens must be rented (from 50 kr) if you don't have your own with you. Call ahead to check availability and reserve, especially during the summer when there's a large influx of walk-in guests from the hiking trails. Aside from hotel booking sites, there's little online presence, so reserving by phone helps you get into the 1990s mindset ahead of your arrival.

Pension Elmehøj Bed-and-Breakfast
Kirkebakken 39, Elmelunde, 4780; tel. 55 81 35 35; www.elmehoj.dk; high season from 499 kr d
Elmehøj's bed-and-breakfast opened 32 years ago in a former retirement home that was built in the 1930s (if you look closely, you can still see the door buzzers in some of the rooms). It has been run as a family business ever since by owner Brit Olifent, who says that the advent of the Camøno has brought an influx of diverse new guests, keeping her as busy as ever. It is located next to Elmelunde Church, famous for its 15th-century frescoes. Facilities include Wi-Fi, a guest kitchen, and a clothes-drying

Pension Elmehøj Bed-and-Breakfast

room. The 23 rooms with 50 beds are modern, clean, spacious, and comfortable. Linens must be rented (70 kr) unless you bring your own; breakfast costs 95 kr, and packed lunches (69 kr) can be ordered in advance.

Tiendegaarden Bed-and-Breakfast

Sønderbyvej 29, Borre, 4791; tel. 55 81 21 26; www.tiendegaarden.dk; high season from 500 kr d

Also popular with Camøno hikers is Tiendegaarden, a bed-and-breakfast set in a handsome old farmhouse close to Møns Klint—the quiet at night is striking, and it's also a good place from which to stargaze into Møn's famously clear sky. Breakfast costs 100 kr and must be ordered by 9pm the preceding evening or on arrival. Quiet time starts at 10pm, but in return you might get a visit from one of the resident cats, which are allowed to come and go as they please.

500-1,000 Kr
Klintholm Bed-and-Breakfast

Klintholm Havnevej 4, Magleby, 4791; tel. 55 81 24 50; www.klintholm-bb.dk; high season from 895 kr d; 10 rooms

Klintholm Bed-and-Breakfast is another of the numerous friendly family-run options on Møn. This one includes a cozy lounge area with a fireplace, an outside terrace, and a bar and games room with a pool table. It has been run by Belgian couple Sophie and Steven since 2021, giving it a European feel. Breakfast is included in the rates, and for an extra 45 kr you can make a packed lunch from the buffet, with packaging provided.

Camping
Møns Klint Resort and Camping

Klintevej 544; tel. 55 81 20 25; www. moensklintresort.dk; Apr.-June 26 and Sept.-Oct. tent site 24 kr, trailer or RV site 35 kr, plus adults 126 kr, under age 12 87 kr, June 26-Aug. tent site 68 kr, trailer or RV site 90 kr, plus adults 126 kr, under age 12 87 kr, plus 27 kr per day environment fee, electricity 44 kr per day

An extensive campground that also has family and smaller cabins, the well-rated Møns Klint Resort and Camping has three large clean service buildings with kids play and sports facilities, a heated swimming pool in late summer, and a guest kitchen. There's a restaurant and a small shop with a laid-back welcoming feel. Tents, trailers, and RVs are welcome at the 400 campsites. It is close to the countryside and not a bad place to see Møn's night sky: Wandering around the sprawling campsite can be a memorable way to take in the dusk and wait for the stars to appear.

GETTING THERE
By Public Transit

You can reach Møn by public transit from Copenhagen by first taking the regional train service from Copenhagen Central Station to Vordingborg. From there, switch to bus 660R, and in about 45 minutes you reach **Stege,** Møn's largest town. From Stege, take bus 667 to Busemarke (Klintholm Havnevej/ Klintholm Harbor), which leaves every 10 minutes during peak season but hourly during winter. May-September you can transfer here to bus 678, which goes all the way to the stop at the **GeoCenter** (use the same ticket; around 15 minutes). Rejsekort users should only ever check out at the end of their journey, but always check in again when making a transfer. When bus 678 is not running, you have to walk (be prepared with boots and warm waterproof clothes) a distance of around 6 km (4 mi), or arrange for a taxi. The full journey costs 132 kr, or 98 kr using a Rejsekort.

By Car

To drive to eastern Møn and Møns Klint from Copenhagen and Zealand, take the E47 and exit 41 toward Vordingborg, before following Route 59 to Stege on Møn and then Route 287 toward Borre. From here, signposts will direct you to Møns Klint. The road leads up through the hilly forest and becomes surprisingly steep and gravelly before reaching the top. Here, you can head for the forest path and the steps down to the beach, or visit the GeoCenter.

Stege

Stege has the feel of a market town with a large tourist industry, with a sense that residents are acquainted with each other and well versed in accommodating visitors. The town is charming and nicely maintained, with timbered buildings, narrow streets, and hidden yards around its central market square and the former town hall, as well as at Mølleporten, the old town gate. There's a regular Tuesday market during the summer, and a string of specialty shops run by local producers.

SIGHTS
Mølleporten

Storegade 75, Stege, 4780

The 15th-century Mølleporten (the Mill Gate) was once part of the fortifications defending medieval Stege, along with two others like it that have not survived, and a moat that is still visible. A sturdy square redbrick tower with white bands of limestone, innumerable vehicles have passed under its vaulted entrance through the centuries. It gives the impression of loyally insisting on performing the task it was built for, dutifully watching over the town limits.

Mølleporten

Møns Museum

Storegade 75, Stege; tel. 70 70 12 36; www.
moensmuseum.dk; Apr.-June Tues.-Sat.
10am-2pm, July-mid-Aug. daily 10am-4pm,
mid-Aug.-Sept. Tues.-Sat. 10am-4pm, Oct.
Tues.-Sat. 10am-2pm; adults 65 kr, under
age 18 free

Møns Museum is a modest local history museum archive in Empiregården, a merchant's house built in 1813 right by the medieval city gate. It has an information desk with resources for the Camøno walking trail. Permanent exhibitions on subjects such as Møn's history 1660-2000, migration on Møn, and a collection of oil paintings provide a look at local history with a focus on personal stories. There are also rotating exhibitions. One of the museum's most unusual objects is an organ-like instrument that is both a normal and a barrel organ and is said to have been used at many special occasions on the island.

✪ Thorsvang Collector's Museum

(Thorsvang Samlermuseum)

Thorsvangs Allé 7, Stege, 4780; tel. 40
46 91 46; www.thorsvangsamlermuseum.
dk; Jan. mid-Mar. Thurs.-Sun. 10am-5pm,
mid.-Mar. late-Oct. daily 10am-5pm, late
Oct.-Dec. Thurs.-Sun. 10am-5pm; adults 70
kr, ages 5-18 40 kr

This remarkable local history museum is a collection of odds and ends gathered over the course of decades. The owner, a local chef who has lived his entire life on Møn, began collecting the objects now displayed in the museum at age seven. Decades later, the result is a nostalgic cross between an exhibition and a flea market. The affectionately presented museum is a hoarder's dream, with 18 small shops stocked with 1960s biscuit tins, stacks of crockery, and vintage beer bottles crowding shelves; rooms full of old-fashioned TV sets, a garage of Model T Fords, Volvos, and motorbikes in various states of repair; a barber's salon, a carpentry workshop, telephone boxes, a post office—I could go on and on. On the grassy plain out front that also serves as a car park, wooden allotment houses and inoperable fairground stalls add to the charm. The staff, mostly retired volunteers, are happy to chat and tell you a bit about the island and the museum's history. A visit here is always memorable and a must-see on Møn.

Definitely stop in to the on-site café (noon-3pm) for lunch to round out your visit with a traditional feast. This is particularly rewarding on weekends, when there is a buffet of herring fish fillets, salad with curried dressing, relish, and fresh bread available (adults 169 kr, children 75 kr), or there's coffee and cake (65 kr). Smørrebrød (45 kr) is available weekdays.

Damsholte Observatorium

Grønsundsvej 251, Stege; tel. 38 71 97 18;
www.damobs.dk; May-Aug. hours vary,
Sept.-Apr. daily 8pm-11pm; 50 kr pp

This small observatory is run by a society of enthusiasts and was opened in 2016. Much pride is placed on Møn and Nyord's status as an International Dark Sky Community—one that doesn't use poor-quality outdoor lighting that can result in glare and light pollution. If skies are clear, the observatory opens for visitors for a couple of hours in the late evening when the sky is darkest, giving you the opportunity to try out some serious telescope equipment. Remember not to take out your phone or use your flash—you'll reset your and others' night vision. Always call ahead to check the hours before setting out; if conditions aren't right or if no one is coming, the observatory stays closed. A good rule of thumb is if you can see the Milky Way in the sky with the naked eye, you should be in luck. Note that conditions are better in the winter when the sky is darker, and the observatory only opens occasionally May-August. Wheelchair access is available, unusual at observatories and which resulted in Damsholte receiving an award from the local government in 2019.

RECREATION
Hiking
✪ Camøno: The
  Juniper Section
(Enebæretapen)

Start: *Møns Museum, Storegade 75, Stege*
Distance: *15 km (9.3 mi)*
Time: *2.5-4 hours*

The stretch of the Camøno known as the Juniper section begins at Møns Museum in Stege, which also functions as the main tourist information point for the trek, making it an ideal place to start. Friendly staff will help you plan and prepare your route. While you're here, take a look at the old merchant's yard behind the museum. The route itself is flat, family-friendly, and designed as a soft start to the Camøno.

As you leave the museum, turn left and walk through **Mølleporten,** the medieval tower that was once part of the town's fortifications. You'll also pass the excavation of the old moat encircling Stege. Following the road out of town, you'll reach **Stege-Udby Forest.** This wooded area has an easy-to-follow path, bushes and trees, and a small log shelter. At the right time of year, you can pick cherries from the overgrowth by the path.

Emerging from the forest, you have a stunning view across a flat landscape with grazing cattle, and across Stege Bay. A long stretch of open countryside follows, with wide sky and a view out over the fields. This is **Ulvshale Marshes and Heath.** Eventually, the land ends as path reaches the **Nyord Bridge.**

The bridge is a simple concrete single-lane structure with a retro-looking traffic light. Hikers can walk across the flat bridge and watch flocks of birds soaring above the marshy landscape while ducks and geese bob in the strait separating Møn and Nyord.

After you reach the **Nyord** side, a long straight section of the path leads through the heart of the island and provides a sense of how much of it is wilderness. If your legs are tiring, options are at hand. Turn left onto a dirt trail to find **Hyldevang Shelter,** an octagonal wooden structure open to the elements where you can sleep for free (if there's space). You may meet one of the volunteers who help maintain the area. There's a wood-chopping machine for the bonfire, and the **Nyord birdwatching tower** is nearby.

If you are staying over and want a little more comfort than sleeping in the shelter, you can finish the hike to Nyord and rest for the night at **Nyord Cabin** (Nyord Havnevej 10; tel. 23 31 32 70; 200 kr per bunk, whole cabin 500 kr), a white-painted hut with four bunks. Call ahead to reserve. Don't expect luxury, but you will find a kitchenette with a kettle and hot plates and access to a patio garden overlooking the sea.

Nyord itself is great reward for finishing the trek. The car-free hamlet, with its fishing houses and little harbor with a view of Stege Bay and the Queen Alexandrine Bridge to Zealand, is even more idyllic when you've spent several hours walking to get here. There's a designated **Camøno Pause,** a rest spot with restroom facilities, electricity, and water where you can recharge for the next leg of the Camøno.

This leg of the Camøno, at 15 km (9.3 mi), takes 2.5-4 hours, depending on your pace.

Bicycling

Møn can be explored by bike with a number of well-signposted routes. Møn's bicycle routes are all well supplied with cafés, shops, and ice cream kiosks, but they are also notable for Denmark's first two bicycle-friendly churches, **Borre Church** and **Magleby Church,** which offer free water bottle refills, tire pumps, and a rest on the church pews.

Fri Bikeshop Stege

Storegade 91, Stege, 4780; tel. 55 81 42 49; www.fribikeshop.dk/cykler-stege; Mon.-Fri. 8am-4pm, Sat. 9am-1pm; standard bicycles 100 kr daily, electric bicycles and mountain bikes 250 kr daily

Standard, electric-assisted, and mountain bikes can all be rented at this friendly bicycle store in Stege, which has a range of equipment and also makes repairs. A deposit is required when you pay for the rental. Reservations are recommended from early spring to September, preferably by email (info4780@fribikeshop.dk); alternatively, you can reserve over the phone.

Beaches and Watersports
Ulvshale Beach

Ulvshalevej, Stege; free

This child-friendly, low-water beach on the spit between Stege and Nyord has some nice sand dunes and access for wheelchairs, as well as restrooms and a kiosk. Its blue-turquoise water and white sands

The Camøno: A Trek Around the Island

on the Camøno walking trail

The **Camøno** (http://camoenoen.dk) is a 175-km (109-mi), 250,000-step hiking trail across Møn, Nyord, and Bogø. The name is a lighthearted pun that pays homage to the Camino de Santiago pilgrimage trail in Spain. Møn's version is a well-signposted route split into **10 sections** (plus two shortcuts if you want a reduced schedule) directing you along country paths, tracks, fern forests, and, naturally, to Møns Klint. The trail was established in 2016 and has become one of the island's biggest draws, with tens of thousands of people stepping onto its paths every year.

Denmark might not be known for spectacular geological scenery like Norway's fjords or the ice of Sweden's Lapland, but the Camøno and Møns Klint draws high marks from hikers of multiple nationalities. Arriving at Møns Klint is a worthy payoff for the long hours of walking; the peaceful sound of the waves on the shore directly below a towering wall can look positively Mediterranean in summer. It has Blue Flag certification, which means quality is assured.

Naturen Kalder Kayaking

Moenavej 4, Borre, 4791; tel. 50 96 11 10; www.naturenkalder.com; naturenkalder@ gmail.com; hours vary; tours 300-750 kr, children 150 kr

If paddling is your thing, Møn can be seen from a kayak, with various guided tours available for beginners and experienced kayakers. Stand-up paddleboards can also be rented (2 hours 450 kr, minimum 2 people). It's best to call or email the company directly to reserve and check tour information. Tours leave from Stege or near Klintholm or Ulvshale, depending on where you will be kayaking.

of white, cream, and yellow chalk cliffs makes the experience an overwhelmingly beautiful one.

Physical maps (135 kr) can be purchased via the Camøno website. The website and map is currently only in Danish, so if your web browser's translator is not up to it, **Møns Museum** (Storegade 75, Stege, 4780; tel. 70 70 12 36; www.moensmuseum.dk) is the place to go for all the tourist information you will need. The staff is happy to provide advice and words of encouragement.

There are several places along the route where supplies can be bought, including at or near the nine designated break stations known as **Camøno Pauses,** where hikers can relax, refill water bottles, and chat with residents and other hikers. These break areas are located about one day's walk from each other and are marked on the maps and with signposts. Many bed-and-breakfasts sell packed lunches, and the small supermarket in Borre (Dagli' Brugsen Borre; Klintevej 381; tel. 55 81 20 04) is a great place to restock and support a local business.

Some tips to bear in mind:

- Make sure you have a good pair of **broken-in waterproof hiking boots.** You won't be making any challenging mountain ascents, but you will be walking for a long time, and your feet will thank you for taking care of them.

- Plan **where to stay** in advance. There are free shelters and cheap camping sites along the route; information on these is available at Møns Museum. Hostels, bed-and-breakfasts, and hotels on the island are all used to seeing hikers.

- **Ease yourself in** and gradually increase your daily distance. Walking 12-16 km (7.5-10 mi) on the first day is fine; this can then be ramped up to 20 km (12.4 mi) per day.

Be sure to say hello to the Mønboer (Møn islanders) you pass along your way—people are generally sympathetic to the tired feet of the hikers of the Camøno.

SHOPPING

Ympelys

Klintevej 110, Stege, 4780; tel. 55 81 30 05; http://ympelys.dk; Apr.-Oct. Mon.-Tues. 10am-5pm, Thurs.-Fri. 10am-5pm, Sat. 10am-4pm, Nov.-Mar. Thurs.-Fri. 10am-5pm, Sat. 10am-4pm

This homey shop is packed with Nordic-style crafts and clothing, starting with a huge selection of handmade candles as well as ceramics, textiles, clothing, and home goods. Ympelys is located on the main road heading east, just outside Stege.

Lene Evers Chokolade

Storegade 39, Stege, 4780; tel. 29 71 15 19; https://leneeverschokolade.dk; Aug.-June Fri. 11am-6pm, Sat. 10am-2pm, July-early Aug. Tues. 10am-5pm, Fri. 11am-6pm, Sat. 10am-2pm

Bike Routes on Møn

landscape of Møn

BERLIN TO COPENHAGEN

The **Berlin-Copenhagen Bikeway** bicycle route (www.bike-berlin-copenhagen.com and www.cykel-ruter.dk) traverses Møn. Note that the main bicycle routes on Møn are marked by their national bicycle lane designation, **N8 and N9,** but these two routes are not exhaustive of the side trips included in the Berlin-Copenhagen tour. By following this route you can see a large part of the island. As it's part of a longer route, the N8 can be picked up anywhere on Møn, but if you want to cycle it in its 75-km (47-mi) entirety, you can pick it up at car road 287 near the Bogø Bridge, and take it across the southern half of the island. The route eventually turns north on the eastern end, heading back across the northern

With a splendid selection of lovingly made confectionaries, Lene Evers Chokolade is worth stopping by for both the intricate tastes and creative designs of the chocolates. Ingredients include limoncello, figs, berries, rhubarb, coconut, and port. Look for topical designs—witches at Halloween, skippers pipes on Father's Day, and eggs at Easter.

Galleri Warrer

Hovedskovvej 20, Ulvshale, 4780; tel. 23 61 18 77; www.warrer.dk; high season daily 11am-5pm, low season Thurs.-Sun. 11am-5pm; free

At 1,000 sq m (10,760 sq ft), Galleri Warrer is the largest gallery on Møn, with art, furniture, ceramics, sculpture, glass, jewelry, and clothing. As many of 50 artists from various disciplines have contributed to part of the island to Stege. The terrain is a mixture of asphalted roads and bicycle lanes with some gravel tracks. Unlike most other parts of Denmark, there are some challenging uphill and undulating sections, notably on the Klintholm panorama route, at the eastern end of the island near Klintholm.

The best way to plan bicycling on any iteration of the Berlin-Copenhagen route is to use the website's online maps on your smart phone. The website contains a wealth of other resources too, such as downloadable data for GPS devices and written turn-by-turn navigation. All routes are clearly signposted: Look for the little white bicycle and route numbers N8 and N9.

PANORAMA ROUTES

Excellent options for those wanting to see Møn by bike are Møn's three Panorama Routes, designed as sightseeing side trips that can be added to the main Berlin-Copenhagen journey. These include **On Top of the World** (18 km/11.2 mi), around Klintholm and Liselund; **Life Is Sweet** (21 km/13 mi), circling Stege Cove; and **Take The Family Exploring** (29 km/18 mi), covering the Stege-Nyord stretch. The three routes encapsulate the nature and landscape that make Møn great: the open marshes, chiseled cliffs, beech forests, and expansive shorelines.

Look for the designation "Panoramarute" on the blue road signs. Maps and information can also be downloaded from the Berlin-Copenhagen Bikeway website (www.bike-berlin-copenhagen.com).

REFRESHMENTS

Møn's bicycle routes are all well supplied with cafés, shops, and ice cream kiosks, but they are also notable for something that is possibly unique: Denmark's two first bicycle-friendly road churches, **Borre Church** and **Magleby Church,** which offer free water bottle refills, tire pumps, and a chance to rest on the church pews.

the rotating exhibitions. Its location in Ulvshale makes it a convenient stop between Stege and Nyord.

DINING
Danish and New Nordic
Bryghuset Møn

Søndersti 3, Stege, 4780; tel. 30 74 04 00; www.detgamlebryghus.dk; daily noon-3:30pm and 5pm-7:30pm; burgers from 145 kr, 3-course menu 429 kr

In a quiet yard set back from Stege's main street, walking into Bryghuset Møn feels like wandering into a secret alley. There is decking for outside seating in the summer and a spacious high-ceiling interior that echoes its connection to the local brewery Bryghuset Møn. On the menu is a three-course meal, hearty burgers, steaks, and fish dishes, but few options for vegetarians. Any of the mains can be paired with locally brewed craft beers.

Eating Møn Ice Cream

Møn's locally produced ice cream comes from cows that live on the island, and the ice cream is 100 percent organic. This means that your ice cream will be made from milk less than eight hours old, giving it a genuine rich taste, whichever flavor you choose.

Møn Is and the Camøno

As you make your way across the island, you'll find plenty of chances to sample the ice cream. Wherever it's sold, you'll see the characteristic logo—an outline of the island turned into a blob of vanilla ice cream on a waffle. Here are a few places around the island where you can find ice cream stands:

- **GeoCenter Møns Klint** (Stengårdsvej 8, Borre)

- **Grab and Go** (Thyravej 14, Klintholm)

- **Daglì Brgusen Borre** (Klintevej 381, Borre)

- The farm shop at the **Møn Is** dairy (Hovgårdsvej 4, Stege)

International
Støberiet

Storegade 59, Stege, 4780; tel. 55 81 42 67; https://slagterstig.dk; Mon.-Sat. noon-4pm and 5pm-8:30pm; sandwiches 89-99 kr, evening buffet 145 kr

Støberiet is simultaneously charcuterie and brasserie. You'll find a traditional butcher counter in one half of the restaurant, where you can select a cut of meat to be prepared with your meal. Pair it with side dishes from the buffet and take a seat in the rustic informal surroundings. The buffet includes herring, fish fillets, cold cuts, and salads, and there are a range of meats to choose from for your main dish, from traditional steaks to occasionally more eclectic choices such as kangaroo or crocodile. There's also a lunch buffet and a solid range of meaty sandwiches, including pork belly and meatball. Reservations must be made by phone.

Cafés and Light Bites
David's

Storegade 11, Stege, 4780; tel. 33 13 80 57; www.davids.nu; Tues.-Fri. 10am-5pm, Sat.-Sun. 10am-4pm; sandwiches from 98k, salads from 135 kr, tapas 150-220 kr

Located on Stege's main street, David's prides itself on its fresh ingredients and has a range of carefully crafted sandwiches, including roast beef with bearnaise mustard, salmon and crème fraîche, and brie with crispy ham. There are also salads and vegetarian dishes as well as options for kids. A cozy courtyard, from where the church spire is visible over the rooftops, makes for a great place to enjoy your lunch on sunnier days.

Ice Cream

✪ Møn Is Farm Shop and Dairy

Hovgårdsvej 4, Stege, 4780; tel. 23 26 38 19; www.moen-is.dk; June-Sept. and holidays daily 11am-5pm, Oct.-May Sat. noon-4pm; from 22 kr for 1 scoop

Whatever you do, don't miss Møn's locally made ice cream, Møn Is. And where better to sample it than at the source? In the summer, visit the producer's farm shop and dairy, located in rural surroundings where you can enjoy the freshly made flavors and see the animals that provide the raw ingredients. There's a children's play area including a hay-bale fort, toy cows that can be bounced around on, and miniature tractors. You can also tap some fresh cow's milk to take home as well as choose from the many varieties of award-nominated Danish ice creams. If you enjoy the ice cream enough, you can even thank the animals that produced the milk. Highly rated flavors include the classic vanilla, pistachio, coffee with salted caramel, and rhubarb trifle.

NIGHTLIFE

Ba'ryhl

Storegade 70A, Stege, 4780; tel. 25 70 75 70; www.baryhlbar.dk; Wed. noon-6pm, Thurs. noon-8pm, Fri.-Sat. noon-1am, hours may be longer in summer; cocktails from 65 kr, beers from 40 kr

Aimed at islanders and tourists in equal measure, Ba'ryhl is both a bar and a café—you can stop for a coffee and panini during the day or enjoy one of the full range of Bryghuset Møn beers or expertly made cocktails in the evening. Informal and welcoming, there are comfy armchairs, board games, and cushions, and an outdoor deck area in summer.

ACCOMMODATIONS

Motel Stege

Provstestræde 4, Stege, 4780; tel. 31 44 40 35; www.motel-stege.dk; high season from 815 kr d; 12 rooms

Owned by Brit Olifent, the proprietor of Elmehøj Bed & Breakfast, Motel Stege is located right next to Stege Church and is conveniently close to the bus station and tourist information center. Room options include private and shared baths, and some rooms also have their own kitchenettes. There's a large garden where you can put your feet up at the end of a long day of walking or cycling.

Hotel Præstekilde

Klintevej 116, Stege, 4780; tel. 55 86 87 88; https://moengolfresort.dk/en; high season from 995 kr d; 41 rooms

Hotel Præstekilde is a comfortable

hotel, conference center, and restaurant with a golf course right next door. Breakfast is included in the rates, and the restaurant serves highly rated New Nordic-inspired fare (2-course menu 295 kr).

Residens Møen

Langelinie 44, Stege, 4780; tel. 70 40 48 50; www.residensmoen.dk; high season from 1,075 kr d; 31 rooms

The regal Hotel Residens Møn has a selection of different rooms, including doubles, apartments, and suites with balconies overlooking Stege Bay and Queen Alexandrine Bridge. Built in 1703, the building is a former navigation college that later became a prison for convicts of means—members of the nobility and even a princess were incarcerated here. It was opened as a hotel in 2016. There are also hotel suites and family apartments, which have their own kitchens. Apartments can accommodate up to seven adults and two children.

TOURIST INFORMATION

The best and most accessible spot to find broad tourist information, including detailed assistance for the Camøno, is the **Møns Museum** (Storegade 75, Stege, 4780; tel. 70 70 12 36; www.moensmuseum.dk;

Apr.-June Tues.-Sat. 10am-2pm, July-mid-Aug. daily 10am-4pm, mid-Aug.-Sept. Tues.-Sat. 10am-4pm, Oct. Tues.-Sat. 10am-2pm).

GETTING THERE
By Public Transit

You can reach Møn by public transit from Copenhagen by first taking the regional train service from Copenhagen Central Station to Vordingborg. There are frequent trains, though in some cases you might need to transfer at the mid-Zealand town Næstved. At Vordingborg, transfer to bus 660R. Buses depart from outside the rail station. Show your ticket to the driver or use your Rejsekort. Bus 660R takes 45 minutes to reach Stege, with the total journey including transfers around 2 hours. A ticket for the full trip costs 128 kr, with a Rejsekort 95 kr.

By Car

From Copenhagen, take the O2 circular road to reach the E20 highway toward Odense, later merging onto the E47, before taking exit 41 to Vordingborg on Route 59. That road will take you all the way to Møn via the striking Queen Alexandrine arch bridge and then to Stege. The journey should take around 1 hour, 30 minutes.

Nyord

Nyord is a 5-sq-km (2-sq-mi) island connected to Møn by a quiet concrete bridge that feels like the backdrop from a whimsical movie set. The island has a calmingly desolate feel despite its meadows being home to a large and diverse bird population. Black-tailed godwits, ruffs, and dunlins are some of the rarer species that have been spotted here, and waders, terns, ducks, and gulls also all come in numbers to breed. The flat landscape and sandy coastline can be enjoyed on foot—most easily by following the marked Camøno trail—and you might see people wading in the water to fish or fishing from skiffs in the shallow waters off the coast.

The town Nyord By has a smattering of streets on the southwestern part of the island; the meadows take up the eastern and northern parts. It feels secluded and remote from Stege, never mind Copenhagen. The town is minuscule, with a population in 2023 of just 43, according to Denmark's official statistics agency. There were a few more than that when I visited on a warm August evening—many were also visitors, come to enjoy the car-free streets and time-forsaken bending roads. If you're lucky, you could find yourself being invited to

Nyord Church

✪ Stargazing on Møn and Nyord

Møn and Nyord are certified dark-sky preserves—areas with restricted light pollution that provide optimal conditions for astronomy. That means there's just as much reason to experience the island at night as in daylight. Up to 14,000 stars can be seen in Møn's skies on a clear night; by contrast, no more than 100 can be seen in Copenhagen.

Stargazing on Møn doesn't require a huge amount of preparation, but here are a few tips:

sign to stargazing areas at Møns Klint Resort and Camping

- The summer season is the worst time of year for stargazing, as the short nights reduce the visibility of the stars.

- If it's raining, you won't be able to see any stars.

- You'll want to bring binoculars, a telescope, or photography equipment, but you won't be able to use a flash.

a summer party at the small harbor, with old-fashioned Danish pop music on the stereo and pork on the grill.

SIGHTS
Nyord Church

Søndergade 1, Nyord By, 4780; www. nyordkirke.dk/forside; summer daily 7am-7pm, winter daily 8am-5pm; free

At the center of Nyord By's handful of twisting improvised-looking streets is the eight-sided Nyord Church. With a model ship hanging from its ceiling, the traditions bound to this diminutive place of worship are clear. Built in 1846, the inspiration for architect Jens Otto M. Glahn's design are a little mysterious, with the archives not open

to the public at the time of writing. However, there are some common characteristics with medieval and neoclassical churches built elsewhere in Denmark as well as in Europe and the Middle East, including Rome's Pantheon, which is a circular structure that might just be a distant relative of the church in Nyord.

Birdwatching Tower

Ulvshalevej 401, Nyord; daily 24-7; free

Nyord's approximately 400-ha (988-acre) meadow and bird habitat has a birdwatching tower by the only road that cuts through the island. There are open and sheltered areas in the two-tiered tower along with a platform for wheelchair

- Warm clothes are required—do not underestimate the chilliness of the Danish weather.

- Bring a beach towel to sit on, a lamp, and a bag to carry away your garbage.

- Mosquito repellent is handy in the warmer months.

BEST SPOTS FOR STARGAZING

In addition to the Observatorium, there are plenty of other spots dotted around the island where views of the galaxy are striking.

- **Birdwatching tower** (Ulvshalevej 401, Stege) on Nyord has wheelchair accessibility and a sheltered section. It's as useful for seeing stars at night as it is for seeing birds during the day.

- **Liselund Park** (Langebjergvej 6, Borre) is free to enter and open year-round, so you can crank up the romance level with a bit of stargazing.

- **Møns Klint Resort and Camping** (Klintevej 544, Borre) is possibly the best place to stay if you want to step outside your door in the small hours to check out the constellations.

- **Rytsebæk beach** on the quiet south coast might give you the Milky Way all to yourself.

users, providing a great view over the meadow. It also has potential as a stargazing spot.

Lodsmuseet Møllestangen

Nyord; Easter-Nov. morning-sunset; free

Also worth keeping an eye out for is a brick cabin on the edge of Nyord's town known as "Denmark's tiniest museum," more officially Lodsmuseet Møllestangen (Flagpole Pilots Museum). This micro museum is filled with posters that tell the story of the old ports and tough stevedores and pilots that worked it. Located on high ground, this is an ideal place to stop for a rest on your walk around Nyord to enjoy the views of the sea, as well as a bit of local history and charm. Visitors are asked not to shut the door on the way out; the latch will lock out subsequent passersby.

SHOPPING

Noorbohandelen

Nyord Bygade 1, 4780; tel. 31 18 71 61; www.noorbohandelen.dk; Easter-Oct. daily 11am-5pm, Oct.-Dec. Sat. 1pm-5pm, Sun. 11am-4pm

Eagle-eyed visitors to the Torvehallerne food market in Copenhagen might recognize the Noorbohandelen name, but the specialty spirits vendor is at home on Nyord (Noorbo is the word used to describe someone who lives on the island). Herbs and fruit grown on Nyord are used to produce the homemade bitters and schnapps sold here. The spirits can be tasted in the store, decanted from specially designed bottles. Imported whisky, rum, cognac, and grappa are also available. If you stop for a sandwich and coffee, try the locally made Nyord jam and mustard in the Noorbohandelen café.

DINING

Lolles Gård

Hyldevej 1, Nyord, 4780; tel. 53 88 67 53; high season Mon.-Wed. and Fri. noon-4pm, Sat. noon-9pm, Sun. noon-4pm, closed off-season

This Nyord restaurant opened in 1947 and continues the theme of both nostalgia and island life with its traditional kro (inn) style design—striped wallpaper and thick tablecloths. You can also sit in the garden in good weather and be surrounded by trees, flowers, and white wooden tables. The food is as traditional as the decor: Danish rye bread with fish fillets, prawns, cheeses, and red peppers; warm staples such as roasted pork with parsley sauce; and coffee to help it down. Fresh fish like eel keep things exciting and introduce a local influence, while desserts like the white chocolate mousse won't leave you wanting.

GETTING THERE

From Copenhagen, take the O2 circular road to reach the E20 highway toward Odense, later merging onto the E47, before taking exit 41 to Vordingborg on Route 59. That road will take you all the way to Møn via the striking Queen Alexandrine arch bridge and then on into Stege. To drive from Stege to Nyord, simply follow Ulhavevej out of the town heading north and keep going until you reach the Nyord bridge. To find Ulhavevej, leave Stege through Mølleporten, and turn left after 300 m (0.2 mi) or so onto Katedralvej. This leads to a junction with Ulhavevej; turn right.

Malmö

Just a 25-minute train journey from Copenhagen across the dramatic Øresund (Öresund to the Swedes), breezy Malmö is a destination that offers something entirely different to its Danish neighbor—different country, different language, different scale. Yet you only need a ticket from Copenhagen to get here and back.

Rooted in its history as an international harbor town, Malmö's most attractive areas include a cobblestoned old city and a smart redeveloping harbor area. Its many parks

Highlights

⭐ **Malmöhus Castle:** Wander dungeons and royal apartments, see spiders, and learn about dinosaurs, all in the grounds of one castle (page 293).

⭐ **Västra Hamnen:** Cycle along the coast, sit by the sea, and enjoy the sight of two wonders of engineering, the Öresund Bridge and the Turning Torso tower (page 296).

⭐ **Malmö's Parks:** Get a lungful of fresh air, stroll in romantic copses, and watch a free concert in an amphitheater; Malmö is the city of parks (page 299).

⭐ **Fika:** Sweden's version of high tea is a national institution. Be sure to take time in the afternoon for coffee and cake at a cute café (page 307).

and proximity to the sea mean you are never far from fresh bracing air, and a visit to the moat-and-masonry Malmöhus Castle will leave you in no doubt as to the city's role in Swedish and Scandinavian history.

ORIENTATION

Exiting **Central Station,** where you arrive by train from Copenhagen or elsewhere in Sweden, the first thing you are likely to notice is the proximity of water in all directions. A network of canals surrounds the historical **Gamla Staden (Old City),** separating it from the Harbor (Hamnen) District, where the station is located. One of these canals is in front of you as you head out the station's south entrance.

To the northwest of the station, past **Universitetsholmen,** the small island on which Malmö University is located, is **Västra Hamnen (West Harbor),** which was originally part of the still substantial main harbor and is now a reenergized area with a sea promenade. It's easy to navigate—the 190-m-tall (623-ft) Turning Torso building, the largest in Scandinavia (it can be seen from Copenhagen), is right in the center.

Previous: sunset in Malmö. **Above:** Västra Hamnen; Malmöhus Castle.

Just west of the Central Station and surrounded by a moat is the **Malmöhus Castle.** Beyond the castle, to the immediate south, east, and west, **Kungsparken, Slottsparken,** and **Slottsträdgården** are among the best of Malmö's numerous green areas, with their rolling slopes, wooded areas, and high stone bridges.

In Gamla Staden, as you cross Mälarbron from the station, which leads directly onto **Stortorget (Great Square),** you'll find an expansive 16th-century marketplace. A statue of King Karl X Gustav, who conquered the once-Danish provinces of Skåne, Blekinge, and Halland and united them with the Swedish Empire in 1658, symbolically marks it.

Just around the corner from Malmö's largest square is its most charming, **Lilla Torg (Little Square),** where some very old buildings are now home to modern bars and restaurants, and people gather on the benches and cobblestones in summer. The third major square in Gamla Staden is **Gustav Adolfs Torg,** at the opposite end of the Södergatan main street. A large public space adorned with sculptures and fountains, the square borders a cemetery adjoined to the Södra Förstadskanalen, a canal you can walk alongside toward the city library and Kungsparken.

On the opposite side of the canal, the central shopping street continues outside the old city on Södra Forstadsgata, which leads south for around 500 m (0.3 mi) before terminating at **Triangeln,** the location of a large mall and railway station. This area has many lodging options as well as one of the city's major museums, Malmö Konsthall. Southwest from here is the expansive **Pildammsparken,** while **Folkets Park** lies to the east in working-class Möllevången.

PLANNING YOUR TIME

Malmö's sights are close to each other, and it is quite easy to be able to navigate around the city on foot. Västra Hamnen is a little farther away, however, and taking a bus to and from this area will save time and strain on your legs. The castle and associated museums take an afternoon to explore, as does the old city, so to experience Malmö at a leisurely pace, an overnight stay is likely to be a decision you'll not regret.

Malmö

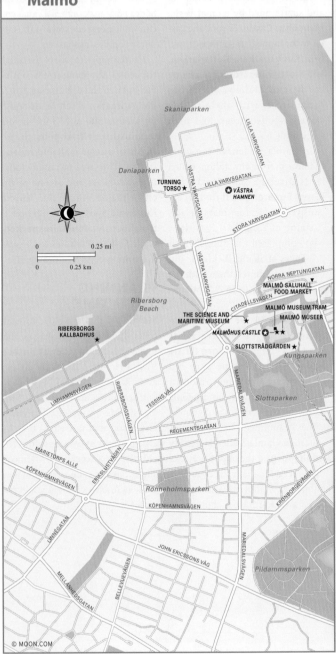

Skaniaparken

Daniaparken

LILLA VARVSGATAN

VÄSTRA VARVSGATAN

TURNING TORSO ★

LILLA VARVSGATAN

✪ VÄSTRA HAMNEN

STORA VARVSGATAN

VÄSTRA VARVSGATAN

0   0.25 mi

0   0.25 km

Ribersborg Beach

CITADELLSVÄGEN

NORRA NEPTUNIGATAN

MALMÖ SALUHALL FOOD MARKET

MALMÖ MUSEUM TRAM

THE SCIENCE AND MARITIME MUSEUM ★

MALMÖ MUSEER

MALMÖHUS CASTLE ✪ ★★

RIBERSBORGS KALLBADHUS ★

SLOTTSTRÄDGÅRDEN ★

Kungsparken

MARIEDALSVÄGEN

LIMHAMNSVÄGEN

RIBERSBORGSVÄGEN

TESSINS VÄG

Slottsparken

REGEMENTSGATAN

ERIKSLUSTVÄGEN

MARIETORPS ALLÉ

KÖPENHAMNSVÄGEN

Rönneholmsparken

KÖPENHAMNSVÄGEN

KRONBORGSVÄGEN

LINNÉGATAN

JOHN ERICSSONS VÄG

MARIEDALSVÄGEN

MELLANHEDSGATAN

BELLEVUEVÄGEN

Pildammsparken

© MOON.COM

MALMÖ

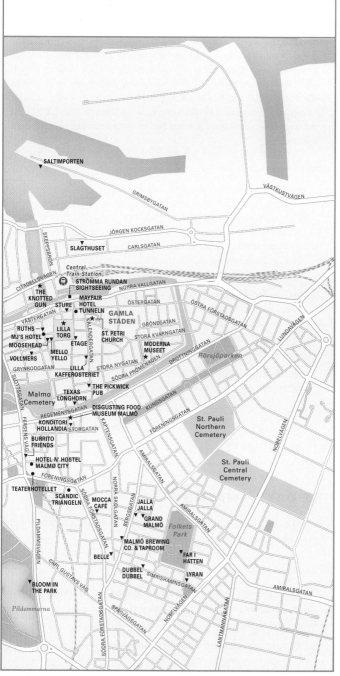

SALTIMPORTEN

GRIMSBYGATAN

VÄSTKUSTVÄGEN

SKEPPSBRON

JÖRGEN KOCKSGATAN

SLAGTHUSET

CARLSGATAN

Central
Train Station

CITADELLSVÄGEN

STRÖMMA RUNDAN
SIGHTSEEING

NORRA VALLGATAN

THE
KNOTTED
GUN

MAYFAIR
HOTEL

STURE

TUNNELN

ÖSTERGATAN

ÖSTRA FÖRSTADSGATAN

VÄSTERGATAN

GAMLA
STADEN

GRÖNEGATAN

LUNDAVÄGEN

RUTHS

MJ'S HOTEL

MOOSEHEAD

LILLA
TORG

ST. PETRI
CHURCH

STORA KVARNGATAN

KALENDEGATAN

ETAGE

MODERNA
MUSEET

VOLLMERS

MELLO
YELLO

Rörsjöparken

LILLA
KAFFEROSTERIET

STORA NYGATAN

SÖDRA PROMENADEN

DROTTNINGGATAN

GRYNBODGATAN

SLOTTSGATAN

THE PICKWICK
PUB

TEXAS
LONGHORN

KUNGSGATAN

Malmo
Cemetery

DISGUSTING FOOD
MUSEUM MALMÖ

St. Pauli
Northern
Cemetery

FÖRENINGSGATAN

REGEMENTSGATAN

KONDITORI
HOLLANDIA

STORGATAN

KAPTENSGATAN

FERSENS VÄG

BURRITO
FRIENDS

NOBELVÄGEN

HOTEL N' HOSTEL
MALMÖ CITY

St. Pauli
Central
Cemetery

FÖRENINGSGATAN

AMIRALSGATAN

TEATERHOTELLET

SCANDIC
TRIANGELN

MOCCA
CAFÉ

NORRA SKOLGATAN

JALLA
JALLA

BERGSGATAN

PILDAMMSVÄGEN

SÖDRA FÖRSTADSGATAN

GRAND
MALMÖ

AMIRALSGATAN

Folkets
Park

BELLE

MALMÖ BREWING
CO. & TAPROOM

FAR I
HATTEN

CARL GUSTAVS VÄG

DUBBEL
DUBBEL

SIMRISHAMNSGATAN

LYRAN

BLOOM IN
THE PARK

Pildammarna

SÖDRA FÖRSTADSGATAN

SPÅRVÄGSGATAN

NOBELVÄGEN

AMIRALSGATAN

LANTMÄNNAGATAN

MALMÖ

Crossing the Danish-Swedish Border

Traveling between Copenhagen and Malmö means crossing the Danish-Swedish border. This border is within the Schengen visa-free zone, but in recent years ID spot checks have been carried out by both Danish and Swedish authorities. Border guards may enter trains or check the IDs of motorists and bus and ferry passengers arriving from Denmark. In general, you should always bring your passport or national ID card when crossing Schengen borders and to ensure you are never caught without it.

Aside from the border itself, there are a few other things to keep in mind when crossing the Öresund:

- **Border control:** The border control carried out on the Öresund crossing is ID spot checks. That means an acceptable form of ID is required when crossing from Denmark to Sweden, with spot checks carried out on trains, buses, and cars. The extent of these controls varies by location and the general assessment of authorities at the time of travel. Your passport will not be stamped; this is not required regardless of whether your ID was checked on entry.

- **Forms of ID and visas:** Put simply, bring your passport with you. National identity cards from countries that issue them are also accepted. If you need a visa to visit Denmark, the visa will also be valid for other Schengen countries, including Sweden. In this case, you should carry your passport.

- **Crossing by train:** Border checks are conducted not at Malmö's Central Station but at Hyllie, on the outskirts of the city and the nearest

Itinerary Ideas

ONE DAY IN MALMÖ

If you're heading in and out from Copenhagen in a day, this itinerary will help you best experience Malmö.

1 After an early breakfast, take the train from Copenhagen's Central Station to **Malmö's Central Station.**

2 Head straight to the 16th-century **Malmöhus Castle** and spend the morning exploring the varied exhibits inside, from the king's antechamber to the aquarium and dinosaur exhibit.

3 Have lunch at **Malmö Saluhall Food Market,** an artisanal market station to the Öresund Bridge. Police officers sometimes board the train to check IDs.

- **Crossing by bus:** Bus passengers are also subject to ID spot checks on arrival on the Swedish side of the bridge.

- **Crossing by car:** Passport control for travelers arriving by car takes place at the Öresund Bridge toll stations at Lernacken at the Swedish end of the bridge. Police have the right to search cars.

- **Currency exchange:** Like Denmark, Sweden does not use the euro, so you will need to exchange or withdraw some **Swedish kronor** (SEK). Exchange rates at the time of writing are 1 SEK = 0.65 Danish kr = US$0.10 = €0.09 = £0.08. Cash can be exchanged at the Forex exchange bureau at Malmö Central Station (Lokgatan 1; tel. 040 30 40 31; Mon.-Fri. 8am-8pm, Sat.-Sun. 10am-6pm). If you are going to return to Denmark, consider holding on to your Danish kroner to avoid a poor exchange rate when using SEK to buy Danish currency.

- **Using your phone:** Phones that can roam in Denmark will also do so in Sweden, but make sure you've checked ahead with your service provider for your international options before traveling in order to avoid excessive roaming charges. This won't be a problem if your phone has an EU number. The EU abolished roaming charges in 2017, so if you arrive in Sweden or Denmark with, for example, an Irish phone number, you'll pay the same rates as you do at home (although there can be limits on data usage—check with your service provider). The country code for Sweden is +46. If you want to call Denmark from Sweden, dial +45 or 0045 followed by the full Danish phone number.

in a converted warehouse near the harbor. You'll have a vast choice of options, but you can't go wrong with a falafel or a bowl of noodles.

4 Walk off lunch at the expansive **Slottsparken,** one of Malmö's gorgeous green spaces. Meander around the lakes and admire the Castle Mill, a charming windmill.

5 Do as the locals do and go for fika at **Konditori Hollandia.** The buns and tarts are scrumptious.

6 Any remaining afternoon time can be spent walking around the old city as well as the extremely old and equally appealing **Lilla Torg,** with its cobblestones and wooden buildings, home to a slew of modern restaurants and bars.

7 Settle down at **Ruths** for dinner. It's one of the best restaurants the city has to offer. Be sure to book ahead.

Itinerary Ideas

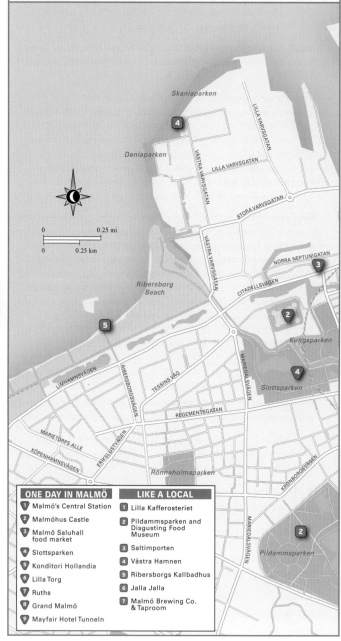

Skaniaparken

Daniaparken

LILLA VARVSGATAN

VÄSTRA VARVSGATAN

LILLA VARVSGATAN

STORA VARVSGATAN

VÄSTRA VARVSGATAN

NORRA NEPTUNIGATAN

CITADELLSVÄGEN

Ribersborg Beach

Kungsparken

MARIEDALSVÄGEN

Slottsparken

0   0.25 mi

0   0.25 km

LIMHAMNSVÄGEN

RIBERSBORGSVÄGEN

TESSINS VÄG

REGEMENTSGATAN

MARIETORPS ALLÉ

KÖPENHAMNSVÄGEN

ERIKSLUSTVÄGEN

Rönneholmsparken

KRONBORGSVÄGEN

MARIEDALSVÄGEN

Pildammsparken

ONE DAY IN MALMÖ

1 Malmö's Central Station

2 Malmöhus Castle

3 Malmö Saluhall food market

4 Slottsparken

5 Konditori Hollandia

6 Lilla Torg

7 Ruths

8 Grand Malmö

9 Mayfair Hotel Tunneln

LIKE A LOCAL

1 Lilla Kafferosteriet

2 Pildammsparken and Disgusting Food Museum

3 Saltimporten

4 Västra Hamnen

5 Ribersborgs Kallbadhus

6 Jalla Jalla

7 Malmö Brewing Co. & Taproom

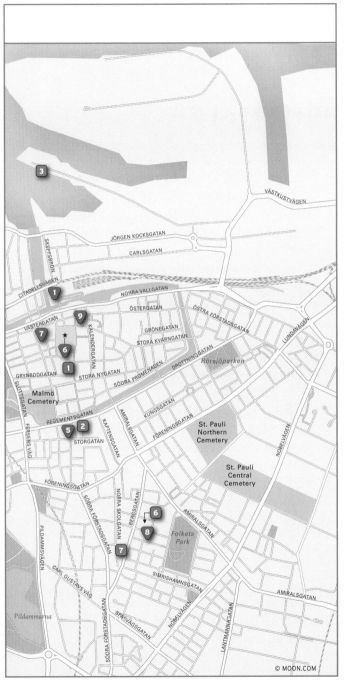

© MOON.COM

8 Partake in Möllan's nightlife scene with a drink or two at **Grand Malmö.**

9 If you're staying the night, **Mayfair Hotel Tunneln** is a great choice. The building is steeped in history, but thankfully the rooms are not.

MALMÖ LIKE A LOCAL

Head outside Gamla Staden and visit the Swedish spots you might not have had time to savor on your first day in town.

1 Get a morning pick-me-up at **Lilla Kafferosteriet.**

2 See more of Malmö's famed green spaces, and go for a morning jog, stroll, or bicycle ride through the expansive **Pildammsparken.** Alternatively, give your taste buds a workout at **Disgusting Food Museum.**

3 Head to **Saltimporten** at the port—one of the best spots in the city for lunch—for a "meat and two veg."

4 Walk off lunch along the **Västra Hamnen** seafront promenade. Stop to take in the goings-on and views of the Öresund Bridge in the distance.

5 For a bit of relaxation Swedish-style, visit the **Ribersborgs Kallbadhus** public bath for a dip, some sauna time, and light refreshments at the restaurant.

6 Across town, it doesn't get much more local than **Jalla Jalla.** End your day with some shawarma or falafel.

7 Unwind with a beer at the **Malmö Brewing Co. & Taproom** just down the street.

Sights

GAMLA STADEN
Malmö Museer

Malmöhusvägen 5-8; tel. 040 34 44 00; https://malmo.se/museer; Tues.-Wed. 11am-5pm, Thurs. 11am-7pm, Fri.-Sun. 11am-5pm; adults 100 SEK, students 50 SEK, under age 20 free (Malmö Museer ticket)

Malmö Museer is the umbrella term for museums located in and around the Malmöhus Castle. The museums within the castle include an aquarium, a dinosaur exhibition, and art museum Malmö Konstmuseum in addition to the historical exhibits within the castle. Nearby is the Science and Maritime Museum. Although a little worn-looking—its entrance is reminiscent of a local library built in the 1980s—it contains several interesting exhibits that are well worth your time.

✪ Malmöhus Castle

Reedy moats form a citadel reminiscent of Copenhagen's Kastellet. In the middle sits the 16th-century Malmöhus Castle, the oldest Renaissance Castle in the Nordic region and where Denmark's coins were once minted when the Kalmar Union briefly brought the Scandinavian nations under a single banner. It was built by the same King Erik of Pomerania who founded Kronborg Castle in

Malmö Museer

Malmöhus Castle

Helsingør as he fortified the coasts of the Öresund. The low deep-red cannon towers and broad moat are the most striking features of the Malmö castle; its appearance contrasts to the thin, almost delicate spires of Kronborg.

The castle's interior successfully conjures medieval and Renaissance Sweden, with the king's antechamber, carved furniture, tapestries, portraits, and marble floors on the upper level and, in the dark stony dungeon, a strong exhibition on the long years of war with Denmark in the 17th century and the history of prisoners incarcerated, and executed, at the castle. This murky section, with its ghost stories and tales and portraits of woe, is the highlight of a visit to the castle.

You'll find more than just history at the castle. In attached museum galleries, built within the castle grounds in the 1930s as it

was restored to be opened to the public, there are exhibitions on geology and natural history, as well as a somewhat arresting taxidermy collection, which includes species native to Sweden. There's also an exhibition on dinosaurs and a small aquarium with reptiles, fish, and spiders. In the upstairs section of the galleries, there's a modern art museum with temporary exhibitions and a section on the history of Malmö, and another covering the city's role in taking in Jewish refugees during World War II. There are also a number of temporary exhibitions at any one time: Notable topics in 2023-2024 included "The Year Is 2084" and "From Idea to Nobel Prize." All these exhibits are included in the castle's main ticket price and provide excellent value and a lot to see, although don't feel you need to see everything. Some of the exhibitions don't have English labeling, so take a guide booklet from the information desk (there are no audio guides) and pick and choose what interests you most.

The Science and Maritime Museum

The Science and Maritime Museum is located just 200 m (660 ft) west of the castle bridge; keep walking as you pass the castle and you'll see it on the right. It contains an entertaining selection of old cars, airplanes, and trains along with a submarine in the backyard, which you can enter to experience the claustrophobic engine room and look out at Malmö through the periscope. Look for the corner on the upper floor dedicated to the old Malmö-Copenhagen ferry, rendered obsolete by the opening of the Öresund Bridge in 2000. There's a ticket office, old seats from the boat, a retro price list from the ferry canteen, and a video showing a typical morning for travelers on board in which a decades-old Copenhagen slips by the portholes as waiters serve breakfast and coffee to passengers.

Other areas of the museum are dedicated to important scientists from the Skåne region, such as 18th-century botanist, physician, and zoologist Carl Linnaeus, also known as the father of modern taxonomy. There are collections of various animal skulls and butterflies along with a diorama of the man himself. Astronomer Tycho Brahe, born in Skåne when it was part of Denmark, is one of the region's most famous scientists. The Heaven and Earth exhibit pays tribute to him with an interactive dark room where you can navigate the solar system. The Wisdome, a dome-shaped cinema screen, shows 3-D films on topics like space, dinosaurs, and coral reefs. An interactive section will keep kids entertained with activities related to sustainable energy and human health science.

Overall, there's enough in the science museum to hold your interest for 2-3 hours. Just outside (turn left as you exit and take the first street on the left) you'll find **Fiskehoddorna** (www.fiskehoddorna.se), traditional-style fishing huts, which are also part of the museum. Freshly caught raw fish and shellfish are sold here Tuesday-Saturday 7am-1pm. Try a piece of herring, smoked salmon, or eel from the sellers, who display their catches in flatbed refrigerators in front of wooden shacks painted in reds and blues. In summer, sit-down service is sometimes set up outside the huts.

Malmö Museum Tram

Banérskajen; www.mss.se; June-Sept. daily 2-3 departures hourly noon-5pm; adults 30 SEK, ages 6-16 10 SEK, under age 6 free

In summer, visitors can take the nostalgic Museum Tram (Museispårvägen Malmö) between the Science and Maritime Museum and Malmö City Library. Restored with its olive-green livery and Victorian paneling and with uniformed conductors and wooden interiors reminiscent of a boat cabin, tram no. 100, built in 1906, dings and whirrs its way from the stop at the Banérskajen fishing huts area next to the Science and Maritime Museum, through the green surroundings of Slottsparken and Malmöhus Castle, and then on to the library. The trip takes around 20 minutes. You can use the tram to get from the castle and museum area to the city center, a few minutes' walk across the Södra Förstadskanal, but it's worth taking the tram for the fun of the short journey, enjoying the ride down treelined avenues.

Tickets can be purchased at the Banérskajen ticket office as well as on board the tram. It operating season is usually June-September.

Lilla Torg

Lilla Torg

The most camera-friendly of many handsome spots at the center of the Gamla Staden (Old City) is the cobblestoned Lilla Torg, which is flanked by bars and restaurants in wood-framed buildings. Created as a marketplace in the 16th century and still a popular meeting spot, Lilla Torg comes alive on weekends as locals fill the nightspots, which include popular places like Moosehead and Mello Yello. In summer, small free concerts are sometimes held on the plaza. All around the square, the centuries-old buildings are stunning. Of particular note are the red post-and-beam houses in the southeastern corner that join Skomakaregatan and the neighboring yellow-stuccoed building. These are Malmö's best-preserved timber structures.

St. Petri Church

Göran Olsgatan 4; tel. 040 27 90 56; www. svenskakyrkan.se/malmo/stpetrikyrka; Fri.-Tues. 10am-6pm, Wed. 8am-6pm, Thurs. 10am-7pm; free

The oldest building in Malmö, the early-14th-century St. Petri Church is open daily for visitors to admire its polygonal Gothic spires from the outside and the minimalism inside. The Krämare Chapel breaks with this theme with intense vault paintings, the only ones to have survived from the church's medieval heyday.

OUTSIDE GAMLA STADEN
✪ Västra Hamnen

Västra Hamnen; https://malmo.se/ Stadsutveckling/Stadsutvecklingsomraden/ Vastra-Hamnen.html; free

Västra Hamnen was once the

Västra Hamnen

city's shipping yard. After heavy investment and redevelopment into a boardwalk and promenade, it has become a hugely popular destination for locals and visitors. The centerpiece is the towering **Turning Torso,** the highest building in Scandinavia until 2022, when construction of Gothenburg's Karlatornet overtook it. The part-boardwalk, part-concrete seafront promenade feels wide open, with grass on one side and the sea on the other. It's a great place to go for a bracing afternoon walk in the cold, and then pop into one of the many restaurants and cafés to warm up with views of the Öresund, including the bridge. Summertime can bring a Mediterranean vibe, with music blaring from boom boxes and salsa and yoga classes on the promenade. Don't miss **Stapelbäddsparken,** a molded

moonscape of a skateboarding park designed by architect Stefan Hauser.

Turning Torso

Lilla Varvsgatan 14; www.hsb.se/malmo/ om-boende/hyreslagenhet/turning-torso- malmos-landmarke/in-english; not open to the public

Twisting its way 190 m (623 ft) into the Öresund coastal sky, the Turning Torso is unlike any other building in Malmö or Copenhagen (from where it can be seen on a clear day). Yet somehow it manages to fit in, like a daydreamy vision of a science-fiction Scandinavia. Its white neofuturist facades bend through seemingly impossible angles, and the center of the roof is not directly above the center of the ground floor. Up close, it's slightly easier, if still not entirely straightforward, to comprehend how its nine segments of five-story pentagons fit together. It is a residential building and cannot be visited except through prearranged tours of at least 10 people (http://skyhighmeetings.com/en/studiebesok). A small board placed outside the building entrance provides some information. It is well worth passing as part of a walk around the Västra Hamnen area.

Moderna Museet

Ola Billgrens plats 2-4; tel. 040 685 7937; www.modernamuseet.se; Tues.-Wed. and Fri.-Sun. 11am-5pm, Thurs. 11am-7pm; adults 50 SEK, seniors and students 40 SEK

Contemporary art specialist Moderna Museet Malmö is a part of the state-owned Stockholm-based Moderna Museet but has its own independent exhibition program. Located in a former power station with a distinctive bright-orange extension added on, its perforated facade clashes to agreeable effect with a gray Romanesque archway, making it stand out on the quiet Gasverksgatan in the southeastern part of the old city. At a manageable size of 809 sq m (8,700 sq ft), the exhibition spaces include Swedish and international contemporary art. Recent exhibitions have covered the struggles of a family from the Sámi indigenous community as it clashed with Swedish authorities for the right to practice reindeer husbandry, and a solo exhibit by prominent Swedish interdisciplinary artist and designer Moki Cherry.

Disgusting Food Museum Malmö

Södra Förstadsgatan 2; tel. 040 101 771; https://disgustingfoodmuseum.com; daily 11am-5pm; adults 220 SEK, seniors and students 175 SEK, ages 6-16 75 SEK, under age 6 free (two per adult)

The Disgusting Food Museum riffs on Sweden's famously rancid delicacy surströmming, a type of fermented herring, to present over 80 of the world's most off-putting foods. There's a tasting bar where visitors can put this to the test, although reports suggest that it's actually salted licorice, a favorite Swedish candy, which makes people retch the most. Displays are not just an unflattering exercise in finger-pointing, but look at the science behind why you might react with disgust at a certain type of food and include a lot of things Swedes consider edible but others definitely do not. As a thoughtful extra touch, the entry ticket is printed on a sick bag.

The Knotted Gun

Bagers plats; free

On the opposite side of Suellshamnen from the Central Station, Carl Fredrik Reuterswärd's iconic pacifist sculpture is an admirable first impression of Malmö, and it's no less pertinent given that some parts of the city, and elsewhere in Sweden, have had problems with gun violence in recent times. Officially named *Non Violence,* it is more commonly referred to as the Knotted Gun.

Reuterswärd created the bronze monument after the assassination of one of the most famous pacifists of all time, John Lennon, in 1980. The barrel of the weathered oversize Colt Python .357 Magnum turns around on itself; the muzzle, rendered apparently harmless, points toward the sky. There are around 30 copies of the work in various locations around the world, including one famously gifted by Luxembourg to the UN headquarters in New York City. Malmö's, installed in 1985, is one of the originals.

Recreation

✪ PARKS

Malmö is sometimes referred to in Sweden as the "City of Parks," and not without reason. You're never far from at least one, making it easy to go for a run, a walk, a picnic, or, if you're lucky, to sunbathe. There are lakes, small canals, amphitheaters, broad fields, skateboard parks, and ball courts. It's little wonder the Swedes look so healthy.

Slottsparken

Kung Oscars väg; https://malmo.se/ Uppleva-och-gora/Natur-och-parker/ Parker-i-Malmo/Slottsparken.html; daily 24 hours; free

Running adjacent to Kungsparken and between the castle and the city library, the expansive Slottsparken (Castle Park) is replete with lakes of various sizes with ample stretches of woodlands. The two most recognizable landmarks are the **Castle Mill** (Slottsmöllan), a large windmill, and Carl Milles's 1950 statue *Man and Pegasus,* with man and his flying horse atop a 10-m-tall (33-ft) granite pillar overlooking the big lake (Stora dammen). At the lake, you can spot black-headed gulls, herons, and swans. The center of the park is the 2.5 sq km (1 sq mi) Lördagsplanen (Saturday Field), where mini festivals and other events are sometimes held during summer. There are also rockeries and shaded areas with trees and bushes.

Slottsparken

Kungsparken

Slottsgatan 33; https://malmo.se/Uppleva-och-gora/Natur-och-parker/Parker-i-Malmo/Kungsparken.html; daily 24 hours; free

Kungsparken is connected to Slottsparken via the Kommendantbron Bridge (the two parks shared the name Slottsparken until 1881 and are still often confused). The calm leafy park with its lake, paths, and idyllic bridges is like a serene smaller version of New York City's Central Park. Its 3.4 ha (8.4 acres) boast more than 100 species of trees. A 19th-century **iron-cast three-tiered fountain** is the most impressive human-made sight in the park, and a very small and peculiar **cave,** with a snake's head peering down from its apex, spitting water into a stone tray underneath, is a hidden spot for discovery. The fountain and the cave are close to each other near the end of the **Lovers' Alley,** which makes its romantic way east from Trädgårdsbron alongside the canal, flanked by tall shade trees.

Slottsträdgården

Malmöhusvägen 8; https://malmo.se/ slottstradgarden; daily 24 hours; free

Completing a triumvirate of green areas near the castle with Kungsparken and Slottsparken, Slottsträdgården, with its many plant beds, is an ecological garden reminiscent of a lovingly tended city allotment. It's run by a society of local garden lovers. It has 14 different sections of both vegetables and ornamental elements and up to 400 types of plants. Visitors are welcome to walk among the flower beds on the paths. It is also home to the **Slottsträdgården Café** (https://slottstradgardens-kafe.se), which uses produce from the garden.

Pildammsparken

Pildammsparken; https://malmo.se/ Uppleva-och-gora/Natur-och-parker/ Parker-i-Malmo/Pildammsparken.html; daily 24 hours; free

At 45 ha (111 acres), Pildammsparken is Malmö's largest park. The name translates to Willow Pond Park, an accurate representation of the leafy thickets and two large ponds for which it is known. A domed pavilion with slender columns, Margareta pavillon is a relic from the 1914 Baltic Exhibition, from which Pildammsparken sprung. The park was finished in 1926, after it had been used to grow potatoes during the World War I. The pavilion is just west of the largest lake, Pildammarna, a great place for a morning jog or an afternoon walk (there'll be others out doing the same thing, but there's enough space for everyone). The western section of the park is dominated by a large amphitheater, where free concerts and performances often take place during summer. These are normally listed on Malmö's city website (https://evenemang2. malmo.se).

Folkets Park

Malmö Folkets Park, Malmö 205 80; tel. 040 34 10 00; http://malmofolketspark.se; daily 24 hours; general admission free

Located south of the city center, Folkets Park blurs the lines between green space and amusement park. It was partly inspired by Copenhagen's Tivoli Gardens, which can be seen in the design of the **Moriska paviljongen** (Moorish pavilion). Founded at the end of the 19th century, the park was closely associated with the Social Democratic Party, which bought it in 1891 and sold it to the city 100 years later in 1991. In the intervening years, it was commonly used as a gathering place for workers. Today, the park is a family-oriented diversion with a playground, a paddling pool, miniature golf, and a roller-skating disco; events and activities vary by season. These are generally free and do not need to be booked in advance, but during summer a section of the park is sometimes closed off for small concerts and other activities with an entry fee. If you're hungry after all the kid-friendly activity, the on-site

Far i Hatten restaurant (tel. 040 61 53 651; www.farihatten.se; Tues.-Thurs. 5pm-11pm, Fri. 4pm-2am, Sat. noon-2am, Sun. noon-10pm; pizza from 135 SEK) has excellent pizzas to restore your energy levels.

BATHS

Ribersborgs Kallbadhus

Limhamnsvägen, Brygga 1; tel. 040 260 366; www.ribersborgskallbadhus.se; summer Mon.-Fri. 9am-9pm, Sat.-Sun. 9am-6pm, winter Mon.-Tues. and Thurs.-Fri. 10am-7pm, Wed. 10am-8pm, Sat.-Sun. 9am-6pm; single entry 80 SEK

If you want to take some time out to relax while learning about Swedish culture, head to the Ribersborgs Kallbadhus public bath. It is a great destination, with a pier location and a distinctive boardwalk.

pier at Ribersborgs Kallbadhus

Take a sauna (there are five types) with a sea view, an ice-cold sea bath (known as "winter bathing"), go for a refreshing swim in the summer, or simply get a massage. The restaurant includes a range of fish, chicken, and vegan dishes as well as a lunch of the day at a very modest 130 kr. In true liberated Swedish style, saunas and winter baths are experienced in the nude. There are segregated areas for men and women and one mixed-gender sauna. As with a number of other recognizable Malmö locations, the baths show up in an episode of *The Bridge* TV series.

BICYCLING

Malmö is superbly equipped for cycling, with broad bike lanes and favorable traffic rules. There has been heavy investment in bicycle lanes in the city since the mid-2000s, providing things like designated parking areas, underpasses designed for optimal visibility, and even apartments with elevators designed to accommodate bikes so they can be stored in homes.

Many of the city's 510 km (300 mi) of bicycle lanes are separated from roads, so you often don't have to share the asphalt with cars. In traffic, if you are cycling straight ahead through an intersection and a car is turning right across your lane, you have the right of way, so the car should stop and wait for you. Be alert nonetheless; cars occasionally edge forward or fail to spot cyclists coming from behind. Despite the favorable conditions,

it's important to cycle safely at all times, and I strongly recommend always using a bicycle helmet. Almost all bike rental companies offer these. The city's biggest park, **Pildammsparken,** where the wide paths and open spaces mean there is ample space for bikes and pedestrians but keep things at a leisurely pace, is a prime spot for cycling in Malmö.

Västra Hamnen to Ribersborgs Kallbadhus

Start: *Scaniaparken*
Distance: *4 km (2.5 mi)*
Riding time: *30 minutes*

Västra Hamnen, a redeveloped part of the city, does not suffer from a lack of bicycle lanes found in some other places and is a good place to set out on a short trip from the center of the city. Parts of the area still have an industrial look, but when you reach the coast, you can bicycle along the scenic **Ribersborg** path or **Scaniastigen,** where you can view the Turning Torso and the Öresund Bridge and stop for a picnic on the beach or by the promenade. Continuing around the coast in a westerly direction, you will eventually reach the treelined **Limhamnsvägen,** a beautiful coastal area with a designated bicycle lane that runs alongside a flat grassy plain, a sandy beach, and several jetties where you can walk out and take in the sea air. It is also here you will find **Ribersborgs Kallbadhus,** a public sea-bathing facility that is open year-round. The distance around the coast from

bikes in Malmö

Västra Hamnen to the Ribersborg baths is around 4 km (2.5 mi).

Kungsgatan
Kungsgatan, south of the historical center, is a 3-km (1.8-mi) stretch of road with long winding cycle lanes that undulate under bridges and swerve around trees. There's lots of green space, playgrounds, and fresh air. It's such a pleasant place to ride and is so close to the city that it's worth trying out, even if it's not on a route between points of interest.

Malmö By Bike
www.malmobybike.se
Malmö By Bike is a rental service that allows you to rent a bike for an hour. You can purchase an annual subscription (250 SEK) or access to the system for 72 hours (165 SEK) or 24 hours (80 SEK), meaning you can make as many hourly rentals as you like within the time you purchased. These can be bought on the website or at selected charging stations. Once you've signed up and bought a pass, you get a PIN code that is used to unlock the bikes. Make sure you return and connect to a charging station: Look for the slot with the green light. The 100 stations, where the bikes can be picked up and returned, are spread across the city and can be located using the Malmö by Bike website or app, which you can also use as a journey planner.

Donkey Republic
www.donkey.bike
Donkey Republic is a Europe-wide app, available in Malmö, that allows you to find, unlock, and rent a bicycle using an app.

TOURS
Strömma Rundan Sightseeing

Norra Vallgatan 3; tel. 040 611 74 88; www.stromma.com/sv-se/malmo; ticket booth Apr.-June daily 11am-3pm, July-Aug. daily 9am-8pm, early Sept. daily 10am-6pm, mid-late Sept. daily 10:30am-4pm; 209 SEK

Stromma's Malmö canal tour takes advantage of the compact size of the city. The historical center is surrounded by a complete canal loop that allows for comprehensive sightseeing tours. The canal tour sails close to Malmöhus Castle next to the Old City, passes the Turning Torso, and loops into the harbor before returning to its starting point by the Central Station. Seeing the city from this angle, which sometimes requires ducking as you pass under the old stone bridges, is complemented by guided commentary and anecdotes in Swedish and English. Bring dry warm clothes if the weather is not agreeable—there's no hiding from the elements on the flat open canal tour boats.

Dining

GAMLA STADEN
Scandinavian
Ruths

Mäster Johansgatan 11; tel. 040 12 13 18; https://ruthsmalmo.se; daily breakfast 7am-10:30am, lunch noon-2:30pm, dinner 5pm-midnight; breakfast from 55 SEK, lunch from 55 SEK, dinner from 165 SEK

Deli, bakery, and restaurant Ruths remains one of the most popular and best-value spots to eat in Malmö after a rebranding from its previous identity as Restaurant Bastard. There are three separate menus for breakfast, lunch, and dinner, all of which carry a strong Swedish identity while also being infused with more southern European styles. Examples include rye bread with a boiled egg and fig marmalade for breakfast, cod with leeks and aioli for lunch, and duck or buffalo mozzarella with crushed chickpeas for dinner. There's a relaxed vibe with brickwork walls and arched windows, but there's no doubting the care that goes into the preparation of the dishes. You don't just have to eat at the restaurant—you can buy bread, produce, and condiments from the deli and take them out with you. It's often busy, so booking ahead isn't a bad idea, but some spots are kept for walk-in diners to maintain a sense of spontaneity.

Vollmers

Tegelgårdsgatan 5; tel. 040 57 97 50; https://vollmers.nu; Jan.-Nov. Wed.-Sat. from 6pm, Dec. Tues.-Sat. from 6pm; set menu 2,695 SEK excluding wine pairing

Vollmers received two Michelin stars in 2018 and is currently the only restaurant in Malmö bestowed with the accolade. The surprise menu comes with some dishes which are "inspired by the owners'

Ruths

childhood memories," according to the guide. It's located in a 19th-century townhouse tucked away on a side street a stone's throw from Kungsparken. Local ingredients are held in high regard, and the tasting menu is named The Granary, after a colloquial name for Scania, the southern Swedish region that includes Malmö. Book ahead to ensure a table, and set aside around 4 hours.

Mello Yello

Lilla Torg 1; tel. 040 30 45 25; www.melloyello.se; Mon.-Thurs. 3:30pm-1am, Fri. 1:30pm-1am, Sat.-Sun. noon-1am; mains from 195 SEK

Mello Yello is a popular restaurant-bar in a busy location on Lilla Torg that heats up on weekends. With alfresco seating and plenty of blankets and heaters during winter, Mello Yello features a range of bistro fare, including moules frites, confit duck, rigatoni pasta, and burgers. However, the prime location pushes prices up a little.

French
Sture

Adelgatan 13; tel. 040 12 12 53; https://sture1912.com; Mon.-Thurs. 11:30am-11pm, Fri. 11:30am-midnight, Sat. noon-midnight, Sun. 1pm-10pm; dish of the day from 165 SEK, starters from 85 SEK

Brasserie-style restaurant Sture returned with new owners in 2021 after a pandemic closure, allowing it to reopen the doors to its huge, largely French wine cellar. The extensive menu mixes contemporary and traditional European influences. There are excellent-value daily dishes from the remarkably cheap price of 165 SEK, examples of which might include a grilled leg of rooster with tomato sauce or fusilli with sunflower seeds and ratatouille. First established in 1912,

Sture is in the heart of the old city in a building with an Ottoman-style look, with large arched windows, balconies, and stone pillars on the exterior. Inside, there is a relaxed feel to the modernized interior, and the service is highly rated.

Fika and Cafés
Lilla Kafferosteriet

Baltzarsgatan 24; tel. 040 48 20 00; www.lillakafferosteriet.se; Mon.-Fri. 8am-6pm, Sat.-Sun. 10am-6pm; espresso from 28 SEK

Lilla Kafferosteriet is the perfect place to try fika. It's not just any old coffee, though: Specialty coffee beans from Guatemala, Indonesia, and Peru, among others, are roasted on-site and steamed by specialist baristas. The café can be found in one of Malmö's oldest houses, close to Lilla Torg. Traditional Scandinavian cakes are on offer, such as the dry almond and marzipan kransekaka or sugary cinnamon buns kanelsnäcka. There is also a carrot cake, a range of cheesecakes, buns, and muffins. If you fancy something savory and are missing Denmark, try the honey-roasted brussels sprouts on rye bread.

Burgers
Texas Longhorn

Kanalgatan 5; tel. 040 18 21 40; www.texaslonghorn.se; Mon.-Thurs. 11am-9pm, Fri. 11:30am-10pm, Sat. noon-10pm, Sun. 1pm-8pm; starters from 89 SEK, burgers from 195 SEK, lunch 105 SEK

Swedish burger chain Texas Longhorn has several dozen restaurants spread across the country. The branch at Kanalgatan is in a handy location near the central shopping districts with a nice canal-side view, making for a pleasant and calming summer city spot to stop for a meal. The simple order-at-the-bar service is stress-free, and the courteous staff keep comfort at the fore. The burgers are satisfying, and side snacks are a slight variation on the usual—the fried cauliflower is a delicious alternative to fries. A second Malmö outlet can be found at the Triangeln shopping mall (St. Johannesgatan 1B).

OUTSIDE GAMLA STADEN
Scandinavian
Saltimporten

Hullkaj en, Grimsbygatan 24; tel. 070 651 84 26; www.saltimporten.com; Mon.-Fri. 11am-2pm; lunch of the day 125 SEK

Saltimporten has a somewhat hidden location in the old Frihamnen harbor area behind the Central Station, but it is no secret that this is one of the best spots for lunch in the city. The concept is straightforward: There's a daily lunch menu with a flat fee. Ingredients are sourced from local producers, and the menu changes daily. The busy hustle more than makes up for the rugged industrial look inside and out. There is excellent value and delicious Scandinavian dishes, which pack as much taste as possible into the "meat and two veg" format. Vegetarian options are also available.

○ Fika: The Swedish Coffee and Bun Tradition

Anyone who has spent more than a few days in Sweden will probably be aware of the concept of **fika,** the quintessentially Swedish daily afternoon coffee break—with an all-important sweet nibble—that is just as important as a cup of tea in Britain or an espresso in Italy. The 10-million-strong population of Sweden accounts for almost 1 percent of the world's coffee drinkers, a surprising statistic that is, in part, due to fika.

Malmö buns

Pronounced "fee-ka" and used as either a noun or a verb, fika is also one of the first contacts with the Swedish language visitors are likely to have, drawing parallels with Denmark's hygge.

Although coffee is drunk at other times of the day, it is the crucial afternoon combination of coffee with a delicious sweet cinnamon bun that makes fika the phenomenon it is. People at home, at work, or hiking in the mountains are rigorous about making space in their schedules for this afternoon break. The basic idea is simple and rooted in the Scandinavian commitment to good living: It's all about making sure you take some time out of your day to slow things down and not get too caught up in the rush of daily life.

WHERE TO FIKA IN MALMÖ

- **Lilla Kafferosteriet** (Baltzarsgatan 24; tel. 040 48 20 00; www.lillakafferosteriet.se; Mon.-Fri. 8am-6pm, Sat.-Sun. 10am-6pm). This coffee specialist has a range of delightful pastries behind the counter.

- **Konditori Hollandia** (Södra Förstadsgatan 8; tel. 040 12 48 86; www.hollandia.se; Mon.-Fri. 8am-7pm; Sat.-Sun. 9am-7pm). Thought to be the oldest patisserie in town, with an enticing range of buns and tarts, it's a great place to fika.

MALMÖ
DINING

Lyran

Simrishamnsgatan 36 A; tel. 076 324 52 28; www.lyranmatbar.se; Tues.-Sat. first seating 5pm and 5:30pm, second seating 8pm and 8:30pm; from 650 SEK pp excluding wine

Lyran is a great way to try out fine dining without breaking the bank. In the lively Möllan neighborhood, this self-styled urban inn has a low-key look from the outside, but the four tasting menus (mixed, vegetarian, pescetarian, and vegan) are anything but basic. Each menu consists of 7-8 servings, including smaller dishes and a dessert. Wine (625 SEK) or nonalcoholic drink parings (300 SEK) can be added. Allergies can be accommodated if the restaurant is advised in advance. Swedish beef potatoes, caviar with mash, and pumpkin with foamed smoked hazelnuts are just a smattering of the dishes with which you might be presented.

Bloom in the Park

Pildammsvägen 17; tel. 040 793 63; https://bloominthepark.se; Mon.-Sat. 5pm-11pm, Sun. noon-4pm; 2-course menu 495 SEK, 3-course dinner menu 695 SEK excluding wine

Bloom in the Park has a reputation for surprise: There is no menu, and diners experience tasting dishes without being given prior information—according to the concept. Vegan, vegetarian, and allergy needs are fully catered to with prior notice, and the menu is eventually presented with the help of a QR code or physical card. The constantly evolving

kitchen and wine cellar reflect the season and availability, so each visit is likely to be unique. Located in Pildammsparken overlooking Pildammarna Lake, the black-painted wooden building that houses the restaurant is part of the charm, with a congenial atmosphere filling the minimalistic interior of carefully designed lighting and tasteful paneling. Booking ahead is essential.

Fika and Cafés
Konditori Hollandia

Södra Förstadsgatan 8; tel. 040 12 48 86; www.hollandia.se; Mon.-Fri. 8am-7pm; Sat.-Sun. 9am-7pm; tart for 5 people 295 SEK

Quaint Konditori Hollandia, which opened in 1903, is thought to be the oldest patisserie in town, and its delightful cinnamon buns, cream cakes, and tarts are certainly testament to its years of perfecting the trade. It also has the elegant and charming tearoom look down, making it a fantastic and atmospheric place for fika.

Markets
Malmö Saluhall Food Market

Gibraltargatan 6; www.malmosaluhall. se; Mon.-Thurs. 11am-8pm, Fri. 11am-9pm, Sat.-Sun. 11am-5pm; coffee and pastries from 45 SEK

An artisanal food market in a converted warehouse near the harbor, Malmö Saluhall is an ideal place to stop for fika or falafel, coffee or noodles. You could start with fika in the form of a coffee and an outstanding example of a semla bun, the traditional Swedish brioche filled with marzipan and cream, at St. Jakobs Stenugnsbageri. Do you have kitchen access at your lodgings? Pick up some premium raw ingredients such as fresh raw salmon or trout from Söderholmens Fisk. You could also pick out some handmade pralines, caramel, and fudge from Chocolatte to take home as a souvenir. Hawaiian poke bowls with lukewarm rice and marinated fish are served up at Påris, and hipster sandwich specialist Poms offers sauerkraut and pastrami, pickled onions, and feta among its fillings. There are plenty of other stands too. The atmosphere is laid-back, and summertime sees outdoor tables brought out. Make sure you have a credit or debit card—cash is not always accepted.

International
Burrito Friends

Fersens väg 14B; tel. 040 615 32 78; https://burritofriends.se/city; Mon.-Thurs. 11am-9pm, Fri. 11am-10pm, Sat. noon-10pm, Sun. noon-9pm; from 99 SEK

Bar Burrito is a solid stop for an inexpensive filling snack. Its rather ordinary-looking interior and display of meats and salads behind the glass counter contains a surprisingly tasty variety of fillings, including pulled pork that's more Mexican than Scandinavian and lightly spiced achiote chicken. Bowls, tacos, and salads are all available as alternatives to the burrito.

Far i Hatten

Folkets Park 2; tel. 040 615 36 51; www. farihatten.se; Tues.-Thurs. 5pm-11pm, Fri. 4pm-2am, Sat. noon-2am, Sun. noon-10pm, pizza from 135 SEK

Inside Folkets Park you can find Far i Hatten (Father in the Hat) in an inviting-looking white-planked building with red trim, a restaurant that also has a late-opening bar on weekends. You can get snacks like fried zucchini wedges or more filling offerings like burrata or fried pumpkin with ricotta, so there's plenty to choose from. It is best known for its pizza, which makes it an ideal place to eat after a day of activity in the park with children when you need a good spot close at hand. There are five variations on the menu with authentic ingredients like buffalo mozzarella, mortadella, and roasted pistachios; gluten-free and vegan versions are available.

Belle

Södra Skolgatan 43; tel. 073 155 76 36; https://bellemalmo.se; Mon.-Thurs. from 5pm, Fri.-Sun. from 4pm; light dishes from 65 SEK

Near the lively Möllevångstorget square in the Möllan neighborhood, Belle serves burgers, taco bowls, and salads as well as bar dishes like nachos, chicken bites, and club sandwiches that can be shared in a group while you enjoy something from the cocktail list. After this, you are invited to stay and experience Malmö nightlife at the bar and dance floor

(Wed.-Sat.), where there are regular events and special offers.

Mocca Café

Friisgatan 4; tel. 076 709 50 62; www.instagram.com/moccacafemalmo; Mon.-Thurs. 11am-8pm, Fri.-Sat. 11am-10pm, Sun. noon-8pm; sandwiches from 120 SEK

One of several good options on the semi-pedestrianized Friisgatan near Triangeln, Mocca's generous roast beef halloumi sandwiches or smoked salmon baked potatoes make it a preferable location for lunch or coffee while you're in the central part of the city.

Dubbel Dubbel

Simrishamnsgatan 14; tel. 040 12 58 55; https://dubbeldubbel.se/simrishamnsgatan; Sun.-Thurs. 5pm-10pm, Fri. 4pm-11pm, Sat. 5pm-11pm; starters from 55 SEK, dumplings from 95 SEK

Dumplings and dim sum are served in authentic bamboo bowls with a Tsing Tao beer or Chinese-inspired cocktail. Dubbel Dubbel is highly popular with locals and influenced by the street-food roots of its Chinese cuisine. Takeaway is available, or you can sit inside among the tasteful Swedish lighting and furniture fused with Chinese square-table, low-stool seating culture. In summer, the backyard garden is open to diners.

Jalla Jalla

Bergsgatan 16; tel. 040 623 70 00; https://jallajallamalmo.se; Mon. 11am-1am, Tues.-Thurs. 11am-2am, Fri.-Sat. 11am-5am, Sun. 11am-midnight; falafel wraps from 45 SEK, kebab wraps from 65 SEK

One of Malmö's most popular spots for a late-night shawarma or falafel, Jalla Jalla has an authentic Middle Eastern feel with ingredients such as pickles and halloumi and is easily recognizable from the colorful shop front in Swedish yellow and blue. The restaurant even makes a brief appearance in hit TV series *The Bridge*.

Entertainment and Events

FESTIVALS

Malmöfestivalen

Gamla Staden and around; https://malmofestivalen.se; mid-Aug.; free

The creaking streets of the old city become awash with colorful sights and exotic tastes during the Malmö Festival, a week of diverse music, food, and drink events scattered across Gamla Staden. More than 1 million people attend the traditional mid-August festival every year, making it the largest street party of its kind in Northern Europe. The program in 2023 included the likes of art installations, DJs, street basketball, kids activities, circus shows, animal rights talks, a container for creating TikTok content, virtual reality, and good old-fashioned concerts. A huge street food and drinks market fills Gustav Adolfs torg and Södergatan, creating a festival atmosphere in the city streets. An information point for visitors can be found on Gustav Adolfs torg throughout the duration of the festival, providing guidance on the program. Entry is free, and with its sustainability-conscious outlook, care is taken not to leave Malmö in a mess once the fun is over.

NIGHTCLUBS AND LIVE MUSIC

Etage

Stortorget 6; tel. 040 40 23 20 60; www. etagenightclub.com; Wed.-Thurs. 11:30pm-4am, Fri.-Sat. 11:30pm-5am; cover charge Fri.-Sat. 160 SEK

If you plan to go big while in Malmö and can mix with a younger crowd, long-standing multi-floor club Etage might be the place to start. There are four dance floors and six bars. Tables can be booked in advance if you want to have your own space. There's no dress code but shorts and sandals are not looked upon favorably.

Grand Malmö

Monbijougatan 17; tel. 040 12 63 13; www. grandmalmo.se; Wed.-Thurs. 5pm-midnight, Sat.-Sun. 5pm-3am, cover charge after 11pm 120 SEK

The Möllevången neighborhood—shortened to "Möllan" by locals—is located south of the old city and includes Folkets Park. This traditionally working-class neighborhood is emerging as a popular location for going out, with Grand a part of making it an increasing draw away

from the city center. As well as a nightclub, it functions as a restaurant and bar with frequent concerts; check upcoming listings on the website or Instagram. Usually concerts finish by 11pm or midnight, and the venue then switches to nightclub mode. Genres vary from indie to pop to disco and house. There may be a cover charge, but entry is likely to be free before 11pm.

Slagthuset

Jörgen Kocksgatan 7A; tel. 040 611 80 90; https://slagthuset.se/en; check program online for events and prices

Slagthuset is a concert venue that doubles as a theater, hosting plays and stand-up comedy along with private events. Located in a former slaughterhouse, from where it gets its name, the high ceilings and minimalist brickwork interior are topped off by details such as pallets used as seating. An on-site restaurant offers set lunches (from 139 SEK) most days, and is sometimes open in the evening when concerts are on. Details are usually on the tickets. Concerts are a mix of tribute acts and Scandinavian rock bands, some of which are known outside Sweden. Check the website for upcoming concerts and ticket availability—you might be pleasantly surprised.

BARS

The Pickwick Pub

Malmborgsgatan 5; tel. 040 23 32 66; https://pickwickpub.nu; Mon.-Thurs. 4pm-midnight, Fri. 3pm-2am, Sat. 1pm-2am, Sun. noon-11pm; draft beers from 77 SEK

A pub in the English tradition, the Pickwick tries with good effect to go for the tavern look, with a dark-green color scheme and wood paneling. Any English pub that references Dickens in its name has a decent claim to authenticity in my book, but Pickwick backs this up with a decent selection of ales and beers. There's a quiz night on Wednesday at 8:30pm.

Malmö Brewing Co. & Taproom

Malmö Brygghus, Bergsgatan 33; tel. 073 392 19 66; https://malmobrewing.com; Mon.-Thurs. 4pm-midnight, Fri. 4pm-3am, Sat. noon-3am, Sun. 4pm-midnight; small draft beers from 60 SEK

Malmö Brewing Co. & Taproom merits recommendation for the 35 different beers on tap at any one time, including ciders, imperial stouts, IPAs, seltzers, and other brews that are hard to come by elsewhere. Tours of the on-site microbrewery (90 minutes; Sat. 4:30pm; 300 SEK), which was launched in 2010 on the site of an older brewery, end in a tasting session. Although these tours are in Swedish, similar private tours in English can be arranged.

Moosehead

Lilla Torg 1; tel. 040 12 04 23; Mon.-Thurs. 3pm-1am, Fri. 2pm-1am, Sat. noon-1am, Sun. noon-midnight

There's rustic brickwork interior, antlers mounted on the walls, and a large outside seating area at Moosehead, a tourist-friendly Lilla Torg bar and restaurant with an eclectic menu of beer and cocktails as well as pub food, including elk stew and a range of Thai dishes. It's a good place to take in the local Gamla Staden action; it heats up on Friday and Saturday evenings.

Accommodations

500-1,000 SEK

Hotel n' Hostel Malmö City

Rönngatan 1; tel. 040 655 13 00; https:// hotelnhostel.se; from 650 SEK s with shared bath, from 905 SEK d with private bath

This large facility provides good standard budget lodging in the form of both private and "hostel" rooms—which are actually private rooms too, but with shared baths. There's a common area and living room good for socializing, and a shared kitchen that's free to use, with a refrigerator for storing food. Towels and linens are included in the room rates, and a continental buffet breakfast (100 SEK per person, children 55 SEK) is on offer. It's conveniently located a short walk from the Central Station and near the central sights.

1,000-2,000 SEK

Teaterhotellet

Fersens väg 20; tel. 040 665 58 00; www. teaterhotellet.se; high season from 1,036 SEK d

Located near the corner of Pildammsparken, Teaterhotellet is a solid budget hotel option close to the city with a hearty buffet breakfast (including a juice presser). The theatrical connection is not immediately obvious, apart from elevator doors being painted like stage curtains, but the functional rooms and efficient service don't leave anything wanting for the cost.

Mayfair Hotel Tunneln

Adelgatan 4; tel. 040 10 16 20; www. mayfairtunneln.com; high season from 1,025 SEK d

Stepping into the Mayfair Hotel Tunneln is a travel experience in itself, given that the building dates in part from the beginning of the 1300s, when the cellar—where breakfast is now served—was built by Danish knight Jens Uffesen Neb. The step-gable Gothic house on top of the cellar was built in the 1500s. History literally drips from the corridors of the hotel, with framed pictures describing the building's and the city's roles in each other's histories. The rooms are anything but 15th century and are well equipped for a peaceful night's sleep. Wheelchair access is limited due to the building's age, but otherwise this is a highly recommended option.

Scandic Triangeln

Triangeln 2; tel. 040 693 47 00; www. scandichotels.com/hotels/sweden/malmo/ scandic-triangeln; high season from 1,228 SEK d

The tall glass-fronted Scandic Triangeln building looks like it might feel more at home in New York City than in central Malmö. But it provides a good orientation point in, and a view above, the central shopping streets. Amenities include a cocktail bar, a gym, and a spa area with saunas. As you'd expect from a Scandic hotel, the comfort and quality levels are high.

MJ's Hotel

Mäster Johansgatan 13; tel. 040 664 64 00; www.mjs.life; high season from 1,005 SEK d

First impressions count at MJ's Hotel, with its entrance on the corner of Mäster Johansgatan and Isak Slagergatan given a glamorous twist with golden pillars and "Hotel" written in bright lightbulbs reminiscent of the Moulin Rouge. Just a block away from both Stortoget and Lilla Torg, the plush interior and exterior fit with the Old City splendor. There's a lively lobby bar with regular events. Rooms have mahogany furniture and thick carpets or patterned rugs, with marble sinks and copper faucets in the baths.

Information and Services

The City of **Malmö** (https://malmo.se/Welcome-to-Malmo/Visit-Malmo.html) has tourist "info points" scattered around the city, where you can pick up maps and brochures, and staff can help answer your questions. Various locations include **Travelshop** (Centralplan 10, Cykelgaraget, Malmö Central Station), **Pressbyrån** (Södergatan 11), **City Hall** (Stadshuset, August Palms plats 1), **Skånetrafikens Kundcenter** (Malmö Central Station), and **Moderna Museet Malmö** (Ola Billgrens plats 2-4).

In an emergency, dial 112 for ambulance and fire services or 11414 (nonemergency) for police.

Sweden's postal service is run by PostNord, the same private company responsible for Denmark's. That means that in lieu of regular post offices like the type seen in the United States, Britain, and elsewhere, stamps can be purchased and letters and packages sent at "postal service points," which are desks located in places like supermarkets, convenience stores, and gas stations. These are easily identified: Look for the yellow horn and crown symbol on a blue background. Postage stamps and labels can also be bought from PostNord's online store (www.postnord.se/en/shop-online/products), and letters, once stamped, can be dropped into regular mailboxes.

Getting There and Around

GETTING TO MALMÖ FROM COPENHAGEN

It's easy to forget that until 2000, traveling between Malmö and Copenhagen involved a ferry voyage. These days it's much simpler.

By Train

The quickest way is by train from either **Copenhagen Central Station** or **Copenhagen Airport.** Tickets can be bought online, via the **Skånetrafiken** app or website (www.skanetrafiken.se), or by using the **Rejsekort travel card.**

If you go with the latter option, don't forget to check out at Malmö Station. There are only two check-in and check-out points, at the far end of the concourse by the exit. The trip to **Malmö's Central Station** is a 25-minute journey from Copenhagen Airport or 40 minutes from Copenhagen Central Station. Tickets cost 135 SEK for a one-way ticket or 94 kr with the Rejsekort, and you can bring a bicycle on the train for free provided there's enough space (there are nine slots for bicycles, strollers, and similarly sized items).

By Bus

If you'd rather see the Öresund from a bus, **Flixbus** (www.flixbus.com; from 59 kr) offer tickets less expensive than the train at the cost of some of the convenience. Flixbuses leave from the long distance bus departure terminal in Copenhagen, close to the central rail station, and there are also departures from the airport. In Malmö, the Flixbus will drop you off at Central Station. It's not normally possible to transport bicycles by bus.

By Car

Before you begin your drive, remember your wallet: There's a toll to cross the Øresund by road, and it's not cheap, at 440 kr for a passenger car (up to 6 m/19 ft). Cash and credit cards are accepted. A small discount of 22 kr can be had by purchasing in advance from www.oresundsbron.com. You can also register for the annual "ØresundGO" rate, which costs 349 kr per year and reduces the bridge toll to 170 kr.

From central Copenhagen, take the O2 ring road, which runs close to the harbor near Central Station and south of Vesterbro, where it meets Sydhavnsgade. Follow signs for Malmö E20. This road will take you across to Amager via the Sjællandsbroen Bridge. Merge right and continue to follow signs for Malmö E20, crossing Amager from west to east. The sea will come into view, and you'll enter the tunnel section of the Öresund crossing, the 4 km (2.5 mi) Drogden Tunnel. You'll emerge on the artificial island of Peberholm before continuing on the vast Öresund Bridge for the next 8 km (5 mi); enjoy the view. Once you reach the other side of the bridge, you'll approach the toll gates. Passport control spot checks take place at these toll stations at the Swedish end of the bridge. Continue on the E20 until you reach the exit for Limhamn/Malmö V. Take this exit into the Swedish city. The entire journey is just over the length of a marathon, at 44 km (27 mi), and should take around 45 minutes to drive.

GETTING AROUND
By Public Transit

City buses and trains in Malmö are operated by **Skånetrafiken** (tel. 0771 77 77 77; www.skanetrafiken.se). The most straightforward way to buy tickets is via Skånetrafiken's app, but there are also ticket machines on train station platforms, including at Copenhagen Central Station and Copenhagen Airport. The Skånetrafiken app can also be used to plan journeys.

If you are planning extensive use of public transportation in Malmö, consider buying a 24-timmarsbiljett, which gives unlimited use of the public transit system in the city, including buses and trains, for a 24-hour period. The 24-hour pass covering Malmö can be purchased for 62 SEK on the

Skånetrafiken website (www.ska-netrafiken.se) or on the app.

Most of Malmö's attractions are close to each other, but public transportation can be useful to save time. From the central Gustav Adolfs Torg in Gamla Staden, buses 1, 2, 4, 8, and 35 go to Pildammsparken, an 8-minute journey that costs 31 SEK. From Gustav Adolfs Torg to Västra Hamnen, bus 8 goes directly. The ticket price is the same, and the journey is longer, at around 14 minutes. Buses leave every few minutes during the day for either journey.

By Car and Taxi

Driver's licenses valid in Denmark are also valid in Sweden. If you are driving a rental car, make sure your agreement allows you to cross international borders.

Malmö's traffic is user-friendly and orderly, and there is ample parking. There is a handful of multistory parking garages in the center of the city, with the Triangeln area and Caroli shopping mall (Östergatan 12) both good bets if you want to get close to the old city.

Read more about parking charges in Malmö on the city's parking information website (www.pmalmo.se).

Sweden's taxi market is deregulated, so you can hail cabs and prearrange fixed prices with companies that have such policies. Arranged prices are entered into taxi meters at the start of your journey. Normally, the step-in fare for a taxi is 59 SEK and then 18 SEK per kilometer. A trip from the Central Station to Västra Hamnen costs around 100-150 SEK.

Unlike in Denmark, Uber ridesharing is legal in Sweden and is therefore an option in Malmö.

On Foot and By Bicycle

Walking and cycling are a breeze in Malmö. There are bicycle lanes, many well away from corresponding roads. Wide paths, coastal promenades, and parks everywhere all contribute to near optimal conditions. Take care when cycling in heavy traffic and watch for right-turning cars, which sometimes don't see cyclists and turn in front of them. Always wear a bicycle helmet.

Essentials

Transportation
....

GETTING THERE
From the United States

International flights arrive at **Copenhagen Airport (CPH),** also known colloquially as Kastrup. Direct flights are available from almost anywhere in Europe as well as many Asian and North American cities. Booking air travel as far as possible in advance is recommended. Traveling directly from East

Coast cities such as **New York** or **Miami** is generally the most cost-efficient, with direct round-trip economy tickets from these cities to Copenhagen Airport ranging $300-800. **Skyscanner.com** is a good starting point for searching round-trip tickets. Copenhagen Airport is the largest airport in Scandinavia. **Scandinavian Airlines** (SAS, www.flysas.com) operates flights from a number of US cities, including New York, Boston, Chicago, and San Francisco.

From Europe
By Air

Budget flights to Denmark are usually less expensive and almost certainly quicker than going anywhere by train or by car, given Copenhagen's awkward location on a smallish island at the northern end of the continent. As such, check all transport options before buying a ticket. **Ryanair** (www.ryanair.com), **Norwegian** (www.norwegian.com), and to a lesser extent **EasyJet** (www.easyjet.com) all operate budget services out of Copenhagen, making much of Europe accessible via a relatively inexpensive nonstop flight.

By Train
Copenhagen Central Station (Hovedbanegården, often abbreviated to Hovedbanen; Bernstorffsgade 16-22), is linked to the European rail network via

Stockholm (5 hours, 30 minutes; from 449 kr) to the north and Amsterdam (12 hours; from 433 kr), Hamburg (4 hours, 30 minutes; from 220 kr), and Berlin (7 hours; from 319 kr) to the south and east. International tickets can be booked via Denmark's national rail operator **DSB** (tel. 70 13 14 18; www.dsb.dk). If you are planning an extended trip around Denmark, it makes sense to look into the two main European rail passes, **Eurail** (www.eurail.com) for non-Europeans, and **Interrail** (www.interrail.eu) for residents of European countries. Both are particularly useful for travelers under age 25.

Travel times and fares to Copenhagen from:

- **Stege, Møn:** 2 hours via bus 660R Stege-Vordingborg, train Vordingborg-Copenhagen; 128 kr; hourly departures

- **Helsingør:** 45 minutes; 88 kr; departures every 20 minutes

- **Humlebæk** (Louisiana Museum of Modern Art): 35 minutes; 74 kr; departures every 20 minutes

- **Roskilde:** 25-30 minutes; 66 kr; departures every 5-10 minutes

- **Dragør:** 40 minutes via bus 250S Dragør-Tårnby, train Tårnby-Copenhagen; 30 kr; every 10 minutes

- **Klampenborg:** 18-20 minutes; 40 kr; every 10 minutes (the S-train also serves Klampenborg)

Previous: Marmorkirken metro station, Copenhagen.

By Bus

German company **Flixbus** (www.flixbus.com) operates international bus services to Denmark from both Sweden and Germany. Travelers to Copenhagen from within Denmark can use **Flixbus** or **Kombardo Expressen** (www.kombardoexpressen.dk). As of June 2024, buses arrive at a terminal close to Central Station and Dybbølsbro S-train station.

By Car

Coming by car from either mainland Europe via Germany or from Sweden via the Øresund Bridge is straightforward, given that all three countries are within the EU's Schengen common visa area. Denmark retains the right to carry out checks on its border with Germany and has done so since 2016 under the "exceptional circumstances" exemption permitted under the Schengen Agreement. This does not mean there's a hard border, and the controls are unlikely to affect tourists. Nevertheless, there is a chance you could be stopped for a random spot check. In short, make sure you carry your passport.

By Ferry

Ferry operator **DFDS** (+44 8718 820 881; www.dfds.com/en/passenger-ferries) offers daily overnight ferries between Copenhagen and Norwegian capital Oslo for €43 per person (not including a car). Exact departure times vary, but the ferry from Copenhagen normally departs at either 3pm or 4:30pm, depending on whether a stop is made in northern Danish city Frederikshavn, arriving in Oslo at 10am the following morning. A similar timetable applies for the reverse journey. The ferries have restaurants, play areas, and bars, and a cabin is included in the fare, with various cabin sizes and comfort options available. A "mini cruise" option allows you to buy a two-night return ticket at a discounted fare (from €42 per person), giving you 24 hours to spend in the Norwegian capital, and bumps up the standard of your cabin. The ferry terminal is located at Dampfærgevej 30, close to the Langlinie pier.

GETTING AROUND
By Train

Copenhagen's public transportation system is comprehensive, consisting of bus and Metro networks as well as an overground metropolitan network known as the S-tog (S-train).

Metro

The Copenhagen Metro provides excellent coverage of the city thanks in part to two new lines and 17 new stations that opened in 2019.

The **M3 City Ring** connects the Inner City, Østerbro, Nørrebro, and Frederiksberg districts and includes a stop at Copenhagen Central Station. The other new 2019 line, **M4,** is a short branch from the M3 heading out to two stations at Nordhavn and

Orientkaj. The two original lines, **M1** and **M2,** connect Amager and Christianshavn directly to the Inner City and Frederiksberg. **Line M2** terminates at the airport and also stops at Amagerbro and the Amager Strand beach and lagoon area; **M1** has stations at Islands Brygge and Vestamager, from where you can access the Amager Fælled national park and Amager Nature Center. They also both stop at Nørreport Station, the main hub for local rail in Copenhagen, where you can transfer to rail and S-train services.

Open **24 hours,** Metro trains run every 2-4 minutes at peak times, 3-6 minutes during the day, 15-20 minutes on weeknights, and 7-8 minutes during the night on weekends.

S-Train
S-trains go through Central Station and run regularly throughout the day around 5am-12:30am. On weekends, there are all-night services. The S-train's 7 lines and 86 stations comprehensively cover the metropolitan area, including Klampenborg, but with the notable exception of Amager, which has Metro coverage.

Regional Trains
For travel between Copenhagen and other cities, towns, and regions in Denmark, there is one rail option: state operator DSB. The trains are comfortable and quiet and normally run on time, but they are not always viewed favorably

by Danes, possibly due to their high fares. Sample fares include Odense (1 hour, 11 minutes; 319 kr) and Aarhus (2 hours, 46 minutes; 429 kr). Other destinations include Roskilde (22 minutes; 66 kr), Helsingør (46 minutes; 88 kr), and Malmö (39 minutes; 94 kr).

Planning and Fares
The **Rejseplanen app,** which is available in English, is a must-have for instant planning of journeys that combine all three of these transportation networks. The prepaid travel card **Rejsekort** is the easiest way to pay fares. It can be bought from machines in stations. The same machines (look for their neon-blue cladding) can be used to add credit to the cards. Alternatively, single tickets can be bought in Metro and S-train stations and from bus drivers.

When using the Rejsekort, you must "check in" by holding the card over the sensor inside the bus or train at the beginning of your journey. Then, "check out" by using the separate checkout sensor when you are about to reach your destination. If you connect to a different bus or train, you do not check out but must check in again on the second bus or train after transferring. You then check out for the entire journey when you reach your destination. The Rejsekort card costs 180 kr from machines, of which up to 100 kr can be used as credit, although you will have to add value before the balance reaches zero.

The physical Rejsekort is

gradually being phased out to be replaced by an app, but both card and app will be valid in the transitional phase. More detail will be made available on the Rejsekort website (www.rejsekort.dk).

By Bus

There are currently two companies competing for passengers who eschew DSB's more expensive rail fares for less expensive coach services between Danish cities. These are **Kombardo Expressen** (www.kombardoexpressen.dk) and **Flixbus** (www.flixbus.com). Bus fares are far lower than the train, balanced out by the cramped space and slightly longer journey times. Sample fares for a trip from Copenhagen to Aarhus can range 99-189 kr, and from Copenhagen to Malmö 59-199 kr, although going by train is preferable.

Outside Copenhagen, local buses are generally simple and convenient to cover short distances within towns. Companies awarded contracts by regional authorities operate city buses in Denmark as well as in Malmö in Sweden, so there's only one type of bus. The Rejsekort can be used anywhere in Denmark in the same way as in Copenhagen, as can the Rejseplanen app for checking departure times and planning journeys. Buses usually run at least hourly on principal routes. On Møn, it can be a little difficult to rely on buses alone to get around the island, particularly in the off-season when services are cut back.

By Car
Traffic and Driving Conditions

As far as major cities go, Copenhagen isn't bad to drive in as a newcomer. Traffic can get heavy at peak times (Mon.-Thurs. 7am-9am and 4pm-5pm, Friday 7am-9am and 3pm-4pm), but it is generally forgiving; sitting in gridlock for long spells is uncommon.

Driving from Copenhagen to the other destinations in this book is quite straightforward and not at all time-consuming by US standards. The most distant location is Møn, with a journey time of 1 hour, 30 minutes. The major roads and highways are well maintained, clearly marked, and toll-free (not including bridges).

When traveling from Copenhagen to **Malmö** by car, there's a toll to cross the Øresund Bridge (440 kr for a standard car, cash and cards accepted). A discount of 22 kr can be had by purchasing in advance from www.oresundsbron.com. You can also register for the annual "ØresundGO" rate, which costs 349 kr per year and reduces the bridge toll to 170 kr, thereby making it worthwhile for anything more than a one-way journey across the straits. Cancel your annual subscription once you're done with it.

Road Rules

Like most European countries, apart from Britain, Ireland, Cyprus, and Malta, driving in Denmark is on the right-hand side. International Driving Permits are not required for residents of EU countries, the United States, Canada, or Australia. Driver's licenses from other **countries outside the European Economic Area** are also accepted provided they are printed with Latin letters or accompanied by a translation to Danish, English, or French. **International Driving Permits** are also valid. It's important to note that an International Driving Permit is not a license on its own—you still have to carry your actual driver's license alongside it.

Drivers from most other countries are unlikely to be used to seeing so many bicycles on the road, and you will need to adapt your driving style to accommodate this. Although the bikes have their own lane, they have the right of way on right turns: When you are turning right, you must wait until all non-turning bicycles have passed on your curbside before turning. The same applies with pedestrians: Right-turning cars must wait for them to clear traffic crossings before making the turn. This isn't the case in many other countries.

Parking

All cars in Denmark display a **parking disc,** which looks like an analogue clock (some cars have automatic digital ones), on the inside of the windshield. This must be set at the time you leave your car if you are parking in an area that does not have a parking charge but does have a time limit. If there is a time limit for parking, it will be displayed on a signpost on the street or parking lot. Failure to set your parking disc or parking illegally can result in your vehicle being issued with a ticket or booted ("clamped").

In Copenhagen, parking fees can be paid using apps that include ParkOne, EasyPark, and APCOA Flow, and sometimes from machines on the street.

Parking in smaller towns is easier than in Copenhagen, both in terms of finding a spot and being able to park for free, but if you do park in a fee-charging parking lot, the apps used to pay are the same as the ones used in Copenhagen.

By Bike

Bicycles can be taken on S-trains and the Harbor Bus for free but are not allowed at the busy Nørreport station or on the Metro during weekday peak times. On the Metro, buses, and longer distance trains, you'll have to purchase a separate bicycle ticket (cykelbillet) or you could end up facing a fine.

Visas and Officialdom

UNITED STATES, AUSTRALIA, AND NEW ZEALAND

For American, Australian, or New Zealand citizens, **no visa** or special documentation is required other than your valid government-issued **passport** that is valid for at least six months past the date that you are scheduled to leave the Schengen Area (of which Denmark is a part). The passport must have been issued no more than 10 years ago. No tourist visa or other kind of visa is necessary for entering and leaving the Schengen Area for a cumulative 90 days within a 180-day period. This does not necessarily mean 90 consecutive days, but rather 90 total days within the 180-day time frame. Note that this includes any country in the Schengen Area, not only Denmark. If you plan to exceed the 90-day limit, you have to obtain a tourist visa or another kind of visa to legally stay in the country.

Two new EU border systems, the **Entry/Exit System (EES)** and the **European Travel Information and Authorization System (ETIAS),** are expected to come into force in 2024 and 2025. EES, a replacement for passport stamps, will record data on non-EU citizens in an EU-wide database every time they enter and exit the Schengen Area, while ETIAS will require non-EU nationals from visa-exempt countries to apply online for a digital authorization before departure. As such, these changes are important to be aware of. ETIAS applications will cost €7 but will be free under age 18 and over age 70. Detailed information on EES and ETIAS is available on the EU's website (https://travel-europe.europa.eu).

EUROPEAN UNION AND SCHENGEN

For citizens of countries that are members of the European Union, you only need a valid **passport** or government-issued **national identity card** that is valid during the length of your stay in Denmark to enter the country. It is important to have this with you when crossing the land or sea border from Sweden or Germany, as spot checks are possible, and you can be sent back if you do not produce the relevant ID.

EMBASSIES AND CONSULATES

- **US Embassy Copenhagen:** Dag Hammarskjölds Allé 24; tel. 33 41 71 00; https://dk.usembassy.gov

- **British Embassy Copenhagen:** Kastelsvej 36-40; tel. 35 44 52 00; www.gov.uk/world/organisations/british-embassy-copenhagen

- **Australian Embassy in Denmark (Copenhagen):** Dampfærgevej 26; tel.

70 26 36 76; https://denmark.embassy.gov.au

- **New Zealand Consulate-General Copenhagen:** Skarpögatan 6, Stockholm, Sweden; tel. +46 8 400 17 270; https://www.mfat.govt.nz/en/countries-and-regions/europe/sweden/new-zealand-embassy

- **South African Embassy Copenhagen:** Strandøre 15; tel. 39 18 01 85; https://dirco1.azurewebsites.net/copenhagen

- **Embassy of Canada to Denmark (Copenhagen):** Kristen Bernikows Gade 1; tel. 33 48 32 00; https://www.international.gc.ca/country-pays/denmark-danemark/copenhagen-copenhague.aspx?lang=eng

- **Embassy of Ireland in Denmark:** Østbanegade 21; tel. 35 47 32 00; www.ireland.ie/en/denmark/copenhagen

Festivals and Events

SPRING

Things start to warm up in Denmark in May, when **Ølfestival** brings the city's strong craft beer game and other lovers of fine ales out of winter hibernation. **CPH:DOX** is a widely praised documentary film festival that lasts 11 days in March and will inspire you the rest of the year.

SUMMER

Copenhagen comes alive in the summer with what seems like a festival every weekend. **Distortion,** at the end of May and beginning of June, turns the streets of the city into a hedonistic mess often bemoaned by residents. The **Roskilde Festival,** though it takes place in a nearby city and not in Copenhagen itself, is the country's most famous festival and the largest live music event in Scandinavia.

Copenhell is a heavy metal festival that takes place in mid-June on Refshaleøen. **Copenhagen Jazz Festival** is 10 big days of big jazz and intimate bar music in early July. By August, things calm down a bit, exemplified by the world-class offerings of the **Copenhagen Opera Festival** near the end of the month. **Kulturhavn** is a 3-day community culture festival on the waterfront with scores of activities and cultural performances. **Copenhagen Cooking & Food Festival,** Scandinavia's biggest food festival, also takes place in August. In the middle of all this is **Skt. Hans Aften** (St. John's Eve), when the celebration before the Feast Day of Saint John the Baptist is marked in a community spirit and Danes come out to sing in unison and light bonfires. **Copenhagen Pride** is in the middle of August. In Helsingør, the **Elsinore Shakespeare Festival** brings open-air theater to the real-life location of the events depicted in *Hamlet*. Down the coast, **Louisiana Literature** is calmer but perhaps no less dramatic, as famous international authors come to the picturesque town of Humlebæk to give readings of their works.

AUTUMN

Copenhagen Blues Festival keeps the summer music vibe hanging in for a little while longer into autumn. **Culture Night** (Kulturnatten) is a late-night art and culture festival in October. Although it's not a traditional celebration in Denmark, **Halloween** has now been enthusiastically adopted by the country, so you can brace for a plentiful supply of spooky happenings and decorations.

WINTER

Christmas in Copenhagen is almost synonymous with **Tivoli**, the iconic 19th-century amusement park at the heart of the city that spares no expense when it comes to yuletide fun. **Winter Jazz** (Vinterjazz) at the beginning of February has intimate concerts—sometimes even held in people's front rooms—as well as events in the city's cafés and jazz bars. **Fastelavn,** in February or early March, is the Danish version of Carnival but has as much in common with Halloween, as kids dress up in funny costumes and hit a piñata-like wooden barrel to win sweets.

Conduct and Customs

LOCAL HABITS

Danes can often come across as taciturn and withdrawn in their meetings with strangers. They commonly avoid making eye contact with neighbors when passing them on steps and are unlikely to acknowledge people sharing public transportation with them, for example. Though this may seem cold, it should not be taken personally. It is part of Danish culture and makes established friendships feel all the more genuine.

ALCOHOL AND SMOKING

The minimum age for purchasing cigarettes in Denmark is 18, and the minimum age for purchasing alcohol is 18 for beverages with an alcohol percentage more than 16.5 percent and age 16 for percentages less than that. A surprisingly high number of Danes smoke: some 13 percent of the adult population were daily smokers in 2022, according to figures from the Danish Cancer Society. A partial but not complete ban on smoking in bars has been in place for years, and supermarkets are now obliged to keep cigarettes out of the view of customers, thereby preventing advertising in any form. Smoking is still allowed in bars with less than 40 sq m (430 sq ft) of floor space, not including staff areas: The old-fashioned pubs known as bodegas remain as smoky as they have been for decades.

There are diverse, inventive, hip, traditional, and innovative nightlife venues in the form of nightclubs, cocktail bars, wine bars, and cheap grimy pubs (the aforementioned bodegas) spread all over the city, particularly in the Inner City, Nørrebro, and Vesterbro districts. Nightlife action peaks Thursday-Saturday, with weekend parties often not finishing until the sun has come up again and everyone has had a morgenfest (morning party), but Copenhagen has something to do every night of the week.

DRUGS

Recreational drugs, including marijuana, are illegal to use, purchase, and sell in Denmark, although, as in many countries, you may see people in the general population under the influence. That is particularly the case in Christiania, the nonconformist enclave in the city, which began as a hippie commune in the 1970s and for years saw cannabis openly sold on its Pusher Street market. Police tolerated this for intermittent periods over the decades, but it appears to be on borrowed time now: Increasing encroachment on the illicit market by rival crime gangs has led to increasing violence, including a handful of shootings in the last few years. Police, politicians, and Christiania residents are now in broad agreement and there is a shared will to permanently shut down Pusher Street. The legislative process to this end has already begun.

Using drugs in public can result in a fine from law enforcement. However, you probably won't be fined unless you are disturbing public peace or disobeying law enforcement, or if you are in the wrong place during a period when police are cracking down on, for example, Christiania. Harder illicit drugs such as cocaine and amphetamines are illegal in Denmark, and being caught with such drugs can lead to prosecution under criminal law.

Health and Safety

EMERGENCY NUMBERS

The following numbers can be used to call emergency services in Denmark:

- **112** is a direct number to emergency services if you require immediate response, for example, an accident or if someone's life is in danger. Use 112 to call an ambulance, the police, or the fire service.

- **114** is a direct number for police across the country, that is, if you have a query but your concern is not an emergency.

- If you have a possible medical emergency and want to call an on-duty medic for advice, you can use the Danish public health system's regional direct system. The number is 38 69 38 69 in Greater Copenhagen, including Helsingør, Klampenborg, and Dragør, and 1818 in the rest of the Zealand region, including Roskilde and the smaller island Møn. Check your travel insurance for coverage.

In almost all cases, operators can speak in English. In the unlikely scenario that they can't, will quickly transfer you to somebody who can.

MEDICAL SERVICES

Travel medical insurance is recommended on any type of trip, so arrange this before departure or check what your current health insurance covers internationally. If you need medical attention while in Denmark, you can call 112 for medical emergencies or if an ambulance is needed. Denmark has public health care, meaning the government provides free health care to all Danish citizens and legal residents. This is part of a larger integrated health system in the European Union, so if you are an EU resident, any medical costs that you incur in Denmark can be fully refunded by the medical system in your home country (so keep your receipts).

Regardless of where you are from, if you fall ill during your stay in Denmark, you are entitled to free emergency hospital treatment in accordance with the normal rules applied in the area.

Foreign travelers from countries outside the European Economic Area and Switzerland have the same rights as Danish citizens when it comes to emergency health care, meaning that emergency medical treatment is free of charge in the emergency rooms of public hospitals. Nonemergency medical bills must be paid, however. Prices start from 800 kr for a consultation.

PHARMACIES

The Danish word for pharmacy is apotek. Pharmacies are marked with green plus signs and can be found every few blocks in built-up areas and all smaller towns. The law requires a small number of pharmacies to remain open outside normal business hours. In Copenhagen, Steno Apotek (Vesterbrogade 6; tel. 33 14 82 66; www.stenoapotek.dk), located close to the Central Rail Station, is open daily 24 hours.

All Danish pharmacists speak English well or adequately and are willing to help you find the medications you need if you are able to describe your conditions or symptoms. If you know the generic name of your prescribed medication, they can sometimes find them for you. Unlike in the United States, medications such as over-the-counter headache treatments and nasal sprays are not readily available on the shelves, so you have to ask the pharmacist for it at the counter.

If you travel with medications, pack them in their original containers. Separately, pack other documentation or information that may help you in case of emergency.

CRIME AND THEFT

Crime rates are relatively low in Denmark, although the number of reported crimes was higher in 2022 than in the two preceding COVID-19 impacted years, as was the total number of police charges for all types of crime, according to national statistics. In Copenhagen, 3 percent of residents in the city said in a 2023 municipal survey that they'd been the victim of a break-in or theft. One of the biggest hazards is bicycle theft, with 19 percent saying their bike had been lifted during the last year. Around 1 in 5 was offered drugs or witnessed someone else buying them, 5 percent said they'd been sexually harassed, and 4 percent had been victims of violence or attempted violence.

Visitors should be mindful of pickpocketing and bag theft. At the beginning of 2022, Copenhagen Police said such incidents were making a comeback after declining during the pandemic. People in their early 20s are frequent targets, as are those over age 70. Keep your belongings secure when you are in busy places, particularly in and around Copenhagen Central Station and on the Strøget shopping thoroughfare. Although it is sometimes said that you can leave your computer on the table in a café while you go to the restroom, I advise very strongly against it: Always keep valuable items close to you.

Muggings and other forms of assault are also rare but not unheard of. Take the same precautions you would in any big city. Don't take unlicensed taxis anywhere at any time.

The alternative enclave of Christiania was the setting of a flare-up of violence between organized crime gangs in 2023. This seemed to culminate when a 30-year-old gang member was shot and killed in August that year, and residents and politicians are now working toward a permanent closure of the Pusher Street market around which the gang conflict revolves. Christiania is often a draw for tourists, but the spate of incidents has noticeably worsened its reputation and popularity. The situation is concerning but it should be noted that gun crime in Denmark remains rare and is extremely unlikely to affect visitors.

The poorer suburbs in Malmö, including Lindängen, Rosengård, and Southern Sofienlund (Seved),

have also seen gang-related violence, and 2023 was a particularly bleak year for gang violence in Sweden in general. However, areas of Malmö such as Gamla Staden and Västra Hämnen, where visitors are likely to find themselves, are less likely to see any incidents than the marginalized suburbs. Overall, neither Copenhagen nor Malmö are any more dangerous than any other big city.

Practical Details

PASSES AND DISCOUNTS

There are savings to be had when visiting museums in Denmark. Some museums are free, such as the acclaimed Islamic art museum the David Collection; others offer discounts on certain days or off-season. The following museums have free entry on specific days: **Ny Carlsberg Glyptotek** (last Wed. of each month), **Thorvaldsens Museum,** and **Nikolaj Copenhagen Contemporary Art Center** (Wed.).

Senior citizens and students often qualify for reduced rates on museum entry and transportation, but you'll need to show proof of your student status or age.

The **Copenhagen Card** (https:// copenhagencard.com) is a prepaid card that provides admission to over 80 attractions in the city and nearby. It includes travel on public transportation throughout the

capital region as well as on hop-on, hop-off sightseeing buses. Two children under age 12 can be added free to an adult's card.

A full list of the discounted attractions can be found via the Copenhagen Card website and app. It's quite extensive, so if you already have an idea of what you want to see while in the city, or are planning to pack in a lot of sightseeing, there is a good chance the card will save you money.

MONEY
Currency and Exchange Rates

Denmark's currency is the krone (plural kroner); only the krone can be used to pay for goods and services. You may occasionally find businesses that accept the euro, but you should never expect this.

The value of the Danish krone is intentionally kept close to that of the euro by the central bank,

Danmarks Nationalbank. At the time of writing, exchange rates were 1 krone = €0.13 = US$0.15 = £0.12.

Currency Exchange

There are several desks at Copenhagen Airport where money can be exchanged. **FOREX Bank** has several branches in Copenhagen, including at the Central Station, in the Inner City (Nørre Voldgade 90; tel. 81 95 81 14), and Frederiksberg (Falkoner Allé 12b; tel. 81 95 81 15).

It's worth bearing in mind that Denmark is a relatively cash-free society. Most people make payments using a smartphone app, **MobilePay,** connected to their bank account, or with their debit cards. Foreign debit and credit cards can be used to make payments with almost every business and store in Denmark, with the exception of some, but not all, supermarkets.

Bargaining

Haggling is not common practice in Denmark beyond second-hand trade apps and flea markets. Retailers all have set prices. In thrift stores and charity shops, you may be able to agree on a reduced price with a staff member, depending on the store's policy and the inclination of the person in question. At flea markets, feel free to ask if the price is negotiable (although the answer may well be no).

Tipping

Tipping is not expected in Denmark, even in expensive restaurants, because Danish labor market practices ensure staff are paid a negotiated salary. It is, however, always appreciated—10 percent gratuity is plenty, should you wish to tip.

ATMs and Banks

ATMs, commonly referred to as pengeautomater (money machines) or hæveautomater (withdrawal machines), are commonplace on streets outside shops and banks as well as within banks. They can also occasionally be found within small stores such as minimarkets: These should be avoided if possible as they are more likely to levy a withdrawal fee on top of any fees you already face for international withdrawal.

Check ahead with your bank to see if they have partnerships with Danish banks for waived or reduced fees. If they do not, a fee of around 30-35 kr is likely to be charged for each ATM withdrawal.

Credit and Debit Cards

Visa and Mastercard are accepted almost everywhere in Denmark; American Express and Diners Club cards are not always accepted. In general, very few businesses don't accept card payment, and fewer and fewer Danes use cash. Occasionally, you may find a store (for example, some Netto supermarkets) that has a system that doesn't accept cards that aren't linked to Denmark's Dankort debit card payment system. This is rare, however. Any

Stretching the Krone in Copenhagen

Copenhagen can be an expensive place to visit, but there are ways to offset the expense while still enjoying the country to its fullest.

- The **Copenhagen Card** (page 40) offers potential savings on museum entry along with transportation if you plan your itinerary to maximize the use of the card.

- The **Parkmuseerne** multiple-entry ticket (page 40) can also be a money-saver if you want to visit at least three of the six attractions it covers.

- **Visit museums for free:** For example, the **Ny Carlsberg Glyptotek** (page 53) art museum offers free entry on the last Wednesday of each month, while the **David Collection** (page 47) is free every day.

- Like many Danes, you could alternate inexpensive or free outdoor activities where you take along packed lunches to the more expensive sights. Copenhagen and its surroundings have a plentiful supply of **parks** and **beaches.**

- To get city views for the price of a coffee, head to the **rooftop café** at the **Illum department store** (page 92).

- There are some cafés in the city that are focused on students. These have lower prices while retaining spades of charm and character. Try looking around the University of Copenhagen in the Inner City for cafés with a heavy student presence, for example **Paludan Bog & Café** (page 101).

- You can save substantially—often half—by using **happy hour** offers. In central Copenhagen, **The Jane** (page 126), **The Bird & the Churchkey** (page 128), **Little Green Door** (page 128), and **Jolene** (page 134) are good bets. You can also look for chalkboards outside bar entrances promoting their special offers.

business that caters to tourists will accept card payments, including for small amounts. Surcharges are sometimes imposed on foreign cards. If this is the case, customers must be notified about the surcharge, for example at hotel reception or on restaurant menus.

OPEN HOURS

Open hours can vary among businesses, and seasonal businesses reduce hours during the off-season, but the following hours generally apply:

- **Shops:** Monday-Friday 10am-6pm; some close earlier

Saturday (between 2pm and 4pm); some are open Sunday

- **Supermarkets:** Monday-Saturday 8am-10pm; many are open Sunday, and some close at 11pm or midnight; some convenience stores are open daily 24 hours

- **Department stores:** daily 10am-8pm

- **Bars:** Sunday-Wednesday 4pm-10pm, Thursday-Saturday until midnight-6am

- **Cafés:** daily 8am-7pm, some café-bar crossovers are open as late as midnight

- **Restaurants:** daily noon-10pm; some close at 11pm or midnight

- **Banks:** Monday-Friday 10am-4pm; sometimes Thursday 10am-5:30pm or 6pm

PUBLIC HOLIDAYS

- **New Year's Day** (Nytårsdag): January 1

- **Holy Thursday** (Skærtorsdag): Thursday before Easter

- **Good Friday** (Langfredag): Friday before Easter

- **Easter Sunday** (Påskedag)

- **Easter Monday** (2. påskedag)

- **Ascension Day** (Kristi Himmelfartsdag): 6th Thursday after Easter

- **Pentecost** (Pinsedag): 7th Sunday after Easter

- **Whit Monday** (2. pinsedag): day after Pentecost

- **Constitution Day** (Grundlovsdag): June 5

- **Christmas Eve** (Juleaften): December 24 (from noon)

- **Christmas Day** (Juledag): December 25

- **Boxing Day** (2. juledag): December 26

International Workers' Day, also known as Labor Day or May Day (May 1), is not an official public holiday, but many employers, especially in the public sector, give employees the day off. In Copenhagen the annual occasion is marked by speeches, workers' songs, and red banners as workers organized by profession or trade union head to the Fælledparken park in Østerbro, where there's a spirited festival atmosphere as people join together to drink coffee and beer and support workers' rights.

COMMUNICATIONS
Phones and Cell Phones

Denmark's country code is +45. All numbers have eight digits after the country code, and there are no area codes, so it's simple to dial once you're in the country.

If you're coming from outside Europe, check that your cell phone works on the European GSM 900/1800 network—some Asian and American phones only work on different frequencies.

Prepaid, refillable SIM cards can be bought at retailers and supermarkets without showing identification, but this is no longer widespread. They can also be ordered online for free from service providers such as Lycamobile (www.lycamobile.dk), but you will need a Danish address.

Useful numbers:

- **118:** directory assistance
- **113:** international directory assistance

Internet Access

Although the city of Copenhagen doesn't provide public Wi-Fi access, you can log onto Wi-Fi at the vast majority of cafés, restaurants, and hotels as well as at many attractions. You may need to ask for a password, although there is often also free access. City buses and intercity coaches also have onboard Wi-Fi, although it's not always reliable.

Shipping and Postal Service

Denmark's postal service has been privatized, and the traditional post offices of days gone by have been fully replaced by **postbutikker** (post shops), which are counters at supermarkets run by operator PostNord. Packages are now sent from and can be collected at these counters as well as other package service providers in minimarkets and newsagents. Find your nearest one via www.postnord.dk. Open hours are normally those of the store hosting the postal desk. Parcel delivery to home addresses still exists but is slow, and delivery to a nearby **pakkeshop** (parcel shop) is usually the more convenient option. A pakkeshop may be a kiosk, convenience store, or even a gas station counter. PostNord does not have a monopoly: Companies including GLS, DAO and UPS all operate in Denmark for sending and receiving packages from a pakkeshop.

Costs for sending packages internationally from Denmark start from 36 kr for up to 2 kg (4 lbs) with PostNord; registered parcels can be sent from 132 kr. Delivery times are advertised as 6-10 days but are always longer in my experience, with around 2-3 weeks to be expected.

WEIGHTS AND MEASURES

Denmark uses the metric system. Many Danes struggle to name US or imperial units; others find them quirky. A few basic conversions are as follows:

- 1 kilometer = 1,000 meters = 0.62 miles
- 1 meter = 3.3 feet = 1.1 yards
- 1 liter = 0.26 US gallons = 0.22 imperial gallons
- 1 ounce = 28.4 grams
- 1 kilogram = 2.2 pounds

LEFT LUGGAGE

Luggage storage is available at **Copenhagen Airport,** where baggage lockers are placed near car park P4. Three sizes are available, ranging from 60 kr for 4 hours to 120 kr for 24 hours.

At **Copenhagen Central Station,** lockers are located at the bottom of the steps inside the western entrance of the station at Istedgade. Luggage storage is open Monday-Saturday 5:30am-1am and Sunday and public holidays 6am-1am. The cost is 75-95 kr for 24 hours, depending on the size.

TOURIST INFORMATION
Tourist Offices
Copenhagen Visitors Center
Vesterbrogade 4B; tel. 70 22 24 42; www.visitcopenhagen.com; low season Mon.-Tues. 9am-4pm, Wed.-Sun. 9am-6pm, high season Mon.-Fri. 9am-4pm, Sat.-Sun. 10am-3pm

Physical tourist information centers have become a rarity, but Copenhagen's main bureau is still firmly in place as a smart and user-friendly resource located a few minutes' walk from the Central Station and opposite the main entrance to Tivoli. There's a café and lounge with free Wi-Fi. You can buy the Copenhagen Card, book tours, use the digital guide or speak to staff, and pick up a library of brochures.

Internet Resources and Apps
The **Rejseplanen app** is essential for planning journeys in Copenhagen and all over Denmark. It tells you the easiest route to your destination, where and how to transfer, and how much the fare is. It also provides a link to buy the ticket online (this is more expensive than using a Rejsekort). The app is available in English. Train tickets can also be purchased on DSB's app. Local transportation operator DOT has its own straightforward app on which tickets for buses, trains, and the Metro in Greater Copenhagen can be purchased. Google Translate is handy for understanding written Danish, if not for the language's nuances.

Maps
Apple Maps and **Google Maps** are as reliable in Denmark as anywhere, especially if you need a turn-by-turn GPS navigation when driving, bicycling, or walking around. Both are available in offline mode and work well in rural areas like Møn.

Traveler Advice

ACCESS FOR TRAVELERS WITH DISABILITIES
Accessibility for travelers with disabilities at tourist attractions is still not guaranteed in Denmark, but it is fast improving.

Tourist information website **Visit Copenhagen** (www.visitcopenhagen.com) lists sights, restaurants, and hotels with good accessibility in its "Accessible Copenhagen" section.

God Adgang (www.godadgang.dk)

is another good resource, listing service providers approved and registered as accessible.

TRAVELING WITH CHILDREN

With its open spaces and cargo bikes, Copenhagen is a child-friendly capital city. Attractions like Experimentarium and Tycho Brahe Planetarium, as well as GeoCenter Møns Klint on Møn, mean there are plenty of stimulating and educational places for kids. Some of the major museums, such as Louisiana Museum of Modern Art, make sure there is something for kids to do while parents are gazing at contemporary art. In fact, Louisiana has an entire section dedicated to daily activities and workshops for children. Vintage amusement park Bakken is a great day out for children, and Tivoli Gardens is a timeless experience that has a bit of magic about it, not least at Christmas.

Using public transportation with children is made as easy as possible with family areas on trains and reduced fares. Most restaurants below Michelin-starred class have children's menus.

WOMEN TRAVELING ALONE

Women should take precautions when traveling alone, especially at night. There are no specific dangers that set Copenhagen apart from other major European cities. Danes are generally reserved in the public sphere, so catcalling is less prevalent than in some other countries. Overall, the prospect of traveling alone as a woman should not act as a deterrent to visiting Denmark.

SENIOR TRAVELERS

Copenhagen can feel like a young city to the point of exclusivity at times, given the stylish beautiful appearance of so much of its population. However, many museums and attractions are senior-friendly, offering discounts on admission. There are also discounts on public transportation for those over age 65. Although it's a cyclist's city—many senior Copenhageners also bicycle—it's compact and easy to get around on foot too. Outside Copenhagen, public transportation discounts also apply. Louisiana, perhaps somewhat surprisingly, does not offer a senior discount, but it is otherwise perfectly accommodating. Møns Klint and the Cannon Tower at Kronborg Castle may prove difficult for senior travelers due to the physical demands of climbing hundreds of steps at each attraction.

LGBTQ+ TRAVELERS

Denmark was the first country to legalize same-sex civil partnerships in 1989 and unilaterally declassified trans identities as a disorder in 2016, three years before the World Health Organization (WHO). The annual Copenhagen Pride is attended by the leaders of all the major political parties on the right and the left. The leader of the

Conservative party is the highest-profile of many politicians who are openly gay.

There are plenty of gay-friendly or gay-focused bars and clubs in Copenhagen, particularly in the area around Kattesundet and Studiestræde in the Inner City, underlining why the city is sometimes referred to as Northern Europe's gay village.

Denmark has a good record on LGBTQ+ issues in public life going back to the 1970s, and there is a deep-rooted national culture of acceptance and equality. However, hate crimes based on sexual orientation do occur, and I have witnessed one in Copenhagen: I would be sugar-coating if I didn't mention it. In general, they remain rare and are totally rejected by society in general.

TRAVELERS OF COLOR

Compared to most other parts of Denmark, Copenhagen has a high level of diversity and multiculturalism, but this is relative: It might feel homogeneous to some. Around 15 percent of the country's population were born abroad or have foreign parents as of 2023, but this proportion is higher in Copenhagen at around 25 percent. Away from the capital, there is less diversity, but people may be more friendly to passersby, as there tends to be more willingness to talk to strangers, or at least greet them politely. Danes of older generations can have a tendency to use outdated, racially

loaded, and offensive Danish words and pass them off as "Danish humor."

Political trends going back to the 1990s have left a lot of Danes with immigrant backgrounds feeling not fully accepted by Danish society. This stems from the emergence of national conservative political parties and their ideology, a highly influential factor in Denmark's multiparty political system, to the adoption of the so-called "Ghetto Law" in 2018 (the word "ghetto" was later replaced in government terminology with "parallel society"). These laws are a broad range of policies ostensibly designed to reduce crime and improve integration and socioeconomic mobility in underprivileged neighborhoods, but their methods—which have included forced rehousing, doubling sentences for certain crimes if they are committed in neighborhoods covered by the law, and forcing children to attend day care—have been criticized as discriminatory and ineffective.

Also in 2018, the government adopted the so-called "Burqa Ban" that imposes a 1,000-kr fine for wearing any face-covering garment, essentially targeting the Islamic burqa and niqab (but not the hijab). Very few women in Denmark wear the niqab and almost none wear the burqa. As a result, the law has rarely been used, but its adoption served to make many Danish Muslim women—regardless of whether they wear a head covering—feel more marginalized than before. Such policies, while they exist primarily in the political sphere, can seem hostile to Muslims and other minority populations. In general, Muslim travelers are not more likely to experience Islamophobia in Denmark than in other Western and Northern European countries.

In late 2023, the government said it was concerned about a rise in antisemitism. The justice minister called fighting antisemitism, including through application of hate speech laws, the government's "highest priority."

The National Police recorded 521 hate crimes in 2021, and the Danish Institute for Human Rights has called for a more rigorous registration system.

Essential Phrases

Hello: *goddag*
Hi: *hej*
Bye: *hej hej*
Good-bye: *farvel*
See you: *vi ses*
Thank you: *tak*
Thank you very much: *mange tak*
Good morning: *godmorgen*
Good evening: *god aften*
Good night: *godnat*
How much does this cost?: *Hvor meget koster det?*
Where is . . .: *Hvor er . . .*
the toilet: *toilettet*
the bathroom: *badeværelset*
the rail station: *banegården*
the museum: *museet*
the beach: *stranden*
the restaurant: *restauranten*
the café: *caféen*
What would you recommend?: *Hvad kan du anbefale?*
I would like to have . . .: *Jeg vil gerne have . . .*
Could I get . . .: *Må jeg få . . .*
the soup: *suppen*
the fish: *fisken*

the sandwich: *sandwichen*
the chicken: *kyllingen*
potatoes: *kartofler*
vegetables: *grøntsager*
pork: *svinekød*
bacon: *bacon*
butter: *smør*
cake: *kage*
coffee: *kaffe*
tea: *te*
milk: *mælk*
water: *vand*
What is your name?: *Hvad hedder du?*
My name is . . .: *Jeg hedder . . .*
I come from . . .: *Jeg kommer fra . . .*
How are you?: *Hvordan går det?*
I don't understand: *Jeg forstår ikke.*
Do you speak English?: *Taler du engelsk?*
Sorry: *sorry/undskyld*
Excuse me: *undskyld*
Look out!: *Pas på!*
Good luck!: *Held og lykke!*
Goodness me!: *Det må jeg nok sige*
Cheers!: *Skål!*

Index

List of Maps

Photo Credits

Stunning Sights Around the World

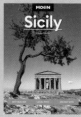

Guides for Urban Adventure

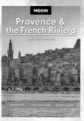

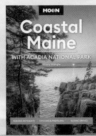

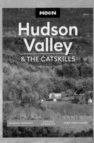

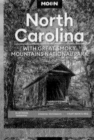

Road Trip Guides

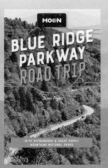

City Guides

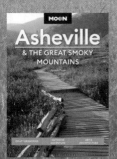

Gear up for a bucket list vacation

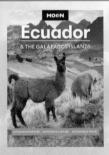

or plan your next beachy getaway!

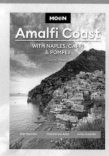

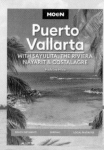

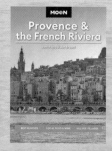

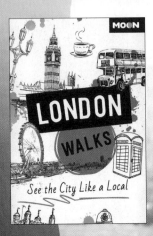
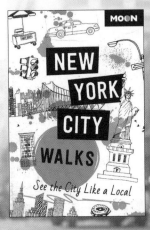
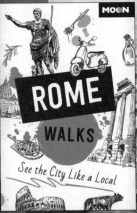
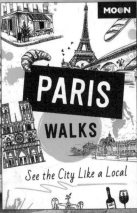

MAP SYMBOLS

═══ Expressway	▪▪▪▪▪▪ Unpaved Road	▬▬▬ Railroad
─── Primary Road	▬▬▬ Trail	▓▓▓ Pedestrian Walkway
═══ Secondary Road	▬▬▬ Ferry	▪▪▪▪▪ Stairs

○	City/Town	🛈	Information Center	🌲	Park
◉	State Capital	🅿	Parking Area	⚑	Golf Course
✹	National Capital	⛪	Church	✦	Unique Feature
✪	Highlight	🍇	Winery/Vineyard	🌊	Waterfall
★	Point of Interest	TH	Trailhead	Λ	Camping
●	Accommodation	🚉	Train Station	▲	Mountain
▼	Restaurant/Bar	✈	Airport	⛷	Ski Area
■	Other Location	✗	Airfield	🕶	Glacier

CONVERSION TABLES

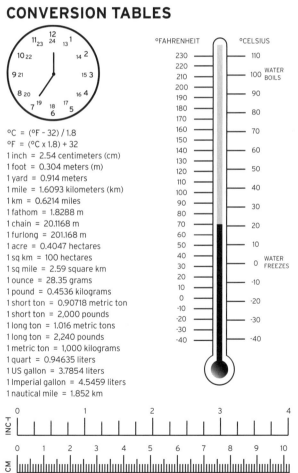

$°C = (°F - 32) / 1.8$
$°F = (°C \times 1.8) + 32$
1 inch = 2.54 centimeters (cm)
1 foot = 0.304 meters (m)
1 yard = 0.914 meters
1 mile = 1.6093 kilometers (km)
1 km = 0.6214 miles
1 fathom = 1.8288 m
1 chain = 20.1168 m
1 furlong = 201.168 m
1 acre = 0.4047 hectares
1 sq km = 100 hectares
1 sq mile = 2.59 square km
1 ounce = 28.35 grams
1 pound = 0.4536 kilograms
1 short ton = 0.90718 metric ton
1 short ton = 2,000 pounds
1 long ton = 1.016 metric tons
1 long ton = 2,240 pounds
1 metric ton = 1,000 kilograms
1 quart = 0.94635 liters
1 US gallon = 3.7854 liters
1 Imperial gallon = 4.5459 liters
1 nautical mile = 1.852 km

MOON COPENHAGEN & BEYOND

Avalon Travel
Hachette Book Group
555 12th Street, Suite 1850
Oakland, CA 94607, USA
www.moon.com

Editor: Rachael Sablik
Managing Editor: Courtney Packard
Copy Editor: Christopher Church
Graphics and Production Coordinator: Rue Flaherty
Cover Design: Faceout Studio, Charles Brock
Interior Design: Megan Jones Design
Map Editor: Karin Dahl
Cartographers: Brian Shotwell, Karin Dahl
Proofreader: Callie Stoker-Graham
Indexer: Hannah Brezack

ISBN-13: 979-8-88647-075-8

Printing History
1st Edition — 2019
2nd Edition — November 2024
5 4 3 2 1

Text © 2024 by Michael Barrett.
Maps © 2024 by Avalon Travel.
Some photos and illustrations are used by permission and are the property of the original copyright owners.

Front cover photo: Rosenborg Castle Gardens, Copenhagen © Maurizio Rellini / Sime / eStock Photo
Back cover photo: Amagertorv, Copenhagen © Laurentiuz | Dreamstime.com
Back flap photo: Inderhavnsbroen, Copenhagen © Radioval | Dreamstime.com

Printed in China by RR Donnelley APS